PEASANTS, PROPHETS, &
POLITICAL ECONOMY

PEASANTS, PROPHETS, & POLITICAL ECONOMY

The Hebrew Bible and Social Analysis

Marvin L. Chaney

CASCADE Books • Eugene, Oregon

PEASANTS, PROPHETS, AND POLITICAL ECONOMY
The Hebrew Bible and Social Analysis

Copyright © 2017 Marvin L. Chaney. All rights reserved. Except for brief quotations in critical publications or reviews, no part of this book may be reproduced in any manner without prior written permission from the publisher. Write: Permissions, Wipf and Stock Publishers, 199 W. 8th Ave., Suite 3, Eugene, OR 97401.

Cascade Books
An Imprint of Wipf and Stock Publishers
199 W. 8th Ave., Suite 3
Eugene, OR 97401

www.wipfandstock.com

ISBN 978-1-5326-0441-6 (PAPERBACK)
ISBN 978-1-5326-0443-0 (HARDCOVER)
ISBN 978-1-5326-0442-3 (EBOOK)

Cataloguing in Publication data:

Names: Chaney, Marvin L., author.

Title: Peasants, prophets, and political economy : the Hebrew Bible and social analysis / Marvin L. Chaney.

Description: Eugene, OR: Cascade Books, 2017 | Includes bibliographical references and indexes.

Identifiers: ISBN 978-1-5326-0441-6 (paperback) | 978-1-5326-0443-0 (hardcover) | ISBN 978-1-5326-0442-3 (ebook).

Subjects: LCSH: Bible. O.T.—Social scientific criticism | Sociology, Biblical | Palestine—Social life and customs—To 70 A.D. | Title.

Classification: DS112 C44 2017 (print) | DS112 (ebook).

Manufactured in the U.S.A.

Contents

Preface | vii

Abbreviations | ix

1. Ancient Palestinian Peasant Movements and the Formation of Premonarchic Israel | 1
2. Joshua and the Deuteronomistic History | 51
3. Coveting Your Neighbor's House in Social Context | 67
4. Systemic Study of the Israelite Monarchy | 83
5. Debt Easement in Israelite History and Tradition | 106
6. The Political Economy of Peasant Poverty | 121
7. Bitter Bounty: The Dynamics of Political Economy Critiqued by the Eighth-Century Prophets | 147
8. Whose Sour Grapes? The Addressees of Isaiah 5:1–7 | 160
9. Accusing Whom of What? Hosea's Rhetoric of Promiscuity | 175
10. Producing Peasant Poverty: Debt Instruments in Amos 2:6b–8, 13–16 | 191
11. Micah—Models Matter: Political Economy and Micah 6:9–15 | 205
12. Korea and Israel: Historical Analogy and Old Testament Interpretation | 220
13. Some Choreographic Notes on the Dance of Theory with Data: A Response to Roland Boer, *The Sacred Economy* | 243

Acknowledgments | 251
Bibliography | 253
Scripture Index | 277
Author Index | 290

Preface

I feel a certain ambiguity in consenting to this republication of a number of my previously published articles—some decades old, others as recent as last year. Several distinguished colleagues have overcome my reticence by arguing that the essays here collected were often first published in venues less than obvious, and thus have been difficult to access. Many of the analyses, they add, become clearer and more complete in concert than in splayed, separate publication. All of the articles, moreover, share an explicitly social-scientific dimension, a perspective now deemed increasingly pertinent by a wide variety of biblical interpreters.

Most of the essays were occasioned by requests to address a given subject in a particular venue, and thus bear clear markers of their origins. These venues usually entailed strictures of space—sometimes severe—that truncated the more detailed discussion I often would have preferred. Each of the papers sought to speak to the situation of its time. The citation of secondary literature in the older articles is now woefully dated, but full revision of the older discussions would erase their contextual dimension. The flood of publication on the subjects of the older chapters has chastened my naïve and unnuanced statement of certain issues and added important new dimensions to the discussions. It has not, however, convinced me that any of my more innovative suggestions is demonstrably false or implausible. After carefully considering major revision of the older essays, therefore, I have decided to present them here in their original form, warts and all.

Because the venues for which I originally wrote required me to summarize assumptions that were more fully substantiated elsewhere, the articles evidence some redundancy. That is particularly true in the significant portion of the book that addresses texts and contexts of the so-called eighth-century prophets. This redundancy, however, allows the reader interested in a certain biblical text to explore my analysis of that text with some systemic understanding, but without the necessity of reading the whole book to grasp my operating assumptions and their sources. Readers interested in the fuller picture can read each chapter secure in the knowledge that it will summarize and refresh important points elaborated elsewhere.

Three categories of minor changes have been made. Citation of secondary sources has been revised to conform to one consistent format. Typographical errors introduced into the original publications after the manuscripts left my control—including classical examples of both dittography and haplography—have been repaired where found. In a handful of cases where copyediting made the text deviate slightly from my intended meaning or nuance, I have restored wording—however infelicitous—that expresses my actual understanding of the matter under consideration.

Two sets of inconsistency that have been allowed to remain in the various chapters deserve brief comment. One involves how to refer to the biblical canon primarily in view in these essays. It was long called the "Old Testament," but such nomenclature privileges a specifically Christian perspective and can be read as having denigrating supersessionist connotations. As a result, the "Hebrew Bible" has been a frequent substitute. I welcome that usage for nonconfessional and interfaith discourse. In an explicitly Christian theological context, however, "Old Testament" still seems appropriate. These tensions are sometimes glossed today by the cumbersome "Hebrew Bible/Old Testament." In the republication of these essays, I have allowed my usage in the originals to stand, since they variously participate in the several universes of discourse delineated. Other instances simply bear witness to my growing awareness—or lack thereof—of the problematic involved.

A similar issue surrounds the divine name in ancient Israel. It is written in Hebrew by four consonants, *YHWH*, and thus is frequently referred to as the tetragrammaton. Already in antiquity pious Jews regarded this name as too sacred to pronounce. When vowel points were added to the purely consonantal Hebrew text, therefore, the vowels for a circumlocution, "the Lord," were used to remind readers not to pronounce the divine name itself. As a result, the tetragrammaton is usually translated as "the LORD" in the English Bible. The combination of the consonants of one word with the vowels of another also gave rise, in certain circles, to the linguistically impossible "Jehovah." Critical scholars later arrived at "Yahweh" as the likely vocalization of the tetragrammaton, and that convention was common in scholarly discourse for several decades. More recently, many critical scholars who are also practicing Jews have come to honor ancient sensibilities by using "YHWH" or "Yhwh" in their writing. Scholars of all perspectives have embraced this usage increasingly, since it is unambiguous and mutually respectful of all parties to the conversation. The mixture of usage in these essays reflects the history just rehearsed. I have allowed it to stand as a part of preserving the articles' contextual dimensions.

The first chapter of the present volume, "Ancient Palestinian Peasant Movements and the Formation of Premonarchic Israel," is the oldest essay here republished. In fact, it is older than its publication date of 1983. It was accepted for publication and passed out of my hands in the spring of 1978, but complications involving the exact mode and venue of its presentation delayed publication for five years. During that interim, Norman K. Gottwald's landmark, *The Tribes of Yahweh*, was published. The editors of *Palestine in Transition* added the last sentence in footnote 10 of my essay to make reference to Gottwald's magnum opus, but, in fact, I had no access to its final, published form in my article. I had had access to Norman's many preparatory articles, and, more important, to Norm in person—first as my senior colleague in the Graduate Theological Union in Berkeley beginning in the fall of 1969, and, after he left for New York, in several program segments of the Society of Biblical Literature. No words can express the depth of my gratitude for his graciousness and generosity in our interaction and friendship across now many years.

Since I wrote on the emergence of ancient Israel, the topic has enjoyed a long season of scholarly attention. That discussion is far from reaching any consensus, but many dimensions of the current discussion were not on anyone's radar in 1978. Still, several overtures in my essay have not been fully integrated into the conversation and, in my judgment, retain their cogency. In a section titled, "Conditions Conducive to Peasant Revolt," I review the theoretical and comparative work of Henry A. Landsberger, Gerhard E. Lenski, Barrington Moore Jr., and Eric R. Wolf and apply it to the world of Israelite origins. Although this initiative has attracted occasional positive mention (e.g., Dever 2003:184–89), to my knowledge it has never been fully integrated into the discussion of the emergence of ancient Israel. Similarly, the Excursus, "The ʿApiru and Social Unrest in the Amarna Letters from Syro-Palestine," explicates the Amarna ʿapiru in terms of Eric J. Hobsbawm's analysis of social banditry. Linguistic scholarship on the Amarna archive has proceeded apace since 1978, but the historical interpretation of these texts in that same period has shown little interest in social-scientific categories such as those articulated by Hosbawm. How fortunate I am that my master teacher in matters Amarna, William L. Moran, was open to such categories.

Chapter 2, on the biblical book of Joshua, analyzes Joshua in terms of how it functions in the larger Deuteronomistic History. Basic to my analysis is the hypothesis of Frank Moore Cross concerning the composition of this larger work. The particulars of that composition have once again occasioned the flow of much scholarly ink since 1989. Notwithstanding that extended and controverted discussion, I continue to find Cross's hypothesis compelling, not because I revere his memory as my doctor father—although I do, profoundly—but because I find his hypothesis to have greater explanatory power when tested in detail against texts such as Joshua. Both Cross and my other doctoral teacher in Hebrew Bible, G. Ernest Wright, were remarkable in honoring their graduate students' independence. We learned that loyalty to them meant using the rigorous scholarly tools they helped us to acquire honestly and to the best of our ability, not blindly following what they had previously taught or written. Were I to undertake a fresh introduction to the book of Joshua today with greater space available, I would add an exploration of the fact that the received Hebrew text and the Old Greek text tell slightly different versions of the same narrative. The difference involves more than individual textual variants. The two texts often represent slightly different redactions of the same book.

I first treated the Tenth Commandment, the subject of Chapter 3, in my inaugural lecture as Nathaniel Gray Professor of Hebrew Exegesis and Old Testament at San Francisco Theological Seminary. That form of this essay, subsequently published in *Pacific Theological Review* in 1982, was expanded and revised for *The Ten Commandments: The Reciprocity of Faithfulness* in 2004. The latter version is republished here. It seeks to illustrate how taking social context seriously—behind, in, and in front of the biblical text—can add important dimensions to the disputed interpretation of an iconic passage of Scripture.

"Systemic Study of the Israelite Monarchy," Chapter 4 in this volume, was written for the 1981 session of "The Sociology of the Monarchy in Ancient Israel" Seminar of the Society of Biblical Literature. It was published in 1986 in a special number of *Semeia*, "Social Scientific Criticism of the Hebrew Bible and Its Social World: The Israelite Monarchy." Highly schematic and somewhat polemical, it was designed to counteract what I regarded to be the overemphasis on religious ideology as causal explanation in the historiography of the ancient Israelite monarchy. My analysis made particular use of the neoevolutionary and technoenvironmental social theory of Gerhard E. Lenski. I had spent the academic year 1977–78 as a Visiting Scholar in the Sociology Department of the University of North Carolina at Chapel Hill dialoguing with Lenski about his analysis of "agrarian societies" and its relevance for study of the Hebrew Bible and the ancient Fertile Crescent. I felt—and continue to feel—that his theoretical work is profoundly pertinent to the understanding of ancient Israel and Judah in their wider social and economic contexts. I welcome this opportunity to express my deep appreciation to Gerry for his extraordinary hospitality and for the generosity of his mentoring me in matters social-scientific.

By 1991, when I wrote Chapter 5, "Debt Easement in Israelite History and Tradition," Robert B. Coote had been my subject area colleague at San Francisco Theological Seminary and the Graduate Theological Union for some years and had begun a steady production of significant publications. I cite Bob's work approvingly in the biblical portion of this essay, but that citation and similar references elsewhere are only a very partial acknowledgment of what I learned from and with him in co-taught courses and frequent collegial discourse. Virtually everything I have written from that point on is different and better because I was privileged to have such an erudite and innovative colleague just down the hall.

Chapters 6 and 7 overlap considerably, but were written on different occasions with different audiences in view. Chapter 7, "Bitter Bounty: The Dynamics of Political Economy Critiqued by the Eighth-Century Prophets," was first drafted in 1984 as the first part of a longer paper for "The Sociology of the Monarchy in Ancient Israel" Seminar of the Society of Biblical Literature. A predecessor of the current Chapter 10 appeared with it as extended illustration. A slight revision of that paper was subsequently shared with a seminar on "Reformed Faith and Economics" at Ghost Ranch. When selected papers from that seminar were then published under the title, *Reformed Faith and Economics*, my paper was included, but minus the second, illustrative section. In my preparation of the section then published, I learned much—as I have continued to do—from the superb, pioneering work of David C. Hopkins on agrarian economics in the biblical world.

Chapter 6, "The Political Economy of Peasant Poverty: What the Eighth-Century Prophets Presumed but Did not State," was drafted in 2013 for a symposium on "The Bible, the Economy, and the Poor," sponsored by the Kripke Center at Creighton University. Participants, who all enjoyed the genial hospitality of our host, Ronald A. Simkins, included scholars from a variety of religious disciplines. The revision of my contribution to the symposium, subsequently published with the other papers in the *Journal of Religion and Society* Supplement Series, constitutes my most recent comprehensive treatment of the subject matter of chapters 6 and 7. Because it presumes a more general audience, however, it has been placed first here, out of chronological sequence. The older essay (Chapter 7) covers much of the same ground in greater detail, but does not address the issue of gender roles. This topic is discussed briefly in Chapter 6, mostly along theoretical lines delineated by Laurel Bossen. This more recent treatment also includes a brief discussion of "Some Implications for Considering Poverty Today," as well as an extended excursus that summarizes and critiques recent publications by Philippe Guillaume, Avraham Faust, and Walter J. Houston.

"Whose Sour Grapes? The Addressees of Isaiah 5:1–7," here republished as Chapter 8, was first drafted for the "Social Sciences and the Interpretation of the Hebrew Scriptures" Section of the Society of Biblical Literature. It was subsequently published in a special number of *Semeia* celebrating "The Social World of the Hebrew Bible: Twenty-Five Years of the Social Sciences in the Academy." In the context of the present volume, it is the first of four chapters, one on each of the four eighth-century prophets, that seek to show how the perspectives developed in Chapters 6 and 7 inform the detailed interpretation of specific prophetic texts.

Chapter 9, "Accusing Whom of What? Hosea's Rhetoric of Promiscuity," was read in several forms and venues before it was published in a Festschrift in honor of my esteemed New Testament colleague of many years, Antoinette Clark Wire. The meticulous, groundbreaking work of Phyllis A. Bird, a friend since graduate school days, was instrumental in clearing the way for such rereadings of the book of Hosea. My discussion is also indebted to the work of Alice A. Keefe and to extended dialogue with Bob Coote, my Old Testament colleague. This chapter, and the many other publications that now argue some version of the same basic perspective, would have been impossible, in my opinion, without the existence a critical mass of women in the field of Hebrew Bible. Only that inclusion of the experience of half the human community allowed us all to see that Hosea's dizzying collage functions to hoist Israel's upper-class males with their own petard. This breakthrough also allows Hosea to be read of a piece with the other eighth-century prophets.

As noted above on Chapter 7, my interpretation of the Israel oracle in Amos 2 was first drafted as an illustrative example of how texts from the eighth-century prophets reflect and reflect upon the "bitter bounty" of Israel and Judah in their time. Because this material was more technical, it was excluded from the publication of "Bitter Bounty" in *Reformed Faith and Economics*. I finally published a revised form in a Festschrift in honor of my esteemed colleague and friend, Bob Coote. It is here republished as Chapter 10. As explained in the essay, the oracle is significantly typical of the oldest materials in the book of Amos.

The book of Micah, the fourth of the eighth-century prophets, bristles with textual and philological difficulties. Chapter 11 of this volume examines one particularly difficult passage, Micah 6:9–15, deploying standard textual and philological tools, but utilizing them in full concert with what is known or knowable about the dynamics of political economy presumed and reflected in the text. This essay was prepared for the "St Andrews Conference on Old Testament Interpretation and the Social Sciences," held at the University of St Andrews in Scotland in 2004, and was published in

Ancient Israel: The Old Testament in Its Social Context along with other papers from the conference. I remember with great warmth and appreciation the extraordinary hospitality extended to all members of the conference in St Andrews by its chair and organizer, Philip F. Esler.

When I arrived at San Francisco Theological Seminary and the Graduate Theological Union all-but-dissertation from Harvard in the fall of 1969, I had many surprises in store. One was that a year's interim appointment would become a thirty-seven year career. Another was the number of international students with whom I would be privileged to interact. Many of these students were Korean and Korean-American. In an effort to understand better the experience and background of these students, I began to read about Korean history. A sabbatical term spent at the Presbyterian Theological Seminary in Seoul in the spring of 1985 greatly heightened my interest. During those months, my learned host, Kim Yong Bock, graciously tutored me in Korean history, society, and culture. I began to see significant parallels between preindustrial Korea and biblical Israel, with potential for extended comparison to benefit the historical understanding of both.

Upon my return to San Francisco Theological Seminary, I was unwilling to treat this experience as mere personal enrichment, but wary of undertaking on my own a curricular offering half of which would focus on Korea. Full of trepidation, I asked my Korean-American colleague, Warren W. Lee, if he would consider co-teaching a course with me that would compare the agrarian monarchies of Israel and Korea. The alacrity with which he responded remains one of the great joys of my life. Warren and I taught the course together every other year until my retirement. Each time was different. We learned with and from each other and a succession of highly motivated students. The publication of pertinent literature on Korea swelled to floodtide during those years. We were also greatly encouraged by Eugene E. C. Park, who arrived to become our wise and erudite New Testament colleague.

Early in retirement, I was invited to be a Visiting Professor at The United Graduate School of Theology of Yonsei University in Seoul. Chapter 12 in the present volume, "Korea and Israel: Historical Analogy and Old Testament Interpretation," was mostly written during my time at Yonsei in the spring of 2010. A form of the essay was given as a public lecture there, and another form at the International Conference in Celebration of the Jubilee Year of the Korean Society of Old Testament Studies. An expanded and revised version of the latter was subsequently published in *The Korean Journal of Old Testament Studies*. Republished here in that form, this essay relies on social-scientific theory, particularly that of Gerhard E. Lenski, for methodological control. The discussion is exploratory and preliminary, designed to stimulate correction and further work, especially by Korean and Korean-American colleagues.

Chapter 13 was written when I was invited to be part of a review panel for Roland Boer's important new book, *The Sacred Economy of Ancient Israel*, in the Ideological Criticism Section of the annual meeting of the Society of Biblical Literature in 2015. It was subsequently published in revised form in 2016 in *Horizons in Biblical Theology*. Space limitations precluded a full review of Boer's tour de force. After my expression of my heartfelt appreciation for the many achievements of this book, I outline a few of my differences. Boer's consistently Marxian theoretical focus allows him many insights, but, in my view, it also blinds him to certain data and their most salient interpretation. The ghost of Marx's Asiatic Mode of Production haunts Boer's analysis, causing him to build a virtually impenetrable wall between agrarian societies that occurred before the rise of capitalism and those that occurred after. This separation obscures comparison of the role of maritime societies on both sides of the watershed and makes Boer unnecessarily wary of the disciplined comparison of agrarian institutions in ancient Southwest Asia and in various parts of the world since the rise of capitalism. My discussion in this chapter represents my most current understanding of maritime trade and of pressure on the availability of arable land in eighth-century Israel and Judah.

Most of the essays in this volume first took their rise in materials I prepared for students. Anything of value here owes much to the intelligence, diligence, curiosity, patience, and wisdom of the generations of students it has been my privilege to "teach." I am sure that I got the better of the transactions, learning far more than I taught. I am profoundly grateful to and for my students.

A number of colleagues in biblical studies have repeatedly urged that I republish in one volume the works herein contained. I think particularly of Walter Brueggemann, Robert B. Coote, Norman K. Gottwald, Richard A. Horsley, and Herman C. Waetjen. I thank them for their confidence and hope that this volume proves worthy of their encouragement.

This collection of essays would never have happened without the patience and persistence of K. C. Hanson of Wipf and Stock. His work in suggesting this volume and bringing it to fruition has greatly exceeded anything that could reasonably be expected of an Editor in Chief. No words are adequate to express my gratitude for his selfless labor on this volume.

My last and greatest expression of gratitude must go to my wife of fifty-three years, Rilla McCubbins Chaney. She has been my supportive partner through the birth pangs of each and every one of the projects here represented. Ever candid and with unfailing love, she has routinely proved my best sounding board and truest critic. Although her life has always brimmed with her own full complement of professional and familial activities, she is never too busy to strengthen my weaknesses and make good my lapses. I thank God for the grace of her grace!

Abbreviations

AB	The Anchor Bible
ABD	*The Anchor Bible Dictionary.* Edited by David Noel Freedman. 6 vols. New York: Doubleday, 1992
AHw	Wolfram von Soden, *Akkadisches Handworterbuch.* 3 vols. Wiesbaden: Harrassowitz, 1965–81
ANEM	Ancient Near East Monographs
ANET	*Ancient Near Eastern Texts Relating to the Old Testament.* 3rd ed. Edited by James B. Pritchard. Princeton: Princeton University Press, 1969
BA	*Biblical Archaeologist*
BASOR	*Bulletin of the American Schools of Oriental Research*
BDB	Francis Brown, S. R. Driver, and Charles A. Briggs, *Hebrew–English Lexicon of the Old Testament.* Oxford: Clarendon, 1907
Bib	*Biblica*
BZAW	Beihefte zur Zeitschrift für die alttestamentliche Wissenschaft
CAD	*The Assyrian Dictionary.* Edited by I. J. Gelb et al. Chicago: Oriental Institute, 1958–
CBQ	*Catholic Biblical Quarterly*
CTA	A. Herdner, ed., *Corpus des tablettes en cuneiformes alphabetiques.* Mission de Ras Shamra 10. Paris: lmprimerie Nationale, 1963

DCH	David J. A. Clines, ed., *Dictionary of Classical Hebrew*. 9 vols. Sheffield: Sheffield Academic, 1993–2012
EA	texts from el-Amarna, Egypt, as numbered in J. A. Knudtzon, *Die El-Amarna Tafeln*, 2 vols. 1908–1915. Reprint, Aalen: Zeller, 1964; and Anson F. Rainey, *El Amarna Tablets 359–379: Supplement to J. A. Knudtzon, Die El-Amarna Tafeln*, Alter Orient und Altes Testament 9. Neukirchen-Vluyn: Neukirchener, 1970
FOTL	The Forms of the Old Testament Literature
GKC	*Gesenius' Hebrew Grammar*. 2nd English ed. Edited by E. Kautzch and A. E. Cowley. Oxford: Clarendon, 1910
HALAT	Ludwig Köhler and Walter Baumgartner et al., *Hebräisches und Aramäisches Lexikon zum Alten Testament*. 3rd ed. Leiden: Brill, 1967–1990
HALOT	Ludwig Köhler and Walter Baumgartner, *The Hebrew–Aramaic Lexicon of the Old Testament*. Leiden: Brill, 1994–2000
HSM	Harvard Semitic Monographs
HTR	*Harvard Theological Review*
HUCA	*Hebrew Union College Annual*
ICC	International Critical Commentary
IDB	*The Interpreter's Dictionary of the Bible*. Edited by George Arthur Buttrick. Nashville: Abingdon, 1962
IDBSup	*The Interpreter's Dictionary of the Bible Supplementary Volume*. Edited by Keith Crim. Nashville: Abingdon, 1976
IEJ	*Israel Exploration Journal*
JB	Jerusalem Bible
JBL	*Journal of Biblical Literature*
JESHO	*Journal of the Economic and Social History of the Orient*

JNES	*Journal of Near Eastern Studies*
JSOT	*Journal for the Study of the Old Testament*
JSOTSup	Journal for the Study of the Old Testament Supplements
KTU	*The Cuneiform Alphabetic Texts from Ugarit, Ras Ibn Hani and Other Places.* 2nd ed. Edited by Manfried Dietrich et al. Alter Orient und Altes Testament 360. Münster: Ugarit, 1995
LAI	Library of Ancient Israel
LHBOTS	Library of Hebrew Bible/Old Testament Studies
NAB	New American Bible
NEB	New English Bible
NIB	*The New Interpreter's Bible.* Edited by Leander E. Keck. 13 vols. Nashville: Abingdon, 1994–2004
NJB	New Jerusalem Bible
NRSV	New Revised Standard Version
OBT	Overtures to Biblical Theology
OTL	Old Testament Library
PEQ	*Palestine Exploration Quarterly*
PRU	Jean Nougayrol, ed., *Le palais royal d'Ugarit*, vol. 3. Mission de Ras Shamra 6. Paris: Imprimerie Nationale, 1955
RSV	Revised Standard Version
SBLDS	Society of Biblical Literature Dissertation Series
SBLSP	*Society of Biblical Literature Seminar Papers*
SBT	Studies in Biblical Theology
SJOT	*Scandanavian Journal for the Old Testament*
SWBA	Social World of Biblical Antiquity Series
UF	*Ugarit-Forschungen*
VT	*Vetus Testamentum*
VTSup	Vetus Testament Supplements
ZAW	*Zeitschrift für die alttestamentliche Wissenschaft*

1

Ancient Palestinian Peasant Movements and the Formation of Premonarchic Israel[1]

INTRODUCTION

Few biblical scholars would deny that ancient Israel, prior to its coalescence as a monarchic state at the tranisition from the second to the first millennium BCE, constituted for some time a recognizable society, resident in the hill country of Palestine. An equally broad consensus would probably agree that this premonarchic period proved normative for much in later Israel, but that its detailed, sequential history cannot be written from the information currently available. Although questions concerning the process by which Israel became established in the Palestinian uplands are too important to ignore, the data, of themselves compel no particular historical reconstruction. As a result, three contending gestalts are presently championed for the historical interpretation of these data.

1. This paper was written while the author was a Visiting Scholar in the Department of Sociology of the University of North Carolina at Chapel Hill on a sabbatical leave supported by the Association of Theological Schools in the United States and Canada, the Andrew W. Mellon Foundation, the Arthur Vining Davis Foundation, and his home institution, San Francisco Theological Seminary. He gratefully acknowledges the hospitality and support of these institutions. In addition, he also wishes to thank Professors C. Calhoun, R. B. Coote, F. M. Cross. N. K. Gottwald, H. A. Landsberger, G. Lenski, W. L. Moran, J. M. Sasson, Mr. T. Sayer, and his wife, R. M. Chaney, from whose critical reading the entire manuscript benefited materially. All errors, whether inadvertent or obstinateiy maintained in the face of learned critique, remain the sole responsibility of the writer.

No full rehearsal of the data is possible or intended here. This study will instead examine the adequacy of the paradigmatic—and frequently contolling—assumptions made by the proponents of each of the three models, while advocating a nuanced version of one. Since these assumptions frequently pertain to societal processes more fully attested in the history of other agrarian societies, a further modicum of control will be sought in the disciplined comparison of such societies by historical sociologists.

The latter expedient is not a methodological commonplace in biblical studies and hence deserves a word of explanation. To readers more familiar with the linguistic tools correctly regarded as indispensable to biblical research, the role granted here to the social sciences can be expressed by the following proportion: philology:comparative linguistics::history:historical sociology. The first and third of these fields are primarily concerned with the humanistic interpretation of delimited data—in this case, a given text or a given historical period and location. Utilizing a broader database, the second and fourth disciplines seek to analyze commonalities of structure, process, and causation. While a tendency to find patterns and make generalizations is thus inherent in the tasks of the two comparative fields, their more delimited counterparts partake of an equal and opposite proclivity for particularism. Only when the tension intrinsic to this division of labor occasions mutually corrective dialogue, rather than polarization, can any of the four disciplines remain healthy.

For example, a difficult form or vocable in the text of the Hebrew Bible routinely prompts a controlled comparison with related phenomena in the other Semitic languages, even though their attestation may be at a great chronological and/or geographical remove. Any study of comparative Semitics is, in turn, dependent upon the fullest possible philological description of Biblical Hebrew. Similarly, when a given event or process in ancient Israelite society is difficult to interpret historically because of sparse or ambiguous data, recourse is properly had to a disciplined comparison of related phenomena in other agrarian societies just as the comparative analysis of such societies should take account of the most nuanced histories of ancient Israel.

The time is particularly propitious for this dialogue. After a long period of neglect by both anthropology and sociology, agrarian societies—those whose primary means of subsistence is a cultivation of fields which utilizes the plow but not industrial technology—are once again receiving serious attention from social scientists, who, from their side, are expressing renewed interest in interdisciplinary cooperation with historians in the investigation of such societies (Lenski and Lenski 1978:30, 88–141, 177–210).

Before each of the three models is reviewed in light of this broader methodology, points of congruence among their respective reconstructions need to be sketched, for they are presupposed in the discussion of disputed areas. All would agree that Late Bronze Canaan comprised a miscellany of agrarian city-states, each with its own petty kinglet, but under the nominal suzerainty of Egypt. The power and control of the local dynasts were centered in walled cities which clustered near the steady water supplies of the piedmont springline and the rich, alluvial soils of the plains. Connecting these concentrations of population with each other and·the world beyond were overland routes, also favored by the relatively level topography. While constituting only a small minority of the population, the ruling elite were able to dominate the other inhabitants of these plains because they alone could field chariots armed with composite bows. Conversely, premonarchic Israel's poor and mostly unwalled towns and villages were concentrated where the control of the Canaanite kings had never been strong—in the rugged terrain and scrub woods of the hill country. Although this territory was less desirable economically because of its steep, brushy hillsides, thin soils, and relative lack of perennial water sources, it effectively neutralized the tactical advantage of the chariots and composite bows with which the ruling classes held sway on the plains.

With these elements of consensus[2] as background, the conflicting models may be examined.

---

2. One partial exception to this consensus is the work of de Geus (1976:153 and n126), who seems to posit the priority and greater density of highland settlement and thereby to explain that "the ancient towns of the Canaanites usually lie on the edge of the plain, at the foot of the mountains" (153). He quotes the work of Baly (1963:60–76) in support. Baly, however, affirms the consensus position and states the real reasons for the location of the cities of Bronze Age Canaan, as follows:

> Almost all the towns mentioned [in Judges 1 as untaken by Israel], it should be noticed, lie in the piedmont region between the still thickly forested uplands and the often marshy districts of the lower-lying plains, for here, water is most easily available along the piedmont springline, and where the movement is less hindered by the nature of the terrain, the greatest settlement had taken place. The only alternative, as Joshua is represented as making clear to the people of Manasseh and Ephraim (Josh 17:18), was to wrestle with the only partly inhabited plateau. (62)

The integration of such geographic and demographic factors with those of social stratification and military technology and tactics has been undertaken both historically and sociologically (Yadin 1963:1–31, 77–356; Rowton 1965:375–87; Lenski 1966:189–296; Sjoberg 1960:80–144 et passim).

A MODEL OF NOMADIC INFILTRATION

Developed by such scholars as Alt (1966b:135–69), Noth (1960:66–84), and, more recently, Weippert (1971:1–146), what may be termed the nomadic infiltration model posits that the Israelites, prior to their founding of a monarchic state, were land-hungry nomads and semi-nomads in a process of gradual sedentarization in the sparsely inhabited hill country.

> We may think of it as having proceeded rather in the way in which even today semi-nomadic breeders of small cattle from the adjoining steppes and deserts pass over into a settled way of life in the cultivated countryside ... The Israelites were land-hungry semi-nomads of that kind before their occupation of the land: they probably first set foot on the land in the process of changing pastures and in the end they began to settle for good in the sparsely populated parts of the country and then extended their territory from their original domains as occasion offered, the whole process being carried through, to begin with, by peaceful means and without the use of force. (Noth 1960:69)

The latter point is linked by this school with a judgment that Joshua 1–12 is constituted mostly of traditions that were aetiologically generated and hence of little value to the modern historian regarding the events of which they purport to tell (Alt 1936:13–29; Noth 1953:7–13; 20–69; Weippert 1971:136–44). Archaeological evidence for the destruction of many of the cities named in Joshua 10–11 is denied relevance by the judgment that the time and agent(s) of the destruction cannot be ascertained accurately. With military conflict thus largely excluded, the tension between Canaanites and Israelites is understood essentially as that between farmers and nomads, respectively.

Although both past and present exponents of this view exhibit prodigious learning and exert broad influence, their synthesis and its assumptions now stand under heavy and—it would appear to this writer—decisive criticism. The essentials of that critique may be summarized in the following points:[3]

---

3. Mendenhall joined several of these issues, albeit in abbreviated form (1962:66–87; 1973:174–97; 1976a:152–57; 1976b:132–51). More extensive documentation for much of the summary offered here may be found in several articles by Gottwald (1974:223–55; 1975:89–100; 1976b:629–31; 1978b:2–7) and the literature that they cite. Access to relevant works by Rowton—in addition to those cited by Gottwald—may be gained through Rowton's recent paper (1977:181–98). Note should also be taken of the recent work of de Geus (1976:124–33); and Dever (1977:102–20).

Weippert's attempt (1971:102–26) to answer Mendenhall's critique of his understanding of nomadism is largely a precis of the earlier monograph by Kupper (1957).

(1) Neither the tribalism of early Israelite society nor the itinerancy of some of its members *necessitates* desert or pastoral origins. Tribal organization is well documented among various tillers of the soil, while tinkers, merchants, bandits, and caravaneers itinerate without being desert pastoralists.

(2) In a sharp break with nineteenth-century concepts which still dominate OT scholarship, modern prehistorians and anthropologists no longer regard pastoral nomadism as an evolutionary interval between hunting and gathering and plant cultivation. Instead, it is viewed as a marginal specialization from the animal husbandry that came to be associated with horticulture and agriculture. Thus, although some pastoral nomads might later sedentarize, the evolutionary flow was from the cultivated areas of the Near East "*toward* the steppe and desert, not out of the desert to the sown" (Luke 1965:24).

(3) So-called "full nomadism," such as that associated with the Midianites or the modern Bedouin, depends upon extensive, mounted use of camels or horses, which alone allow significant penetration of the Syro-Arabian desert by a preindustrial society. Before the camel saddle made possible the first such penetration, the asses and flocks of "semi-nomads" clung of necessity to the fringes of the fertile crescent. Modern proponents of the nomadic infiltration model recognize that "full nomadism" appeared too late in antiquity to bear upon the discussion of Israelite origins, but their frequent appeal to such intentionally vague phrases as "nomads and semi-nomads" or "(semi-) nomads" endeavors to salvage a paradigm based upon the priority of a nomadism completely at home in the desert. This attempt to win a reprieve for long-cherished assumptions, however, only succeeds in confounding chronological periods, evolutionary sequences, and discrete ecosystems, which can and should be distinguished.

(4) Contrary to the dichotomy unusually drawn between nomad and farmer, the relationship between cereal cultivation and pastoralism, particularly in its "semi-nomadic" form, was symbiotic. Grain harvest in spring and early summer coincided with the drying up of winter pastures in the steppes. When wetter uplands such as Carmel also proved insufficient, the hungry flocks needed to graze upon the stubble of the harvested grainfields and drink from the perennial waters available where hill met plain. In return, they served as roving manure spreaders, fertilizing the fields for the

---

Perhaps most significantly, Weippert (1971:111 n37) indicates awareness of the work of Luke (1965), but states that he has been unable to consult it. Could he have done so, his reply might have been different in kind, for Luke programmatically challenges the assumptions, methods, and conclusions of Kupper. With regard to the Shosu recently discussed by Weippert (1974:265–80, 427–33), the reader is referred to Gottwald's discussion (1974:248–51).

autumn sowing. At the very least, then, herder and cultivator lived hard by one another several months of each year and were economically interdependent; at most, they were one and the same.

(5) Judging from technological parameters and evidence from later periods, the number of pastoral nomads in comparison to the sedentary population would have been quite small. Before the development of a satisfactory camel saddle—which occurred after the initial formation of Israel—the number of pastoralists lacking significant intercourse with cultivators may be regarded as historically negligible. The romantic image of the Syro-Arabian desert as a vast womb, producing wave upon wave of Proto-Semites, is as demographically fallacious as it is long-lived in historiography.

(6) Similarly, the portrait of pastoral nomads as the major agents of change in every agrarian society of the ancient Near East has been grossly overdrawn. "Their restiveness and conflict with the state was not due to their invading or infiltrating from the desert but rather to their rural-based resistance to the drafting and taxing powers of the state" (Gottwald 1976b:629).

(7) OT traditions view the desert as strange and hostile—a place where Israel required special assistance. The motif of "return to desert" has been shown to express a threat against covenant breakers rather than harking back to an idealized past. Other supposed vestiges of a nomadic ideal in the Hebrew Bible, such as the Rechabites, have been plausibly explained in other terms (Riemann 1963:passim; Talmon 1966:31–63; Frick 1971:279–87).

(8) The land hunger evinced in so many OT texts is far more characteristic of peasants than pastoral nomads (Wolf 1966:passim).

(9) The primacy of the aetiological element in Joshua 1–12 posited by Alt and Noth has been convincingly challenged on literary grounds (Seeligmann 1961:141–69; Childs 1963:279–92; 1974b:387–97; Long 1968: passim).

(10) Modern archaeology has successfully established at more than one site a poor but distinct stratum between the late thirteenth-century destruction of the Late Bronze "Canaanite" city and the appearance of quantities of pottery characteristic of the Philistines. Such strata evidence some building in the ashes of the previous stratum and a material culture consistent with that of the poor, unwalled towns in the hill country which were founded in the same period or refounded then after a long hiatus in occupation. Thus, the likelihood of "Israelites" rather than Philistines or the kings of other Canaanite city-states being the agents of destruction is enhanced (Lapp 1967:286–87, 292, 298).[4]

---

4. Mendenhall (1976a:152–57) now appears to find the agency of the destruction outside Israel. He fails to account adequately, however, for the fact that the cities of the old Canaanite heartland were not destroyed at this time. Only sites located in or near

Because they stand under this combination of strictures, the axiomatic presuppositions of the nomadic infiltration model fail to inspire confidence.

A CONQUEST MODEL

A second interpretive framework has been forged in polemical dialogue with the nomadic infiltration model. Proponents of this conquest model,[5] as we shall call it, take umbrage, not at the positing of nomadic origins for Israel, but at the treatment of the conquest narratives in Joshua by their opponents. Archaeology has vindicated the essential historicity of these narratives, they argue, by demonstrating that numerous cities stated in the text to have been destroyed do in fact evidence massive destruction: "the stratigraphic evidence . . . outside the coastal cities and the Plain of Jezreel, points . . . strongly to the thoroughgoing destruction of nearly all important cities in the last half of the thirteenth century" (Lapp 1967:295). While Jericho, Ai, and Gibeon are candidly acknowledged as problems because they provide no evidence of occupation at the time,[6] the concatenation of destruction layers

> certainly suggests that a planned campaign such as that depicted in Josh. 10–11 was carried out. Its purpose was evidently the destruction of the power of the city-states, though some of these states were carefully avoided, presumably because they were too strong. We may safely conclude that during the 13th century a portion at least of the later nation of Israel gained entrance to Palestine by a carefully planned invasion, the purpose of which was not primarily loot but land. (G. E. Wright 1962:84)

These destructions and the "poor unfortified occupations that follow, plus the large number of sites with new occupation or with occupation that followed centuries of abandonment," moreover, are thought to "point to a large group of intruders" (Lapp 1967:295, 299). For the source and nature of these intruders, appeal is had once again to the denizens of the desert or its fringes: "Thus we must conceive of the movement of Hebrew tribes from

---

the hill country or otherwise isolated from the main cluster of fortified Canaanite settlements witness destruction late in the thirteenth century. To state that "such destruction levels are virtually universal at this time throughout the whole of the eastern Mediterranean area" (Mendenhall 1973:22) glosses over important geographical distinctions.

5. Prominent here would be the names of Albright, Wright, Bright (especially in the first edition of the work cited below), and Lapp. Most of the relevant bibliography has been collected by Bright (1972:127 n54). Reference may also be made to works of Lapp (1969a:107–11) and Dever (1974:44–46) not listed there.

6. Arad and the Negev, too, raise their own set of problems (Aharoni 1976:55–76).

their nomadic existence into the settled area of urban and agrarian activity, as a movement of uncultivated 'barbarians' into scenes of self-conscious civilization" (G. E. Wright 1962:70).

Although the two mutually antagonistic reconstructions thus share a supposition of Israel's nomadic derivation, the conquest model not only views the intruding Israelites as far more militant, but as more politically self-conscious as well. At the outset of his attempt to give the archaeological evidence historical interpretation, Lapp makes the primacy of political categories a matter of explicit, historiographic theory:

> Two observations appear in order in regard to *historical* meaning. First, historical meaning includes political, economic, and cultural aspects. The above evidence has been confined primarily to evidence relating to the political sphere. Cultural objects have been ignored, although the possibility of their shedding light on the political situation has not been overlooked. The second observation is that the bearers of history are not simply people but historical groups, such as Israelites, Philistines, and Canaanites. This observation justifies the focus here on the political sphere. Until the various stratified deposits of archaeological evidence can be confidently attributed to a particular historical group, that evidence can have little specific implication for interpreting economic and cultural history. (Lapp 1967:296)

According to Lapp, then, conflict between Canaanites and Israelites should be understood primarily in political terms. Even though this writer does not join those who denigrate the archaeological evidence amassed by adherents of the conquest model,[7] he still finds their larger interpretive scheme unconvincing for the following reasons:

(1) Its presumption of the prior existence of "a large group of intruders" as nomads and semi-nomads in the desert suffers all the liabilities already catalogued for such a view.

(2) While insisting that the material culture of Israel's earliest settlements must be intrusive, proponents have been totally unable to find its antecedents outside Palestine in a manner parallel to that possible, for instance, with the Philistines. On the other hand, they are forced to admit that within Palestine, "the basic general typology is virtually identical in the 13th and 12th centuries B.C." (Lapp 1967:295). Beyond the specifics of this particular case, an issue of theoretical importance is at stake. Syro-Palestintian

---

7. While most earlier excavations and some recent ones have lacked sufficient methodological control, the judgments of Weippert (1971:127–36) and de Geus (1976:48–53 et passim), following the earlier lead of Noth (1960:42, 46–48), appear far too sweeping and extreme.

archaeologists have tended to explain changes in material culture by the intrusion of new peoples from outside. This tendency is understandable, since much of the hard-won stratigraphy of historical times is fixed by destructions that are attributable to foreign invasions known from literary sources. The broader perspective of important modern theories of sociocultural evolution, however, regards technological innovation as a far more frequent and powerful engine of social change than the intrusion of whole new populations.[8] When the external source of a change in material culture is no more apparent than the ubiquitous but highly questionable "(semi-)nomads" of the archaeological literature, the cause of that change is better sought in innovations or conflicts within the society itself or common to all societies in the area.

(3) In their linkage with archaeological evidence, the biblical narratives of conquest have been treated selectively. Archaeology has remained necessarily mute on most of the text and openly embarrassing with regard to Jericho, Ai, Gibeon, and Arad, leaving only parts of Joshua 10–11 and Judges 1—the latter exhibiting decidedly gradualist proclivities—to be connected with the evidence of material remains.

(4) Treatment of the remaining narratives has tended to be general and unidimensional, as illustrated by the following statement from Lapp:

> ... the "conquest" by a sizable group is reflected in the Biblical record. It is hard to see how this tradition could have been invented in later times, which could be expected to expand traditions related to the founding of the kingdom by David but hardly to have invented a conquest narrative. This Biblical picture may be stressed without pressing any of its details. The literary stratification is diverse, but it is consistent in indicating a substantial conquest in a rather short period of time. (Lapp 1967:299)

Far from the consistent viewpoint attributed to the text by Lapp, however, the picture of a rapid onslaught from outside, in which all the inhabitants of captured cities were put to the sword, is conveyed primarily if not exclusively by the "Deuteronomistic" framework into which the older literary materials have been set (cf. Miller 1977:220-21).[9] Moreover, if the "first

8. Gottwald (1975:89-100) makes both this point and the fifth one in the discussion that follows. Important theoretical statements of the primacy of technological innovation in social change, couched in probabilistic rather than deterministic terms, have been made by Lenski (1976:548-64). Lenski and Lenski (1978:65-85), and Harris (1968:passim). Note, too, the role attributed to technology by Sjoberg (1960:7-13 et passim).

9. The "Deuteronomistic" framework and glosses can be isolated on literary grounds with considerable consistency. Note, for example, the substantial agreement between

edition" of the "Deuteronomistic History" is viewed as a programmatic piece written to support the Josianic reform (Cross 1973:274–89; Freedman 1976:226–28), its framer's propensities are readily understandable. For that archaizing reform of the late seventh century BCE sought to weld Judah and the remnants of the northern Kingdom into a united, centralized, pure, and militantly independent nation, realizing its manifest destiny under both Mosaic and Davidic covenants. This program could hardly have been better legitimated than by an interpretation of pre-Davidic history that emphasized the unfailing success of Israel's national and territorial aspirations if and when political cohesion and military discipline were maintained and all vestiges and bearers of "foreign culture" eradicated. Faced with northern suspicions of the centralized leadership of a Davidide, the "Deuteronomistic Historian" urged that the paradigm for such national leadership and its success predated the Davidic monarchy in the person of a northerner—Joshua, the Ephraimite.

(5) Proponents of the conquest model have been inconsistent and imprecise in conceptualizing Canaan, Israel, and their mutual antagonism. On the one hand, Canaan is understood to comprise various agrarian city-states with ever-shifting alliances and enmities, while Israel is envisaged as nomadic tribes, invading from the desert. At a more tacit level, however, following the lead of the "Deuteronomistic Historian," the language used to speak of both seems to presuppose the nation-state as prototype. Lapp's "historical group," a "political" entity to which stratified deposits must be attributed before they can have any "specific implication for interpreting economic and cultural history," appears to be the nation-state in disguise. Wright's "carefully planned invasion" by "a portion at least of the later *nation* [italics mine] of Israel" is cut from the same cloth. But if Canaan was a collection of jealous *city*-states, each with its own petty king, the *nation*-state mold fits premonarchic Israel even less well. Prior to its thirteenth-century occupation of the hill country, it had no territorial definition; prior to David, its poor, unfortified towns and villages witness neither centralized political control nor the extraction and redistribution of a significant economic surplus. In short, the tenuous unity of premonarchic Israel, its lack of sharp social stratification, and its enmity for the city-states of Canaan cannot be explained by the tacit assumption of Israel's prior existence as a nation-state in the desert.[10] The "Deuteronomistic Historian" and many moderns notwithstanding, the nation-state is not always the primary category of history.

Noth (1953:9–10 et passim) and Bright (1953:543 et passim) in the delineation of this material, despite their sharp disagreement about the nature of the *pre*-Deuteronomistic text.

10. The attempt of de Geus (1976:156–64) to describe early Israel's unity as

As with the nomadic infiltration model, an examination of the conquest model has uncovered many implicit assumptions. Once again, however, these paradigmatic assumptions do not appear viable in the form enunciated.

A MODEL OF PEASANT AND FRONTIER REVOLT

Mendenhall's Hypothesis

Many of the shortcomings of both previous models were first exposed by Mendenhall in his schematic but landmark essay (1962:66–87).[11] He went on to offer a new hypothesis which sought to evade the pitfalls of the other two:

> The fact is, and the present writer would regard it as a fact though not every detail can be "proven," that both the Amarna materials and the biblical events represent the same political process: namely, the withdrawal, not physically and geographically, but politically and subjectively, of large population groups from any obligation to existing political regimes, and therefore, the renunciation of any protection from these sources. In other words, there was no statistically important invasion of Palestine at the beginning of the twelve tribe system of Israel. There was no radical displacement of population, there was no genocide, there was no large scale driving out of population, only of royal administrators (of necessity!). In summary, there was no real conquest of Palestine in the sense that has usually been understood; what happened instead may be termed, from the point of view of the secular historian interested only in socio-political processes, a peasant's revolt against the networking of interlocking Canaanite city-states. (Mendenhall 1970:107)

The catalyst for this movement is seen in a numerically small but ideologically potent Exodus group: "A group of slave-labor captives succeeded in

---

"primarily ethnic" does not give an adequate causal explanation for the anomalies of Israelite society nor for its hostility toward the kings of Canaan. See n1, above, for a critique of de Geus's notion that Bronze Age Canaan witnessed a denser population in the hill country than in the plains.

11. Mendenhall's later works (1973:ix–31, 122–214; 1976a:152–57; 1976b:132–51) elaborate his views somewhat. Gottwald (1974:223–55; 1975:89–100; 1976a:465–68; 1976b:629–31; 1978b:2–7) has followed Mendenhall's lead, but with significant distinctions. In his large volume on the *Tribes of Yahweh: A Sociology of the Religion of Liberated Israel, 1250–1050 B.C.E.* (Gottwald 1979) a thorough discussion is provided of the issues raised by the three models.

escaping an intolerable situation in Egypt. Without any other community upon which they could rely for protection and support, they established a relationship with a deity, Yahweh, who had no antecedents except in human traditions about ways in which God manifested himself to human beings" (Mendenball 1970:107–8). The Sinai covenant then provided these ex-slaves a minimal blueprint for the formation of a new community in Palestine:

> Common loyalty to a single Overlord, and obligation to a common and simple group of norms created the community, a solidarity which was attractive to all persons suffering under the burden of subjection to a monopoly of power which they had no part in creating, and from which they received virtually nothing but tax-collectors. Consequently, entire groups having a clan or "tribal" organization joined the newly-formed community, identified themselves with the oppressed in Egypt, and received deliverance from bondage. (Mendenhall 1970:108)

This deliverance was effected when "the appearance of the small religious community of Israel polarized the existing population all over the land; some joined, while others, primarily the kings and their supporters, fought ... The kings were defeated and forced out" (Mendenhall 1970:113–14).

The broad contours of this hypothesis are attractive because they avoid those weaknesses and inconsistencies that plague the competing reconstructions. Mendenhall's positions have been subjected to numerous criticism, however, some but not all of which would appear merited.

Mendenhall's Hypothesis Amended

To begin with the former, his heavy, almost exclusive emphasis upon religious ideology as the explanation of premonarchic Israel's social mutations has tended to obscure other important factors. Although Mendenhall speaks of some groups which "migrated to the fringe areas from the more populous regions" (Mendenhall 1970:114), his gestalt appears far more dominated by "the withdrawal, not physically and geographically, but politicaliy and subjectively, of large population groups from any obligation to the existing political regimes" (Mendenhall 1970:109). The geographic factor in the withdrawal should not be so easily dismissed. As witnessed by both biblical tradition and archaeology, Israel was not able to take and hold the plains until David's time. The rugged, scrub-covered uplands which it occupied prior to Davidic expansion were, in the Late Bronze Age, the traditional haven for marginal elements who had incurred official disfavor or chosen to withdraw from a more regularized niche in the agrarian society of the plains.¹² Even the language of "official" religion at Ugarit reflected this situation. In a mythic text in which Baal Haddu functions in many regards as a city-state king writ large (KTU 1.4:7.35–37):

> Baal's enemies take to the woods,
> Haddu's foes to the sides of the mountain crag.

As shown by the excavations and surface explorations summarized above, such terrain in Palestine sustained a striking growth of unwalled "Israelite" villages on widely dispersed hilltops at the beginning of Iron Age I.¹³

Technological factors were probably responsible for rendering this frontier area habitable by a denser population (Gottwald 1975:95; Aharoni 1967:219; de Geus 1975:65–74; Forbes 1972:229–32, 244–48; Maddin, Muhly, and Wheeler 1977:122–31). The introduction of even relatively small amounts of iron, after the Hittite monopoly on smelting techniques was broken, greatly facilitated the clearing and cultivation of the hill country.¹⁴ Rock terraces were also instituted to hold the thin soils and precious seasonal rains of the highland ridge.

> These were best suited to vine, olive, and nut cultivation. But the earliest terrace farmers at Ai and Khirbet Raddana grew cereals. This inefficient use of terraces suggests an attempt by the highlanders (probably "Israelites" during the period of the Judges) to maintain a subsistence cereal agriculture free from the Canaanite and Philistine spheres, where the primary "bread baskets" were located. (Stager 1976:13)

(It might suggest in addition that these terrace-farmers had previously grown cereals in the plains.) Yet another technological innovation used to be credited with the growth of population in the hills.

---

12. Rowton (1965:375–87) has argued persuasively that *'apiru* bands, including those of the Amarna Age in Palestine, were centered in just such relatively inaccessible terrain and comprised mostly men who had "withdrawn" from the adjacent city-states.

13. Campbell (1976:37–45) and Miller (1977:252–62) also provide recent summaries of the evidence. Even Weippert (1971:135) acknowledges the remains of these villages as the one "archaeological fact which can, with a great degree of probability, be connected with the settlement of the 'Israelite' tribes," although he finds the source of this population in sedentarizing semi-nomads.

14. While 1 Sam 13:19–22 is frequently taken to indicate that the Philistines first introduced iron into Palestine, Aharoni (1967:219) is probably correct that this Philistine attempt to monopolize iron manufacture "proves that the use of iron tools was already in vogue then in Israel." The Philistines clearly wished Israel to have iron agricultural tools, but under Philistine control and for Philistine profit.

> Thanks to the rapid spread of the art, then recent, of constructing cisterns and lining them with waterproof lime plaster instead of the previously used limy marl or raw-lime plaster, the Israelites were able to settle in any site where there was rain, whereas their earlier Canaanite precursors had been forced to restrict their occupation in general to sites near springs or perennial streams. (Albright 1960:113)

While it now appears that this technology was not of such recent origin (Lapp 1969b:33 n53; Paul and Dever 1973:161; de Geus 1976:153 n127), it was at least available to be expanded and combined with the new technologies, their combination, in turn, allowing the highland ridge to sustain a denser population.

Taken as a whole, these data suggest that the settlements of premonarchic Israel be seen as occupying an opening *frontier* of the old city-states. Such frontiers in agrarian societies have attracted the interest of social theoreticians

> because they provide a unique opportunity for departures from the sociocultural patterns so deeply entrenched in agrarian societies. Those who respond to the challenge of the frontier, to its dangers and its opportunities, are primarily men with little to lose, with little stake in the established order. Thus they are likely to possess a willingness to take great physical risks and a proclivity for independence and innovation. As a result, new ways of life commonly develop in frontier areas, innovations are readily accepted, and older rigidities give way.
> One of the most significant changes that occurs is the breakdown of the traditional class system ... Having risked their lives to establish themselves in a new territory, frontiersmen are not prepared to hand over their surplus to anyone. Thus, frontier conditions often break down the sharp inequalities and exploitative patterns characteristic of agrarian societies. (Lenski and Lenski 1978:229)

Dimensions of this sort would seem to constitute an important and necessary complement to Mendenhall's more subjective and ideologically based notions of withdrawal.

His focus on religious ideology has also prompted Mendenhall virtually to equate early Israel's rejection of the forms of socio-political power typically exercised by agrarian states with outright repudiation of the use of socio-political power per se, so that "religion" and "politics" are seen as "reciprocals" (Mendenhall 1973:198–214; 1975a:169–80). Early biblical texts, such as Judges 5, corroborate Gottwald's more realistic assessment of the situation: "1) Israel challenged one form of power by means of another form of power, and 2) Israel consciously exercised power even as it consciously attributed the source of all power to its deity" (Gottwald 1975:94).[15] A less dichotomous understanding of religion and political power also allows the formation of the Israelite monarchy to be viewed less moralistically than "The Fall" depicted by Mendenhall.[16] While kingship and its concomitants were undoubtedly a reversion toward forms more typical of agrarian societies, frontier conditions in such societies are *usually* temporary.

> As ... the land begins to fill up with people, as roads are built and governmental authority is established, there is a waning of the spirit of independence and individualism, opportunities for resistance decline, and the traditional system begins to assert itself. (Lenski and Lenski 1978:229)

Had Israel not forged its own, separate monarchy upon the anvil of the Philistine crisis, the innovations of its frontier society might have been crushed forever beneath the tyrant's heel. As it was, those innovations—particularly in their prophetic expression—not only bent Israelite monarchy significantly, but also outlived it to exert influences still strongly felt today.

While it would be unfair to press the language of Mendenhall's brief article too hard, such statements as, "the appearance of the small religious community of Israel polarized the existing population all over the land" (Mendenhall 1970:113), appear to many readers to adhere more closely to ideological predilection than historical reality. Peasant movements typically involve long periods of smoldering unrest with much if not most of the populace neutral, conservatively indifferent, or involved in cleavages and conflicts that crosscut and attenuate a polarization between peasants and ruling elite (Landsberger 1973:1–64). Early Israel's lack of territorial contiguity, its abundance of natural barriers even within contiguous areas, its inclusion of many microclimates, each with its own variations in the means of subsistence, and its biblical description as a "mixed multitude" all suggest that no polarization of "Israelite" peasantry could be quick, easy, or complete. Since archaeology and biblical traditions also witness great turmoil *internal* to premonarchic Israel, categories designed to investigate these cleavages belong in any framework for the analysis of early Israelite society.

---

15. In this regard, note should also be taken of Mendenhall's own reluctant acknowledgment (1973:137 n72) and Holladay's review (1973:472–74).

16. In addition to the works of Mendenhall already cited, note his explicit treatment of the monarchy (1975b:155–70). That his more schematic formulations, including that of the "tenth generation," sometimes involve this same moralizing has been noted by reviewers (Sasson 1974:294–96).

Although each of these attempts to nuance or supplement Mendenhall's model of a peasant revolt involves matters of significance, seen in the broader context, they amount to "praising with faint damns," for they serve to reaffirm the basic cogency and heuristic value of such a model. Other critics have sought to find more fundamental flaws in this paradigm, however, and they deserve reply.

Response to Criticisms of Mendenhall's Treatment of Nomadism and the Amarna Letters

As already noted (n2, above), Weippert's attempt to rehabilitate a notion of Israel's nomadic origin in the desert reiterates the older position and its assumptions, without really confronting the mounting critique which renders it untenable.

The critique of Mendenhall's use of the fourteenth-century BCE diplomatic archive, discovered at El-Amarna on the middle Nile and commonly known as the Amarna letters, must occupy us longer, even though only a summary of the complex issues involved is possible here. Particularly crucial is his interpretation of the social dynamics associated with the term 'apiru/SA.GAZ as it is employed by the petty kinglets of Syro-Palestine in correspondence with their nominal suzerain, the Pharaoh of Egypt. Since the nature and identity of these 'apiru and their possible relation to the "Hebrews" ('ibrî) and "Israelites" of the Hebrew Bible have been the subject of a voluminous and polemical literature,[17] areas of general consensus among Mendenhall, his published critics, and the majority of informed opinion are probably best stated first: (1) The Amarna 'apiru were autochthonous in Syro-Palestine, rather than constituting an invasion—nomadic or otherwise—from outside (Weippert 1971:71; de Geus 1976:184, 186). (2) Despite recent attempts to revive earlier notions, 'apiru is not primarily or originally an ethnic designation.[18] (3) Instead, it refers basically to various elements in the population who were declassed, fugitive, uprooted, or who otherwise stood outside the acknowledged social system (Weippert 1971:58, 65; de Geus 1976:182–83; Rowton 1976a:13–20; Mendenhall 1973:122–24). (4) In a semantic generalization probably assisted by the ambiguity of such a

---

17. Access to this literature may be had through the recent work of Rowton (1976a:13 n2) and de Geus (1976:182–83 nn236–43).

18. While some scholars have recently reverted to an ethnic understanding of 'apiru (Astour 1976:382–85; de Geus 1976:182 n237), the bases for such an interpretation have received decisive crirtique (Weippert 1971:70; de Geus 1976:182–83; Rowton 1976a:17; Mendenhall 1973:122–24).

negatively defined appellation, 'apiru was not infrequently broadened in the Amarna correspondence to serve as a pejorative designation of one's enemies, vilifying them to the Egyptian court (Weippert 1971:72–74; Mendenhall 1973:123–24, 130–35; Campbell 1960:13–15). (5) Early discussion of the 'apiru often focused upon the term's etymology. While there is some continuation of that trend, a growing consensus views the etymological arguments as moot and of little *historical* significance (Weippert 1971:82–83; de Geus 1976:184–85; Rowton 1976a:13–15).[19]

Beyond these areas of broad agreement lie major disputes. Reacting in part to the unnuanced brevity of Mendenhall's initial suggestion that the Amarna 'apiru were engaged in a "peasant's revolt," Weippert has sought to demonstrate that the movement was "purely political":

> The texts clearly state that city kings, princes, countries, 'mayors' (ḫazannūtu), cities (communities of citizens), ḫupšu belong to the 'apiru or join with them ... The tenor of all the references ... indicates that the writers of the letters, who remained faithful to the Egyptian crown or at least wished to appear faithful in their letters to the Pharaoh or to high officials, mean by 'apiru, amongst whom they classify many of their colleagues (mostly their personal enemies), simply rebels against Egyptian sovereignty and are able, at the same time, to give the term an additional pejorative sense. (Weippert 1971:71–72)

Weippert then concludes that

> our observation of the fact that local kings and their followers took part in the rebellion, shows us beyond all shadow of a doubt that the 'apiru revolt in the Amarna period was not an uprising on the part of the oppressed population of the plains against the ruling feudal classes of the cities and is certainly not to be understood on the basis of a comparison with the great German Peasants' Revolt of 1525/26. (Weippert 1971:74)

Unlike Weippert, de Geus wrote after the publication of Mendenhall's essay, "The 'Apiru Movements in the Late Bronze Age" (1973:122–41), but his refutation with regard to Amarna is limited to one sentence: "To speak, with Mendenhall, of social revolt, is going too far" (de Geus 1976:184 and n245).

While mere expressions of opinion require no answer, Weippert's objections do. As stated, they are both semantically and sociologically simplistic because they assume a completely consistent use of the term 'apiru in

---

19. Mendenhall has recently discussed etymology again (1973:128–41), but his etymology builds upon his historical description, not the reverse.

the Amarna archive and an unalloyed homogeneity in their constituency, motivation, and leadership of the social and political movements to whose members it was applied. Both assumptions are intrinsically improbable and demonstrably false with regard to the Amarna 'apiru. Weippert himself recognizes that 'apiru is basically a socio-economic designation outside Amarna and that its supposed use there to specify "simply rebels against Egyptian sovereignty" is derived (Weippert 1971:65–74). Although one would hardly expect the extension of the term to a political slur to abandon or erase completely all remnants of its former meaning, such subjective judgments need not bear the burden of the argument. For even Weippert (1971:68, 73) grudgingly admits that 'apiru was employed in the Amarna letters explicitly to denote declassed elements who served as mercenaries *in the Egyptian cause* (EA 195:24–32), as well as brigands who took advantage of the troubled times (EA 318:8–15).[20] To these passages should be added EA 112:43–47, not mentioned by Weippert, in which Rib-Adda of Byblos, purportedly the staunchest of all supporters of Egyptian hegemony in Syro-Palestine, rewards an 'apiru for serving as his messenger.

Exceptions to Weippert's monolithic understanding of the Amarna 'apiru do not stop there. While instances of political opportunism on the part of groups and leaders called 'apiru certainly abound in the letters, their intrigue and hostility are directed only partially and often tangentially against Egyptian suzerainty. The major targets of 'apiru activity are the petty dynasts of the Syro-Palestinian city-states (cf. EA 68:12–18; 73:14–33; 74:19–41; 75:10–11; 76:7–20; 77:21–37; 79:7–29; 81:6–13; 85:63–82; 88:29–34; 90:5–25; 91:3–26; 104:17–54; 117:35–40, 56–64, 92–94; 118:21–39; 130:36–42; 144:22–32; 246 rev.:5–10; 271:9–21; 272:10–17; 273:8–24; 286:16–60; 287:14–24; 288:36–46; 299:17–26; 305:21–24; 318:8–15; 366:11–26), who are under fire from elements of what is ostensibly their own population (basic sense of 'apiru), from other such dynasts taking advantage of chaotic conditions for self-aggrandizement at their neighbors' expense (derived sense of 'apiru), or some combination of the two. Although Rib-Adda sought to convince his suzerain that the 'apiru-linked activities of Abdi-Ashirta and Aziru were blatantly anti-Egyptian, the court policies of "balance of power" and "divide and rule" apparently viewed Rib-Adda's constant appeals as alarmist and self-serving: they were largely ignored as being Rib-Adda's concern, not Pharaoh's (cf., e.g., EA 106:13–16). EA 101:29–31 and 161:51–53, moreover, speak of the placement of Abdi-Ashirta and Aziru in their positions *by the Egyptian crown* (cf. Mendenhall 1973:125–27; EA 60; and, on EA 101,

---

20. For 'apiru as mercenaries, see also EA 71:10–31; 246 rev:5–10. Citation of the Amarna archive follows the numbering of Knudtzon (1915) and Rainey (1970).

Moran 1969:94–99). That Aziru later defected to the Hittites does not alter the fact that both he and his father served by Egyptian appointment and regularization of their de facto power while Rib-Adda accused them of being or consorting with ʿapiru. On the other hand, the self-righteously "loyal" Rib-Adda not only threatened to make a pact with Abdi-Ashirta (*EA* 83:23–27), following the pattern of other dynasts in the area (*EA* 82:5–13; 85:63–69), but, it would now appear (McCarter 1973:15–18), actually attempted such collusion with Aziru. In short, both the term ʿapiru in Amarna usage and the activities to which it was applied are far more complex than simple rebellion against Egyptian sovereignty.

Similarly, Weippert's claim that the Amarna materials cannot reflect popular uprisings because the term ʿapiru is applied to local kinglets and their followers is specious on any of three grounds: (1) Such application of the term is easily explained as political slurring, which proves nothing about the possibility of its use elsewhere in a more specific, socioeconomic sense. (To refer to a modern analogue, the status and attributes of persons to whom the terms "communist" or "fascist" have been hostilely applied could hardly be used to deny any particular trait to social and political movements more specifically designated by these names.) (2) Peasant movements enjoying more than localized and momentary success have always involved and allied with other, non-peasant elements—the more successful, the less "pure" (Landsberger 1973:1–64, esp. 57–60). (According to Weippert's historiographic principles, the English Peasant Revolt of 1381 could not have involved a peasant revolt because prominent landowners—including Sir Roger Bacon—and three of London's aldermen are known to have been participants and/or allies.) (3) Most important, while the sparse contexts of many of the Amarna occurrences of ʿapiru might permit various understandings of the term, other passages slighted or ignored by Weippert clearly reflect social unrest.[21] Because of the importance and complexity of this material, a representative sample has been translated and discussed in an excursus: "The ʿApiru and Social Unrest in the Amarna Letters from Syro-Palestine" (see below, pp. 38–50).

Even presuming the social agitation documented there in connection with the Amarna ʿapiru, their exact relation to the "Hebrews" (ʿibrî) and "Israelites" of the Hebrew Bible remains to be treated. Weippert himself concludes from a full investigation of the relevant phonological and morphological data that "the equation ʿapiru = Hebrews can certainly be substantiated with linguistic proofs" (1971:82. cf. 74–82, 101). He then surveys

---

21. Nor has this unrest gone unnoticed in the secondary literature (Artzi 1964:159–66; Astour 1964:6–17; Moran 1967b:878–80; Liverani 1965:267–77; 1974:352–55).

by category the thirty-three biblical occurrences of *'ibrî(m)*, agreeing that the "Hebrew slave" of OT legal texts can be compared with the *'apiru* in slavery contracts from Nuzi, and allowing some analogy between the Amarna *'apiru* and the use of "Hebrew" in 1 Samuel to designate both Israelites who serve the Philistines as mercenaries and the opposing Israelite forces themselves (Weippert 1971:101, cf. 85–88). Otherwise, he regards all connections with grave suspicion: "The passages in the Joseph story and the exodus narratives, as well as the examples from late Old Testament and subsequent writings, seem to understand the word *'ibrî* as an archaic way of describing the 'Israelite' nation. The connection with the *'apiru* is extremely indirect" (Weippert 1971:101). From this fact and the occurrence of *'ibrî(m)* only in certain circumscribed groups of texts, Weippert concludes that it "seems out of the question to regard without closer examination the terms "Hebrews" and "Israelites" as synonyms and to lump the "Israelites"/"Hebrews" together with the *'apiru*-people" (1971:101).

Although the brevity of Mendenhall's initial article might be read as failing to make such distinctions adequately, recent discussions provide nuanced answers to Weippert's objections (Mendenhall 1973:135–38; Rowton 1976a:19). Rowton (1976a:19) cites both old and new evidence for the employment of *'apiru* labor on Egyptian building operations, paralleling the use of *'ibrî(m)* in several of the Exodus narratives. Regarding the alternation of "(Yahweh), God of the *'ibrîm*" with "Yahweh, God of Israel" in these narratives, he writes:

> these detribalized Israelites who, to an Egyptian or or [sic] a Philistine, amounted to little more than tribal scum and renegades, would have been viewed in Israelite tradition as tribal expatriates. Hence from this view, "God of the *'ibrîm*" is simply equivalent to "God of the tribal expatriates," meaning, of course, in the context in which it occurs, Israel's expatriates. And could it be seriously suggested that Jahwe would not have been credited with the power to protect an Israelite living among foreigners? (Rowton 1976a:20)

In these Exodus passages and those where Weippert admits some relationship with *'apiru*, the term *'ibrî(m)* would appear to reflect its socioeconomic and politico-legal roots. All these "Hebrews" were *'apiru*, in that sense, though, of course, not all *'apiru* were "Hebrews," the former term finding a much wider expression geographically and chronologically. When the monarchic state of Israel coalesced about David and his "Hebrew" band, however, this formerly social designation could gradually have acquired an "ethnic" connotation. Rowton offers cogent parallels for such a development, and terms the resulting appellation a "social ethnonym" (1976a:9–20, esp. 19; cf. Mendenhall 1973:137). Since virtually all texts in the Hebrew Bible which employ 'ibrî(m) were written after the advent of the monarchy, it should occasion no surprise that many of them evidence ambiguity between social and "ethnic" meanings for the term, with some knowing only the latter.

Several conclusions seem clear: (1) There is no definitive bar to connecting 'apiru and 'ibrî(m) linguistically. (2) Quite apart from any etymological link, many of the 'ibrî(m) of the Hebrew Bible occupy social roles analogous to the 'apiru of cuneiform and Egyptian sources. (3) Other occurrences of 'ibrî(m) appear to witness the term's development into a "social ethnonym," a process well documented elsewhere and readily intelligible within the historical context. Development in the opposite dirction is implausible. (4) Because of this development, OT texts taken as a whole are ambiguous about the relationship between "Hebrews" and "Israelites." From the perspective of *monarchic* "Israel," *all* Israelites, particularly those in foreign contexts, could be called "Hebrews" as an archaic, "ethnic" name, or some Israelites could be called "Hebrews" to designate their social role. As seen above, however, *most* members of the premonarchic federation known as "Israel" were "Hebrews" in the socioeconomic and politico-legal sense. (5) All names and their possible linguistic associations aside, premonarchic Israel held in common with the Amarna 'apiru of an earlier time their geographic, social, and tactical location, significant forms of social organization, and the enmity of the kinglets of the same Canaanite city-states. (6) Since major interventions in the Palestinian hill country by Egypt or other monarchic states are unknown between the Amarna Age and the appearance of premonarchic Israel, considerable continuity of social dynamic is probable. (7) In the historical reconstruction of premonarchic Israel, therefore, reference to the social unrest unequivocally attested for Syro-Palestine by the Amarna archive is legitimate on *historical* grounds, and does not rest upon a semantically simple-minded equation of 'apiru, "Hebrews," and "Israelites." All three terms entail decided ambiguity, and their referents vary with the context; no two are completely synonymous; each is closely related to the others in the manner outlined.

Archaeological Objections to the Revolt Model Considered

Even when Mendenhall is granted use of the Amarna materials, however, his hypothesis still faces criticism from proponents of the conquest model, who have argued that archaeological evidence weighs against notions of a peasant revolt. Lapp is most explicit:

> But the massive destructions and the complete reorientations of fairly prosperous cities could hardly have resulted so consistently, I would expect, if the primary matter was the elimination of a few Canaanite overlords. The employment of so many silos (not known in the Late Bronze age), the new kind of ceramic ware, the architectural poverty, and the new occupations on so many sites combine to suggest a social change that is more than the result of social upheaval. These things point to a large group of intruders. The "revolt of the masses" seems to be a modern construct forced on ancient traditions in opposition to the archaeological evidence. (1967:298–99)

As we have already seen (n3 above), Mendenhall's current answer seems to be that the agent of destruction was not Israel. He has recourse instead to what he terms the virtual universality of destruction levels at this time in the whole eastern Mediterranean area.

Painting with that broad a brush glosses over important distinctions that may be briefly summarized: (1) In the late thirteenth and early twelfth centuries BCE, the destruction in Palestine took place at sites in or near the hill country or otherwise isolated from the main group of Canaanite city-states, which were *not* destroyed at that time. (2) Away from the coast, more than one site evidences the sequence: Late Bronze Canaanite, "Israelite" (material culture consistent with the unwalled villages of the hill country), and Philistine. Some such "Israelite" towns were built in the ashes of the previous Canaanite city (Lapp 1967:286–87, 292, 298). (3) At least some cities in the coastal plain have no "Israelite" stratum in the period concerned, but passed directly from the destruction of the "Canaanite" city to Philistine occupation (Lapp 1967:293–94; Miller 1977:257). (4) In other instances (e.g., Shechem and Khirbet Rabûd), no layer of destruction separates the "Canaanite" and "Israelite" strata (Campbell 1975:152–53).

Although these distinctions tend to erode Mendenhall's position on the archaeological evidence, they aid in formulating an alternative answer to Lapp's objections which is consistent with Mendenhall's hypothesis as amended here. This answer may be developed by discussing seriatim the categories of data which Lapp thinks to necessitate "a large group of intruders" and tell against a popular uprising.

He looks first to "the massive destructions and complete reorientations of fairly prosperous cities," phenomena that also trouble E. F. Campbell (1975:152), who is considerably less hostile to Mendenhall's approach. But one must ask what was destroyed, and what, for that matter, has been excavated. With few exceptions, the answer is the same—the city fortifications and the temple-palace-garrison-store house-elite housing complexes.

These structures were instruments and symbols of the power and social control of the governing class, requiring corvée labor to build. As in most agrarian societies, they stood as architectural manifestations of a system of stratification in which an elite of probably no more than two percent of the population controlled up to half or more of the total goods and services produced (Lenski 1966:189–296; Lenski and Lenski 1978:177–230; Sjoberg 1960:80–107, 110 et passim).[22] An internal revolt against this small governing class and any of its retainers who remained loyal, therefore, would have involved an attack upon these very structures for reasons both "instrumental" and "expressive."[23] All but the briefest fighting would have resulted in the destruction of some non-elite structures as well, for the forces that ultimately won would probably have sustained reverses in the process, and fire, once unleashed in the preindustrial city, would have been almost impossible to control. In any reoccupation by the "revolutionaries," architectural poverty and reorientation would certainly have been the order of the day, since, at the level of technology then current, to do otherwise would have meant the reimposition of the very exactions and corvée they had fought to abolish. Cities where the governing class fled, or where it chose to conciliate its people and the loose federation known as Israel, would not have experienced such radical architectural disruption, but the marked reduction in social stratification and division of labor would have resulted in material culture similar to that of the people who reoccupied the destroyed cities and founded the many new villages of this period.[24]

Let us now examine that material culture more closely. Lapp argues that the pit silo, whose profusion is the virtual trademark of the earliest "Israelite" sites, was unknown in the Late Bronze Age, and that it was therefore introduced from outside Palestine, even though he cannot point to antecedents elsewhere. Although pit silos may have been as rare in Late Bronze Canaan as they were frequent in early Iron I "Israel," they *did* exist. Albright reports finding several at Tell Beit Mirsim in strata unequivocally belonging

---

22. To those who would protest that no such statistical data are available from Late Bronze Canaan, it must be answered that these figures have been developed on a broadly comparative basis for agrarian societies as a type of social and economic organization. The system of stratification described is *generic* to societies based upon a cultivation technology that knows the plow but not the industrial revolution. For all their cultural and historical diversity, therefore, the variations within any such society are far greater than between any two such societies.

23. Landsberger (1973:21–22) provides a convenient explanation of these terms and a convincing argument that they properly represent two separate dimensions, which are by no means mutually exclusive.

24. Campbell (1975:152–53) makes a similar assessment of the evidence from such sites as Shechem and Khirbet Rabûd.

to the Late Bronze Age (Albright 1932:51; 1938:64–65; 1943:1–4). Nor is the rapid proliferation in earliest "Israel" of this minor form of "Canaanite" grain storage difficult to explain in terms of a model of peasant and frontier revolt. Because the surrender by the peasants to the ruling class of a large proportion of their cereal harvest would have been a major source of conflict (for the Amarna Age, cf. Albright 1975:106), one would expect peasants who had overthrown or driven out their lords to institute a radically decentralized means of storing the grain which they had thereby redeemed from the tax-collector. The pit silo, which is found in most, but not all early Israelite towns and villages (Callaway 1976:29–30) would have represented one cheap and available method for keeping precious cereals hard by the dwelling of the peasant who had produced them.

Similar considerations readily explain the rapid growth in the population of the hill country witnessed by the founding of many new and widely dispersed villages and the reoccupation of other sites long vacant. Retention by the peasants of surpluses formerly surrendered to the ruling elite of the few upland cities would have been partially responsible, for as Mendenhall rightly states, "peasant populations tend to invest economic surpluses in population increase" (Mendenhall 1976a:157). Another cause of this denser population has already been outlined in terms of the technological innovations which rendered the highland ridge a more economically viable haven for disgruntled peasants from the plains. Callaway provides a specific example. In a discussion of the early "Israelite" village founded upon the long-deserted mound at Ai, he notes the similarity between a terrace-creating retainer wall there and "barriers built in valleys or wadi beds to slow the flow of water and trap eroded soil ... Because of the similarity of the terraces and barriers built in valleys, one may conjecture an origin for the villagers in the lowland region west of the hill country" (Callaway 1976:29–30). Flight to the hill country would have put such villagers beyond the effective control of their former lords, for the terrain itself helped to neutralize the dread chariots with which those lords dominated the plains. Thus free from high taxes and rents on their agricultural production and from the imposition of corvée in order to build city walls and monumental architecture, these newcomers to the hills would also have retained economic surpluses, thereby adding to the process of "swarming" noted by Mendenhall (1976a:157).

Lapp's final objection concerns pottery, regarding which his own masterful summary (1967:295–96) marks the following salient features: (1) "The basic general typology is virtually identical in the 13th and 12th centuries B.C." (2) "Both periods are characterized by very heavy vessels"; but "the Late Bronze ware seems to be much more finely levigated, and many of the diverse particles characteristic of Iron I ware do not seem to occur in the Late Bronze ware." (3) Differences in color "suggest different kiln traditions." (4) By the twelfth century, both imports and their local imitations cease outside the coastal and Esdraelon plains. Once again, this evidence no more necessitates "a large group of intruders" than it precludes the paradigm developed here. In the highly stratified society of the Canaanite city-states, artisan skills were relatively specialized and foreign trade, consisting principally of luxury and strategic goods, had been developed by and for the ruling elite. One would expect imported pottery under such circumstances, with local, full-time potters throwing well refined clay and utilizing relatively sophisticated and consistent techniques of firing. If premonarchic Israel constituted the kind of frontier counter-formation from this Canaanite society here presumed, it could be expected to employ part-time potters who would carry on the same basic ceramic typology in utilitarian vessels, but with cruder execution. Local clay, often less well refined, would be fired under more rudimentary and less consistent conditions. Since this subsistence economy would not produce major concentrations of wealth or trade in either luxury wares or commodities, imported pottery would not appear. In short, a model of peasant and frontier revolt accounts for this and the other archaeological evidence cited by Lapp at least as well as, if not better than, a large group of conquerors from outside. Since the antecedents and subsistence of any such group outside Palestine are problematic in the extreme, the balance of probability in accounting for the archaeological data falls to a model of revolt and withdrawal toward an opening frontier.

Conditions Conducive to Peasant Revolt

Yet another frequent objection to such a model contends that it "seems to be a modern construct superimposed upon the biblical traditions" (Miller 1977:279; cf. Lapp 1967:299), and that it "seems altogether too idealistic and romantic" (de Geus 1976:186)! But these opinions are merely asserted rather than argued, and ignore both the Amarna evidence cited here and the fact that the history of agrarian societies is replete with peasant rebellions (Lenski 1966:274–75; Wolf 1969:279; Landsberger 1973:1). Particularly pertinent is a burgeoning literature which studies comparatively those far fewer peasant movements which have grown to more than localized extent and significance. While such comparative studies cannot prove that ancient Israel emerged from a Palestinian peasant's revolt, they can allow us to determine whether there existed in Late Bronze and Early Iron I Palestine a concatenation of conditions which in other agrarian societies have proved conducive to broader peasant revolts.

What, in summary, are some of those circumstances, as they have been delineated by historically minded social scientists? Wolf argues convincingly that the "tactically mobile" segment of a peasantry is the most likely to revolt because such peasants "are able to rely on some external power to challenge the power which constrains them" (1969:290). Furthermore, "any factor which serves to increase the latitude granted by that tactical mobility reinforces their revolutionary potential" (1969:293). Although controversy abounds concerning which stratum of the peasantry in areas under close landlord control best meets the revolutionary criteria (Landsberger 1973:17–18, 26), there is broad agreement that "peripheral location with regard to the center of state control" *does* grant such latitude (Wolf 1969:293; cf. Lenski 1966:274). "The tactical effectiveness of such areas is strengthened still further if they contain defensible mountain redoubts" (Wolf 1969:293). Both the Amarna 'apiru and premonarchic Israel, of course, occupied the mountainous periphery of the Canaanite city-states.

More romantic notions notwithstanding, the unequal economic relationship between elite and peasantry has not, of itself, produced peasant revolution. Landlords have frequently provided protection and other services necessary for the agricultural cycle and social cohesion of the village, thus forming manystranded bonds with their peasants. "Where the links arising out of this relationship between overlord and peasant community are strong, the tendency toward peasant rebellion (and later revolution) is feeble" (Moore 1966:469). The failure of the aristocracy to perform such compensatory services for the peasantry, however, reduces the relationship to a single strand, one of economic exploitation. This turn of affairs is both obvious to peasants and conducive to revolt (Moore 1966:468–71; Landsberger 1973:29–30). As the Amarna letters (see below, pp. 38–50) and anepigraphic archaeology both make clear, Palestine, just prior to and during the emergence of Israel as a society, was embroiled in a chronic state of petty warfare, with none of the local dynasts able effectively to protect his peasants or their fields.

These constant hostilities would have had results other than imposing additional economic burdens on the peasantry and undermining the strength and effectiveness of the ruling class. "Indeed, wars in general are associated with, and often precede the outbreak of peasant unrest" (Landsberger 1973:52). Of particular relevance here is the consciousness-arousing aspect of peasant involvement in warfare, for "individuals and groups most likely to participate in peasant organizations are those whose traditional values have been modified . . . through such circumstances as participation in military service and war" (Landsberger 1969:41). As a result of this experience, "skill in the disciplined use of force is acquired, the fruits of organization and cooperation [are] observed and often the incompetence of the upper strata demonstrated" (Landsberger 1973:52). The descriptions of certain *ḫupšu* in the Amarna letters indicate that some Syro-Palestinian peasants gained such experience and acted accordingly. That the term apparently means both "peasant" and "peasant soldier" also seems to reflect the enlistment of numerous peasants into armed service (see below, pp. 38–41, and n31).

Structural considerations are also significant. "The great agrarian bureaucracies of royal absolutism . . . have been especially liable to the combination of factors favoring peasant revolution" (Moore 1966:478; cf. 472–74, 478–79; and Landsberger 1973:30). They have tended to take over the protective and judicial functions of the local overlord, and thus to weaken the crucial ties between peasants and the upper classes. Where their assumption of these functions has been only partial and/ or when royal power has waned, two overlapping and competing layers of administration have usually developed, each exacting an economic surplus from the peasants, but neither able or willing to protect their persons or production. Corruption and bribery have run rife under such conditions. Due partially to environmental factors, Egypt provides the most striking example from the ancient Near East of royal absolutism and its attendant bureaucracy (Parsons 1977:53–63). When the Pharaohs of the New Kingdom period extended Egyptian rule into Palestine, compromises were struck between the kind of bureaucratic control which was possible in the Nile valley and the exegencies of distance, terrain, and entrenched local overlords—a situation which was repeated a millennium later under Ptolemaic administration (Helck 1962:109–621; Lorton 1974:176–79 et passim; Albright 1975:102–16; Tcherikover 1959:59–73; Bagnall 1976:11–24). As a result, neither the Egyptian "commissioners" nor the local Canaanite "governors"—*rabiṣūtu* and *ḫazannūtu*, respectively, in Amarna parlance—could effectively maintain order in the absence of an Egyptian army, but both could and did extract resources from the peasants of Canaan. "The extent to which both official and irregular exaction went is almost unbelievable" (Albright 1975:106).

In addition to this situation of double taxation without compensation, "reinforcing cleavages," such as national, religious, ethnic, and linguistic divisions, have been found to enhance the revolutionary potential of peasants. "Cleavages other than economic ones may be of critical importance both in strengthening and weakening peasant movements, depending simply on whether or not they coincide with, or cut across class lines" (Landsberger 1973:54; cf. Wolf 1969:293). One such reinforcing cleavage of an ethnic nature is suggested for Canaan by the fact that "a high proportion of the Palestinian chiefs bore Indo-Aryan names," while "the proportion of Indo-Aryans decreases as we go downward in the social scale" (Albright 1975:104, 109).

This reinforcement of a stark vertical differentiation was linked with a relative lack of horizontal differentiation in the structure of Canaanite society—that is, economic, political, religious, and other institutions were quite incompletely distinguished. Such a combination favored profound and wide-ranging goals in any peasant movement which might arise, for "the more the social institutions confronting the peasant were themselves interconnected—so that in order to tackle one, they all had to be dealt with—the broader would be the movement's goals" (Landsberger 1973:25; cf. 1969:31–35).

The revolutionary tendencies of peasants have also been shown to vary in relation to the institutional structure of the peasant village itself. "In a rebellious and revolutionary form of solidarity, institutional arrangements are such as to spread grievances through the peasant community and turn it into a solidarity group hostile to the overlord" (Moore 1966:475). Landsberger writes of "a history of communal cooperative effort" favoring a "common reaction to low status" (1973:27). Recent, detailed studies of the documentary evidence from Syria for village life in the Late Bronze Age have emphasized the collective nature of many obligations.

> Villages, as collective units, were obligated to meet all taxes and duties placed upon them by the royal government. This demonstrates the communal character of the Ugaritic village, which should thus be considered a rural community. (Heltzer 1976; 47)

> The rural communities were responsible for corvée, ... [and] in various legal actions. (Heltzer 1976:63)

Heltzer (1976:1, 102) is undoubtedly correct that these conclusions may be extrapolated, *mutatis mutandis*, to Palestine, since the pressures of commercialization, which tend to erode such arrangements, were stronger at Ugarit than in Palestine.

Perhaps the most significant such institutional arrangement was a system of land tenure wherein the fields were held by the village as a whole and were periodically redistributed among its members to take account of demographic changes. "One of the main consequences of the periodic redivision of property in the ... peasant commune ... seems to have been to generalize land hunger, to align the richer peasants with the poorer ones" (Moore 1966:475–76). Although seriously attenuated by elite and mercantile encroachments, some vestiges of this system seem to be reflected in the

Syrian evidence (Heltzer 1976:65–71; Diakonoff 1975:121–33). Moreover, as virtually all students of the subject have concluded (Alt 1955:13–23; 1959:348–72; Bess 1963:passim), only the postulation of this repartitional domain for premonarchic Israel and of its unequal conflict with the combination of patrimonial and prebendal domain[25] introduced in conjunction with the monarchy can adequately account for scores of allusions in the Hebrew Bible. The origins of this system and the accompanying generalization of land hunger should not be sought, with Alt and his followers, among sedentarizing nomads, for such an explanation is predicated upon a model the evidentiary bases of which have been almost completely eroded. Since repartitional domain is well attested in the historical record of agrarian socieites[26] and administrative texts seem to support its prior existence in Syro-Palestine, the roots of this phenomenon in Israel are best traced to the villages of Canaan. The ideology of the Exodus group added the potent notion that all the land ultimately belonged to Yahweh, the only legitimate overlord, thereby stripping of legitimation any absolute claim of property right by a mere human. The more concrete demands of "Israelite" peasants probably involved some remembrances of earlier village communes. In Landsberger's words, "Goals will be more specific when past institutional structures can serve as a reference point, for example, the restoration of communal lands" (1969:36). Finally, this redistributional system of land tenure may provide one more reason why the earliest terrace-farmers in Israel grew cereals, rather than the grapes, olives, and nuts to which their hillside plots were better suited (see above, p. 13). For "where a piece of land changes hands periodically, few cultivators will make permanent improvements on it. The system thus reinforces the traditional and relatively extensive cultivation of annual crops and discourages the introduction of intensively produced perennials" (Wolf 1966:79).

There is broad agreement that a final factor—outside leadership—not only favors organized peasant unrest, but is essential in transforming local peasant rebellions into broader agrarian revolt. "By themselves the peasants have never been able to accomplish a revolution . . . They . . . have to have leaders from other classes" (Moore 1966:479; cf. Landsberger 1973:47–49; Wolf 1969:294–96). *It is this factor, in the persons of the leaders of the Exodus group, which—along with the technological and demographic changes already noted—spells the difference between the peasant unrest patent in the Amarna letters and the broader revolt hypothesized as a crucial component*

25. Wolf (1966:50–59) provides a convenient discussion of these terms as used here.

26. Perhaps the two best attested examples are the *mir* of prerevolutionary Russia and *mušaʿa* tenure in the Near East (Wolf 1966:78–79, 86, 90; Moore 1966:475–76; Blum 1961:510–12; Latron 1936:passim).

in the formation of Israel as a society. No matter who else was involved, the "Levites" of the earliest strata of biblical tradition have the strongest claim to this role, since a number of their names—including that of Moses—are Egyptian in etymology (Bright 1972:119 and n28). Although the traditions concerning these premonarchic Levites are relatively sparse, they make reference to most of the characteristics which the leaders of peasant revolts are known to have exhibited.

The consciousness-arousing effects of military service for peasants were discussed above. A parallel break with traditional values would have been facilitated for future leaders by their living in a foreign country (Landsberger 1973:27, 52; 1969:41), in this case, sophisticated Egypt. In the biblical traditions of the Exodus from Egypt, the figure of Moses probably represents both the ideological fountainhead of later Israel and a generic composite of its leadership. As such, he manifests a related attribute frequent among the leaders and supporters of movements to change society, namely, "status inconsistency." This means that he is portrayed as ranking low in society according to one criterion, but high according to another: he was born a "Hebrew," but raised the son of Pharaoh's daughter. Lenski has articulated the cogent theory that the tensions and conflicts born of such inconsistent status often "lead individuals to react against the existing social order" (1966:87; cf. 86–88, 288–89, 408–10).

The lineal and ideological descendents of the Moses group had potent seeds to sow and fertile soil in Canaan in which to sow them. As the root metaphor of their faith, they asserted that Yahweh had saved them from slavery by the defeat of Pharaoh and the elite of his troops. At Sinai, they believed, this same God had declared himself the only legitimate suzerain and bound them to a covenantal blueprint for a just society.[27] If some of the harried peasants of Palestine found this ideology and its bearers appealing, they fit a common pattern:

> A peasantry which finds itself increasingly economically exploited by superior groups and institutions providing it no service in return, and with an ideology which provides no plausible justification for this, will be more susceptible to other ideal designs for society. (Landsberger 1973:40)

---

27. Such statements, of course, presume some historical connection between Exodus and Sinai—a matter much debated. Although far too complex to be rehearsed here, the issues and literature have been surveyed recently for the interested reader (Nicholson 1973:1–84; Campbell 1975:141–51).

> Its leadership, particularly its outside leadership, imparts to peasant movements such ideologies as they have, particularly in the case of radical ideologies. (Landsberger 1969:52)

Nor did these outside leaders lack means of initiating their "Canaanite converts" into the paradigmatic experiences of their faith. Although thinly historicized and heavily encrusted with later accretions, Joshua 3–5 and 24 reflect at heart the liturgical recapitulation of the Exodus and Sinai events in rites that instructed and incorporated new members, inculcated discipline and unity against the common enemy, and celebrated and reinforced the power and legitimacy of their covenant with one another and with their divine overlord. Both Gilgal and Shechem, the sites of these observances, were broadly accessible from the frontier areas occupied by premonarchic Israel.

In the kind of goal-oriented organization here envisaged, however, "the leader may be more prepared than his followers to use 'secondary' violence as a premeditated means to vanquish the enemy, . . . or to unify and animate a divided and sagging movement" (Landsberger 1969:55). "The adoption of violence as a means," moreover, "requires a paramilitary type of organization" (Landsberger 1969:55). Old traditions embedded in Gen 34:25–31; 49:5–7; and Exod 2:11–15; 32:25–29 cast Moses and the Levites in just this mold.

Such militancy and wide-ranging goals for the reconstruction of society are not the only prerequisites of an organized movement. Networks of communication are imperative, though necessarily difficult in a rural setting (Landsberger 1969:55–56). Without their bonding function, actions cannot be coordinated, and the parochial interests and sectional jealousies which typify peasant communities dissolve any larger unity or effectiveness. Biblical tradition leaves little doubt that such centrifugal forces operated powerfully in early Israel, and that most of the Israelite tribes constituted separate cantons. The one conspicuous exception to this regionalism was the Levites, who occupied no single area, but were spread as resident aliens throughout the territories of the various other tribes (cf. Judg 17:7–9; 19:1). One may plausibly infer that, aided by the disarray of the upper classes in Canaan and the protection afforded by the terrain, they provided the loosely knit organization called Israel with both ideology and channels of communication in their role as non-elite priests. If so, they served a function frequently performed by members of the inferior clergy in other peasant revolts (Landsberger 1973:49; Landsberger and Landsberger 1973:123–24, 127–30; Lenski 1966:263).

This brief attempt to delineate factors known on the basis of comparative investigation to foster significant agrarian revolt and to document their occurrence in the world of Israel's emergence has been far from exhaustive. It does suffice, however, to demonstrate that a model for the formation of ancient Israelite society that includes an element of peasant revolt fits established socio-historical parameters for agrarian societies and is not merely a romantic, modern fabrication, foisted without warrant upon the evidence.

The Revolt Model and Biblical Tradition

A final objection to such a model appeals to biblical tradition:

> The theory that Israel emerged from a Palestinian peasants' revolt finds no basis in the biblical materials, whether one considers the oldest discernible strata of the conquest tradition or the final canonical account ... There is not the slightest hint in the biblical traditions regarding the revolution which supposedly brought Israel into existence. Surely one would expect to find some allusion to it in the book of Judges if such a revolution had in fact occurred. (Miller 1977:279; cf. Lapp 1967:299)

While a full analysis of the biblical text in light of the revolt paradigm still remains to be undertaken, this working hypothesis *does* find support in the biblical materials as well as providing a plausible explanation for certain anomalies within the tradition. Only the briefest summary is possible here, but even it should serve to encourage the vigorous pursuit of such analysis rather than its a priori foreclosure.

That a connected narrative of a peasant revolt is not to be found in the Hebrew Bible can hardly occasion surprise. In their present form, virtually all OT narratives are the product of royal functionaries and/or priestly elites who could not be expected to transmit traditions of peasant uprisings in a sympathetic and unrefracted form. The "conquest" account in Joshua, as noted above (p. 10), probably owes its present framework and orientation to the intense nationalism of the Josianic reform. From that perspective, "Canaan" and "Israel" were understandably viewed as nation-states and their conflict moralistically interpreted in terms of Deuteronomistic ideology. Even when the Deuteronomistic "mortar" and glosses are isolated on literary grounds (cf. n8, above) and bracketed, the older materials betray shaping from a number of different viewpoints, including that of the early monarchy (Noth 1953:11-13; Tucker 1972:71-86). Traditions more reflective of a revolt of the lower classes in Canaan have thus been abridged and muted, but not completely suppressed.

In the saga of Rahab the harlot in Joshua 2, for instance, only the first person plurals of the Deuteronomistic additions to Rahab's speech in vv. 9b–11 understand her as just another loyal subject of the king of Jericho, along with all "Canaanites" paralyzed with fear at the approach of large numbers of Israelite intruders. While the pre-Deuteronomistic remainder of the chapter has been truncated and edited, so that it abounds with tensions and unanswered questions, it basically reflects instead a conflict between the king and his retainers on the one side, and Rahab and the Israelite spies (or "messengers"; cf. Josh 6:17b, 25b) on the other. Nor can there be any question of the narrator's hostility toward the former or sympathy with the latter. These attitudes go far in placing the earlier narrator, his audience, and their enemies in terms of social roles and cleavages, the more so since characters in saga are often more generic than specific. Seen as such generic types, Rahab and the spies represent the urban lower classes and "outside agitators" against royal authority, respectively, for her "profession" places the harlot among the debased and vulnerable "expendables" of an agrarian city, while the Israelite representatives seek refuge in the hills (vv. 16, 22, 23), the traditional haven for anti-royal elements.[28] Not only would such groups not agonize over the morality of Rahab's lying or her means of subsistence, as have so many commentators since antiquity, but they would relish each repetition of the tale of her making an utter fool of the king. For the rest, the narrative emphasizes what would most concern the urban poor and those from outside who might seek to organize them. The former would require assurance that the movement would succeed (vv. 9a, 14b, 24a) and that they would survive the hostilities (vv. 12–14, 18–19); the latter would seek to guarantee that their secret plan not be exposed (vv. 14, 20–21). In short, the oldest kernal of the Rahab saga gives literary expression to one of the basic dynamics presumed by the revolt hypothesis, and would once have served to reinforce and legitimate the somewhat tenuous alliance between the groups typified by Rahab and the spies.

The literary linkage of this saga with the account in Joshua 6 of Jericho's fall is almost universally recognized as secondary, though

---

28. The socioeconomic role of prostitution in an agrarian city is well known (Lenski and Lenski 1978:214–15; Sjoberg 1960:134–37, 203–4). While Tucker (1972:84) is correct that the present narrative does not specifically picture the spies enlisting a fifth column, "this business of ours" (vv. 14, 20) which they are so concerned not to have divulged can hardly have referred to anything else originally, for according to vv. 2–7, the king already knew of the presence of spies. In v. 18, moreover, LXX has the spies speak of when they will enter "a part of the city." MT's bland reading of "the land" at this point is surely a secondary harmonization with Joshua 6. Note, too, the strategic location of Rahab's house in the city wall (v. 15). Soggin (1972:37–38) discusses these and other indications of what the current torso implies or presupposes, but does not state.

pre-Deuteronomistic (Tucker 1972:72). Compared with chapter 2, chapter 6 exhibits quite a different genre. Like Joshua 3–4, its thin historicization poorly conceals liturgical origins (Cross 1973:103–5, 138–44; Soggin 1972:83, 86–88; see above, pp. 31). These origins, in turn, can account for the lack of remains from the "conquest" period at Jericho. Just as the march "from Shittim to Gilgal" (cf. Mic 6:5) could epitomize and celebrate escape from bondage, solemn procession around the nearby ruins of the ancient and once proud city of Jericho could symbolize the defeat of the elitist power (cf. Josh 6:2) manifested by *any* walled city (see above, pp. 22–23). Jericho's role as the cultic archetype for the fall of the governing classes and the architectural expressions of their control would have been far less congenial to official celebrants and tradents of monarchic times, who could be expected to historicize this paradigmatic ritual into the miraculous capture of a specific enemy city.

As has long been noted, the Hebrew Bible contains no "conquest" narrative for much of central Palestine—a region marked in the Amarna period by the 'apiru-linked activities of Labaya. This area *is* represented in biblical tradition by accounts of covenants involving the Gibeonites (Joshua 9–10) and Shechemites (Joshua 24). Although these narratives have been embellished and refracted by any number of tradents and polemics, they seem at heart to reflect covenants between the "Israelites" and friendly "Canaanites" against the kings of Canaan (G. E. Wright 1962:76–78). As Halpern has recently argued,

> the Israelite treaties with Gibeon and Shechem may reflect the general process of defection by indigenous peoples from their aristocratic Canaanite overlords to an insurgent camp. Gibeon and Shechem, ruled by their elders, chose to make common cause with the Israelite invaders against the monarchs of Jerusalem and other towns. In so doing, they gave expression to Canaan's social cleavage. The imperial towns of the coastal plain and trade routes could no longer enforce their will in the central hills. (1975:312)

That the dynasts of Canaan were the primary targets of such alliances is also suggested by the list of defeated kings in Joshua 12 (Mendenhall 1973:26). While some of the specifics of this list may date to the Solomonic period (Fritz 1969:136–61), the underlying genre and much of the information are "certainly very ancient" (Soggin 1972:143). Rather than picturing the capture and annihilation of whole cities, this list names the kings—many of whose cities are specifcally mentioned elsewhere as untaken—whose power to control the countryside has been effectively neutralized and whose lands may accordingly be alloted to "Israelites." In this regard, the situation presumed is an accelerated version of that mirrored in the Amarna letters.

Although all these diverse materials from the book of Joshua lend at least circumstantial support to the revolt model, the prose of each has been heavily and repeatedly redacted, leaving the evidence more ambiguous than a modern historian might wish. The relatively unrevised poetry of the Song of Deborah in Judges 5 takes on added significance in this context, for not only is its claim to predate the monarchy more widely recognized in critical scholarship than that of any other composition in the Hebrew Bible, but its subject is the conflict between Israel and the kings of Canaan. Long before Mendenhall's article of 1962, scholars sought to exploit this unusually direct access to the struggle. Already in the nineteenth century, Moore drew the following conclusions from his circumspect analysis of Judges 5:

> The Canaanite city-kings of these [Taanach and Megiddo] and neighboring cities, relying on their chariots and their superiority in arms, gave battle in the open field . . . The Israelites . . . were peasants from the hills, and were armed only with peasants' weapons; a regular military equipment was hardly to be found among them. (1895:134–35)

From the sociological side, Weber also recognized the relationship between topography and social stratification:

> In the fertile plains and on the coast, the military patrician of the cities was the enemy against whom . . . the mountain peasant . . . had to fight.
>
> . . .
>
> The peasant proprietor was the main champion of the battle against the urban patrician. He was most exposed to the imposition of forced labor. The Deborah war was conducted essentially as a peasant war. Praised most highly by the Song is the fact that untrained mountain footmen have fought . . . and have been victorious. (1952:54–55)

A more recent study by the present writer (Chaney 1976: passim) reaches similar conclusions and seeks to demonstrate in detail that such an understanding of the conflict consistently applied also aids in solving many of the song's textual and philological puzzles.

If these passages from Joshua and Judges ultimately derive from various stages of a protracted struggle between the kings of Canaan and "Israelite" peasants, as suggested, the narratives about David in 1 Samuel 23–27; 29–30 depict a logical sequel. By David's time, most of the old Canaanite city-states were part of a Philistine-Canaanite symbiosis under the far more efficient control of a military aristocracy. The Philistine tyrants who had filled the vacuum in political power were unwilling to allow the central hill country a continuance of its separate ways, for its growing peasant population had become an economic base worth exploiting. Utilizing military tactics more appropriate to the uplands, the Philistines sought to subjugate and garrison Israel. Under such circumstances, Israel's unconsolidated peasant revolution partially reverted to the prerevolutionary level of "social banditry" represented by David's "Hebrew" band (see below, pp. 49–50). The unstable conditions, in turn, allowed David, the master strategist, to translate this nucleus of power into an agrarian monarchy.

But aspects of the monarchic state that he founded deviated significantly from the norm for agrarian societies—deviations that find plausible explanation in the reconstruction of premonarchic Israel sketched here. Law is one such area. Since the laws of the Pentateuch exhibit detailed affinities in both form and content with the legal tradition preserved in cuneiform sources, the comparison of Israelite jurisprudence with that typical of other ancient Near Eastern societies can be particularly nuanced (Greenberg 1962:733–44; Paul 1970:36–42). These commonalities also serve to make the contrasts all the more stark. Whereas the collections of cuneiform law "are the product of a secular jurisprudence which recognized the state and the king as the promulgators and ultimate sanction of the law" (Greenberg 1962:737), Yahweh is conceived as the *sole* fountainhead of biblical law, and he "selects the entire corporate body of Israel to be the recipients of his law" (Paul 1970:38). That law rejects any class distinctions in meting out justice. For the cuneiform legal corpora, "social status is decisive in evaluating harms and assessing penalties" (Greenberg 1962:737). "Biblical law [also] diverges from other law systems of the ancient Near East in not regarding any offense against property as a capital crime" (Greenberg 1962:734). In the case of a runaway slave, cuneiform laws seek to protect the owner, with the crime of harboring such a fugitive sometimes punishable by death (cf. Laws of Lipit-Ishtar 12–13; Laws of Eshnunna 49–52; Laws of Hammurabi 15–20; Hittite Laws 22–24). Deuteronomy 23:15–16 (Heb. 16–17), by contrast, *mandates* this harboring and the unprejudiced incorporation of the runaway into the community. No typical agrarian monarch could countenance such a policy, not to speak of promulgating it. At the court of Solomon, for instance, the right of a master to reclaim runaway slaves was a foregone conclusion (cf. 1 Kgs 2:39–40). It has long been recognized, however, that biblical law did not originate with the monarchic state of Israel; it had premonarchic roots in town and village institutions that continued to function alongside royal administrative structures (Noth 1966:1–107;

Mendenhall 1954:26-46; Köhler 1956:127-50). Both the grassroots tenacity and the anomalous content of this legal tradition find cogent explication in the revolt model for Israel's emergence as a society. The polemically deviant ideals which inform Pentateuchal law—God as the sole sanction of the law and all of the people as its recipient, no recognition of class distinctions, rights of persons placed above those of property, and the duty to provide sanctuary and communal inclusion to any fugitive from elite power—are readily intelligible as those of peasant revolutionaries and their leaders. The two contending models do not plausibly explain these anomalies, or even address the issue of their causation.

Israelite prophecy may be viewed in much the same light. While it, too, had antecedents and parallels in the other societies of the ancient Near East, its critique of agrarian monarchy and its concomitants was unprecedentedly vigorous. Particularly scathing invectives were directed toward wealthy landlords and creditors who pressed sharp marketing and foreclosure procedures against previously freeholding peasants, thereby concentrating land ownership in a few hands and creating a large mass of landless cultivators (Alt 1959:348-72). The canons against which the prophets measured these practices were essentially those of the legal tradition just discussed, and like it, they are more fully explained by a heritage ultimately derived from a process of peasant revolt.

In sum, biblical tradition supports the revolt model in two ways. Despite the work of later redactors and editors, it contains numerous allusions to conflicts and dynamics in premonarchic times of the type envisaged by this gestalt. Other traditions evidence a marked departure from more typical agrarian patterns by certain of monarchic Israel's institutions. The revolt model provides a plausible explanation for these mutations; the contending hypotheses do not.

CONCLUSIONS

As paradigms for the formation of premonarchic Israel as a separate society in Palestine, the models of nomadic infiltration and conquest by a large group of intruders both proceed from assumptions which appear fundamentally flawed. While it remains a working hypothesis, a model of peasant and frontier revolt has been found to accommodate and illuminate the data provided by the Amarna archive, Syro-Palestinian archaeology, and the biblical tradition, and to do so within parameters defined by the comparative study of agrarian societies by social scientists. Its heuristic value alone argues that this model and its sociologically derived research strategies be tested in greater detail against each of the sets of relevant data. The writer will consider this paper a success if it serves to enlist new recruits in that ongoing process.[29]

EXCURSUS: THE *'APIRU* AND SOCIAL UNREST IN THE AMARNA LETTERS FROM SYRO-PALESTINE

Perhaps the fullest account of social unrest preserved in the Amarna archive was written by the prolific Rib-Adda of Byblos. It can serve to focus our discussion.

> All my towns which are in the mountains and on the seashore have joined with the *'apiru* troops. Byblos, together with (only) two towns, remains in my possession. And behold, now, Abdi-Ashirta has take Shigata for himself and said to the people of Ammia: "Kill your leader! Then you will be like us and you will have peace." So they acted according to his words and they are like *'apiru*. And behold, now, Abdi-Ashirta has written to the troops: "Assemble in Bit-NIN.URTA and let us fall upon Byblos! Behold, there is no one who will save it from our hand! So let us drive out the 'governors' from the midst of the lands, and let an alliance be formed for all the lands, and then sons and daughters will have peace forever! And if, indeed, the king (of Egypt) does come out, then all lands will be hostile to him, so what can he do to us?" Thus they exchanged oaths. And thus I am very, very fearful because there is no one who will rescue me from their hand (*EA* 74:19–45).[30]

There can be no doubt of Abdi-Ashirta's opportunistic manipulation of the situation, but his program is unintelligible without widespread unrest among the lower classes to be manipulated.[31] In the same vein, while Rib-

---

29. The issue of the *Journal for the Study of the Old Testament* containing discussion of the "peasants' revolt" hypothesis by Hauser (1978a:2–19; 1978b:35–36), T. L. Thompson (1978:20–27), Mendenhall (1978:28–34), and Gottwald (1978a:37–52) appeared after the current article had been accepted for publication. While revision to make direct reference to that discussion is thus precluded, it will be obvious that many of the issues raised there are anticipated and explicitly addressed here.

30. This translation presupposes the readings and interpretations advanced by Mendenhall (1947:123–24) and Moran (1953:78–80, esp. nn4 and 5). The rendering of *ālu* in 11, 19, and 22 as "town" cannot adequately represent the word's range: "city-town–village" (*AHw* 39; *CAD* 1:379–88). That *EA* lacks a separate word for "village" is frequently germane to the discussion that follows.

31. This is also the explicit and unequivocal conclusion of Artzi (1964:165–66. It is difficult to understand how Weippert (1971:74 n72) can cite Artzi as being in basic

Adda clearly desired to vilify a political adversary to the Egyptian court, his proclivity elsewhere for the use of vague slurs to convince Pharaoh of the anti-Egyptian import of Abdi-Ashirta's activities renders this report on specific tactics all the more trustworthy. Such extended reflection on the concerns of the non-elite majority, albeit only in an elite-held mirror, is understandably rare in the diplomatic correspondence of Amarna. Even so, all major aspects of this one, somewhat fuller account are echoed more briefly in other letters.

Time and again the petty dynasts of the city-states, regularly called "governors" (*ḫazannūtu*) in the letters, feared assassination, mostly by the lower classes of their own people. Rib-Adda wrote of it repeatedly with regard to himself and other dynasts (in addition to the passages quoted, see also EA 75:25–34; 82:33–45; 89:10–32; 130:31–33; 131:18–30; 132:43–50; 138:9–14; 139:12–15, 33–40; 140:10–14):

> And all the "governors" seek to have this done to Abdi-Ashirta [to have archer troops advance from Egypt so that Abdi-Ashirta's people, following the greatest might, will defect to the "governors'" side] because he wrote to the people of Ammia: "Kill your lord!" And they joined with the 'apiru. So the "governors" are saying: "Thus he will do to us, and all the lands will join with the 'apiru." (EA 73:23–33)

> Byblos and Batruna (alone) remain mine, and he [Abdi-Ashirta] seeks to take (these) two cities. He has also said to the people of [Batruna]: "Kill your lord!" And they have joined with the 'apiru, like the city of Ammia. (EA 81:9–13)

> I fear the peasants (*awīlūt ḫu-u[p-ši]*), that they will slay me. (EA 77:36–37).[32]

---

agreement with him.

32. Note that the threat of the 'apiru in 11.21–35 (partially broken). While *ḫupšu* will regularly be translated here as "peasants," the larger interpretation being argued does not depend upon the exact equivalence of the two terms. As a matter of fact, the English term is so difficult of sociologically precise definition that no two scholars can agree upon its exact limits or essentials, prompting Landsberger's cogent recommendation (1973:6–18) that the term cover the continuum of "all low-status cultivators" who consititute the large majority of any agrarian society. "Peasants" in that sense translates *ḫupšu* well, for the latter are seen in various contexts as present in large numbers, holding small, rural plots, lacking significant property, and being subject to corvée and military service (Wiseman 1953:10; Weippert 1971:72 n63; Dietrich et al. 1974:26–27: and the literature there cited). In some of the Amarna passages, the latter sense—"peasant troops"—may be primary.

As usually translated, EA 112:10–12 would also constitute succinct proof that

Nor was such activity limited to Syria; it is witnessed for Palestine as well. Abdu-Heba of Jerusalem narrated the following events, also reported in *EA* 335:7–20.

> ... but now 'apiru hold the cities of the king. There is not one "governor" (left) to the king, my lord—all are lost! Behold, Turbazu has been slain in the (very) gate of Sile, (yet) the king is negligent. Behold, (as for) Zimrida of Lachish,[33] slaves/servants who had become 'apiru smote him. Yaptih-Adda has been slain in the (very) gate of Sile, (yet) the king is negligent. Wherefore does the king not call them to task? (*EA* 288:36–47)

Milkilu of Gezer encountered analogous problems:

> Let the king, my lord, know that the hostility against me and against Shuwardata is powerful. So let the king, my lord, deliver his land from the hand of the 'apiru. If not, let the king, my lord, send chariots to fetch us, that our slaves/servants not slay us! (*EA* 271:9–21)

According to Ba'lat-UR.MAH^MES of Sapuna, the threat extended to Milkilu's sons, who probably represented his authority in the towns named:

> Let the king, my lord, know that hostility is practiced in the land and that the land of the king, my lord, is gone through desertion to the 'apiru. So let the king, my lord, attend to his land, and let the king, my lord, know that 'apiru sent word to Aijalon and to Zorah, and the two sons of Milkilu were nearly slain. (*EA* 273:8–24)

A letter of undetermined origin strikes a similar note:

Rib-Adda faced both external hostility and internal rebellion by the lower classes of his own people:
> From whom shall I protect myself? From my enemies or from my peasants (awīlūt ḫu-up-ši-ia)?

Moran (1975:154, 165 n68) has recently argued persuasively, however, that *ištu* means "with" in this and other passages in peripheral Akkadian, and that the lines are therefore ironical:
> With whom shall I protect myself? With my enemies or with my peasants?!

The context of the passages quoted makes obvious why Rib-Adda could expect as little aid from his peasants as from his enemies, but it is unclear here whether the main thrust of his rhetoric is that his peasants would be *unwilling* or *unable* to mount a defense comparable to that of the garrison that he once enjoyed and for whose return he now pleads.

33. Zi-im-ri-da ^{URU}L[a-k]i-si^{ki} is translated here *casus pendens*. For a partial parallel, cf. *EA* 75:25–29.

> Let the king, my lord, know that the "governors," who were in the city of my lord, have come to an end and all the land of the king, my lord, has deserted to the ʿapiru. (EA 272:10–17)

Rib-Adda bemoaned desertion and internal rebellion by the lower classes often (in addition to the passages quoted, see also EA 69:12–28; 91:14–15; 104:37–45; 125:25–30):

> What should I do? Behold, they kill the "governors." There *are* no cities. They are like dog(s), and there is no one who seeks after them. What should I do, I, who dwell amidst ʿapiru? If now I have no provisions of the king, then my peasants (*awilut ḫu-up-ši-ia*) will become hostile.[34] All lands are inimical to me. (EA 130:30–43)

> So let the king concern himself about his city and his servant, for my peasants (*awilut hu-*[!]*-si-ia*) seek to desert. (EA 114:20–22)

The relation between such desertion and the "taking" of cities and lands[35] is tersely delineated in two passages:

> Hostility is powerful against me, and there are no provisions for the peasants (*awīlūt ḫu-up-ši-i*), so therefore they desert to the sons of Abdi-Ashirta and to Sidon and to Beirut. Truly, the sons of Abdi-Ashirta are hostile to the king, and Sidon and Beirut no longer belong to the king. Send a commissioner that he may seize them. Let him not abandon the city and go off to you. Truly, if the peasants (*awīlūt ḫu-up-ši-i*) desert, the ʿapiru will capture the city. (EA 118:21–39)

> Now I am guarding the towns of Byblos, the city of the king, night and day. If I should (attempt to) conquer the lands, then the men would desert in order to take lands for themselves, and there would be no men to guard Byblos, the city of the king, my lord. So may my lord hastily despatch archer-troops or we die. (EA 362:31–42)

---

34. Unfortunately, both the reading of the verb and its meaning involve some uncertainty. The translation here presumes *ul-ta-na*[*-n*]*a*, understood as a Dt of *šanānu* (cf. Knudtzon 1915:555 n. f; Ebeling *apud* Knudtzon 1915:1394–95; AHw 1116a; Rainey 1970:81).

35. ʿApiru are said to be involved in "taking" towns and cities in EA 71:10–32; 76:7–20; 79:7–29; 81:6–13; 90:5–25; 91:13–26; 185:9–64; 288:36–46; 289:5–24. They "take" land in 76:7–20; 83:15–20; 289:5–24.

While the latter passage does not specifically mention ʿapiru, it does name the ʿapiru-linked sons of Abdi-Ashirta (l. 67) and refer ominously to activities characteristic of ʿapiru with the indefinite "they" of several verbal forms. The picture is that of an agrarian elite clinging fearfully to its eroding power base, while finding it impossible to control the cultivated countryside or its population.[36]

Given an opportunity, the lower classes of the cities—some of whom were probably peasants who had been forcibly urbanized due to hostilities (cf. *EA* 81:33–41; 85:10–15)—also deserted to other leaders, whose promised programs had greater appeal, and thereby "joined with" ʿapiru:

> . . . so I cannot go out (of Byblos) or Byblos would join with ʿapiru. They [Rib-Adda's enemies mentioned earlier in the letter] came to Ibirta, and an agreement was made with ʿapiru. (*EA* 104:49–54; for *epēšu pû*, see *CAD* 4:216)

> . . . the hostility is powerful against me. I fear my peasants (ḫu-up-ši-ia). So I have written to the palace for a garrison and men of Meluha . . . Let the king send garrison troops and men of Meluha to guard me, lest the city join with the ʿapiru. (*EA* 117:89–94).

In another instance, this time from the Esdraelon valley, the people of Taanach "took" their own city in the manner counseled by Abdi-Ashirta's speech in *EA* 14, "driving out" their "governor" and attacking his privileged property:[37]

> Let the king, my lord, know that the people of Taanach have moved to attack every last thing which the king, my lord, has given to his servant, and they have butchered my cattle and driven me out! And behold, I am staying with Biridiya ["governor" of nearby Megiddo], and let the king, my lord, care for his servant. (*EA* 248:9–22)

Even though ʿapiru are not explicitly named in Yashdata's account of the revolt, they do appear as the enemies of Biridiya (*EA* 243:19–22; 246

---

36. Both Sjoberg (1960: esp. 80–144) and Lenski and Lenski (1978:186–87, 201–15) delineate the predominantly urban base of agrarian elites and their relationship to the rural population.

37. While it is nowhere explicitly stated that Yashdata, the writer of *EA* 248, was "governor" of Taanach, no other assumption adequately explains the contents of this letter and Yashdata's relationship to Biridya of Megiddo (Helck 1962:189). Note that forms of *dubburu* are used both here and in *EA* 74:34 for the "driving out" or "expulsion" of "governors."

rev.:5–10), with whom Yashdata was closely allied and identified (*EA* 245:11–18). The social dynamics are, in any case, more important than the particular term applied to the group involved, for the nameless masses who "join with, become, desert to," or "are like" ʿapiru, or who otherwise side with them, are variously characterized as "peoples, lands, cities, peasants," and "slaves," with more than one designation often used within a few lines of the same letter.[38]

Many of the elements in this fluidity and complexity can be delineated and integrated within Hobsbawm's conceptualization of "social banditry" (1965:13–29; 1969:11–115; 1973:142–57). His broadly comparative studies of this phenomenon have not previously been applied to the ʿapiru problem, but such application is suggested by the common description of at least some ʿapiru as brigands. Both Weippert's careful rendering of "outlaws" for the non-Amarna ʿapiru (1971:58–65) and Rowton's useful discussion of the "parasocial element" (1977:181–98) grant initial encouragement. Closer comparison reveals significant congruities between Amarna's ʿapiru and social banditry. The latter

> consists essentially of relatively small groups of men living on the margins of peasant society, and whose activities are considered criminal by the prevailing official power-structure and value-system, but not (or not without strong qualification) by the peasantry. (Hobsbawm 1973:143; cf. Mendenhall 1973:130–35)

A "remarkably uniform . . . phenomenon throughout the ages and continents" (Hobsbawm 1969:11), social banditry "is found throughout the wide belt of rural societies which lies between the tribally organized and the modern industrial, excepting only, it would seem, formalized caste

---

38. For "people" joining with, being like, or wholly going over to the ʿapiru, see *EA* 73:26–29; 74:25–29; 81:11–13 (all quoted above); and 179:20–22; cf. 121:19–23. "Lands" joining with, being lost to, or deserting to the ʿapiru are mentioned in *EA* 73:32–33; 74:35–36 (both quoted above); 76:33–37; 77:26–29; 79:18–26; 85:69–74; 88:29–34; 111:17–21; 117:56–58; 148:45; 215:9–17; 272:14–17; 273:11–14 (quoted above); and 290:12–13. "Cities" join with or are lost to the ʿapiru in 68:12–18; 74:19–21 (quoted above); 76:33–37; 81:11–13 (quoted above); 104:51–52 (quoted above); 116:37–38; 117:92–94 (quoted above); 144:24–33; and 207:19–21; cf. 87:18–24; 88:29–34; and 189:9–18. Slaves/servants are said to have become ʿapiru in 288:44, while "peasants" (ḫupšu) are linked with ʿapiru in *EA* 77:21–37; 117:89–94; 118:21–37; 130:30–43 (all quoted above). Although some of the briefer passages cited might be understood as referring primarily to political rebellion against Egypt, the revolt of the lower and peripheral elements of the city-state societies against their top and center as personified in the "governor" is clear in the fuller texts quoted. Because of the linkage between the political and socioeconomic factors, they cannot be neatly distinguished either in the language of the letters or in the underlying reality. Sparser contexts, however, should be read in light of the more amply attested evidence.

societies" (Hobsbawm 1973:148). "Otherwise social bandity is universally found, wherever societies are based on agriculture (including pastoral economies), and consist largely of peasants and landless labourers ruled, oppressed and exploited by someone else" (Hobsbawm 1969:15).

Hobsbawm's description of those who became social bandits and of the ambiguity of their relationship to constituted authority is not only reminiscent of the Amarna 'apiru, it also aids the analysis of their often crosscut role(s). "If we want to understand the social composition of banditry," he writes, "we must . . . look primarily at the mobile margin of peasant society" (Hobsbawm 1969:25). "The overwhelming majority of the normal brigands were peasants, herdsmen or—what comes to the same thing—ex-soldiers" (Hobsbawm 1965:29). Whether escaped serfs, ruined freeholders, pastoralists denied access to sufficient pasturage, or low-ranking servicemen who had been discharged or had deserted, they all shared an economic marginality and official opprobrium, without having violated the values and norms of the groups from which they constituted "seepage" and whose continued empathy they enjoyed (Hobsbawm 1969:27; for "seepage" cf. Rowton 1967a:14–15). If the Amarna 'apiru are viewed in this light, the widespread sympathy which they found in the countryside and the constant threat that the ḫupšu—viewed in either their socioeconomic or military role—would desert to them are both easily understood.

An assumption that many of the Amarna texts reflect social banditry also allows the unstrained interpretation of links between 'apiru and portions of the non-peasant population. "Since the bandits' fundamental loyalty was to peasants, with their permanent opposition to the actual authorities, even the most traditionalist brigand had no difficulty in making common cause with other oppositionists and revolutionaries, especially if they were also persecuted" (Hobsbawm 1965:28–29). The ability of this paradigm thus to integrate the social unrest and political opportunism witnessed in the texts extends to a phenomenon evidenced in a letter from Yapahu of Gezer:

> Let the king, my lord, know that my youngest brother is estranged from me, and has entered Muhhazu, and has made an agreement with (lit.: "given his two hands to"; see Greenberg 1955:49) an 'apiru. (*EA* 298:20-27)

Hobsbawm has written appositely that "where landowning families fight and feud, make and break family alliances, dispute heritages with arms, the stronger accumulating wealth and influence over the broken bones of the weaker, the scope for bands of fighting men led by the disgruntled losers is naturally very large" (1969:82). Such disaffected or impoverished nobles easily adopt the bandit's life because "arms are their privilege, fighting their vocation and the basis of their systems of values" (Hobsbawm 1969:30).

In specifying the conditions that tend to multiply bandits, Hobsbawm could hardly have described Late Bronze Canaan more aptly: "The ideal situation for robbery is one in which the local authorities are local men, operating in complex local situations, and where a few miles may put the robber beyond the reach or even the knowledge of one set of authorities and into the territory of another, which does not worry about what happened 'abroad'" (1969:17). One is reminded of the protests of Mayarzana of Hazi (*EA* 185; 186) that Amanhatbi of Tushulti consistently harbored 'apiru after they harrassed and plundered Mayarzana's territory. Situations "where the central state apparatus is absent or ineffective and the regional centres of power are balanced or unstable, as in conditions of 'feudal anarchy,' in frontier zones, among a shifting mosaic of petty principalities" (Hobsbawm 1969:82), foster banditry. So do harvest failures—whether due to natural causes or the disruption of cultivation by hostilities (cf. *EA* 74:17–19; 75:10–17; 81:33–41; 90:36–44)—and wars, both of which reduce the peasant's economic viability (Hobsbawm 1969:18).

In such chaotic circumstances, a robber band, even though it is relatively small, constitutes a political force, because it forms a nucleus of armed strength. "Where the state is remote, ineffective and weak, it will indeed be tempted to come to terms with any local power-group it cannot defeat. If robbers are successful enough, they have to be conciliated just like any other centre of armed force" (Hobsbawm 1969:44; cf. 1973:156). Such considerations surely functioned in the Egyptian crown's failure to respond with alacrity to the "governors'" repeated appeals for campaigns against the 'apiru in their region. That even Abdi-Ashirta's recognition by the Egyptian state (*EA* 101:29–31) represented something of this dynamic is suggested by Rib-Adda's fulminations.

> What is Abdi-Ashirta, the slave, the dog, that he takes the land of the king himself? What is his auxiliary force, that it should be strong? (Only) by means of 'apiru is his auxiliary force strong! So send me fifty teams of horses and 200 infantrymen in order that I may resist him in Shigata. (*EA* 71:20–26)

Furthermore, as noted by Mendenhall (1973:123), none of the six letters of Abdi-Ashirta or the eleven of his son, Aziru, ever mentions the term 'apiru—a fact that places them in a distinct minority at Amarna. Were these leaders sensitive about their origins?

A paradigm of social banditry also allows the Amarna 'apiru to be related plausibly to the use of the term in other texts. "Elsewhere they are settled in cities, serving in the armies of states or supported by private individuals—in all cases a recognized element in society" (Greenberg 1955:76). The difference lies in the relative strength or weakness of centralized authority, for "retainers, policemen, mercenary soldiers are ... often recruited from the same material as social bandits" (Hobsbawm 1965:13; cf. 1969:61–62). Those elements who became the "landlords' bandits" and the "states' bandits" in more settled times and places were propelled into "social banditry" by the anarchy of Syro-Palestine in the Amarna Age.

A profound ambiguity, however, was inherent in this new role.

> For the crucial fact about the bandit's social situation is its ambiguity. He is an outsider and a rebel, a poor man who refuses to accept the normal roles of poverty, and establishes his freedom by means of the only resources within reach of the poor, strength, bravery, cunning, and determination. This draws him close to the poor: he is one of them. It sets him in opposition to the hierarchy of power, wealth and influence: he is not one of them ... At the same time the bandit is, inevitably, drawn into the web of wealth and power, because, unlike other peasants, he acquires wealth and exerts power. He is 'one of us' who is constantly in the process of becoming associated with 'them'. The more successful he is as a bandit, the more he is *both* a representative and champion of the poor *and* a part of the system of the rich. (Hobsbawm 1969:76)

The Amarna 'apiru are better served by recognition of this intrinsic ambiguity than by attempts to force them into a straitjacket of political, social, or lexicographical consistency.

In quantitative terms, too, the Syro-Palestinian 'apiru fit Hobsbawm's picture of social banditry. Brigand bands are normally small, "larger operations being undertaken by coalitions of such groups" (Hobsbawm 1973:155; cf. 1965:18–19). Despite images of nomadic hordes or massive military operations conjured up by some discussions of the Amarna 'apiru, the specific information provided by the letters themselves points to bands of modest size. One of these is said to have had forty survivors after action in which some of its members were killed (*EA* 185:42–49). The requests of the "governors" for special, outside forces to control the 'apiru are often for less than 100 men and never more than 400 (on 132:56–57, see Pintore 1972:103 n9). Only at Byblos do the numbers exceed 200 (Greenberg 1955:75; Campbell 1960:21; Pintore 1972:101–31; 1973:299–318). Since the bands appear to have operated from rugged terrain with a sparse but sympathetic population, the conventional troops needed to control them effectively would have outnumbered the 'apiru themselves. Greenberg's conclusion that they usually roamed and raided "in groups of perhaps 50–100 men" (1955:75) is therefore well within the evidence. Such figures lend support to Mendenhall's observation that, for all the rhetoric of the letters, very few cities are reported actually to have been captured in battle by 'apiru troops (1973:126, 129; cf. Campbell 1960:21). Far from the clash of major armies, the process reflected is rather the harassment and intrigue typical of bandits operating with the sympathy of those social elements from which they sprang. The somewhat larger troop requests, moreover, came from Rib-Adda of Byblos, whose letters contain explicit references to *alliances* with or among the 'apiru (*EA* 74:36–37, 42; 104:52–54). While the Egyptian court chose to acknowlege the strength of the coalitions formed, it did so, not by sending the troop contingents for which Rib-Adda continually begged, but by granting de facto legitimacy to forces which it could not control, at least, not at a cost deemed reasonable.

Hobsbawm's analysis illumines the *nature* of the pleas by the "governors" for troops and mercenaries from Egypt as well as the numbers involved, for he states as a general principle what the letters illustrate so profusely: at the local and sometimes even regional level, "everybody has to come to terms with large and well-established bandits" (Hobsbawm 1969:78). The compromised stance in which local officials thus inevitably find themselves "explains why in really bandit-infested areas campaigns against banditry are so often carried out by special forces brought in from the outside" (Hobsbawm 1969:79).

Geographic factors, however, usually work against the outsiders. "For obvious reasons" social banditry "has always flourished best in remote and inaccessible areas (e.g., mountains, forests . . .), and under inefficient administration" (Hobsbawm 1973:149; cf. 1969:16, 61, 79, 82). We have already noted Rowton's argument that the 'apiru of Syro-Palestine operated in and from such terrain, where the chariots of the elite were disadvantaged (1965:375–87; 1976b:29–30). Further illustration may be found in *EA* 292, in which Baal-Shipti of Gezer writes that "there is hostility towards me from the mountains" (ll. 28–29), and alludes to paying brigands a standard price of thirty pieces of silver to ransom someone "from the mountians" (ll. 48–50).

In similar regions elsewhere, "where agents of authority enter only on occasional forays, the bandit may actually live in the village" (Hobsbawm 1969:39). "Indeed in the real back country, . . . the bandit may be not only tolerated and protected, but a leading member of the community" (Hobsbawm 1969:40). The latter statement does not accord ill with the picture of Labaya and his sons which the letters afford (cf. *EA* 243:19–22 with

244:8–33; 246: rev. 5–10; 250; 253; 254; 287:29–31; 289:5–29). Their 'apiru-associated activities radiated out from the thinly settled, mountainous region around Shechem at least as far as the territory of Megiddo, Gezer, and Jerusalem. One gains the impression that they moved about the wooded uplands with impunity, prompting some of the "governors" into uneasy and shifting alliances with them. Although Labaya can write grandiloquently of his fealty to Pharaoh when he is explaining away his relative's involvement with 'apiru (EA 254:31–46), the truculent tone and barbarous language of EA 252 express the backwoods independence that he really enjoyed in his mountain domain.

Finally, it may be observed that philological obscurity and semantic ambiguity are characteristic of the terminology applied to social bandits (Hobsbawm 1965:21; 1969:61; 1973:154–56). The orthography of the letters makes this doubly true of 'apiru, for not only is the etymology mooted, as seen above, but the ideogram SA.GAZ and its variants, by which 'apiru is represented in a large majority of its occurrences, also represents Akkadian *ḫabbātu*, "robber, bandit, raider" (Rowton 1965:386; 1976a:14–15; Greenberg 1955:88–90). We have noted as well that ambiguity is inherent both within the social role described and in the expansion of the term in political name-calling. Even when 'apiru was not being used by one "governor" merely to malign another, however, the ambiguity of the social phenomenon designated was matched by the variety of social perspectives from which it was viewed and evaluated, and these differences were reflected in the use of language. Because most of the letters were written by the ruling elite of the city-states, Hobsbawm's remark that "bandit" has "become a habitual term ... governments use to describe revolutionary guerrillas" (1965:21) has significance for the identity of at least some 'apiru. (Note once again that Abdi-Ashirta and Aziru eschewed any use of the term.)

Since Hobsbawm's delineation of social banditry has proven apt in analyzing many of the intricacies of Amarna's 'apiru, his understanding of the relationship between such activities and broader peasant movements warrants exploration. By itself, "banditry is not so much a form of peasant movement as a symptom of peasant unrest" (Hobsbawm 1973:153), but it "may be regarded as a precursor, and a primitive form of, wider peasant agitations" (Hobsbawm 1973:146). Hobsbawm sees three kinds of relationship between the terms.

"*First,* banditry and more ambitious types of peasant movement tend to flourish in the same areas, if not actually to live in symbiosis" (Hobsbawm 1973:146). In the Amarna Age, it was the hinterlands of Palestine and Syria—particularly those in the mountains—which spawned and harbored both 'apiru bands and more broadly based movements against the "governors."

The Israelites later occupied the Palestinian portion of this zone and had the dynasts of the same Canaanite city-states as enemies. Concurrent with the appearance of premonarchic Israel in Palestine, technological developments made the traditional areas of resistance to these kings' authority economically viable for a much larger population. That the poor, unwalled, "Israelite" towns and villages that came to dot the old 'apiru territory were peopled by peasants who had revolted is not thereby proven, but it is rendered plausible in the absence of cogent hypothesis or definite evidence to the contrary.

"Second, at times when mass unrest grips the peasantry, banditry merges with these larger movements, and notable increases in banditry may indeed prepare and announce them" (Hobsbawm 1973:146). Such a merger appears to be reflected in at least some of the declarations that "peasants, slaves, peoples, lands," and "cities" "join with, become," and "desert to" the 'apiru. It also reconciles the reports of large-scale participation by these groups in 'apiru-like activities with the relatively small size of the 'apiru bands proper. As any student of the comparative study of peasant movements knows, however, "the more extensive and . . . permanent the movement becomes, the less likely it is to be, or at least remain, in the hands of peasants" (Landsberger 1973:47). Abdi-Ashirta and Aziru, for instance, seem to have manipulated the widespread social unrest in their region much as they played the Egyptian and Hittite empires against one another—toward their own opportunistic ends. Thus, when Hittite power was able to intervene decisively in the area, it "plucked with little difficulty the fruits of the SA.GAZ movement" (Mendenhall 1973:129). No comparable interruption of the ferment in Palestine is known. With regard to notable increases in banditry preparing and announcing larger movements, we need add to the picture of rampant 'apiru outlawry already sketched only that still other Amarna letters speak of the harrassment and interdiction of caravans in Syro-Palestine (*EA* 7:73–82; 8:13–41; 16:37–42; 148:20–23; 255:8–25; 264:5–25).

"Third, banditry may itself provide the model or cadre of certain kinds of primitive peasant insurrection or guerrilla activity" (Hobsbawm 1973:147). Particularly "likely is the systematic use of bandit tactics and experience for the technically very similar activities of guerrilla warfare" (Hobsbawm 1973:147). In that sense, the letters speak accurately enough of the lower classes being "like 'apiru" when they assassinate or harass their lords, appropriate their land and property, form alliances with other folk in the countryside, and generally rely upon intrigue and psychological warfare rather than frontal attack.

Nor is this tactical link between social bandits and broader movements absent from the traditions of early Israel. As has been pointed out frequently

(Alt 1939:58–61; Greenberg 1955:75–76 and n73; Campbell 1960:14), the narratives about Abimelech (Judges 9), Jephthah (Judges 11), and especially David (1 Samuel 23–27; 29–30) provide excellent *social* parallels to the Amarna 'apiru in this regard. The description of 1 Sam 22:1–2 is classic:

> David departed from there and escaped to the cave of Adullam. When his brothers and all his extended family heard it, they went down to him there. Then every man who was in straits, every man who had a pressing creditor, and every man who was embittered gathered to him, and he became their leader. About 400 men were with him.

With this band David extorted "protection money" from the rich, plundered Judah's traditional enemies, shared the spoil with the village elders, curried the favor of cities and kings as their mercenary and enfeoffed vassal, (always playing "both ends against the middle"), and thereby built the nucleus of power around which the monarchic state of Israel was formed.

Neither the Amarna corpus nor the Hebrew Bible provides as much information about such activities as one might wish because the ultimate composers of each were primarily concerned with other matters and perspectives. Even so, this brief investigation has found unequivocal evidence in the letters of both flourishing social banditry and a broader social unrest. The former served the latter as symptom, symbiotic ally, and tactical model. Although the Syrian movement apparently eventuated in little because of opportunistic leadership and cooptation and intervention by Hittite power, what Egyptian presence there was in Palestine hardly touched the hinterlands, even at moments of maximum strength. Can there have been no continuity, therefore, between the social dynamic of Amarna Age Palestine and that of the formation of Israel, when premonarchic Israel's primary areas of strength, its enemies, and its forms of social organization were all congruent with those of the Amarna 'apiru and their allies?

2

Joshua and the Deuteronomistic History

When read through in one sitting, the book of Joshua exhibits both unity and disunity. An analysis of each is intrinsic to modern attempts to understand the finished work in the context of the ancient setting in which it was composed.

Much of the unity of Joshua comes from two discrete sections which together account for the bulk of the book—a narrative of Israel's conquest of Canaan west of the Jordan in chapters 1–12, and an account in chapters 13–21 of the distribution of the land thus taken among the various tribes of Israel. Both these sections contain introductory, concluding, and summary passages (1:1–18; 10:40–43; 11:16–23; 12:1–24; 13:1–7; 14:1–5; 18:1–10; 19:51; and 21:43–45) that tie the sections together and help to orient the reader. The relationship between taking the land and allotting it is articulated already in chapter 1, which also prepares the reader for Joshua's leading role in both functions.

Apart from these two sections on the conquest and the allotment of the land, and the passages that organize them, the book of Joshua appears to disintegrate into a diversity of constituent parts in which unity and organization are much less obvious. A series of appendixes ends the work. Chapter 22 narrates the departure of the Transjordanian tribes who live east of the Jordan River and a dispute between them and the Cisjordanian majority west of the river over an altar built at the river's edge. Cast as the farewell speech of Joshua, chapter 23 seems to conclude what was begun in chapter 1. Undeterred by this apparent finale, the book of Joshua in its present form continues on to chapter 24, which contains an account of a covenant at Shechem, partially parallel to chapter 23, and ends with a series of burial notices.

JOSHUA AS PART OF THE "DEUTERONOMISTIC HISTORY"

In the last half century, attempts to understand the unities and disunities within the book of Joshua have led to the conclusion that it was composed as but one part of a larger whole. A growing consensus of biblical scholars believes that the books of Deuteronomy, Joshua, Judges, 1 and 2 Samuel, and 1 and 2 Kings were written in their present form as a "Deuteronomistic History"—a single entity intended to be read as such.

Earlier treatments of this larger "history" followed the pioneering lead of Martin Noth (1943; 1981) and sought to relate it to the experience of the exiles in Babylon in about 550 BCE. Since the first chapters of Deuteronomy introduce a work that concludes with the release of King Jehoiachin from a Babylonian prison in 2 Kgs 25:27–30 (ca. 560 BCE), Noth reasoned, the Deuteronomistic History as a whole was written in and for the period immediately following this event. Some scholarly work on the book of Joshua continues in this vein, on the assumption that older literary materials showing a wide diversity of origins, genres, and modes of preservation were edited together as a Deuteronomistic History for the first time during the exile.

Following Frank Moore Cross (1973), a growing number of scholars now believes that the Deuteronomistic History was composed essentially in the manner posited by Noth, but in at least two stages. The earlier and major composition occurred before the exile, during the reign of Josiah (640–609 BCE), this being the only context that can account for many of the characteristics of the work.

Even a sketch of this hypothesis can suggest something of its explanatory power. In the whole of the Deuteronomistic History, for example, Josiah is unique in having the particulars of his kingship prophesied some three centuries in advance (1 Kings 13). The account of his reign in 2 Kgs 22:1—23:25a not only narrates the self-conscious and detailed fulfillment of this prophecy but also pictures him as the only king ever to comply in full with the laws found in chapters 12–26 of Deuteronomy. These laws stand as a frontispiece for the Deuteronomistic History and establish the standards by which it evaluates the events and careers it recounts.

Together with other evidence, such data suggest that a major "first edition" of the Deuteronomistic History ended at 2 Kgs 23:25a, with the account of Josiah's "reform" as the climax of the piece, The motive for this work was to undergird and legitimate Josiah's policies. If these political dynamics shaped Joshua as a part of a larger entity, then the basics of Josianic history are of utmost significance for understanding the book.

Before examining this point more closely, however, the parts of the Deuteronomistic History not belonging to the main, Josianic edition must be accounted for. The need for a "second edition" arose not only because of Josiah's death at the hands of Pharaoh Neco (2 Kgs 23:29) and the failure of his "reforms," but because of the subsequent destruction of the Judahite state by the Babylonians and the exile of its upper classes to Babylon.

These events necessitated an addition to the Josianic Deuteronomistic History that completed the story down to a mildly positive event for the exiles, the release of King Jehoiachin from prison and his elevation to pensioner at the table of the king of Babylon (2 Kgs 23:25b—25:30). But the same events mandated more than an appendix, for the "first edition" had spared few pains in preparing the reader for Josiah's reign as its goal and culmination.

The explanation for Josiah's death and the nation's fall given by the addition—that the sins of Josiah's grandfather, Manasseh, were so great as to require the destruction of Judah as punishment (2 Kgs 23:26-27)—was therefore foreshadowed in a series of glosses inserted earlier in the History. A clear case in point within the account of Josiah is the exilic recomposition of 2 Kgs 22:15-20. In its current form, this passage explains that Josiah, because of his penitence and humility, will be "gathered to his fathers," lest he be forced to witness the destruction of Judah.

The clearest example of such exilic insertions in Joshua occurs in 23:13b and 23:15-16, which mute the climax in 23:14 and interrupt a rhetorical sequence similar to 21:43-45. Although it contains much older material, Josh 24:1-27 may be the work of the exilic editor as well (Nelson 1981a:94-98). Alternatively, chapter 24, with its partial parallel in 8:30-35 (cf. Deut 11:29-30; 27:2-8, 11-26; 31:9-13, 24-29), can be understood as an insertion still later than the main exilic editor (Mayes 1983:49-52).

Other traces of the exile in Joshua are possible, but attempts to find extensive evidence of an exilic Deuteronomist in the book have not as yet attracted a wide following (Boling 1982; Peckham 1985). Since the entire book (apart from 8:30-35; 23:13b, 15-16; and 24:1-33) is intelligible as part of the larger Josianic work, it will be explicated here as such.

CONTEXT AND DYNAMICS OF THE JOSIANIC "REFORM"

Discussion of Josiah's "reform" can be organized under six rubrics, but these are merely facets of the same systemic reality. The focus here will be upon their interaction and mutual reinforcement, for that potent combination defined the "force field" that shaped the contours of the book of Joshua within the larger literary context of the Deuteronomistic History.

The "reform" of Josiah involved a reassertion of Judahite national independence in the context of declining Assyrian power. Since the time of Ahaz of Judah (ca. 734–715 BCE) and the mighty Tiglath-pileser III of Assyria (745–727), the small state of Judah had moved mostly in the orbit of imperial Assyria, the dominant superpower of that time. Hezekiah (ca. 715–687) challenged Assyrian suzerainty, but paid dearly for the attempt. During most of the long reign of Manasseh (ca. 687–642), Judah was of necessity an obsequious vassal of Assyria. As is typical in such situations, a measure of cultural imperialism accompanied the political domination, with citizens of the vassal state affecting aspects of the suzerain's "superior" culture.

Late in the reign of Asshurbanapal of Assyria (668–627) and following his death, Assyria went into steep decline. After a century under the Assyrian heel, the petty states of western Asia—including Judah—struggled to regain at least some measure of freedom. These independence movements were strongly nationalistic and anti-Assyrian.

Josiah's repair of the temple in Jerusalem is to be understood in the light of these political realities. The temple was a national shrine, the dynastic chapel of the Davidic monarchy. When the Davidic king became an Assyrian vassal, symbols of that subservience were displayed in his state temple and its forms of worship (2 Kgs 16:10–18; 21:3–7). Removal of the foreign cultic artifacts, conversely, was a consummately political act, a powerful declaration of independence from Assyrian control.

Temple repair, moreover, was the mark of a successful king in the ancient Near East. Symbolically, it was the equivalent of temple-building, one of the strongest assertions of power a monarch could make. Since a century of subservience to Assyrian superpower had discredited the Judahite monarchy among its subjects, such symbolic acts were important if Josiah was to recover the king's authority.

The reassertion of royal prerogatives addressed another problem as well. Not only had Assyrian superpower discredited the Davidids (kings of the Davidic dynasty), it had also served to further divide the local ruling factions in Judah. Josiah's father, Amon, had been killed in the course of factional fighting (2 Kgs 21:19–26), bringing Josiah to the throne when only a child of eight. National independence and resurgent Davidic kingship required the suppression of these factions to mold national identity and unity, with the temple in Jerusalem as its center.

Territorial expansion was a major part of Josiah's program. Three centuries before his time, at the death of Solomon, the "ten northern tribes" had seceded from the rule of the Davidids to form the separate monarchic state of Israel (1 Kings 11–13). Two centuries thereafter (722–721), that same state fell to Assyria. For a hundred years prior to the climax of Josiah's "reform" (622–621), therefore, the land and population of what had previously been the northern kingdom had been parceled out among various provinces of the Assyrian empire. With the crumbling of that empire and its effective control over its western provinces, Josiah reasserted Davidic hegemony over the north.

However, he faced several impediments to his perceived "manifest destiny" there. Solomon's social and economic policies had pushed the northern peasants to the brink of rebellion. When his son, Rehoboam, arrogantly promised more of the same, the northerners rebelled against what they saw as Davidic tyranny (1 Kgs 12:1–20). In Josiah's time, even the intervening centuries had not quieted all northern suspicions of the Davidic dynasty.

Assyrian imperial policy also bequeathed Josiah an obstacle to his policies that outlived Assyrian control in the area. The Assyrians had deported the ruling elite of the fallen northern kingdom to other parts of the empire, thereby severing the roots from which they drew their power to resist. Conversely, they had also moved defeated elites from other portions of the empire into northern Israel. When Assyrian power receded, the descendants of those foreign elites were left in the area as rivals to Josiah's authority.

Against all these impediments, Josiah pursued his objectives with a combination of "carrot and stick." Specifically, he and his officials effected a "lamination" of the Mosaic and Davidic traditions. Much of what was nearest and dearest to the hearts of northern villagers had its traditional fountainhead in the figure of Moses. Josiah's reform appealed to the northerners by adopting Mosaic law and tradition as its legitimating constitution. But in Josianic rhetoric, Mosaic law and tradition were used to support the current Davidid (Josiah) in his claim to be the sole legitimate executor of that law and tradition. This Josianic integration of the Davidic and Mosaic traditions found full elaboration in the Deuteronomistic History.

According to 2 Kgs 22:3–14 and 23:1–3, Josiah's repair of the temple occasioned the finding of a legal document, which he then solemnized as the law of the land in a covenant ceremony. The inference that this book was some form of Deuteronomy 12–26 is one of the longest-standing pillars of modern scholarship. Most of the policies and actions attributed to Josiah in 2 Kgs 23:4-24 find unique sanction in the legal section of Deuteronomy. This section, in turn, is cast as part of the farewell speech of Moses just before Israel's entry into the promised land. As numerous parallels from ancient western Asia demonstrate, however, Josiah's promulgation of this Mosaic law was an assertion of royal authority.

Centralization was the keystone of the Josianic "reform." Politically, the reform involved reassertion of the prerogatives of the monarch and his national government at the expense of the landed nobility, made binding in Josiah's home territory of Judah and in the portions of the north he captured.

Josiah's centralization of religious worship was of a piece with his political policies. Legislation in chapter 12, requiring that Israel worship only at "the place which Yahweh your God will choose, to make his name dwell there" (12:11; RSV emended), heads the laws of Deuteronomy 12-26. In the context of Josiah's rule that place could only be the temple in Jerusalem.

The elimination of cultic installations other than the central sanctuary, mandated in Deuteronomy 12, plays a major role in the Deuteronomistic account of Josiah's "reform" (2 Kgs 23:4-20). This narrative reaches its climax in the destruction of Bethel (23:15-20; cf. v. 4). From a Josianic perspective, Bethel—a royal cult site established by Jeroboam I (ca. 931-910) to rival Jerusalem and legitimize his secessionist state in the north—epitomized all that was evil and all that impeded national unity under a rightful heir to the Davidic throne. As previously mentioned, the Deuteronomistic account of Jeroboam's establishment of the Bethel sanctuary (1 Kgs 12:26-33) is followed by an extended prophecy of its destruction (1 Kings 13), which mentions Josiah by name (v. 2).

Finally, Josiah emphasized the Passover festival (2 Kgs 23:21-23). This carrier of the Exodus traditions had been prized at the grassroots level, particularly in the north. By giving it new prominence and claiming that "no such Passover had been kept since the days of the judges . . . or during all the days of the kings of Israel or of the kings of Judah" (2 Kgs 23:22, RSV), Josiah presented himself as the champion of popular sentiment. By insisting that the observance of Passover be centralized at Jerusalem according to the provisions of Deut 16:1-8, however, he disenfranchised all other cult sites and their personnel and enlisted the Passover in the service of his centralization program.

STRUCTURE OF THE DEUTERONOMISTIC HISTORY

Cast as the swan song of Moses, the ultimate authority figure for northerners, Deuteronomy provides the legal mandate for the specifics of Josiah's "reform." It also enunciates the norms in terms of which the entire history becomes a series of object lessons, leading up to and legitimating the policies of Josiah.

Seen in this light, the book of Joshua becomes an extended, positive object lesson, illustrating how the Josianic objective of territorial expansion can be properly and successfully achieved. The people of Israel must be fully united under one leader who is the sole legitimate successor of Mosaic authority. The policies and actions of this leader must conform to Mosaic law in strict detail, and he must see to it that the people do so as well. All foreign influences are to be expunged, lest they constitute a temptation.

As presented in the finished form of the book that bears his name, Joshua is the historical prefigurement of Josiah. Against northern suspicions of Josiah, the Deuteronomistic book of Joshua argues tacitly but eloquently that the model for Josiah's behavior is none other than a northern hero, Joshua, the Ephraimite. Just as Joshua was successful in capturing and distributing the land because he adhered strictly to the law of Moses, so, too, will Josiah succeed in capturing and distributing the land in his time because he treads in Joshua's footsteps.

Judges and 1 Samuel, which are bracketed together in the Deuteronomistic History, present the opposite side of the same coin. In that period of the "judges"—among whom the Josianic writer includes Saul—Israel was oppressed by foreigners in its own land because of its disobedience to Mosaic law, particularly because of the decentralized and syncretistic forms of worship and the lack of unitary leadership and stability of succession. Historical paradigms for Josiah's opponents and rivals, in other words, are presented as both leading to disaster and breaching the fundamentals of Mosaic law.

Beginning in 2 Sam 1:1, "after the death of Saul," an ideal Davidic king is presented as the sole means of salvation from such ills. From that point on in the "history," each of the Davidids is judged by how closely he adheres to the Deuteronomic ideal. Several provide positive models, but none measures up to Josiah. "Before him there was no king like him, who turned to Yahweh with all his mind, with all his being, and with all his strength, according to all the legal instruction of Moses" (2 Kgs 23:25a; au. trans.).

The kings of the north, on the other hand, are without exception judged to be evil. Because they sundered the unity of state and religion, their history can only serve as a negative object lesson. The eventual fall of this evil nemesis moves the Deuteronomistic Historian to a peroration on the significance of the event (2 Kgs 17:7–18), just in case the reader still has any doubts.

JOSHUA AS A JOSIANIC BOOK

The preceding analysis of the Deuteronomistic History and its multiform address to the dynamics of the Josianic "reform" helps to explain certain features of the book of Joshua. Chapters 1 and 23—both written almost entirely in formulas that the Deuteronomistic Historian uses elsewhere in framing passages and speeches—bracket the diverse materials in chapters 2–22 and shape them to portray Joshua as a legitimating model for Josiah. Chapter 1 obtains this end so effectively that it may serve as a lens to focus and organize further discussion of the Josianic book of Joshua.

The phrase with which Joshua opens, "And it happened after the death of [Moses]," also appears in Judg 1:1 with the name of Joshua and in 2 Sam 1:1 with that of Saul. Part of an obvious pattern here, but rare elsewhere, this formula directs attention to the basic structure and concerns of the Deuteronomistic History. The era of Moses was unique, a time when laws and norms were set down for all time to come. Because of his obedience to those laws and norms, Joshua, in his time, led Israel to realize its manifest destiny. After his death, however, Israel transgressed the law of Moses and as a consequence became unable to withstand its enemies (cf. Judg 2:6–15). Such was the case until Saul's death cleared the way for David—the founder of Josiah's dynasty—to rule a united, enlarged, and powerful Israel.

Following the introductory formula, Josh 1:1–9 reports Yahweh's charge to Joshua. The form of this charge indicates the installation of officeholders, while its emphasis upon obedience to the law reveals that the office in question is royal. Joshua's assumption of power immediately upon Moses' death also conforms to the royal pattern of dynastic succession, and distinguishes it from the charismatic practice of judges or prophets. These same elements appear together in 1 Kgs 2:1–4, a passage whose parallels to Josh 1:1–9 offer trenchant commentary upon the latter's form and purpose.

Portrayed in the Deuteronomistic History as the sole legitimate successor to Moses, Joshua undergoes a double investment—once by Moses (Deut 31:7–8; cf. 1:38; 3:21; 31:3, 14–15, 23), and once by Yahweh (Josh 1:1–9). This succession of authority is repeatedly reinforced in the book of Joshua. As part of his charge to Joshua, Yahweh promises, "As I was with Moses, so I will be with you" (1:5). In Josh 1:17, the Transjordanian tribes echo the sentiment from below: "As in everything we obeyed Moses, so we will obey you; only may Yahweh your God be with you, as he was with Moses!" When Joshua is about to lead Israel across the Jordan to dry ground—a parallel to Moses at the Sea (cf. 4:23)—Yahweh assures him, "This day I will begin to magnify you in the sight of all Israel, so that they will know that, as I was with Moses, so I will be with you" (3:7). After the people have crossed, the narrator reports, "Yahweh magnified Joshua in the sight of all Israel; and they stood in awe of him, as they had stood in awe of Moses, all the days of his life" (4:14). There are dozens of similar references in Joshua where Moses is mentioned by name and his authority invoked to sanction Joshua's—therefore Josiah's—actions.

This explicit Mosaic sanction of Josiah in the person of Joshua is reinforced at the implicit level as well. Joshua's theophanic encounter with the commander of Yahweh's army (5:13–15) recalls Moses' "burning bush" experience (Exod 3:1–6), with verbal parallels between Josh 5:15 and Exod 3:5.

From the perspective of more recent literary criticism, moreover, Robert Polzin argues that the rhetoric of Josh 1:2–9 and its parallels accomplishes by implication two additional purposes:

> First, it presents the narrator as one who can report God's word directly just as Moses habitually did. Our narrator had already prepared us for his practice of directly quoting God in Joshua—2 Kings by beginning to quote God in direct discourse five times toward the end of the Book of Deuteronomy... Thus, the narrator immediately assumes his authoritative role here in Joshua, a role patterned after that of Moses as he is portrayed in Deuteronomy. Second, if the content and context of God's reported utterance exalts now the role of Joshua as the successor of Moses immediately following Moses' death, the phraseological composition of reported and reporting speech in Joshua 1:2–9 impresses upon the reader rather the role of the Deuteronomic narrator as successor to Moses vis-à-vis those readers whom he addresses. (Polzin 1980:76)

Polzin himself does not place the composition of the Deuteronomistic History in a particular historical context. But his analysis of how the narrative structure transfers to the narrator Moses' role as God's definitive spokesperson reveals a dimension of the text that fits Josiah's policies perfectly. The Deuteronomistic Historian's interpretation of history and current events is authoritative because, implicitly, he in his time speaks directly with God, just as Moses did in his time.

Applied to the explicit links between Moses and Joshua in Josh 1:5, 17; 3:7; and 4:14, such an analysis of the implicit dimension of the text reveals a related technique of the Deuteronomistic narrator. Although referring to a different passage, Polzin's words describe the phenomenon exactly: "We see the authorial voice emphasizing a particular theme by placing it in the mouth of now one, now another, authoritative personage in his story" (1980:79). Note that in this particular series, however, the culminating version of the theme (4:14) is voiced by the narrator.

The theme of the authoritative leader is linked with the unity of the whole nation. In 1:2 a singular "you," referring to Joshua, is joined to "all this people." Expressed in the phrases "all the Israelites," "all Israel," "all the men of Israel," and "all the nation," this national unity punctuates the book of Joshua like a drumbeat (Josh 3:1, 7, 17; 4:1, 11, 14; 6:5; 7:3, 23, 24, 25; 8:15, 21; 10:15, 21, 24, 29, 31, 34, 36, 38). In its larger literary context, the emphasis in chapters 3–4 on twelve men and twelve stones representing the twelve tribes of Israel functions the same way. This internal unity, in turn, is matched by enmity toward foreign nations and peoples (4:24; 7:9; 10:21, 42).

Joshua 1:2 sounds another theme central to both the Deuteronomistic History and the "reform" of Josiah—the declaration that Yahweh is giving the land to Israel (Deut 1:20, 25; 2:29; 3:20; 4:1, 21, 40; 5:16, 31; 11:17, 31; 12:9; 13:12; 15:4, 7; 16:5, 18, 20; 17:2, 14; 18:9; 19:2, 10, 14; 20:16; 21:1, 23; 24:4; 25:15, 19; 26:1–2; 27:2–3; 28:8; Josh 1:11, 15; cf. 1:13; 5:6; 9:24; 11:23; 18:3; 21:43; 23:5). This land is repeatedly referred to as "the land which you are entering [crossing over Jordan] to possess" (Deut 4:5, 14, 22, 26; 6:1; 7:1; 9:1, 5; 11:8, 10–11, 29, 31; 23:20; 28:21, 63; 30:16, 18; 31:13; 32:47; Josh 1:11).

In giving further expression to this "manifest destiny" and the Mosaic mandate for it, Josh 1:3–5ab is modeled almost verbatim on Deut 11:24–25. The declaration of these passages to the Israelites that they shall possess "every place upon which the sole of your [plural] foot shall tread" sets the remainder of the book into the context desired by the Deuteronomistic Historian (cf. 14:9) and anticipates the role of the priests' feet in the crossing of the Jordan (3:13; 4:18).

In its repetition of "No man shall be able to stand before you" from Deut 11:25, Josh 1:5 (cf. 10:8) changes the "you" from plural to singular and adds "all the days of your [singular] life." This concentration of Yahweh's promise to the people upon one individual and his military success evinced a royal ideology exactly fitted to Josiah's policies.

Josiah's "historian" had to walk a tightrope in depicting the territory taken by that royal figure. On the one hand, he needed to stake Israelite land claims at their most optimistic and extensive, and picture Josiah's forerunner, Joshua, as virtually irresistible in his drive toward realizing Israel's territorial aspirations. The idealized boundaries as outlined in Josh 1:4—modeled, in turn, on Deut 11:24 (cf. Deut 1:7)—served this purpose, as did generalizing statements, as in Josh 11:23.

On the other hand, the territory actually incorprated into Josiah's realm was decidedly less extensive, and he faced both internal and external rivals for its control. Along with not raising unachievable expectations, the narrator therefore needed to caution his readers against rival leaders and ways, if he was to prepare them for a negative object lesson regarding alien influences in Judges and 1 Samuel. For these reasons, he framed his composite and relatively modest traditions of allotment in Josh 13:14—21:42 with the motif of the land and peoples that remained as a test and challenge (Josh 13:1–13; 23:4–13a; cf. Judg 3:1–6).

Opinions vary regarding what territory Josiah actually controlled. It appears likely, however, that his primary domain and attempts at expansion lay in the Cisjordan. Deuteronomy 2:5, 9, and 19 make clear that the Transjordanian lands of Edom, Moab, and Ammon, which had been part of the Davidic empire, were not included in the "land grant" presupposed by the Deuteronomistic History.

This geopolitical reality may account for a pervasive feature in the Deuteronomistic book of Joshua—the division of the land at the Jordan between the two and one-half Transjordanian tribes and the nine and one-half Cisjordanian tribes (Josh 1:12–18; 4:12–13; 12:1, 6–7; 13:7–12, 15–32; 14:2–4; 18:5–7; 21:5–6, 27; 22:1–34; cf. Deut 3:12–22; 29:7–8). The lands of the former are portrayed as having been taken and distributed by Moses. Only Cisjordan is conquered by Joshua and then allotted to the people. Was such a division intended by Josiah's court historian to voice Israel's historical claims to Transjordan, while at the same time relieving Josiah from pressure to move into territory that he had no realistic chance of taking or holding?

Another note significant for Josiah is struck in Josh 1:5c–7a and 1:9, with the obvious, often literal adumbration in Deut 31:6–8. Joshua is urged repeatedly to "be strong, be resolute, do not tremble, do not be dismayed" (cf. Deut 1:21; 3:28; 31:23; Josh 1:18; 8:1; 10:8, 25; 11:6). At first glance, this rhetoric may appear to protest too much. Why was this repetitive encouragement and reassurance necessary? As Nelson (1981a:122) explains, Josiah's policies would have faced opposition from many quarters: (1) the newly unemployed provincial clergy; (2) the average peasant, whose familiar, local rituals were being abolished; (3) town and city officials—many in the north were foreigners, brought in by the Assyrians—who saw the prestige and influence of their localities being diminished as their sanctuaries were destroyed; (4) the more extreme reformers, who felt that Josiah had not gone far enough; (5) pro-Assyrian elements, who had supported Manasseh's policies; and (6) ardent northern nationalists, who refused to accept a Davidic king.

Against this opposition, the historian urges that Josiah should be resolute, for he, like Joshua his prototype, has been chosen by Yahweh to secure Israel's inheritance of the land promised of old (cf. Josh 1:6 with 11:23 and Deut 1:38; 3:28; 12:10; 19:3; 31:7). His authority to partition the land reflects the king's right to divide his realm into districts and distribute it to loyal followers (1 Kgs 4:7–19).

By emphasizing that success depends upon scrupulous observance of Mosaic law, Josh 1:7bc–8 further underscores Joshua's royal role in prefiguring the program of Josiah. These lines are modeled on the "law of the king" in Deut 17:18–20. In Deuteronomy, *torah*, "law, legal instruction," is always referred to as "this law," stressing its pertinence for the current (Josianic) context. Such is the case not only in the "law of the king" (Deut 17:18–19), but in the introduction (Deut 1:5; 4:8, 44) and various appendixes to the book (Deut 27:3, 8, 26; 28:58, 61; 29:21 [MT 20], 29 [MT 28]; 31:9, 11–12, 24, 26; 32:46).

This Mosaic *torah* becomes, in turn, the mandate for all of Joshua's actions and his legacy to future generations (Josh 1:7, 8; 8:31, 32, 34, 35; 22:5; 23:6; 24:26). *Torah* is not mentioned again in the Deuteronomistic History until David's deathbed instruction to Solomon to keep it (1 Kgs 2:3). Solomon, it should be remembered, was the founding builder of the temple that Josiah repaired and placed at the center of national life. In this regard, note the long, dedicatory prayer which the Deuteronomistic Historian placed in Solomon's mouth in 1 Kgs 8:12–45. *Torah* next appears in 2 Kgs 10:31, which states that Jehu, though a tool of Yahweh's judgment against the dynasty of Omri, shares with every single northern king the onus of breaking the law. One Davidid (Amaziah) is praised (2 Kgs 14:6) for keeping a specific provision of Deuteronomic law (Deut 24:16). Apart from two passages deriving from the exilic editor (2 Kgs 17:37; 21:8) and the chapters regarding Josiah, the only other mentions of *torah* in the Deuteronomistic History concern the fall of Samaria (2 Kgs 17:13) and the unlawful syncretism of those left or placed in the north after its fall (2 Kgs 17:34). Even without the culminating treatment of *torah* in the account of Josiah, the specific relevance of each of these passages for Josianic policies is patent.

The Deuteronomistic Historian, of course, did not leave the matter at that, but presented Josiah's discovery and implementation of the Mosaic *torah* as the climax of his work (2 Kgs 22:8, 11; 23:24–25a). That he portrayed Joshua as a unique prototype for Josiah's strict obedience to Deuteronomic law is shown by the distribution of the admonition found in Josh 1:7 regarding that *torah*: "Turn not from it to the right hand or to the left." This admonition to keep to the legal straight and narrow is used four times in Deuteronomy (5:32; 17:11, 20 [the "law of the king"]; 28:14), and again in Joshua's farewell address to Israel (Josh 23:6). It does not recur in the Deuteronomistic History until Josiah is said to have fulfilled it (2 Kgs 22:2).

Similarly, Joshua "left nothing undone of all that Yahweh had commanded Moses" (Josh 11:15). No such report of complete obedience to Mosaic law occurs again in the Deuteronomistic History until the account of Josiah reaches its climax in 2 Kgs 23:25a.

In addition to these references to the Mosaic *torah* as a whole, Joshua contains many examples of events that fulfill or violate specific injunctions in Deuteronomy. Most remarkable among these is the "holy war" mandate of Deut 20:16–18 (cf. 7: 1–5) that all previous inhabitants of the land given to Israel be "utterly destroyed" or "put to the ban." Explicit references to this statute are found in Josh 2:10; 6:17–18, 21; 7:1, 11–13, 15; 8:26; 10:1, 28, 35, 37, 39–40; 11:11–12, 20–21; 22:20 (cf. 6:19, 24; 8:2, 8, 24–25, 27–29; 9:24; 10:20, 30, 32–33; 11:6, 9, 14, 17, 22). The "nations" so to be exterminated are listed in Deut 20:17 by a formula that is repeated in Josh 3:10; 9:1; 11:3; and 12:8 (cf. Judg 3:5). The kings of certain of these vanquished peoples are treated (Josh 8:29; 10:27) in strict adherence to the regulations of Deut 21:22–23 governing the exposure of the bodies of executed criminals.

Few portions of the Bible so offend many moderns as this grisly tale of divinely mandated genocide. As has been seen, however, this narrative of conquest is not an "objective history" of Joshua's time, but one "historical" object lesson among many legitimating the cause in which the Josianic composer believed so fervently in his own time. Although notions of holy war and putting to the ban are not restricted to this author or his context, the application of the ban to an entire population as ordered in Joshua occurs only in passages that bear every indication of Deuteronomistic composition.

The rhetorical thrust of this apparent mandate for genocide is to give expression to the pent-up national anger felt by a small state whose identity and integrity had been compromised by decades of domination by foreign superpowers. Viewed from the subjectivity of the rage of the oppressed and the passionate hope for national independence and purity, the only good foreigner was a dead foreigner. (Before dismissing such rhetoric as unworthy, citizens of modern superpowers might well ponder if they are ever the objects of such legitimate anger from the smaller nations that serve as their pawns and surrogates.)

Alongside the need for the public expression of unqualified rage against foreign influences, regimes such as Josiah's face the practical necessity of subtly legitimating certain "good foreigners," whose services are essential to the regime. Rahab (Josh 2:1–24; 6:17, 22–23, 25) fits this description, as do perhaps the Gibeonites (Josh 9:3–27), for they, like Rahab, are exempted from the strictures of Deut 20:16–18. Nor can such "creative interpretation" of Deuteronomic law be an unintentional oversight by the narrator, as Polzin has demonstrated on literary gounds (1980:84–91, 117–23). Rahab is, after all, the very first "Canaanite" encountered by representatives of Israel, and the explicit law of the ban is bent by authoritative interpreters—including both Joshua and the narrator—to spare the lives of her family.

This tension between strict and "creative" application of Deuteronomic law to specific cases has been noted by Polzin throughout the Deuteronomistic History as a dialectic between a voice of "authoritarian dogmatism" and one of "critical traditionalism." While Polzin's analysis is ahistorically literary, the dialectic it reveals fits Josiah's policy needs perfectly. When Josiah needed the mandate for his "reforms" to be unyielding and absolute against opponents or subordinates, it was the very law of God delivered to Moses. When administrative exigencies required a certain freedom of royal interpretation, the paradigm of "critical traditionalism" was invoked.

The taking of cattle and spoil as booty in Josh 8:2, 27; and 11:14 may constitute another case of such "creative interpretation," for it would seem to violate a literal application of Deut 20:16. Alternatively, these passages are perhaps to be read in light of Deut 20:14, which allows spoils to be taken from distant cities. (Ai and Hazor, the cities in question, were both in the north.)

Be that as it may, the location of the extensive narratives of Joshua 7–8 in the immediate vicinity of Bethel cannot have been lost on a Josianic audience (cf. 2 Kgs 23:4–20). The story of Achan—a Judahite—reinforces a royal claim to all treasure goods and metals (cf. Josh 6:19, 24) taken in Josiah's campaign against Bethel, while allowing his Judahite troops to appropriate certain livestock and agricultural goods for themselves. Finally, Joshua's rending of his clothes when he discovers that Mosaic law has been breached at Ai near Bethel (Josh 7:6–9) prefigures Josiah's reaction to the discovery and reading of that same law (2 Kgs 22:11–13).

The Deuteronomistic Historian's use of the Passover traditions in Josh 5:10–12 is even more subtle. Although this old material is not Josianic in composition, its mere inclusion in the larger work adds Joshua's authority to the centralized Passover prescribed by Moses in Deut 16:1–8 and effected by Josiah in 2 Kgs 23:21–23.

JOSHUA AND HISTORICAL RECONSTRUCTION

This essay has emphasized the relationship between the book of Joshua and the historical dynamics of Josianic Israel, in and for which it was composed in nearly its present form as part of the much larger Deuteronomistic History. This emphasis is not intended to deny that the Josianic author(s) incorporated previously extant materials—some of considerable antiquity, extent, and cohesion. The exact shape of these pre-Deuteronomistic materials and their relationship to the history that generated and shaped them, however, present a great quandary. The two major attempts in twentieth-century scholarship to address this hornet's nest of issues now stand under heavy—and probably decisive—criticism.

The so-called "nomadic infiltration model" for Israel's origins, associated with such scholars as Alt, Noth, and Weippert (Chaney 1983:41–44), assumes that most of the stories incorporated into the Deuteronomistic narrative of "conquest" were etiologically generated, that is, composed to explain some physical artifact such as an unusual heap of stones beside the Jordan (see, e.g., Josh 4:5–7, 20–24). The assumption regarding the genre of these materials made by scholars of this school denies their usefulness as historical sources. More recent analyses by Seeligmann, Childs, and Long (Chaney 1983:44), however, demonstrate that the etiological element in the Joshua narratives belongs to the latest, not the earliest, stages of the tradition.

A second scholarly model for Israelite origins, often called the "conquest model," is championed by such scholars as Albright, G. E. Wright, and Lapp (Chaney 1983:44–48). In polemical reaction to the nomadic infiltration model, it has sought to demonstrate the "essential historicity" of the Joshua narrative, without insisting that every detail is literally true. During the middle decades of the twentieth century, when this school reached its flood tide, the fledgling discipline of Palestinian archaeology appeared to many to have shown that numerous sites mentioned in the Bible as taken by Joshua were in fact destroyed in the thirteenth century BCE. More recent and fuller archaeological research proved an embarrassment for this point of view, since more and more of the sites said by the text to have been captured by Joshua have been shown to have been uninhabited in Joshua's time.

Mendenhall, Gottwald, and Chaney (Gottwald 1979; Chaney 1983) have still more recently explored a model of "peasant and frontier revolt," which begins with an extensive critique of the two previously regnant paradigms. While preliminary analyses of some of the pre-Deuteronomistic materials in Joshua have been undertaken by these scholars, no commentary on the book exists that works consistently from their methodological stance. Coote and Whitelam (1987) take their point of departure from this model of peasant and frontier revolt, but bracket the biblical text methodologically in order to place Israelite origins in a much larger chronological and geographical context.

The major scholars espousing each of these models all see the book of Joshua in its present form as a Deuteronomistic work. Few seem to have grasped fully the relationships between that text and Josianic society. Only a beginning sketch of those relationships is offered here, but the detailed and rigorous pursuit of such investigation is surely prerequisite to any more certain delineation of the pre-Deuteronomistic materials in the book of Joshua and their possible relationship to any given set of historical dynamics.

3

Coveting Your Neighbor's House in Social Context

A survey of significant attempts to ascertain the meaning of the tenth commandment demonstrates that all such endeavors and meanings have sociocultural contexts. The environment of any given interpreter and the presenting issues of that interpreter's milieu inevitably influence the resulting exegesis. If written in English yesterday in North America, what is broadly conceived to be the earliest kernel of the tenth commandment would have an obvious, literal meaning: "You shall not covet your neighbor's house," especially if, perchance, it was purchased before residential property values soared! The point is made only half in jest, for conscientious American Christians in increasing numbers innocently assume that they can read the entire English Bible meaningfully without once transcending the worldview particular to their own time, social location, culture, and language.

More tutored attempts to understand the commandment in Exod 20:17 and Deut 5:21 have focused upon the verbs usually translated "to covet" and "to desire." This emphasis has been occasioned, at least in some measure, by the realization that *bayit* (the Hebrew word for "house") frequently has the inclusive meaning of "household" (see, e.g., Hoffner 1975a: esp. 113–15). Thus everything else enumerated merely specifies that comprehensive term, as the final cover phrase ("or anything that belongs to your neighbor") also indicates. Since everything that pertains to the neighbor is included in the object of coveting, the real task of exegesis is seen as determining the exact meaning of the action or attitude that is proscribed regarding that totality.

Efforts to specify that meaning most often have embraced one of two polemically opposed options.

One stream of interpretation has seen in these verbs an emphasis "not first of all upon the deed done but upon the disposition of the self in the direction of the deed" (Harrelson 1997:123–24). In contradistinction to the first nine commandments, which concern objective actions, the tenth is viewed as treating a subjective offense of mind, will, feeling, emotion, or attitude. As Harrelson puts it, "no lusting after the lifestyle or goods of others" (ibid.:123).

Such an understanding is at least as old as the translators of the Septuagint. Twice in Exod 20:17 and once in Deut 5:21, the Hebrew uses *ḥāmad*, usually translated as "covet." Only once in the Hebrew of Deut 5:21 does *hit'awwāh* ("to desire") occur, and even there the Samaritan Pentateuch reads *ḥāmad*. The Greek translators, however, rendered all four verbs with ἐπιθυμέω, "to desire, long for." Paul stood solidly in this tradition—his quotation of the commandment in Rom 7:7 and 13:9 expresses no object of the coveting. Luther (*Larger Catechism*) and Calvin (*Institutes* 2.8.49) followed suit, as do many moderns.

With their culture thoroughly permeated by psychological categories, North Atlantic Christians and Jews find this interpretation readily intelligible, if not always congenial. Not a few chafe at such an understanding because for them, acquisitiveness lies at the root of an "entrepreneurialism" they greatly esteem. A powerful and persistent contemporary perspective opines that the health of the world economy, the "American way of life," and the continuance of "Judeo-Christian civilization" are contingent upon an ever-escalating spiral of desiring, acquiring, and consuming—an attitude, dare one say, of "acquisitiveness next to godliness."

But the exegesis of the tenth commandment that prompts Harrelson's "no lusting after the lifestyle or goods of others" is not above question. (1) As already noted, the commandment so understood stands as an anomaly in the context of the other nine. *They* treat objective, overt actions, each of which is the subject of further legislation elsewhere in the law of the Hebrew Bible. It alone would focus on a subjective emotion that could not by its very nature be subject to further legal specification. (2) Even if the particular enumeration of *ten* commandments is quite late, as many scholars now argue, the individual commandments in their short form belong to a genre frequently assumed to be ancient. Is it likely that this policy genre of apodictic law, which is otherwise so spare, would prohibit theft (the eighth commandment) and adultery (the seventh), only to duplicate the subject areas with a prohibition of the coveting of a neighbor's property or wife? (3) Much of biblical law is biased in favor of the "have-nots," not because they are morally superior, but because of their greater vulnerability and lack of power to defend their own vested interests (Greenberg 1962; Paul 1970:37–42). When understood as entirely subjective, however, the tenth commandment almost inevitably gives aid and comfort to "haves" over against "have-nots." Harrelson recognizes this problem (1997:127), but his attempts to mitigate it are ad hoc and fail to address the more systemic stance of biblical law.

At least partially because of such problems, a second stream of interpretation has attempted to understand the tenth commandment as having a far more concrete sense. In a frequently quoted article, Herrmann (1927) sought to show that *ḥāmad* denoted not merely an impulse of the will, but included the corresponding action. He pointed to several passages in which *ḥāmad* was linked with verbs meaning, "to take, seize, rob." In Exod 34:24 and Ps 68:17, moreover, context necessitates a semantic field for *ḥāmad* alone that covers both desiring and taking possession. Understood in this way, the ancient form of the tenth commandment with only *ḥāmad* and *bayit* prohibited both the subjective and objective dimensions of theft: "You shall not covet and take your neighbor's property." Herrmann saw all specifications as later additions, including Deuteronomy's use of *hit'awwāh* ("to desire"), which, unlike *ḥāmad*, referred only to feeling and not to action.

Herrmann's exegesis received support two decades later from Alt (1949:274, 278). In the Phoenician inscription of King Azitawadda of Karatepe, then recently discovered, Alt found a use of *ḥāmad* parallel to Herrmann's proposal for the Hebrew. Four years later, Alt advanced a related interpretation of the eighth commandment, which, though he did not know it at the time, had been adumbrated centuries earlier by the medieval rabbis (1953). Both Alt and the rabbis adduced the same evidence, Exod 21:16 and Deut 24:7:[1]

> Whoever steals a man,
> whether he sells him or is found in possession of him,
> shall be put to death. (Exod 21:16)

> If a man is found stealing one of his brethren, the people of Israel,
> and if he treats him as a slave or sells him,
> then that thief shall die. (Deut 24:7)

Since the verb "to steal" (*gānab*) is the same in both verses and the eighth commandment, it stands to reason that the commandment originally referred to stealing human beings and forcing them to become slaves. Such an interpretation eliminated any overlap between commandments—the eighth

---

1. Biblical quotations in this chapter are the author's.

forbade kidnapping and impressment into slavery; the tenth prohibited an illicit desire for another's property that led to theft.

This Herrmann–Alt position for a time gained wide currency, aided by the popularizations of Stamm (1967:101–5) and Nielsen (1968:passim). Both its general understanding and each of the particulars upon which its interpretation was based, however, have subsequently been challenged. In an oft-cited counterpart to the essays of Herrmann and Alt, Jackson (1975) defends the view that the tenth commandment involves intention only. Jackson's arguments may be summarized as follows.

(1) The Decalogue was understood to be enforceable only by God, not by the legal action of human courts. "Nowhere in the narrative immediately concerning the Ten Commandments do we find any allusion to a method of enforcement to be applied by man" (ibid.:212). "Thus it is valid to draw two conclusions from the biblical texts. First, there is no evidence that liability for mere intention was ever applied in a human court. Second, and equally significant, the idea did exist that merely to intend a wrong was itself wrong. It was a principle employed in God's justice, but not, at this period, in the jurisprudence of man" (ibid.:213).

A frequent variant of Jackson's view holds that the other nine commandments *do* involve concrete deeds actionable in human courts, but that—as a rhetorical capstone—the tenth commandment shifts to address the subjective root of actions such as theft and adultery. Freedman has recently argued that the "Primary History" (Genesis–2 Kings) was edited in its final form to illustrate Israel's descent into the ruin of exile due to its breach of the first nine commandments in order, book by book, beginning with Exodus (1989, 2000). According to Freedman's analysis, only the tenth commandment is not so instantiated because it does not prohibit "a verifiable crime" (2000:20). "What we will discover is that while the coveting addressed by the tenth commandment serves as the impetus for the violation of a number of the preceding commandments, it is never singled out as a crime by itself" (ibid.)

(2) Jackson argues that proponents of the Herrmann–Alt hypothesis have overreached in defining *ḥāmad* "to covet."

> But the conclusion of Herrmann, quoted with approval by Stamm [1967:102] that in view of [several passages where] . . . *ḥāmad* is followed by verbs denoting taking . . . , "evidently the Hebrew understood *ḥāmad* to mean an emotion which with a certain necessity leads to corresponding actions" is unjustified. What he has done is to impute the particular context described in these sources into the very meaning of the verb itself. This

confusion of context and meaning is unjustified, as may be seen from the many occasions when the verb is used in other contexts, and where there is no "certain necessity" that the desire should culminate in action. (1975:204–5)

Jackson himself concedes that Exod 34:24 and Ps 68:17 "support the contention that the verb is capable of a more concrete meaning" (ibid.:205). Cassuto's attempt to deny that ḥāmad even in Exod 34:24 involves action smacks of special pleading (1967:248–49). Even Jackson demurs (1975:206 n12).

(3) Critics of Alt insist that the eighth commandment refers to ordinary theft, not to kidnapping (ibid., 207–9; Crüsemann 1983; Hossfeld 1982; Klem 1976). Among their arguments is the contention that "not all the 10 commandments are capital" (Jackson 1975:208). (Part of Alt's reasoning was that the Decalogue manifested one form of "apodictic" law, all of which he understood to deal only with capital crimes; Alt 1966a.)

Where does this debate between opposing camps of learned opinion leave the innocent reader? Different scholars of the Decalogue would, of course, answer that question differently. While I can speak only for myself, the time has come for me to step out from behind the footnotes to share some of my own tentative perspectives.

(1) As is frequently the case with polemics, this one has driven both sides to more extreme positions than they might otherwise have taken. (2) Polemics tend to foster opposite answers to the same questions. Further interpretation should seek out pertinent approaches that have been neglected. (3) Different learned interpreters representing different communities of faith have read the tenth commandment with different understandings and implications. In most cases, antecedents of these positions stretch back to ancient and medieval times. Perhaps a moratorium should be called on essentialist attempts to ascertain the one timeless and absolute meaning of the commandment. Greater attention to the contexts of interpretation and meaning making is in order.

(4) In the literary context of the Decalogue as a collection of ten commandments, the tenth can be understood as a rhetorical finale that addresses the motivational wellspring of the concrete actions forbidden in several of the other commandments. In many contexts, it undoubtedly was and is so understood. But as I hope to demonstrate, not only can the tenth commandment be readily understood as prohibiting concrete actions paralleling those in the other nine, but solid evidence exists that it was so understood in certain contexts in antiquity.

(5) Alt's delineation of "apodictic law" utilized categories that were probably overly broad and generalizing. Still, the high degree of congruence in subject matter among his three "apodictic" types—one of which is the prohibition form of the Decalogue—should not be dismissed cavalierly. (6) The eighth commandment has been understood by many, from antiquity to the present, to prohibit simple theft. The understanding of Alt and his rabbinic predecessors, however, cannot be proven invalid. Nelson surely overstates matters when he writes regarding the eighth commandment in Deuteronomy, "There is now consensus that v. 19 is not connected with kidnapping."[2]

(7) The polemicists on both sides have overstated their case regarding *ḥāmad*. It is often followed by verbs of seizure, with which it is closely linked. In a few instances, it seems by itself to imply taking possession. Neither, however, is invariably the case: action is not a necessary part of its denotation. On the other hand, virtually all verbs of desiring in the Semitic languages can and often do imply an act of seizure (cf. Moran 1967a; Childs 1974a:425–28; Weinfeld 1991:316–17). (8) Most discussions of the tenth commandment have effectively severed the discussion of *ḥāmad* ("covet") from its object, *bayit* ("house"). As seen above, the common understanding that "house" has an inclusive sense of "household" has lulled exegetes into focusing on the verb alone, without sufficient attention to how this particular verb is used with this particular object. That insufficiency needs to be addressed.

Moran offers a good place to begin. He comes to his investigation of the conclusion of the Decalogue from an intensive study of Deuteronomy. From that perspective, he wishes to take exception to the common presupposition that Deut 5:21 witnesses a higher and therefore later status of women in giving a man's wife a place apart and not simply including her, as does Exod 20:17, in the list of his possessions. In this instance, his evidence comes from certain legal documents from second-millennium Ugarit, written in peripheral Akkadian (Moran 1967a:548–52). These texts deal with transactions involving the transfer of immovable property. The property may be referred to as "house" (*bitu* = Heb. *bayit*) or "field," or, more commonly, by the conjunction of the two terms, "house and field," always in that order. Even by itself, *bitu* in these texts can clearly mean "house," "house and land," or simply just "land." If other properties are specified as appertaining to "house and field," the latter expression always comes first. Finally, an all-inclusive phrase, "everything belonging to him," sometimes follows at the

---

2. Nelson 2002:83 n10. For interpretation of the eighth commandment in a larger context, see, e.g., Gnuse 1985.

end. The high frequency and fixity of these expressions strongly suggest that they are formulaic.

The relevance of this material for the conclusion of the Decalogue is readily apparent. But Moran has a clincher: a royal grant to one Takḫulenu that is valid only in his lifetime, for upon his death, "his houses, his fields, his menservants, his maidservants, his oxen, his asses, everything belonging to him, shall belong to Gamiraddu" (*PRU* III.116). Moran draws the evident inference: "It follows . . . that, typologically, the list of Dt 5,21 is very old and as far as antiquity is concerned need concede nothing to the list of Ex 29,17" (1967:552). He is content to terminate his conclusions there, without further discussion of the commandment's life situation and tradition history. He has, however, prepared the way for both.

In light of Moran's analysis, I now wish to turn to the *only two known* instances in classical Hebrew outside the conclusion of the Decalogue where *bayit* ("house") and its parallels stand as objects of *ḥāmad* ("covet") and its parallels. Sound philological method dictates that these passages be considered the primary evidence for the meaning of the clause, *ḥāmad bayit*. The word study approach, focused on *ḥāmad* alone, has never grasped either this fact or its implications.

Micah 2:2 is the lone such passage in the canonical Hebrew Bible. It castigates the wealthy landlords of eighth-century Judah:

> They covet fields and rip (them) off (*wĕgāzālû*),
>   and houses, and seize (them).
> They oppress by extortion a fellow and his house,
>   a man and his ancestral allotment (*wĕnaḥălātô*).

While the exact relationship of *ḥāmad* with subsequent verbs may be moot in certain prose contexts, the poetic structure of this verse shows that all of the verbs stand in virtual hendiadys, expressing not separate actions but aspects of the one process of coveting, extortion, and expropriation. The same is equally true of the nouns that serve as their objects: "fields, houses, house," and "ancestral allotment of arable land." Of these mutually defining terms for the object of illicit desire and seizure, *bayit* is emphasized, since it stands at the center of a chiasm and is alone repeated.

For the sake of brevity in this context, the story of Naboth's vineyard in 1 Kings 21 must be allowed to stand as sufficient commentary on the meaning and significance of *naḥălāh*, the word used there and in Mic 2:2 for "ancestral allotment of arable land." Micah's linkage of "house" (*bayit*) and "field" (*śādeh*) parallels, of course, the form of the commandment in Deut 5:17b. The Septuagint of Exod 20:17 and the version of the Decalogue in the Nash Papyrus also include both "house" and "field," and in that order. This pair is also found in Gen 39:5; 2 Kgs 8:3, 5; and Jer 32:15. Isaiah 5:8 is particularly significant for the current discussion:

> Alas for those who join house to house,
> who add field to field,
> until there is no place left.
> And you are made to dwell alone
> in the midst of the land!

When combined with Moran's evidence from Ugarit for the formulaic use of "house and field" and even "house" alone to mean first and foremost a plot of arable land, these data from the Hebrew Bible point to the same meaning for *bayit* in the tenth commandment, at least when interpreted in Micah's context.[3]

The only other occurrence of *bayit* and its parallels as the objects of *ḥāmad* outside the Decalogue appears in *The Temple Scroll*, 11QT 57:19b–21: "He [the king] shall not pervert justice, and shall not take a bribe to pervert righteous judgment, and he shall not covet (*wl' ḥmwd*) field, vineyard (*śdh wkrm*), and any property, house (*wkwl hwn wbyt*), and anything of value in Israel, so that he rips (it) off (*wgzl*)."[4] This passage is commonly regarded as a midrashic pastiche of biblical passages, composed to critique Hasmonean royal practice. Wise's notes on the passage read, "midrashic composition of 1 Sam 8:5, Deut 16:18–19, 1 Sam 8:14, and Micah 2:2; cf. also Mic 3:2, Prov 19:14, and Jer 34:8" (Wise 1990:229). Of these passages, only Mic 2:2 uses the operative verb, *ḥāmad*. Surely Exod 20:17 and Deut 5:21 are at least as much in view as several of the other passages cited by Wise. At the very least, this passage from *The Temple Scroll* witnesses that in the Hebrew of the Hasmonean period, *ḥāmad* could be combined with *gzl*, as in Mic 2:2, to excoriate the actions of powerful figures who illicitly "coveted" and "ripped off" agricultural real estate.

In light of this evidence, I propose that the tenth commandment, when understood in biblical history by elements of the agrarian population vulnerable to such actions by the powerful, forbade forms and practices of land consolidation so aggressive and coercive that they deprived a family of fellow Israelites of their ancestral plot of arable land and the subsistence and social

---

3. For the relation of land and family in ancient Israel under the concept of "father's house," see Gottwald 1979:285–92; McNutt 1999:158–62; Perdue et al. 1997; Schloen 2001; and C. J. H. Wright 1990.

4. For the Hebrew text, see Yadin, ed. 1983: 2:259. The English translation is my own, informed by those of Yadin and also Maier 1985:50.

inclusion that it supported. The full significance of this reading of the commandment can be discerned only in the context of a systemic social history of biblical Israel, a context that neither philological nor form-critical study has provided. I turn, then, to that history of sociocultural systems to see how God, people, and land were related.

Just prior to Israel's formation as an independent society at the beginning of the Iron Age, the city-states that dominated the alluvial plains of Late Bronze Canaan related people to land in the manner typical of agrarian societies. Used here in the sense of Lenski (1984:189–296), an agrarian society is one whose principal means of subsistence is a tillage of fields that utilizes the plow and traction animals in some form, but does nor know industrialized technology's extensive use of inanimate energy sources. Since such tillage of the land was the basis of the Canaanite economy, directly involving a large majority of the total population as peasant producers, the system that determined access to arable land effectively controlled access to the economic base and thereby both the production and distribution of goods and services. At one level, all of the arable land of a Canaanite city-state belonged to its king, the proprietary right of the state. At another level, however, much of the land was granted as hereditary estates to a military aristocracy in return for its martial and other services to the crown. Since these aristocratic lands passed as a patrimony from father to son, this pattern of land tenure is often called patrimonial. Other estates were granted to high-level bureaucrats in payment for their governmental duties—a system of so-called prebendal domain (Wolf 1966:50–59).

The holders of patrimonial and prebendal estates did not work the land themselves, disdaining all manual labor save for the chronic, petty warfare from which they derived their principal identity as warriors. The fields that they and their king or warlord were able to conquer and hold by force of arms they let out to peasant producers, who regularly paid half or more of their total production to the landlord in the form of various taxes and rents, in return for access to the land. By means of this system, a ruling elite of 2 percent or less of the population controlled half of more of the total goods and services produced in the society. This elite, in turn, had every incentive to extract the largest possible "surplus" from the peasant majority, leaving it only the barest subsistence necessary to remain productive. As a result, life for the majority was brutish, with peasant families decimated by hunger and disease. Official Canaanite religion legitimated and reinforced this sharp stratification and its inherent values. Such was the socioeconomic system in the alluvial plains of Canaan when Israel emerged as a separate society in the adjacent hill country.

In the essay antecedent to this present one (Chaney 1982), I explicated the emergent Israelite society as the polemical obverse of the Canaanite city-states. I still stand by much of that earlier analysis—as nuanced, of course, by more recent scholarship. In recent decades, the process of Israelite emergence, however, has become the subject of heated and unresolved debate. Since my interpretation of the tenth commandment does not stand or fall with one or another historical reconstruction of premonarchic Israel, I shall prescind from a lengthy and complex discussion of Israelite origins. Suffice it to say that most informed opinion today would agree that in the villages of the early Iron I hill country, land holdings were smaller and more widely distributed, with a higher incidence of freeholding cultivators than in the alluvial plains of Late Bronze Caanan. Indeed, such a configuration of landholding between alluvial plains and upland is broadly characteristic of agrarian history.

Whenever and however the monarchic state arose in biblical Israel, it transformed the political economy of peasant agriculture in Israel and Judah (Cf. Chaney 1986; Hopkins 1983; Dever 1995; Finkelstein 1995; J. S. Holladay 1995; LaBianca and Younker 1995). Plains and hill country, with their different traditions and values of landholding, were brought within the same royal jurisdiction. Many of the agricultural "surpluses" once retained by freeholding peasants in the hill country were extracted by a variety of taxes and rents to fill state coffers and fund an increasingly consumptive lifestyle among the upper classes. Rain agriculture in Palestine was subject to the vicissitudes of periodic drought, blight, and pestilence. As long as the freeholding peasants retained most of their own "surpluses" and were bound together in a covenant of mutual assistance, such crises could be weathered, albeit with difficulty. Once the monarchic state and its ruling elite began to extract "surpluses" to pay for luxury and strategic items, however, the peasants' margin grew slimmer. Peasant producers were forced to borrow if natural disaster struck, and the only surpluses to be borrowed were in the hands of the large landlords. For collateral, a freeholding peasant family had only its land and its persons. Usurious interest rates ensured frequent foreclosures; debt instruments thus served to transfer land from peasant freehold to large estates, reducing previously free and independent farmers to landless day-laborers or debt-slaves. Portions of biblical law sought to retard this process and to ameliorate some of its abuses by prohibiting interest on such loans to the poor, stipulating humane treatment and manumission after a fixed term for debt-slaves, and instituting the role of the *gō'ēl* or "redeemer"—a kinsman who, if and when able, bought back family land or family members when they had been foreclosed upon. Those seeking the taproot of biblical notions of "redemption" must dirty their fingernails with the mundane soil of these dynamics.

Despite all these attempted safeguards—and because they were frequently co-opted by various elites (Chaney 1991)—more and more of what covenantal tradition viewed as *YHWH*'s land passed into fewer and fewer *human* hands. As many small, subsistence plots were foreclosed upon and joined together to form large estates, a change in the method of tillage also took place. Upland fields previously intercropped to provide a mixed subsistence for peasant families were combined into large vineyards and olive orchards producing a single crop for market. The wine and oil produced on these newly consolidated estates played two roles in the new scheme of things. On the one hand, both were central to the increasingly consumptive lifestyle of the local elite. On the other hand, since wine and oil were worth more than grain per unit of weight or volume, they were easier to export in exchange for the luxury and strategic imports coveted by members of the ruling classes.

But the *efficiency* of these cash crops came at a brutal cost to the *sufficiency* of the livelihood that they afforded the peasants who actually produced them. The old system of freehold had provided this peasant majority secure access to a modest but adequate and integrated living. The new system saw them labor in the same fields, but only according to the cyclical demands of viticulture and orcharding and at wages for day-labor depressed by a sustained buyer's market. During lulls in the agricultural calendar, they were as unemployed as they were landless. Jobless or not, they were forced into the marketplace, of which they had little or no experience, to buy wheat and barley, the staples of their diet. They had previously produced these cereals for themselves in their hillside plots, but now these were grown "efficiently" on the large estates of the alluvial plains and piedmont region and shipped to market. In the marketplace, the meager and irregular wages of field hands bought even less sustenance than they should have, because the vulnerable peasants were cheated with adulterated grain and rigged scales.[5] Finally, a suborning of the courts accelerated the processes of foreclosure and expropriation that initiated these dynamics. Instead of stopping foreclosures based upon illegal forms of interest, these corrupted courts sanctioned the proceedings.[6]

The differences in perspective arising from these conflicts within the political economies of Israel and Judah impacted how various audiences

---

5. Cf. Lev 19:35–36; Deut 25:13–16; Hos 12:7–8 (Heb. vv. 8–9); Amos 8:4–6; Mic 6:10–11; Prov 11:1; 16:11; 20:10, 23.

6. For a fuller explication of the dynamics summarized here, see Premnath 2003; Chaney 1989a, 1999, 2004a, and the literature there cited.

understood the tenth commandment. To oppressed peasants and their prophetic defenders, YHWH's covenantal law sought to protect the community of freeholders and to prevent it from reverting to the oppressive structures characteristic of agrarian societies, symbolized biblically by Egypt and Canaan. Enter the tenth commandment in its short form as a defense of upland freehold and the whole society and value system of which it was the material base. *You shall not covet and/or attempt to expropriate your fellow Israelite's fair share of the God-given right of access to a stable, healthy livelihood.* The commandment's closest philological parallels thus speak concretely of the seizure, robbery, and wrongful expropriation of fields and allotments. But as apodictic law, it was also a broad statement of policy, seeking more than grudging, legalistic compliance. Understanding that the hand does not do strongly or for long what the heart does not believe, it was couched in language that intentionally included the more subjective dimension of identification with YHWH's covenantal community, its values, and its total well-being or shalom. We have seen above how *ḥāmad* combines these subjective and objective elements, just as *bayit* signals both a family's means of sustenance and shelter and the network of human nurture that could grow only once these survival needs had been met securely.

Such an interpretation is reinforced by another body of evidence that previous exegesis has not adequately addressed. Already in 1934, Alt noted the close affinities of content among three sets of Old Testament legal materials: (1) the Decalogue; (2) the so-called cursing dodecalogue of Deuteronomy 27, stated in the "cursed-be-the-one-who-does-X" form; and (3) laws throughout the Pentateuch, stated in the participial form and treating crimes punishable by death—"the one who does X shall surely be put to death."[7] Notwithstanding Gerstenberger's later critique (1965) of the inclusion of all three forms in the category of apodictic law, their striking congruence of subject matter merits attention. If Alt's subsequent interpretation of the eighth commandment as the prohibition of stealing persons for slaves is allowed into court (1953, see the discussion above), the entire corpus of biblical law stated in these three forms involves crimes against either God or persons, never against property alone. The only possible exceptions are the tenth commandment and Deut 27:17: "Cursed be the one who moves his neighbor's boundary marker back!" But moving your neighbor's boundary marker back is a particular instance of "coveting" your neighbor's "house," as understood in this stream of interpretation.[8] And as opposed to the theft

---

7. Alt 1966a:119–23. For the relationships of these three bodies of data, see also Phillips 1970, even though the general thesis of the work has deservedly not found wide acceptance.

8. Cf. Deut 19:14: "You shall not move your neighbor's boundary marker, set up

of movable property, which the casuistic law of the Bible regularly punished by multiple restitution, this crime against a neighboring family's means to an adequate livelihood was a crime against their persons. Reference need only be made to Mic 3:1–4, where, with an extended image of cannibalism, the prophet accused the elite expropriators of his own time of fattening upon the flesh of their neighbors. Thus Micah's interpretation of the tenth commandment is in conformity with the entire body of apodictic law in giving God and persons priority over property.

If such was the case for contexts like Micah's, when and how did the various specifying lists of Exod 20:17 and Deut 5:21 arise? While we lack grounds for dating the additions to the tenth commandment in any absolute chronology, they can be placed, I believe, within the generic context of a Yahwistic elite sometime after the rise of the monarchy. Coveting looked different from their perspective. Any prohibition on coveting, in fact, tends to sanction the status quo. In the world of upland freeholders, the old status quo was communitarian and less starkly stratified, and the commandment in its short form sought to protect that reality. While the wording probably stopped with the "neighbor's house," as most scholars agree, an alternative form may have included "his field," as in Deut 5:21, the Nash Papyrus, and the Septuagint of Exod 20:17. Once the custodians of official Yahwism were the beneficiaries of a stratified, monarchic order, however, the subjective dimensions of *ḥāmad* and *bayit* in the sense of "all property" came to the fore. *Bayit* in this latter meaning was then specified by a list of possessions pertaining to an estate, a list that Moran has demonstrated to be ancient and formulaic but not frozen. While Moran stressed the second-millennium date of his Akkadian parallels, their social perspective is at least as important—they derive from royal archives.

In attributing these specifying additions to members of the upper classes sometime after the rise of the monarchic state, I am accusing them neither of conscious malevolence nor of tampering. They merely made explicit what the old words seemed inevitably to mean when viewed from their social location. With the commandment thus reduced to prohibiting a desire for anything not one's own in the current order, the way was opened for the further specification of the neighbor's wife. Recognizing her lack of homogeneity with the remainder of the list, tradents variously placed her first and separately, as in Deuteronomy, or included her as the first specification after *bayit* and before male and female servants, as in Exodus.

---

by former generations, on property that will be allotted to you in the land that YHWH your God is giving you to possess." On this and three other passages In Deuteronomy making the same distinctive use of "your neighbor" as in the tenth commandment, see Rofé 1990:45–65.

If the preceding analysis is at all cogent, both of these contextual understandings of the tenth commandment are irreducibly "canonical," the first in Mic 2:2, the second in the final form of Exod 20:17 and Deut 5:21. But they pull in very different, sometimes opposite directions. How can the resulting tension be parsed? One helpful approach to that question lies, I believe, in the interpreter's careful attention to the dynamics of power in the context of interpretation. When the human relations in view are between or among persons or groups of approximately equal power, interpretation can properly focus on the final form of Exod 20: 17 and Deut 5:21 and its evocation of theological and ethical questions about the nature, context, and proper limits of human motivation and desire.[9] If the persons or groups involved evidence power differentials sufficient to render one significantly vulnerable to the other, however, a hermeneutic of dynamic analogy presses the perspective of Mic 2:2 on the commandment to the fore. Established North Atlantic culture currently grants the former great precedence over the latter. However, given growing inequalities of power and wealth in much of today's world and systemic dynamics that render all human beings increasingly interdependent, the last word here must surely be given to contexts of interpretation like Micah's.

It was in such contexts that YHWH's messengers, the prophets, insisted that the tenth commandment be heard in its most concrete sense by those who, in Isaiah's words, "joined house to house and added field to field until there was no place left" (Isa 5:8). Micah 2, our point of departure for the philology of the tenth commandment, provides as good a summary as any for the dozens of prophetic texts that castigate aggressive land consolidation and its perpetrators, techniques, and consequences.

The pericope in Mic 2:1–5 reads as follows, though in obscure portions of vv. 4 and 5, any proposed translation must proceed in all humility:

> Alas for those who devise iniquity
> > and work evil upon their beds!
> At morning's light they carry it out
> > because it is within their power.
> They covet fields and rip (them) off,
> > and houses, and seize (them).
> They oppress by extortion a fellow and his house,
> > a man and his ancestral allotment.

---

9. For trenchant comments in this regard, see, inter alia, Harrelson 1997:123–29; and Janzen 1997:156–58.

Therefore, this is what YHWH has said:
"Look, I'm just now devising evil against *this 'family'*
from which you shall not withdraw your necks!
And you shall not walk haughtily,
for it will be an evil time!"
In that day a taunt-song shall be raised over you,
and a lament shall be bitterly lamented,
saying: "We are utterly ruined!
The portion of my people he changes—
How he takes away what is mine!
{To the 'splinterer'}[10] he divides our fields!"
{For restoration . . .}
Therefore, you will not have anyone
casting the line by lot
in the assembly of YHWH!

With the double entendre so characteristic of the prophets, Micah accuses Judah's landlords not only of lying awake nights to dream up "iniquity" but of "carrying it out at morning's light." The mention of dawn, as Zeph 3:5 makes clear, alludes to the time when the village court met, supposedly to dispense "justice in the gate." But because of a lack of procedural safeguards, the peasants who constitute the village court face an unenviable choice. They can refuse to sanction a foreclosure against a neighboring family because the debt has involved high de facto interest or other provisions in violation of customary law. Should they choose that course, however, the case will be appealed to a higher court controlled by wealthy landowners. Reversal there of the village court's decision is a foregone conclusion. By opposing the clear desires of the ruling elite, moreover, the members of the court—themselves peasants almost inevitably in debt to the same landlords—will incur the wrath of their creditors. They can, of course, buy time by acquiescing in the illegal foreclosure, but only in the full knowledge that they thereby sell their neighbors into ruin—a ruin they themselves may soon share. Either way, those who already hold landed wealth get more "because it is within their power."

In YHWH's court, by contrast, might does not make right, at least not if the prophet is to be believed. YHWH's judgment instead shows a marked proclivity for the principle of "measure for measure," or—if one

10. What this double translation suggests is that *lšwbb* simultaneously represents both the Polel infinitive of *šwb*, "to restore, for restoration," and the Qal participle of *šbb*, "splinterer." The forms are identical.

prefers Gilbert and Sullivan to Shakespeare—of "making the punishment fit the crime." "You're good at devising iniquity and working evil against peasant households behind a facade of legality," says YHWH. "How about a little of your own medicine? I'm right now devising evil in my court against this whole 'family' of wealthy land-grabbers! You're accustomed to walking haughtily. Try it with an Assyrian yoke on your neck!"

If my translation and interpretation of the difficult lines of vv. 4 and 5 are on target, this measure-for-measure judgment against those who "covet houses" continues. It is the expropriators who lament because YHWH is expropriating them. In a literary device not uncommon elsewhere in prophecy, a quotation from the once-haughty lords of the great estates is introduced without warning to depict them in the pain of their own dispossession. "We are utterly ruined! He [i.e., YHWH, the ultimate landlord] is changing the allotments given to my peasants, calling them his people. How he takes away what is mine! Why, he's dividing the fields of our estates back into subsistence plots for the peasants, splintering asunder what we worked so hard to accumulate—calling it 'restoration!' Really! Why doesn't God just stick to spiritual matters where he belongs? What has proper theology to do with this so-called land reform and its unwise interference with market forces?" If those last two sentences are my extrapolation, the message of v. 5 is not. In YHWH's assembly, when the land that is ultimately God's is apportioned fairly by lot to all who work it for a livelihood, those who have broken the tenth commandment flagrantly and repeatedly will be excluded.

Such words are not easy to hear from a comfortable pew, let alone from the endowed chair I am privileged to occupy. This prophetic reiteration of the tenth commandment disquiets us, not because most of us are exact modern analogues of those whom Micah addressed, but because we are beneficiaries of complex systems of political economy not completely dissimilar from those condemned by the prophet (cf. Brueggemann 1994:852). The hermeneutical and ethical implications of that juxtaposition are far too complex to be treated in this already overburdened essay. They also greatly exceed the competence of this workaday exegete. But labor at those uncomfortable implications we must, for the biblical heritage that we claim insists centrally and irreducibly that the most profound experience of the living God and the most constant concern for our neighbor's well-being cannot be separated. For the definition of one's neighbor, Christians can scarcely improve upon that given in Luke 10:25–37.

4

Systemic Study of the Israelite Monarchy

Abstract

The usual history-as-biography approach to the Israelite monarchy is inadequate; what is mandated is a systemic study of the material conditions reflected in various biblical literary genres and in the archaeology of villages and of regional economies. A systemic approach will enable us to ground ideology in material conditions, to discern the major social conflicts and social structural "watersheds," to grasp social roles and institutions as aspects of a whole system in change, and to compare Israel's monarchic society with other societies exhibiting similar systemic features. Immediately useful in this regard are the neo-evolutionary and techno-environmental approaches of Gerhard and Jean Lenksi and Marvin Harris, which clarify Israel as an "agrarian society" with some distinctive features of its own within that typology.

By way of illustration, the author develops a socioeconomic sketch of the rise of Israel which stresses its initial stateless peasant economy, profitting from the weakened Canaanite political system and introducing metals for agrarian use in contrast to their reservation for warfare and luxury within the surrounding statist societies. Israel adopted monarchy in response to the twofold threat of a Philistine bid to dominate Israelite economy from without and the move of a prospering agrarian elite to dominate Israelite economy from within.

Subsequently, the Israelite state(s) took peasant surpluses in a manner that impoverished cultivators and pushed them into debt on an enlarging scale. Self-sufficient production was threatened by specialization in agriculture for purposes of export trade and upper class indulgence. The critical socially disruptive effects of these "system trends" are shown in traditions about the kings and in the Elijah and Elisha stories. It is argued that biblical texts from monarchic times can only be interpreted with sufficient precision and inter-connectedness when viewed as witnesses to a dynamic social process reverberating through all dimensions of Israel's life.

∼

INTRODUCTION

What follows is far from systematic. It is instead a rather ad hoc advocacy for the inclusion of a robustly *systemic* dimension in any sociological study of the Israelite monarchy. No attempt has been made to duplicate the literature review that is the task of other papers nor to document or nuance the positions taken in more than the sketchiest terms. My intent is rather to provoke investigation of certain systemic avenues of access to the social world of monarchic Israel at the outset of our deliberations as a seminar, lest the flow of ongoing work in more traditional and particularistic channels functionally exclude such research from our purview.

But is a challenge to employ systemic categories and research strategies more than a tempest in a teapot? Do not most investigations of the monarchic society of ancient Israel treat the dynamic interrelatedness of the various structures and functions of that society? My only honest answer is that they do not do so adequately, and that there are important reasons why. A cursory look at those reasons will also help to define what I mean by the adjective, "systemic."

I. SOME FACTORS MILITATING AGAINST AN ADEQUATELY SYSTEMIC INVESTIGATION OF THE ISRAELITE MONARCHY

1. Most of the historiography that treats monarchic Israel does not adequately balance ideological and technoenvironmental factors in assessing historical causation. The former are almost routinely overestimated, the latter given short shrift. Several reasons for this bias suggest themselves. As the principal sources of our information, the works of the Deuteronomistic Historian and the Chronicler both evidence marked, if different, ideological inclinations. These proclivities went far in determining which historical data were preserved and how those data selected for preservation were interpreted (Sarna 1979:3–19). To conterbalance such refraction in their sources, modern historians would need to swim upstream in both their collection and interpretation of data. But the bulk of biblical scholarship is not so disposed. Steeped in the ideology-prone traditions of theological historiography, it finds the penchants of its sources congenial and is content to perpetuate them.

2. In an adequately systemic analysis, the diachronic dimension must focus upon *significant change* which modifies society *as a whole*. But once again, trends in biblical scholarship—each intelligible in its own context—tend to focus attention almost anywhere except upon systemic change. Given the obvious and complex task of determining the chronology of reigns and battles, most studies of the monarchic period proceed from a perspective of historical particularism. The demands of unraveling the maddening detail of changes in personnel leave little time or energy to investigate the underlying changes in institutional integration. The contours of the forest become lost in the description of individual trees. (An analogous treatment of the history of the United States of America would delineate presidencies in full political and military detail, but neglect to mention that society's passage from agrarian to industrial and on to postindustrial modes of organization.) Since an impressive and growing body of social-scientific theory regards technological innovation as one of the most powerful engines of systemic change, the fact that most biblical scholars exhibit greater interest in and knowledgeability of ideology than technology would appear only to exacerbate this tendency.

If historical particularism is the Scylla of scholarship on the Israelite monarchy, synchronic conceptualizations and comparisons are the Charybdis. Such treatments are wont to compare and contrast *the* monarchy in Israel or Judah with *the* monarchy in other ancient Near Eastern societies. Little room is left for discerning change, systemic or otherwise. The studiedly ahistorical interpretation of biblical texts now in vogue in many quarters only lends aid and comfort to this neglect of analysis which is both diachronic and systemic.

3. Few elements loom as large in a systemic study of an agrarian monarchy as an accurate delineation of the lines of conflict and cleavage. With regard to our knowledge of these features in the Israelite monarchies, however, skewing forces have been at work again. Most of our written sources—be they the Deuteronomistic History, the Chronicler's work, the royal annals and other official records which they used, or documents of these latter genres from neighboring societies—are preoccupied with issues of *national* identity and security. Since a majority of modern biblical scholars are citizens of the nations of western Europe, North America, or Israel, their experience and socialization predispose them, too, to see major variation and conflict as occurring between and among *national* entities. Reinforcing cleavages, such as linguistic, ethnic, and religious divisions, variously heighten this sense of political conflict, both in the sources from the ancient Near East and in the experience of modern scholars. A broader comparison of agrarian societies as a generic type of social and economic organization, however, shows that for all their cultural diversity and political conflict, the variations and cleavages *within* any such society are greater than those between any two such societies (Lenski 1966/1984:189–296; Lenski and Lenski 1978:177–230).

That the patterns of social stratification typical of agrarian monarchies manifested themselves in Israel and Judah is both certain and of an importance difficult to exaggerate. In such systems of stratification, a ruling elite of probably no more than two percent of the population controlled up to half or more of the total goods and services (Sjoberg 1960:80–107, 110, et passim; Lenski 1966/1984:189–296; Lenski and Lenski 1978:177–230). Pervasive and complex social mechanisms served to buffer the experience of that small elite from the harsh realities of the peasant majority which supported them. Though seldom reflected in the literature, it is a simple fact that the lives of the ruling elite in Israel and Judah had more in common with the ruling elite of other Near Eastern monarchies than with the peasants, artisans, and expendables of their homelands.

Elites understood each other and their world on the same basic terms. Internally, they took for granted the patterns of stratification just sketched. Conflict that ensued therefrom was regarded principally as a problem to be "managed." As the architects and beneficiaries of state power, their attention was directed mostly toward maintaining and, if possible, expanding by military and/or diplomatic means the land, resource, and population bases that were the foundation of their power and privilege. History as they saw it thus involved primarily the conflict of national powers headed by great personalities. For modern social historians to be content with such a perspective, however, is to leave the experience of ninety-five to ninety-eight percent of the population of those societies out of account. A systemic perspective would urge both a scouring of sources for rare bits of information about this other "silent majority" and a careful analysis of the interface between socioeconomic and political cleavage and conflict. Full investigation of the "guns or butter" issue is an obvious case in point.

4. Systemic sociology includes of necessity *macro*sociology. It insists upon examining total societies and even concatenations of societies. No portion of such a social system is ever regarded as adequately understood until its articulation with the other parts of the system has been described. Many sociological treatments of materials from the monarchic period eschew such considerations, however, at least partially under the impress of social-scientific traditions that are *micro*analytical. A recent and distinguished work, for example, purports to be a study of *Prophecy and Society in Ancient Israel* (Wilson 1980). In fact, one will search its pages in vain for any description or analysis of Israelite *society* as a whole. Wilson's failure to take macrosociology seriously means that the prophetic roles that he delineates with such care are not articulated adequately with the larger web of society, its conflicts, and its changes. Just these latter considerations are demonstrably a major concern of the prophetic texts themselves. The same cannot be said of the prophetic roles in and of themselves, a fact that leads to no little speculation in any attempt to describe such roles. For once, the available data point directly to socioeconomic conflict, systemic change, and the material plight of the masses. Coupled with the tendencies already delineated, however, focus on individual institutions or roles to the exclusion of macrosociological analysis has truncated and distorted studies of great learning and promise.

5. Systemic considerations lead to more rigorous and fruitful criteria of comparison. Any sociological study of the kingdoms of Israel and Judah almost inevitably involves comparison with other social entities. But the comparisons are often piecemeal and ad hoc, failing to appreciate that the institutions compared are but parts of larger wholes. Evolutionary sociologists, for instance, see important systemic differences between the monarchies of the Bronze and Iron Ages, respectively, while students of the ancient Near East appear to compare portions of each with reckless abandon. Sociological and anthropological research into Israelite prophecy frequently utilizes data from hunting and gathering and horticultural societies without recognition that the different systemic matrices involved condition the data compared. Discussion of commerce and trade flits lightly from Israel and

Judah to Phoenicia, leaving obscured the important distinctions between agrarian and maritime societies born of the cost differential between overland and seaborne transportation in a preindustrial context. The systematic analysis of neo-evolutionary theory, on the other hand, with its empirical delineation of societal types, can provide more precise categories for possible analogies and reconstructions (Lenski and Lenski 1978; Parsons 1977).

Other skewing factors undoubtedly exist. Those outlined vary greatly in the intensity and subtlety of their impact upon individual works. But if their articulation here points—however crudely—to realities in which the bulk of previous scholarship on the subject has been involved in some measure, then it also mandates conscious strategies to correct such skewing in any concerted study of the sociology of the monarchy now to be undertaken.

II. SOME RESEARCH STRATEGIES TO CORRECT THE SKEWING FACTORS PRESENT IN MOST PREVIOUS SCHOLARSHIP ON THE ISRAELITE MONARCHY

1. While it is clearly not their primary interest, the Deuteronomistic Historian and the Chronicler *do* preserve information about the materiality of ancient Israel and Judah. Those data should be collected assiduously and collated carefully with information from other sources.

2. Many prophetic and legal texts—the former including prophetic narratives in Samuel–Kings as well as the Latter Prophets—address socioeconomic and technoenvironmental realities directly. Too little use has been made of these texts by historians, largely due to a penchant for political, ideational, and particularist historiography and to the fact that so many of these texts cannot be dated absolutely. A history of the social systems of monarchic Israel and Judah, on the other hand, would focus on the *generic* dimension that these texts so often reflect. Generic change is less frequent than specific change, meaning that the dating of the sources used to reconstruct the generic plane can be less exact with little loss of precision. Conversely, attention to representations of this generic dimension in a given text may allow it to be placed one side or the other of a systemic watershed, thereby fixing more exactly its position in relative chronology.

3. New interests and methods now being pioneered in archaeology should be emphasized and accelerated. For the monarchic period, more traditional archaeology has understandably concentrated upon the artifacts of political and military history, since much of the hard-won stratigraphy of historical times is fixed by destructions attributable to foreign invasions known from literary sources. Linked with the factors discussed in part I

above, however, such archaeology has served to reinforce the notion of history as "what the kings did." Newer trends seek at least limited excavation of the material culture of villagers and the urban poor. Such work will produce few *objets d'art* to dazzle the eyes of museum-goers, but it can provide invaluable information on how that other ninety-eight percent of the population lived. Equally welcome is the effect that technoeconomic perspectives have had upon field method. As opposed to the past tendency to focus upon the political and religious history of one walled site, some more recent work, for example, has attempted to integrate surface surveys and limited, sample excavations with more traditional methods to reconstruct regional economies. Nor should the published excavation reports of more traditional archaeologists be neglected. The data in those reports can sometimes be reexamined profitably, this time posing different questions prompted by systemic perspectives.

4. Whatever its source, no datum should be left isolated or interpreted only in terms of one of its facets. If we have information that a given social factor changed, we should always pursue the probable effect of that change upon other factors in the social system and upon that system as a whole. When interpreted systemically, do seemingly unrelated data point to similar vectors of change in society?

5. Modern theories of social evolution can provide indispensable tools for the recognition and explanation of significant systemic change. With its concentration upon the nature and causes of social change, this body of theory can suggest criteria for fixing the watersheds which will provide the most accurate periodization of social history. Far more than has been the vogue in biblical studies, these criteria probe *infrastructural* operations, viewed within an extensive geographical and chronological framework (Lenski and Lenski 1978; Harris 1968, 1979, 1980).

6. This neo-evolutionary strategy also allows the classification of all human societies into a limited number of societal types, with all exemplars of a given type sharing basic criteria which in turn serve to distinguish them from all other types. The implications of this delineation for comparative study are enormous.

To gain sensitivity to the patterns of social stratification discussed above in I.3 (see above, p. 86), for example, students of the Israelite monarchies should steep themselves in that portion of stratification theory that treats *agrarian* societies comparatively and as a generic type (Lenski 1966/1984:189–296). Historical evidence may demonstrate that Israel or Judah deviated in one or more particular(s) from such generic patterns, and no precast "model" should be allowed to strong-arm specific evidence. But when the data are fragmentary or allusive, as they are so often, to know the *probable* configuration of power and privilege in *any* society of the genus to which ancient Israel and Judah demonstrably belonged is of inestimable benefit to accurate historical reconstruction.

The historical particularists who are quick to disdain such generic patterns in the name of "empirical evidence" are often distressingly *un*empirical in their own use of ad hoc comparisons. Since the social and economic organizations of the industrial world provide the experience of most such scholars and their constituencies, they sometimes retroject the patterns of stratification generic to *industrial* societies onto *agrarian* antiquity. An *empirical* investigation of the comparative data on stratification, however, demonstrates broad similarities *within* both agrarian and industrial types, but striking and ubiquitous dissimilarities *between* them.

Neither historical specialist nor comparative sociologist is intrinsically more empirical in all matters. By focusing upon a smaller database, the former can obviously control those data, as such, in more detail. But the disciplined comparativist, with a far broader base, investigates more empirically the social comparisons that are tacit in all historiography. Each needs the other in order to remain as precise as possible in an integral part of his/her work.

7. Finally, neo-evolutionary strategies are germane for the comparison of narrower systemic differences. The Israelite monarchies are frequently compared with the agrarian city-states of Canaan, the maritime city-states of Phoenicia, and the agrarian national/imperial states of Egypt, Assyria, and Babylonia. When informed by modern evolutionary theory, such comparisons would investigate the variations between and among these forms of monarchic organization and ask how they are related to such environmental, technological, and economic factors as the following: variations in the type and fertility of the soil; rain agriculture versus irrigation agriculture; subsistence intercropping versus commercial agriculture, producing for market; the relative size of the herding component in agrarian societies; the relative costs of overland versus seaborne transportation; the relative ease or difficulty of access to functional harbors; scarce and expensive metals restricted to the military and luxury artifacts of the ruling elite versus relatively plentiful and cheap metals available to farmers, artisans, and infantrymen; guild literacy versus alphabetic notation; and variations in geographical location, such as major riverine valleys, narrow coastal plains or mountain valleys, steppes, or Balkanized hill country.

Once again, many important categories and strategies have undoubtedly been omitted. Those sketched are intended to be preliminary and suggestive only. To continue their proliferation in the abstract would be almost as easy—and as irresponsible—as continuing to tax previous scholarship for what it has not done. The time has come, rather, for the more difficult task of offering specific suggestions for constructive work, a task to which I now turn.

III. SOME ILLUSTRATIVE SKETCHES OF SYSTEMIC ANALYSIS

The particular emphasis that this section places upon the matrix, organization, and dynamics of the peasantry and its agriculture in the monarchic societies of Israel and Judah was not chosen at random. Such a focus was mandated instead by consideration of the factors discussed in parts I and II. Israel and Judah were *agrarian* societies, meaning that their principal means of subsistence was a tillage of fields that knew the plow but not that concatenation of inanimate energy sources whose use in production denotes industrialization. Constituting a majority of from seventy to ninety percent of the population, peasant cultivators thus provided the monarchies in Israel and Judah their primary economic base.

The systems of land tenure that controlled the cost, terms, and security of these peasants' access to arable land went far to determine not only the conditions of life for the peasant majority, but also the distribution of power and privilege in the rest of society. In response to the promptings of evolutionary theory, I have chosen to begin my sketch of these dynamics, not at the inception of the Israelite monarchy, but in those systemic events that set the stage for its rise.

Just prior to Israel's formation as an independent society at the beginning of the Iron Age, the city-states that dominated the alluvial plains of Late Bronze Canaan related people to land with that combination of patrimonial and prebendal domain that typifies agrarian societies (Wolf 1966:50–59). At one level, all of the arable land of a Canaanite city-state belonged to its king or warlord—the proprietary right of the state. At another level, however, much of the land was granted as hereditary estates to a military aristocracy in return for its martial and other services to the crown. Since these aristocratic lands passed as a patrimony from father to son, this pattern of land tenure is often called patrimonial. Other estates were granted to high level bureaucrats in payment for their governmental duties. While such an estate supposedly accrued to a bureaucrat only by dint of the office in which he was incumbent—a system of so-called prebendal domain—both office and estate frequently passed from father to son, and hence became patrimonial in fact, if not in theory. Strong kings, of course, sought to foster just the reverse process and to make all grants contingent upon the crown's good pleasure.

The holders of patrimonial and prebendal estates never worked the land themselves, disdaining all manual labor save for the chronic, petty warfare from which they derived their principal identity as warriors. The fields that they and their king or warlord were able to conquer and hold by force of arms they let out to peasant producers, who regularly paid half or more of their total production to the landlord in the form of various taxes and rents in return for access to the land. By means of this system, a ruling elite of two percent or less of the population enjoyed the privilege of controlling half or more of the total goods and services produced in the society. This elite, in turn, had every incentive and more than sufficient means to extract the largest possible "surplus" from the peasant majority, leaving it only the barest subsistence necessary to remain productive. As a result, life for the majority was brutish and short, with peasant families decimated by hunger and disease. Official Canaanite religion legitimated and reinforced this sharp stratification and its inherent values. Such was the socioeconomic system in the alluvial plains of Canaan when Israel emerged as a separate society in the adjacent hill country.

As Mendenhall (1962:66–87, 1973: passim), Gottwald (1979), and I (Chaney 1983:39–90) have sought to document in somewhat different ways elsewhere, that emergent Israelite society was in many respects the polemical obverse of the Canaanite city-states. At the heart of the contrast was Israel's system of land tenure. In that premonarchic period, Israel's ideology denied legitimacy to any human king. Royal prerogatives were Yahweh's alone, and Yahweh was definitively manifest in the Exodus, which epitomized the defeat of the monarchic power of the agrarian state on behalf of the "have nots." Among these privileges of the king was ultimate ownership of the land or economic base. The land was Yahweh's. Any absolute claim on it was an arrogation of rights appropriate only to God. But premonarchic Israel understood Yahweh to distribute this economic base to peasant vassals in a manner that sought to assure secure and sufficient access to arable land and thereby to livelihood.

Whether as a specific plot, a right to be included in the periodic redistribution of lands held by the village as a whole, or some combination of the two, each extended family of producers was conceived to hold as an inalienable inheritance the land that it worked. Since, as landlord of the hill country, Yahweh left with their peasant producers the "surpluses" greedily extracted by the human overlords of the nearby plains, the extended families that formed the building blocks of Israel's upland society were relatively viable and stable. Called "father's house" (*bēyt 'āb*), the extended family was a patrilineal and patrilocal unit of three or four generations (Gottwald 1979:285-91). The family members shared a dwelling in the village and together held and worked a portion of its arable land. These hill country farmers practiced mixed, subsistence agriculture, producing most of what they consumed and consuming most of what they produced.

This configuration of village life in premonarchic Israel was made possible in part by a political power vacuum in the area, a local condition that partook of the more general decline experienced by the monarchies of the eastern Mediterranean region at the end of the Bronze Age. What caused that decline? All existing answers are tenuous and all probable answers multiple, but the issue is important for sociological analysis of the monarchies of the ancient Near East. Only by knowing what brought the demise of the Bronze Age monarchies can we fully understand the kingdoms and empires of the Iron Age that arose from their ashes and delineate the elements of continuity and change between them. Two avenues of inquiry into the causes of Bronze Age decline—by no means mutually exclusive—deserve more attention than they are given in politically oriented histories. One is Childe's brief but suggestive analysis of the internal contradictions of the economies of the Bronze Age (1964:159-94). The other is the recent inferential argument that bronze became scarce because of an interruption in the supply of its tin component (Maddin et al. 1977:122-23; Waldbaum 1978:65-66, 72-73).

If the part played by technological factors in the demise of the Bronze Age in general bears investigation, so does their role in rendering the hill country of Palestine—a natural refuge for fugitives from the elitist powers of the plains—habitable by a denser population at the beginning of the Iron Age (Gottwald 1979:655-60; Chaney 1983:49-51). Rock terracing to hold the thin soils and seasonal rains of the highland ridge appears to be one such technological innovation. Although not of such recent origin, the use of slaked lime plaster to waterproof cisterns was greatly proliferated in certain upland regions in this period. (There is not infrequently a time lag between a given technological innovation and its impact upon society in concert with other factors.) Concurrently, modest reservoirs and irrigation works may also have been introduced into the hills. But the technology that lent its name to the era was that pertaining to iron.

The introduction of iron tools in even relatively small numbers often has been credited with allowing "Israelite" peasants to clear and cultivate the hill country and to hew out the many new cisterns already mentioned. If iron appeared early enough and in sufficient quantities to have played such a role—both matters of dispute to be discussed below—Gottwald has provided an exemplary schema for the analysis of its impact upon the process and relations of peasant production.

> What increase in efficiency is introduced by iron tools over bronze tools? Can this be calculated in terms of work output per unit of labor invested and in terms of increase of crop yields and consumption of foods? Were some plants cultivated only for the first time with the introduction of iron in conjunction with a better water supply? Which crops benefited most directly from the technological shift to iron? On first thought, it appears that crops requiring yearly ploughing and sowing of fields, such as grains and vegetables—rather than those grown on trees and vines, such as olives and grapes—were the immediate beneficiaries of improved farming tools. A large-scale increase in wheat and barley cultivation in the highlands will have been of critical importance in supplying the food staples that heretofore were cultivable on a large scale only in the feudally dominated estates of the plains. Israelites-to-be, fleeing from their onerous role as laborers in the quasi-feudal system, were enabled to form the material base for a separate economy and an autonomous society only as they found a way to replace the feudally extracted grain surpluses with grain surpluses extracted by free and equal labor. (Gottwald 1979:657)

Two further lines of reasoning tend to corroborate Gottwald's hunch that grains and vegetables, rather than olives and grapes, would have benefited most directly from iron tools, and that the incentive given thereby to annual crops in the uplands might have had important sociopolitical implications. There is archaeological evidence that at least some of the villagers of premonarchic Israel did, in fact, grow cereals in the hill country. Concerning their terraced plots, Stager writes:

> These were best suited to vine, olive, and nut cultivation. But the earliest terrace-farmers at Ai and Khirbet Raddana grew cereals. This inefficient use of terraces suggests an attempt by the highlanders (probably 'Israelites' during the period of the Judges) to maintain a subsistence cereal agriculture free from Canaanite and Philistine spheres, where the primary "bread baskets" were located. (1976:13)

If at least some of these fields were held by the village as a whole and periodically redistributed, as has been suggested on the basis of both textual and comparative evidence (Alt 1955:13–23, 1959:348–72; Chaney 1983:64–65), this system of repartitional domain would also help to explain premonarchic

Israel's preference for cereals. "Where a piece of land changes hands periodically, few cultivators will make permanent improvements on it. The system thus reinforces the traditional and relatively extensive cultivation of annual crops and discourages the introduction of intensively produced perennials" (Wolf 1966:79). The convergence of such seemingly disparate facts and theories illustrates well the possibilities of a systemic approach.

Exemplary and suggestive as Gottwald's sociological analysis of the effects of iron technology has proven in most regards, it still faces two important questions. One concerns Gottwald's apparent presupposition that iron replaced bronze because it was stronger and otherwise more desirable for making weapons and tools. Recent work (Maddin et al. 1977; Waldbaum 1978; Wertime and Muhly 1980; Stech-Wheeler et al. 1981) challenges that presupposition head-on. Until development of steeling, it is now argued, the bloomery iron of the earliest Iron Age was inferior to bronze as a medium for the manufacture of weapons and tools. Thus, the scarcity of bronze already alluded to above is now often viewed as the major impetus for the development of iron technology. While this version of the transition from bronze to iron appears more adequate than Gottwald's on the basis of current, fragmentary evidence, it still shares with Gottwald and all previous scholarship known to me a failure to reckon fully with an important systemic distinction.

By repeatedly referring to weapons and tools in one breath, scholars convey the impression that the metallurgy available to users of one was available to the users of the other. Our knowledge of the social stratification of the Late Bronze Age should warn us to the contrary. Throughout agrarian societies, in fact, the ruling classes found much of their identity as warriors and lavished great time and energy upon procuring and becoming proficient with the dominant weapons of their day. They had no such interest in the tools of productive technology, which they associated with the manual labor of peasants and disdained. (As Childe [1951:180–88] and Lenski and Lenski [1978:188] have argued, this distinction is responsible for the fact that technological innovation was much more frequent in weaponry than in the productive sector for the duration of the agrarian era.) Since the bronze supply was always relatively limited and expensive, it was allocated to those uses having the highest priority for the ruling classes. Some artisans in elite employ may have had bronze tools, but most of those used by peasants were made of wood, stone, and bone (Lenski and Lenski 1978:189).

Bloomery iron, I would suggest, altered this relationship between metallurgy and social stratification. Easily accessible deposits of a smeltable grade of iron ore were more frequent and plentiful in the Near East than those of copper ore, and certainly more common than the tin that royal traders had to import at great cost. Once the techniques for the basic reduction of iron ore became known widely, metal tools of some sort became available to peasants who had never had access to them before. The socioeconomically important distinction for premonarchic Israel, therefore, may have been not that bloomery iron was inferior to bronze for toolmaking, but that it was superior to wood, stone, and bone! Metallurgy would have come at last to the productive technology of peasant agriculture.

But when did iron tools become available in sufficient quantities to make any such impact? The archaeological evidence currently available is spotty and difficult to interpret. As Waldbaum's careful inventory shows (1978:24–27), relatively few iron artifacts have been found in Palestine which can be dated to the beginnings of Iron I. Even if more iron tools such as the remarkably preserved iron pick from Har Adir come to light from that period, they are not likely to alter two configurations of the archaeological data disclosed by Waldbaum's collations (1978:39–42)—bronze tools and weapons outnumber iron until the tenth century BCE, and in the twelfth century, weapons and ornaments outnumber tools among iron artifacts. Both configurations are not infrequently interpreted as precluding any causal role for iron tools in the proliferation of "Israelite" villages in the hill country at the beginning of Iron I.

The raw statistics, however, may convey a false impression due to several factors that skew the archaeological sample. Bronze and iron decompose differently, for example, meaning that bronze is probably overrepresented in the sample. The bias thus introduced into the body of available data should be roughly comparable from one period to another, thereby granting validity to relative comparisons between or among periods. That the archaeological record accurately portrays the proportions of the two metals actually in use in any society *within* a given period, however, is open to grave question.

While this factor is sometimes recognized by archaeologists, they have not, to my knowledge, considered the probable differential in the rate at which various social groups in antiquity lost their metal artifacts, and hence made them available for modern excavation. Is it not probable that those upper class groups long accustomed to metal weapons and ornaments would deem any one such artifact relatively less precious, and that it would thus become concomitantly more susceptible to loss? Ornaments and weapons are also prone to loss due merely to the nature of the activities in which they are used. Frontier peasants who had a few metal tools for the very first time, on the other hand, would hold them dear, particularly if they understood both their livelihood and their independence to be contingent upon their ability to retain and use such tools. Under such conditions, metal tools that became worn or broken would not be discarded, but reworked into new tools. Only as iron became far cheaper and more plentiful—a process commonly acknowledged to have taken centuries—would hill country peasants have relaxed any of the vigilance with which they conserved iron artifacts.

If such considerations are cogent, the current state of the archaeological evidence does not tell against viewing the introduction of limited quantities of iron tools into the hill country of Palestine as one significant factor in the appearance of so many new villages there at the beginning of Iron I. Even the very few extant iron tools that date to Iron Ia are evidence enough if the skewing factors outlined above are understood to be operative. All interpretations, of course, are subject to correction or refutation by new data brought to light either by archaeological excavation or metallurgical analysis. To be understood adequately, however, any such data must be integrated into a plausible social fabric, not just seen in terms of a single strand called metallurgy.

Such perspectives may also shed new light on one of the dynamics which gave rise to the monarchy in Israel. Recent discussion of the subject has reacted healthily against viewing external pressure from the Philistines as the sole cause of that monarchy and has begun significant research into the role of internal forces (Flanagan 1981:47–73). Since a conjoining of both internal and external causes seems most probable, however, the nature and motivation of Philistine incursions into the hill country of Israel need to be understood as precisely as possible. Tsevat insists that we simply cannot know about such things.

> If the Philistines had a long-term policy after they occupied the interior of the country, what was it? Were they interested in tribute, or just loot? [1 Sam] 23:1; 13:17–18. Or were they possibly waging preventive war to keep the Israelites out of the Shephela and the coastal plain? Did they want to secure their rear and prevent the development of a potential rival power to the east? Or was it perhaps their purpose to fashion a political entity embracing the entire country? We do not know. (Tsevat 1979:68)

A systemic approach may allow us to know more than Tsevat thinks. In the late Bronze Age, neither the kings of the Canaanite city-states on the plains nor the Egyptian Pharaoh had had close control over the Palestinian hill country. They did not because they lacked both the incentive and the means. Given the technoeconomic configurations of the period, the meager population and resource bases of most of the highland ridge simply would not repay the cost of conquest. Chariots and composite bows, which were the cornerstone of elite power and the means by which that small elite dominated the population of the plains, were effectively neutralized by the topography of the hill country. By the time that many of the city-states of Canaan had come under the power of the Philistines, both conditions had changed. Organized as a military aristocracy, the Philistines were possessed of weapons, armor, and tactics appropriate to fighting on foot in hilly terrain. If they were thus granted a means for the conquest of the uplands denied to the kings of the Bronze Age, the Philistine overlords also enjoyed a newborn incentive. Using the technological innovations discussed above, Israel's freeholding cultivators had for the first time produced in the hill country an economic and population base worth controlling.

That such control was at least a major objective of Philistine policy is demonstrated by the famous passage in 1 Sam 13:19–22. Had the Philistines wished only military and political domination, their simplest course would have been an attempt to withdraw and withhold *all* metals from Israel. They in fact adopted the more complicated and difficult option of seeking to deny the Israelites their own smiths, capable of producing metal weapons, while allowing the peasants of Israel the metal tools without which they could not produce the agricultural "surpluses" that the Philistine tyrants hoped to milk from the hill country. Though the business practices of Philistine smiths were probably at least as sharp as their tools, thereby providing another mechanism to extract "surpluses" from the Israelite economy, Philistine policy sought to avoid "killing the goose that laid the golden egg."

The details of the process by which David finally thwarted these Philistine aims must be left for other occasions. Suffice it here to state that David not only defeated the Philistines, restricting them to their pentapolis and laying solid Israelite claim to the alluvial plains of Canaan for the first time, but succeeded in subjugating his neighbors on all sides. In that process of empire building, he incurred debts. His military retainers, many loyal to his person since his days as a social bandit, expected to be rewarded when he came into his glory. He had conquered an empire, and its administration necessitated the creation and importation of bureaucrats. In an agrarian context, these categories of obligation were payable in grants of land, that is, in patrimonial and prebendal estates.

But what land did David have to grant? Certainly not most of the hill country, which supported his core constituency as peasant freehold. (The forces that led to the formation of the monarchy had produced some larger estates in the hill country [cf., e.g., 1 Sam 22:6–8], but these were as modest in number and importance as the military professionals whom they supported [Halpern 1981:86–87 et passim; Ben-Barak 1981:73–91]). But the richer plains had never been a secure part of premonarchic Israel, and were David's to grant by right of conquest. Accustomed to the typical agrarian combination of patrimonial and prebendal domain, the estates of the lowlands simply received new overlords, in this case, newly created Israelite aristocrats and bureaucrats. Once ensconced, these groups increasingly assumed values typical of agrarian elites, and sought to broaden their powers of taxation and control. Yahwism was concurrently undergoing transformation into the official religion of the monarchic state of Israel. Most of its institutional expressions above the local level came to be dominated by the newly risen elite and its values.

From that point on, Israel contained two conflicting systems of land tenure that were the material bases of two fundamentally different understandings of society and its proper values. The two did not compete on equal terms. Rain agriculture in Palestine was subject to the vicissitudes of periodic drought, blight, and pestilence. As long as the freeholding producers of premonarchic Israel retained all or most of their own "surpluses" and were bound together in a covenent of mutual assistance, such crises could be weathered, albeit with difficulty. Once the monarchic state and its ruling elite began to extract "surpluses" to pay for luxury and strategic items, however, the peasants' margin grew slimmer. Peasant producers were forced to borrow if natural disaster struck, and the only "surpluses" to be borrowed—however intermediated—were ultimately in the hands of the large landlords.

For collateral, a freeholding peasant family had only its land and its persons. Usurious interest rates insured frequent foreclosures, debt instruments thus serving to transfer land from peasant freehold to large estates and to reduce previously free and independent farmers to landless day-laborers or debt-slaves. Biblical law sought to retard this process and to ameliorate its abuses by prohibiting interest on such loans to the poor, stipulating humane treatment and manumission after a fixed term for debt-slaves, and by instituting the role of the *gō'ēl* or "redeemer"—a kinsman who, if and when able, bought back family land or family members when they had been foreclosed upon. (Anyone seeking the taproot of biblical notions of "redemption" must dirty the fingernails with the mundane soil of these dynamics.) But despite all attempted safeguards, more and more of what had once been considered *Yahweh's* land passed into fewer and fewer *human* hands, with unhappy results for the peasant majority.

The spoils generated by David's imperialistic wars probably postponed the brunt of these dynamics until late in his reign. Solomon's attempts to finish the transformation of Israel into a typical agrarian nation-state, complete with his erection of the temple as a royal chapel to house Yahwism as a state-established and state-legitimizing religion, were minus that flow of booty. To finance ambitious building programs, the importation of military *matériel* and luxury goods on a grand scale, and the maintenance of burgeoning military, court, and cultic establishments, Solomon pressed his agrarian economic base to the breaking point.

The peasant majority, from whose experience the royal court became increasingly buffered and alienated, paid coming and going. Much of their agricultural production was taxed away and either exported to pay for the imports secured from maritime Phoenicia and other trading partners (1 Kgs 5:1-11 [MT 5:15-25]) or consumed by the lavishly provisioned court (1 Kgs 4:22-28). Within the constraints of the situation, the peasantry of Israel had no good options for meeting this increased demand for agricultural commodities.

One means of enhancing productivity would have been to increase the number of person-hours expended in the cultivation of each unit of arable land. Solomon's heavy use of corvée (1 Kgs 5:13-18 [MT 5:27-32]), however, meant that only a *diminution* of labor intensity was possible. Peasants felling and transporting timber in Lebanon or working on public building projects were tormented both by the taskmasters' whips and by their knowledge of the farm work that remained undone at home. Even though they had less time and energy to till their own fields, the tax collectors seemed to demand more of the production of those fields each year.

Another alternative for increasing output would have been to improve somehow the efficiency of production. In this case, too, Solomon's military and building policies allowed only the opposite (Hauer 1980:63–73). Not only were the chariot horses that were his stock-in-trade procured by the export of foodstuffs, but the maintenance of those pampered symbols of elite power put them in direct competition with the peasant population for the grain that remained (cf. 1 Kgs 4:28). To the extent that they consumed pasture, hay, and straw, the horses reduced the only too finite quantities of those resources available to support the oxen that provided peasant agriculture its major tractive power. A marked increase in the use of metal farm tools might have raised production, but Solomon's priorities for iron and bronze clearly ran to military might, cultic ostentation, and tools to produce monumental architecture, not to agricultural implements. Splendor and might in Yahweh's temple and Solomon's palace meant hunger in the bellies of the peasant masses.

When interpreted by careful comparative and theoretical study of stratification in agrarian societies, merely the well-known datum that Solomon depended almost exclusively upon a standing, professional army leads to the same conclusions about the plight of the peasantry during his reign.

> On the basis of both theory and research, a general proposition can be formulated to the effect that *the greater the military importance of the peasant farmer, the better his economic and political situation tended to be, and conversely, the less his military importance, the poorer his economic and political situation.*
> (Lenski 1966/1984:275)

Note, in this regard, the role of Benaiah ben-Johoiada and the "Cherethites and Pelethites" in the accession of Solomon (1 Kgs 1:8, 38, 44). David had maintained a dual military organization, with Joab in command of the citizen army and Benaiah in command of the foreign mercenaries (2 Sam 8:16, 18; 20:23). Violating the sanctuary of the altar, Solomon ordered Benaiah to purge Joab and then consolidated command of a unified, professional army under Benaiah (1 Kgs 2:28–35). The citizen-soldier had become expendable.

Is it mere coincidence, moreover, that of the rival priestly houses that David had balanced with a dual high priesthood (Cross 1973:195–215), Abiathar joined Joab in supporting Adonijah, Solomon's last rival for the throne, while Zadok, along with Benaiah, backed Solomon (1 Kgs 1:5–8)? Abiathar represented cultic continuity with the more egalitarian institutions of premonarchic Israel. Zadok appears much more the religous apologist for the new monarchic order. As with Joab and Benaiah in the military sphere, the duality of Abiathar and Zadok in David's cultic administration balanced the poles of continuity and change. Solomon resolved both tensions in favor of the total embrace of a starkly stratified, monarchic order. Seen in this light, Jeremiah's probable descent from Abiathar (cf. 1 Kgs 2:26–27; Jer 1:1 with Jer 7:12, 14; 26:6, 9) assumes added significance.

Analysis of the generic dimension implicit in the known detail of individual careers also allows us to track the mounting socioeconomic tensions that resulted in the division of the kingdom upon Solomon's death. Adoram/Adoniram does not appear in the list of high officials from somewhat earlier in David's administration (2 Sam 8:15–18; 1 Chr 18:14–17). In a later Davidic list (2 Sam 20:23–26), Adoram makes his appearance as chief of the newly instituted corvée—an office in which he continued throughout Solomon's reign (1 Kgs 4:6; 5:14 [MT 5:28]). When Solomon died, the burdens of taxation and corvée—which had fallen disproportionately on the separately administered north (cf. G. E. Wright 1967 on 1 Kgs 4:7–19), while the Davidides' home tribe of Judah was accorded preferential treatment—led to an open breach between Rehoboam, Solomon's son and heir, and the people of the north (1 Kgs 12:4, 9–11, 14). That forced labor was a primary bone of contention is indicated by the fact that Rehoboam sent the now elderly Adoram—"Mr. Corvée" in Israel—to quell the rebellion

(1 Kgs 12:18; 2 Chr 10:18). Equally pertinent is that Jeroboam, who was named king of the breakaway north, rose to prominence during Solomon's reign from within the institution of corvée in the Josephite tribes (1 Kgs 11:26–28), where he was ideally placed to exploit the grievances of northern peasants. To complete the circle, it need only be observed that Jeroboam received his sacral legitimation from Ahijah *the Shilonite* (1 Kgs 11:29ff.), a bearer of the same cultic traditions as the exiled Abiathar.

The half century between Jeroboam's assumption of the throne and the accession of Omri (ca. 931–883 BCE) saw the north continue to reject the Solominic model for society without apparently finding a stable alternative. Whenever a son tried to succeed to his father's throne, new rebellion opposed dynastic succession. Multiple capitals and cultic sites—something for every faction and region—were preferred over political and religious centralization. According to at least one interpretation of the excavated finds at Tell el-Farʿah (N)—probably biblical Tirzah—the uniformity of the modest but adequate houses of the period points to a lack of sharp social inequality (de Vaux 1967:376). Political instability, however, left the army the only locus of organized power, and Omri emerged the victor in a struggle between rival officers.

Omri's accession marks a systemic watershed, for he reversed the policies—or lack thereof—of the preceding half century to follow in the footsteps of Solomon. Before his death, Ahab, his son, apparently gained a firm grip on the reins of political power, thus quashing thoughts of rebellion. Just as David and Solomon had made Jerusalem the center of the so-called United Monarchy, Omri and Ahab built Samaria as the capital of Israel to which all else became hinterland. The famous royal quarter of Samaria, separated from the rest of the city by its own wall, was but one architectural manifestation of sharply increased social stratification. Omri reactivated the "Phoenician connection" with a vengeance, arranging the diplomatic marriage of Ahab to Jezebel, daughter of Ittobaʿal, king of Tyre. Since Israel and Judah had ended their feud and were in league, the flow of trade and the subjugation of the neighboring states could in many ways parallel Davidic and Solomonic times.

What were the effects of the Omride about-face on the peasantry of Israel? The number of features shared with Solomon's regime suggests that the net impact cannot have been positive. Particularist historians generally agree, but argue that no means exist to measure the severity of the impact. Bright is typical: "the lot of the peasantry had deteriorated. How onerous the regular exactions of the state were we have no way of saying" (1981:244). Systemic considerations and a few known quantitative data allow us to be more specific, I believe. The implications of the procurement and maintenance of chariot horses for peasant agriculture and peasant diet have been detailed above. From 1 Kgs 10:26 (cf. 2 Chr 9:25) we know that Solomon had 1,400 chariots. The annals of Shalmaneser III (*ANET*: 278-79) indicate that at the famous battle of Qarqar, Ahab had 2,000. Shalmaneser's figures deserve to be trusted. They are not inflated stereotypes, and may well reflect intelligence reports. The point with regard to peasant conditions is that on a smaller land, resource, and population base than that controlled by Solomon, Ahab supported more chariots. Since Omride trading ventures and building programs in Samaria and elsewhere were proportionately as ambitious as those of Solomon, peasants were afforded no relief from the pressures that originated from those quarters. Ahab's conflict with Damascus meant that the costs to peasants of warfare—absence of many males from their farms for extended periods; destruction of crops; payment of tribute and economic concessions (cf. 1 Kgs 20:34); increased corvée to build and repair fortifications and water systems; as well as the support of horses, chariots, and horsemen—had *increased* since Solomon's relatively peaceful reign. While agricultural implements made of iron that had been subjected to an intentional process of steeling are a possibility in Omride Israel (Maddin et al. 1977:127-28), their impact upon peasant productivity, if any, cannot have been great enough to offset increased pressures and demands from other sources upon agricultural production. As with Solomonic policy, that of the Omrides had other priorities for metals. And the pathos of the miracle story in 2 Kgs 6:1-7 is occasioned by the fact that the borrowed axe was relatively rare and expensive—an indigent follower of Elisha could not possibly repay the debt he had incurred by its loss. On balance, then, one can conclude with reasonable certainty that the plight of the peasantry in Omride Israel was at least as desperate as under Solomon, and probably more so.

Just that plight is repeatedly reflected in the stereotyped characters that appear in the miracle stories of the Elijah and Elisha cycles. These stories grant us access, not to specific and individual occasions, but to the generic realities of the folk ethos and the severe deprivation that shaped it. Among its many functions, such folklore provides a forum for the expression of needs. If those needs are not met in the mundane sphere, folklore mediates symbolically between the known, mundane needs and the mostly unknown cosmic power from which succor is sought. In the case of these miracle stories, famine, foreclosure, and death stalk the constituency presupposed like spectres. Peasants forced to the brink by the systemic conditions delineated above had been pushed into the void when natural disaster struck in the form of extended and severe drought. Ahab responded with extraordinary measures to save the chariot horses and pack mules, which were the cornerstone of his power (1 Kgs 18:1–6). Talk about guns or butter!

Even the peasants who survived such times frequently lost their land by foreclosure. For historical reasons sketched above, most freeholding peasants in Israel and Judah were located in the highlands. As many small, subsistence plots in this hill country were foreclosed upon and joined together to form large estates, a change in the method of tillage also took place. Upland fields previously intercropped to provide a mixed subsistence for peasant families were combined into large and "efficient" vineyards and olive orchards producing a single crop for market. The increased production of wine and oil resulting from the formation of these plantations or latifundia played at least two roles in the new scheme of things. On the one hand, wine and oil were central to the increasingly consumptive lifestyle of the local elite, epitomized in a sodality called the *marzēaḥ* (Coote 1981:36–39). On the other, since wine and oil were more valuable than most agricultural commodities per unit of weight or volume, they made ideal exports to exchange for the luxury and strategic imports coveted by members of the ruling classes.

But the *"efficiency"* of these cash crops came at a brutal cost to the *sufficiency* of the livelihood which they afforded the peasants who actually produced them. The old system of freehold had provided this peasant majority secure access to a modest but adequate and integrated living. The new system saw them labor in the same fields, but only according to the cyclical demands of viticulture and orcharding and at wages for day-labor depressed by a sustained buyer's market. During lulls in the agricultural calendar, they were as unemployed as landless. Jobless or not, they were forced into the marketplace of which they had little or no experience to buy wheat and barley, the staples of their diet. They had previously produced these cereals sufficiently for themselves in their hillside plots, but now the same grains were grown "efficiently" on the large estates of the alluvial plains and piedmont region and shipped to market. In the marketplace, the meager and irregular wages of fieldhands bought even less sustenance than they should have because the vulnerable peasants were cheated with adulterated grain and dishonest weights and measures. Finally, the processes of foreclosure and expropriation which initiated these dynamics were accelerated by a wholesale suborning of the courts. Instead of stopping foreclosures based upon illegal forms of interest, these corrupted courts sanctioned the proceedings.

Each of the particulars of this process of latifundialization is mirrored in the oracles of the eighth-century prophets—many repeatedly. While these passages deserve sustained exegesis from a systemic stance, this already overburdened paper is not the place. I shall close, rather, with a brief discussion of a related text in 2 Chr 26:10 regarding Uzziah. NAB alone among the modern English translations construes the text in conformity with the known facts of either Hebrew syntax or the economic history and geography of ancient Judah. I would translate: "He built guard towers in the steppe and hewed out many cisterns, for he had large herds; and in the Shephelah and in the plains (he had) plowmen, and vineyard and orchard workers in the hill country and in the garden-land." This text is speaking of the same regional specialization of production to which the prophets of the period allude. Here we learn that under royal tutelage—a command economy?—herding was increased in the steppes of the Negev by means of guard towers and cisterns, plowing—the cultivation of cereal crops such as wheat and barley—was intensified in the plain and piedmont region, and viticulture and orcharding were pressed in the uplands, which were best suited to them. There is no warrant in this text for placing large herds in the Shephelah and the plains—though they may have grazed the stubble fields there in the summer—or plowmen in the uplands, as do RSV, JB, NEB, et al. Systemic analysis is relevant even to the intricacies of philology, and vice versa. Such are some admittedly preliminary and random musings about the sociology of the Israelite monarchy. To be documented and nuanced properly, each would require extensive research. That research might also prove some or all to be in fundamental error. But no complete sociological analysis of Israel's monarchic institutions can ignore the perspectives which have been emphasized and the questions which have been raised.

5

Debt Easement in Israelite History and Tradition

This brief essay is scant compass to discuss even one of the several forms of debt easement evidenced in the Hebrew Bible. Detailed analyses have been and could again be devoted to prohibitions of interest on survival loans to the poor, protection and manumission of debt-slaves, forgiveness of debts, restoration to the debtor of real estate subjected to foreclosure or articles taken in pledge, and various regulations designed to protect debtors from humiliation or loss of the artifacts necessary to daily life.[1] The specifics of that literature—both primary and secondary—are only partially related to the discussion that follows, however.

Rather, I want to address one basic question: Why were extensive traditions of debt easement included and even featured in the Hebrew Bible, when the literary "collages" that preserved them are the obvious work of

---

1. A short list of biblical passages might include Exod 21:1–11; 22:25–27 (MT 24–26); Lev 25:8–55; Deut 15:1–18; 23:19–20 (MT 20–21); 24:6, 10–13, 17–18; Jer 34:8–22; Neh 5:1–13; 10:31 (MT 32). Note, too, Deut 31:10; 1 Sam 22:2; 2 Kgs 4:1–7; 8:1–6; Isa 61:1; Jer 32:6–15; Ezek 18:7, 8, 12, 13, 16, 17; 22:12; 33:15; Pss 15:5; 112:5; Job 24:3, 9; Prov 19:17; 28:8; Ruth 4:1–12, A list of passages that probably refer to these same phenomena would run much longer.

A representative sample of secondary literature might include Baltzer 1987; David 1948; Gamoran 1971; Gnuse 1985:18–47; Hoenig 1969; M. Kessler 1971; Lemche 1975, 1976; Lewy 1958; Maloney 1974; Neufeld 1955, 1958, 1961, 1962; North 1954; Sarna 1973; Stein 1953; Wacholder 1973, 1975; Weill 1938; C. J. H. Wright 1984, 1990.

elites whose vested interests as a class would appear to be jeopardized by such easements?

To treat this issue in a *Festschrift* honoring Norman Gottwald is appropriate for at least three reasons. First, my interest in the subject was first piqued in the process of writing a formal response to one of his many erudite papers (Gottwald 1986). Not the least of Professor Gottwald's enormous contributions is his ability to provoke new questions and to suggest fruitful categories and methods for their investigation.

Second, Gottwald himself has done much to lay a firm foundation for reassessing traditions of debt easement in the Hebrew Bible. Of particular significance is his placement of the discussion of debt in the biblical world into the context of a twofold system of surplus extraction (ibid.). State extraction in kind, in labor, and later in coin, narrowed peasants' economic margins substantially. State policies simultaneously eroded the risk-spreading mechanisms characteristic of traditional village agriculture by pressing for intensive and specialized cultivation of a few preferred crops. Such agriculture in Palestine was also subject to the vicissitudes of periodic drought, pestilence, blight, war, and other disasters. Coupled with the curtailment of risk spreading, the size and consistency of state exactions insured that small producers would be forced to seek frequent survival loans from those privileged with economic surplus by the working of the state. Debt instruments were thus the means of a second and escalating round of surplus extraction in the political economies of Israel and Judah (Chaney 1986; 1989a).

Third, although Gottwald is justly famous for sharpening scholarly focus upon such realities of social stratification, his work provides an additional rubric of great utility for addressing the question posed in this essay. That analytical category recognizes that agrarian societies are not only starkly stratified vertically, but also segmented into factions horizontally, particularly at the elite level (Gottwald 1986; cf. Chaney 1983:52; Coote and Whitelam 1987; Coote and Coote 1990; Carney 1975:47–82; Kautsky 1982). In biblical Palestine, this phenomenon of factionalized elites was intensified by both internal topography and international geopolitical location.

Topographically, Palestine was broken into a number of cantons, each with its own variations in the natural environment, and hence in the means of subsistence. Within the larger genus of agrarian societies, those characterized by such balkanization are particularly prone to factionalized elites. Once an agrarian state was in place, each region provided its own rival(s) for the positions of power and privilege within that state. Biblical examples are too frequent and well known to require rehearsal here.

The larger geopolitical environment, moreover, reinforced this topographical proclivity for factionalized elites. Biblical Palestine was ringed by socieites more populous and powerful than itself. A significant role for these superpowers in the political economies of Palestine did not begin with their defeat and exile of the national leaders of Israel and Judah. Long before they were able to dominate these states outright, they never ceased meddling in the affairs of their smaller neighbors, who occupied the land bridge where superpower interests met and clashed. Under such circumstances, Egyptian, Mesopotamian, and other foreign diplomats sought influence with various factions of the Israelite and Judahite elites. The latter, just as obviously, sought to strengthen their own hands domestically through powerful international connections, while at the same time retaining as much autonomy as possible from their foreign allies. Specific alignments were as intrinsically unstable as the generic dynamic was constant over extended periods.[2]

In understanding those portions of biblical tradition and history that involve debt instruments, attention to these dynamics of factionalized elites can add an important diachronic dimension to what is often a largely synchronic class analysis. According to most scholars who discuss causation at all, biblical traditions such as those prohibiting interest on survival loans to the poor and granting various other easements and protections to debtors find their fountainhead in the communitarian values of premonarchic

---

2. The history of traditional Korea offers an instructive parallel to each of these factors and to their concatenation. As in Palestine, the arable land of Korea occurs in relatively small regional units that are separated from one another by various topographical impediments. City-states under the impress of a larger and older neighbor—in this case, China—dominated the earlier chapters of political history. Regional centers of power then emerged, vying with one another for control of the whole peninsula. National unification involved one region's dominating the others through a combination of military and diplomatic means. Whenever central control weakened in the resulting nation-state, however, regional loyalties born of the geographic environment proffered their own candidates for national leadership.

This factionalization of the elites of agrarian Korea was further exacerbated by the fact that its geopolitical position in East Asia was comparable to that of Palestine in western Asia and northeast Africa. It occupied the "turf" where the regional superpowers—China and Japan, and latterly Russia, the powers of western Europe, and the United States of America—contested claims and influence. Specific links between any given Korean elite faction and one of the large, foreign powers usually proved ephemeral, but the generic pattern of such alliances describes a powerful constant in Korean history.

Perhaps the most stimulating one-volume history of Korea (Lee 1984) takes factionalized elites, so understood, as the single most salient factor in Korean history. In the Korean language original, a concluding chapter, "The Ruling Elite and the Course of Korean History" (not translated in the English version of the book), develops the theoretical point at some length; (cf. p. vi of the English translation; note, too, Palais 1975:15–16, 291–92 n30). Although this note can only hint at the sustained parallels between this phenomenon in Korea and comparable dynamics in agrarian Palestine, the nature and extent of those parallels strongly encourage a testing of the analytical category involved against the biblical widence.

Israel, values that then survived and persisted with tenacity in later, state-dominated periods and tradition (cf. Stein 1953:165; Neufeld 1955:359–62, 407; 1958:57, 69, 71, 75–76, 99; Gamoran 1971:127–29). But what were the mechanisms of this tenacious persistence, and how may one account for its literary and historical particulars?

An analysis that integrates the realities of class conflict with those of elite segmentation and conflict allows a fuller answer to that question. The ultimate source of traditions such as that stipulating interest-free survival loans is likely to be found in the agrarian village, where mutual assistance loans without interest to one's village neighbors are widely attested (Chaney 1989a:25; Lang 1983a:120; Critchfield 1983:345). Within the village, such conventions were a means of risk spreading, a form of "insurance policy." Faced with the state and the exactions of those who controlled it, however, Israelite village courts probably sought to broaden this customary law to cover the survival loans that villagers were forced to seek beyond the village, preponderantly from the urban elites who benefited from the surpluses extracted by the state. The appeal of such legal traditions to debt-ridden peasants in all times and places is obvious. So, too, is the general incentive for the elites, who controlled the state's legal apparatus above the village level (Dearman 1988:85–87, 108–31; Whitelam 1979), to subvert and override such traditions. Yet within the Hebrew Bible, as noted above, these traditions are preserved in several books and literary strata, each of which, in its final form, is demonstrably the work of one or another elite. A focus upon patterns of stratification alone cannot explain why.

Several lines of evidence and reasoning, on the other hand, suggest that conflicts between and among factionalized elites played a frequent role in the official embrace of such measures of debt easement. A faction that was out of power or seeking to consolidate power recently acquired, gained two advantages from espousing—at least temporarily—various forms of debt easement. First, against the faction currently or recently in power, it thereby gained sympathy and support from elements of the peasantry, who teetered perennially on the brink of economic ruin because of the dynamics of political economy discussed above. Second, because members of the faction most recently in power were the primary beneficiaries, not only of state taxation, but also of the secondary cycle of surplus extraction accomplished by debt instruments, any easement of the terms or effects of indebtedness served to diminish that faction's economic base and power. Once the "reform" faction gained and consolidated power, however, programs of debt easement tended to be honored more in official rhetoric than in actual practice.

Evidence from various areas and periods of the ancient world confirms a prominent role for political elites in the promulgation of documents of debt easement. None of this evidence is more striking than the *mīšarum* materials from the Old Babylonian period in Mesopotamia and their probable relationship to the cuneiform "law codes" (Bottéro 1961; J. J. Finkelstein 1961, 1965; Gnuse 1985:41–42; F. R. Kraus 1958, 1965, 1984; Lemche 1976, 1979; Lewy 1958; Weinfeld 1972:148–57; Westbrook 1985). A *mīšarum* or "justice" involved the king's proclamation of an edict or decree that variously canceled debts, suspended taxes, released debt-slaves, returned land seized by creditors, and remitted other economic burdens. Although the *mīšarum* texts proper are restricted to the Old Babylonian period, they almost certainly continue practices that go back to the kingdoms of Isin and Larsa and are adumbrated already in the "reforms" of Urukagina (F. R. Kraus 1958:103–4; J. J. Finkelstein 1961:103–4; Kramer 1963:79–83; Gadd 1971:141–42; 1973:195–96; Edzard 1965:225–26). They are also closely related to texts ranging from the Old Akkadian to Late Babylonian periods that witness an *andurāru*, a "remission of (commercial) debts," a "manumission (of private slaves)," or "the canceling of services illegally imposed on free persons" (*CAD* 1/2:115; Lewy 1958; J. J. Finkelstein 1961:104 n19; Lemche 1976:41 n11; 1979). Though some of the later of these texts may refer to actions of private individuals and not to royal decrees (Lemche 1976:41 n11; 1979), the king's proclamation of a "release" of some kind clearly lies at the heart of this whole cluster of evidence from Mesopotamia.

Beyond this centrality of the royal initiative, several other aspects of the debt easement reflected in these cuneiform documents deserve emphasis. Although the remissions were usually inclusive of various "ethnic" or "national" groups, they were otherwise characteristically partial, often giving special consideration to certain classes or districts. The majority of the documents that witness these easements, in fact, concern practical attempts by creditors to insure that the "release" did not apply to their particular cases. *Mīšarum*-acts customarily occurred at the outset of a king's reign, but monarchs whose tenure on the throne spanned decades often proclaimed "releases" in subsequent years as well. Although some scholars have argued that these enactments were spaced at regular intervals, the current evidence establishes no such pattern, but rather tells against it (J. J. Finkelstein 1965:243–45; Gnuse 1985:41).

Finally, one must ask what motivated Mesopotamian kings to issue such proclamations of debt easement. The answer almost universally given is that these "releases" addressed crises wherein the accumulated burden of indebtedness, particularly among the lower classes, threatened economic, social, and political order. The rulers' intent, then, was not to transform fundamentally the structure of a heavily stratified society, but to mitigate the most extreme imbalances and restore economic equilibrium and viability (Lewy 1958:29; Bottéro 1961:160–61; Oppenheim 1963:157; J. J. Finkelstein 1965:242; Edzard 1965:225; Gadd 1973:195–96; Lemche 1976:41; Gnuse 1985:41–42).

Although few would doubt that these kings acted out of a practical concern for order and a workable economy, closer scrutiny suggests an admixture of other motivations as well. The literary contexts of these documents demonstrate, for instance, that debt remissions, however partial, were given the most positive "spin" possible by those responsible for the king's public image. Royal apologia wasted no effort in presenting the monarch as the enactor of justice, the vindicator of the vulnerable and oppressed (J. J. Finkelstein 1961:100–104). When the ruler was so viewed by his subjects, his grasp on the reins of governance was strengthened. The need to foster that royal image and the political consensus it nurtured was never greater than when a new king began to reign. Monarchs of considerable longevity on the throne, moreover, probably found it necessary to refurbish both image and consensus from time to time. At least such motives coincide perfectly with the timing of the Old Babylonian proclamations of *mīšarum*.

D. O. Edzard both confirms the scholarly consensus regarding the purpose of these proclamations and supplements it:

> The king's intervention in the country's economy, annulling private debts and rescinding certain taxes (both are temporary and not permanent measures), has a twofold aim: to prevent the collapse of the economy under too great a weight of private indebtedness (the normal interest rate for barley was 33–1/3%, for silver 20%); and to prevent excessive accumulation of private wealth in too few hands. (Edzard 1965:225)

The second aim deduced by Edzard from the evidence can be nuanced in light of the theoretical perspective of this essay. *Mīšarum*-acts were partial in their application, and kings controlled to a considerable extent the legal apparatus that determined how and to whom the decrees applied. Is it not plausible to suggest, therefore, that one purpose of the "releases" was to enable kings to weaken potential rivals who were wealthy and powerful?

The timing of the edicts also favors such a purpose. At the beginning of a new king's reign, he had need (1) to ameliorate economic abuses severe enough to threaten the viability of his state, (2) to project a public image as a just statesman who took good care of his subjects, and (3) to weaken the power of elite factions that threatened his firm hold on power. Skillful proclamation and administration of debt easements could accomplish all three goals simultaneously. Long-lived kings found need to repeat the process for all three reasons at intervals dictated by the vicissitudes of history rather than numerical regularity.

Such an understanding of the evidence obviates Finkelstein's insistence that—despite the irregularity of the evidence—

> enactments of this type had to recur *at fairly regular or predictable intervals.* Were this not the case, and had kings been free to announce the *misharum* without warning and at widely disparate intervals, there would have occurred a drying-up of the sources of credit and a virtual paralysis of economic activity every few year. (J. J. Finkelstein 1965:245)

Deuteronomy 15:9–10 and Lev 25:26–27, 50–52 undoubtedly inform Finkelstein's formulation of the issue. But if the royally proclaimed "releases" were administered selectively toward all the purposes articulated above, no general paralysis of economic activity need have occurred—only the economic diminution or ruin of the king's rivals and enemies, actual and suspected.

The world of Greek antiquity also supplies pertinent evidence for the decisive role of political elites in effecting programs of debt easement. Unlike the Mesopotamian data, however, the best-documented Greek example involves, not royal leadership, but the archonship of Solon in Athens in the first decade of the sixth century BCE.[3] By Solon's time, Athens had reached a state of debt crisis. While the wealthy few were becoming wealthier and their estates larger, the small farms of Attica were being mortgaged at a rapid rate. As a result, many of the small proprietors were losing their land, and growing numbers of the landless laborers, the *hektemoroi*, were being sold into slavery (often abroad) because of default on survival loans, or fleeing into exile to avoid this fate. The masses longed for a tyrant to bring relief and agitated for land redistribution.

A moderate member of the aristocracy, Solon rejected both the role of tyrant the *demos* would gladly have thrust upon him and their demand for redistribution of land. He sought instead to mediate the class strife with a series of debt easements. In 594 BCE he was elected archon with extraordinary legislative powers and began to institute economic reforms, though only for Athenians, of course. He canceled all existing debts and prohibited for the future not merely enslavement for debt, but all forms of mortgages

---

3. The following account of Solon's reforms is summarized from: Austin and Vidal-Naquet 1977:70–72, 210–15; Bury 1959:180–89; and de Ste. Croix 1981:281–82. See also the literature they cite; and for the older literature, see Neufeld 1958:53 n2.

and debts in which the debtor's person was pledged as security.[4] As far as possible, he brought home all Athenian debtors sold into slavery abroad. A limit was fixed on the amount of land a single person could own. Because higher commodity prices abroad were leaving an inadequate food supply for the local population, he forbade the export of agricultural products from Attica, except for olive oil. In an attempt to mold public opinion and forge a political consensus for his moderate approach to economic reform, he wrote and distributed pamphlets. Couched in poetry, according to the canons of the day, some have survived as characteristically Greek exemplars of apologia for particular forms of debt easement and their powerful political exponents.

Solon's reforms came in the midst of great conflict. As a moderate, he pleased few Athenians completely. The rich, who were hit hard, were angry. The poor, who had agitated for more radical reforms, were far from satisfied. Party strife broke out again soon after Solon's archonship, with powerful political leaders dividing between the party of the Coast, that favored his new constitution, and the party of the Plain, that opposed it. The division was not simply along class lines, but was often a function of the particulars of Solon's implementation of his program. Those hurt by specific decisions were opposed, those helped in favor.[5]

Although the evidence is perhaps more diffuse than in the case of either Mesopotamia or Greece, ancient Rome, too, offers significant examples of the close relationship between factional conflict among elites and the promulgation of debt easements. Most of the evidence for debt easements in the earlier Republic appears in the context of the Struggle of the Orders. H. C. Boren characterizes succinctly the dimensions of this struggle most pertinent to our discussion:

> Often, historians have viewed the struggle as a general uprising of the lower classes (the plebeians) against the upper class (the patricians). It was not that simple, however. The leaders of the "struggle" were plebeians, true; but they were from important families. In the later stages of the struggle, often these leaders were aristocratic heads of states that had been absorbed by Rome. (Boren 1977:19)

---

4. Bocchoris, a ruler in Egypt during the twenty-fourth dynasty, is also said to have prohibited the person of a debtor from being bonded. See Neufeld 1958:54.

5. For the specifics of these factional conflicts, particularly the rather complicated situation regarding the aristocracy of the Eupatrids, most but not all of whom sought to sabotage Solon's program, see Bury 1959:188–89; and de Ste. Croix 1981:282.

Such leaders depended upon the masses for political support and often espoused economic causes popular with the masses for political reasons. Yet, as P. A. Brunt writes: "There was no identity of economic interest between the masses and their political leaders, but only an alliance of temporary convenience, which was indispensable to the success of the political demands" (1971:56). Even the briefest summary of examples can serve to illustrate the important truths articulated by Boren and Brunt.[6]

Early in the fifth century BCE, the patricians were forced to accept plebeian officials, the tribunes. By the middle of the same century, the patricians acceded to another demand of the plebeians—the reduction to writing of the previously unwritten body of law and its public display on the Twelve Tables. Although the Twelve Tables contained some provisions against the maltreatment of debtors, they allowed that the debtor who would not or could not pay was liable to be sold into slavery abroad by his creditor. Nor did the Twelve Tables alter a political economy that insured that small farmers were constantly falling into debt. Then, too, there was the hated contract called *nexum*, whereby the poor worked in bondage to the rich in return for loans, and creditors were empowered to levy execution upon a defaulting debtor without recourse to a court of law. Large parcels of public land remained under the effective control of the patricians. As a result of such circumstances, the decades following the promulgation of the Twelve Tables witnessed intermittent outcries for land distribution and relief of debts.

This agitation came to a head in 367–366 BCE under the leadership of the tribunes Licinius and Sextius. Laws were passed requiring that one consul be plebeian, limiting the amount of public land any single citizen could hold, restricting the sale of debtors to satisfy debts, and easing the terms for repayment of loans. Forty years later, in 326 BCE, *nexum* was abolished.

Although the lower classes—upon whom the burden of debt fell with crushing severity—probably benefited in the short term from these laws, that reality should be viewed in the light of several others. The relief was short-lived, as various reports of the need for moratoria on debt payments or the cancellation of interest due demonstrate. By 287 BCE, the debt problem again rose to such proportions that it led to the appointment of a plebeian named Quintus Hortensius as dictator. The abolition of *nexum* probably involved more the niceties of legal procedure than any great practical relief for this class of debtors.

The real winners in this struggle, on the other hand, were rich and powerful plebeians. It was they who gained continuing access to the higher

---

6. The following account is summarized from Brunt 1971:42–59; Boren 1977:17–24: and Cary 1960:72–85.

offices and thence into an enlarged governing oligarchy. The Twelve Tables had banned intermarriage between the orders, but this stricture was set aside in 445 BCE after plebeian agitation. "Evidently there were now plebeians rich enough to entertain social ambitions and patricians ready to gratify them, perhaps in greed for handsome dowries" (Brunt 1971:55). The ambiguous position of these upper-class plebeians is epitomized by a story that Licinius himself was fined for violating the law limiting the amount of public land any one citizen could hold.

Thus, although the data from Mesopotamia, Greece, and Rome exhibit myriad differences in specifics, they all confirm the pivotal role of conflicting elite factions in the espousal of debt easements as public policy in the ancient world. Informed by these analogies, we can now turn to an all-too-brief review of the biblical traditions of debt easement and the historical contexts of their promulgation.

If this review moves in roughly chronological order, the first materials encountered occur in Exodus 21–23. Although most knowledgeable opinion concurs in granting this "Book of the Covenant" chronological priority, it agrees about little else. The nature, purpose, genre, composition, and date of this legal collection are matters of continuing dispute, as is its relation to the narrative strands of the Tetrateuch. Space prohibits even a cursory discussion of the varying positions[7] and requires instead that the preferred option be explicated briefly in the operative categories of this essay.

That preferred option is provided by Robert Coote's cogently argued thesis that the laws of Exod 21:1—22:17 (Heb. 16) are the culmination and goal of the Elohistic writings (Coote and Coote 1990:39–40; Coote 1991). According to Coote, "E" never existed as a separate "strand," but came into existence as a polemical recomposition of "J," designed to legitimate the regime of Jeroboam I in northern Israel after that region's secession from the House of David.

Coote's hypothesis helps to explain the placement of laws regarding the manumission of debt-slaves at the beginning of the "Book of the Covenant" in Exod 21:1–11. Such is not the position one would expect on the basis of other slave laws from the ancient Near East. They tend to be scattered under various rubrics in the latter parts of other legal collections, or left to the end (Coote 1991:chap. 12; Kaufman 1987). By placing the laws on debt-slavery first in his promulgation, Jeroboam I emphasized stipulations that in the main otherwise followed legal precedent (Lemche 1975; Turnham 1987).

---

7. For more recent treatments, giving access, in turn, to earlier works, see Paul 1970; Boecker 1980; Crüsemann 1988; Schwienhorst-Schönberger 1990.

Nor are Jeroboam's purposes in so doing difficult for us to discern from his historical situation. Most villagers in the north had been pushed to the brink by Solomon's economic policies. Debt-slavery was the unhappy result for many.[8] Because Jeroboam had ridden to power on the resultant wave of popular resentment against the Davidids, he needed to signal sensitivity to the plight of the peasant masses. He could ill afford their ire.

But their support alone was an insufficient base upon which to consolidate his power. The much larger fish in his ocean included the powerful landholding families of the north, the magnates that headed them, and the holy persons and sites that gave them sacral legitimation. Jeroboam needed the support of these as well for his regime, which meant recognizing the magnates' traditional authority, at least in part, while containing their factional rivalries and infighting. Jeroboam's promulgation of law thus sanctioned much of the magnates' historical jurisdiction, but sought to present their authority as derivative from that of his own successionist and Egyptian-sponsored state. The same laws on debt-slavery that signaled concern for impoverished villagers, therefore, also authorized the rights of those who held debt-slaves "legitimately."

The courts of both Jeroboam and the northern magnates whose favor he curried, however, would have been quick to declare "illegitimate" such debt-slave contracts as profited creditors loyal to the House of David. Because the workings of the Solomonic political economy had placed much of the "surplus" to be lent in the hands of those beholden to the Davidids (G. E. Wright 1967), selective application of Jeroboam's debt easements to creditors oriented to Jerusalem could both disenfranchise his enemies and please his intended constituents—high as well as low.

Elohistic traditions of debt easement shaped in this context almost certainly would have come to the fore again in Jehu's time. To unite various military, landholding, and prophetic factions with a disgruntled peasantry behind a dynasty founded in usurpation and bloodbath, Jehu posed himself as the champion of all those elements against the Omrids, whom he epitomized in Ahab as the "Solomon of the North."

Exodus 22:25–27 (MT 24–26) occurs in a section almost universally regarded to be a later addition to the "Book of the Covenant." Although the date of its composition may always remain open to quibble, Coote argues plausibly that it reflects Hezekiah's time.[9] If so, this articulation of debt easement fits a socio-historical paradigm by now familiar. Hezekiah sought

---

8. On the process, see Chaney 1986:70–71. On the meaning of "Hebrew" in this context, see Chaney 1983:55–57, 72–83; and Na'aman 1986.

9. Coote 1991:chap. 13. In addition to accounts of Hezekiah's reign by the standard histories, see Rosenbaum 1979.

to reassert the hegemony of a Davidic dynasty whose reputation had been severely tarnished by the depredations of Assyrian imperialism. Certain of the power brokers within the traditional Judahite sphere of influence constituted impediments to Hezekiah's policy. In the territory of the recently fallen state of northern Israel, where Hezekiah sought to extend his power, the foreign elites ensconced by Assyria played a similar role. Meantime, the cost of defending against Assyria or paying tribute to it had once again impoverished the peasants of both regions. Hezekiah's promulgation and selective enforcement of traditional village norms for survival loans would have polished his image among hard-pressed peasants of both areas, while weakening those among their creditors who were his rivals for regional power.

Josiah's "reform"—almost certainly the context for the *promulgation*[10] of Deut 15:1–18; 23:19–20 (MT 20–21); 24:6, 10–13, 17–18—shared most of the dynamics just enumerated as characteristic of Hezekiah's time. Rather than recapitulating those elements, a discussion of the functions of debt easement in the Josianic context can concentrate on specific distinctions.

The crumbling of Assyrian power gave Josiah a certain latitude denied Hezekiah. It also freed from Assyrian control descendants of the foreign elites moved into the territory of the fallen northern kingdom as a matter of Assyrian policy. In addition, Josiah inherited a Judahite elite deeply divided. He came to the throne as a child because his father had been assassinated in factional infighting. This grisly event was one of many symptoms that decades of Assyrian imperialism had effaced the prestige of the House of David. Revenues flowing to the royal coffers and the dynastic chapel in Jerusalem had suffered at least as much abridgment as the royal image. When Josiah's assumption of full adult authority coincided with the retreat of Assyrian power, he faced well-ensconced local and regional magnates and their legitimating and revenue-collecting cultic sites as impediments to his policies for rejuvenating centralized monarchic authority. This was especially true in the territory of the former northern kingdom, where Josiah sought to reassert the hegemony of the Davidids after a lapse of three centuries.[11]

All aspects of the Josianic "reform"—nationalism, political and religious centralization; "cleansing" and repair of the Davidic kings' dynastic chapel; extirpation of local, regional, and "foreign" cults and their personnel; territorial expansion; extended court apology; and royal promulgation

---

10. Although a complex legal and literary history almost certainly preceded Josiah's promulgation, explication of its details would far exceed the space available here. The reader is referred to the works listed in n1 above, particularly those of C. J. H. Wright.

11. On these dynamics of Josianic history, in addition to the standard histories, see Claburn 1973; Nelson 1981a; Chaney 1989b; Coote and Coote 1990:59–66.

of law—are to be understood in this context. Legal traditions of debt easement played their part. Once again, a king desiring to consolidate and expand his power at the expense of diverse and entrenched opponents needed to appeal to the debt-ridden peasant farmers who formed the numerical majority of his constituents. Because the dynamics of political economy in the period immediately prior to Josiah had left an increasing proportion of the region's "surpluses" in the hands of magnates and priests opposed to the enhancement of centralized, royal power, these rivals for Josiah's magistracy and tax base would have been the principal creditors. Debt easement administered under the king's jurisdiction thus killed two birds with one stone for Josiah—it weakened rivals and enemies of his reassertion of centralized monarchic authority, while simultaneously wooing most commoners.

Although Jer 34:8–22 is obviously related to Deut 15:1–18, it does not involve a royal promulgation of law about debt easement, as have all the biblical passages previously discussed. Scholars have reached no consensus on this text's complex literary relationship to the laws regarding the manumission of debt-slaves, nor about the various possible motivations for the actions of the masters of such slaves in Zedekiah's time.[12] For purposes of this essay, suffice it to say that Jer 34:8–22 does witness the tendency of several classes of power-holders (cf. v. 19) to manipulate traditions of debt easemeat in order to serve their changing perceptions of their own vested interests.

Leviticus 25:8–55 is a literarily composite complex of debt easement law. Whether or not the factional conflict occasioning its promulgation involved a royal figure, as did the related texts in Exodus and Deuteronomy, its concerns probably witness a priestly elite disputing jurisdiction over land, peasant production, and cult. A clue to the more specific context for which some version of the Leviticus text was formulated may be found in its inclusion of a feature not known from the stipulations of Exodus or Deuteronomy.[13]

That feature is the addition of the forty-nine or fifty-year "jubilee" cycle to the seven-year "sabbatical" cycle attested elsewhere.[14] If, as seems likely,

12. In addition to the works of David 1948; M. Kessler 1971; Sarna 1973; Lemche 1975, 1976, 1979; and C. J. H. Wright 1984, cited in n1 above, see Bright 1965:219–24; Carroll 1986:643–50; and W. L. Holladay 1989:236–43.

13. On Leviticus 25, see the works of North 1954; Neufeld 1958; Wacholder 1973, 1975; Lemche 1975, 1976; and C. J. H. Wright 1984, 1990.

14. The seven-year "sabbatical" may have originated with fallowing practices for individual fields and/or with patterns of individual debt-slave manumission. If so, the linking of either or both with more general debt remission probably occasioned a secondary phenomenon of placing all debt-related matters within the national jurisdiction on the same cycle. Complications such as those addressed by Deut 15:9–10 and Lev

the first exiles to return from Babylon to Jerusalem under Sheshbazzar—a member of the Davidic royal house—left as soon as practically possible after Cyrus' decree in 538 BCE (Bright 1981:361–64), their arrival in Palestine would have occurred forty-nine years after the destruction of Jerusalem and its temple and the attendant deportation of its political and priestly elites.[15]

Upon their return, these elites and their descendants did not find a power vacuum. The intervening half-century had seen other regional and local magnates and their legitimating cults assume jurisdiction over the lands and cultivators previously tied to Jerusalem. The returnees faced an uphill battle to reclaim fields, peasants, and loyalty to their refounded cult. In this battle of conflicting elites for the hearts and minds of the peasant cultivators, traditions of debt easement would have proved a potent weapon. Forty-nine years was more than enough time for most peasants to become heavily indebted to the magnates exercising power on the scene. The espousal of traditions of debt easement by the returnees would have struck deep resonance in the peasants. If implemented, the remissions would have worked to the hurt of the creditors involved.

Returning members of the exiled priesthood would have had at their disposal an ideological reinforcement for this policy. While in exile, they had developed a version of what is now known as the Priestly Tetrateuch. Its unifying category was the Sabbath. Established by God in creation, this holy seventh day of the week was also the sign of the all-important Mosaic covenant.[16] When the legal content of that covenant already included a "sabbath year" remission, could these masters of religious symbolism have missed the symbolic power of "seven times seven years" between the destruction of their beloved temple and the time of the debt easement that they now sought as part of a larger program to reassert their jurisdiction and to rebuild that temple?

If this must remain speculative, though plausible, a later version of the same conflict between rival elites in postexilic Palestine is the certain context of Neh 5:1–13; 10:31 (Heb. 32). Nehemiah represented the interests both of the returnees and of his Persian masters, whose weakening western flank he had been sent to reinforce. The "nobles" and "officials" (Neh 5:7) against whom Nehemiah inveighed were his rivals for regional jurisdiction, who probably also had sympathies and connections with the Athenian-Egyptian

---

25:26–27, 50–52 were the result. For the specific biblical vocabulary referring to the several practices combined in various ways in Deuteronomy 15 and Leviticus 25, see particularly C. J. H. Wright 1984, 1990.

15. If Sarna (1973:147–49) is correct, this timing would also correspond to a sabbatical cycle fixed by the Zedekiah incident in Jeremiah 34.

16. In addition to the standard works on "P," see Coote and Ord 1991.

axis opposed to Persia.[17] As usual, the peasant majority was caught between. Nehemiah's self-righteous embrace of debt remission was classical apologetic, much in the mold of the Greek tyrants.

Each of these biblical examples cries out for fuller explication. Enough has been said, however, to demonstrate that the traditions of debt-easement preserved in the literature of the Hebrew Bible have been shaped by their promulgation in the context of jurisdictional disputes between rival elite factions. Comparative materials from elsewhere in the ancient world confirm this conclusion. Because factionalized elites were a perennial feature of Palestinian history for reasons of both regional topography and larger geopolitical environment, multiple variations on the theme of debt easement are to be expected in biblical literature. Given the political economies in which even the most sincere and well-intentioned of the elite "reformers" was involved, the long-term succor that their policies of debt easement afforded struggling peasants as a class was minimal. Each generation of aspiring elites was motivated to promulgate its own version of debt easement, because each generation of peasants was forced into poverty and debt by the structures of agrarian society. Only the fundamental transformation of those societal structures could address the root problem.

---

17. Coote and Coote 1990:74–84.

6

The Political Economy of Peasant Poverty

What the Eighth-Century Prophets Presumed but Did not State

INTRODUCTION

Passages from the so-called eighth-century prophets—Amos, Hosea, Isaiah, and Micah—voice a substantial portion of the Bible's discourse on peasant poverty. Several factors, however, tend to blur the picture they present for an untutored reader. While each of these books contains units most easily understood as generated in the eighth-century BCE, they all show evidence of having been recomposed significantly during the late Judahite monarchy and again in the Persian period. The concerns of royal "reform," central to the first such recomposition, and of the Second Temple, dominant in the second, shift the focus of the finished text away from peasant poverty and toward monarchic nationalism and client-state cultus, respectively. Much scholarly ink has flowed to clarify these somewhat later dimensions of the text (see Chaney 2006:145–46, and the works there cited).

Much less attention has been paid to another issue that also clouds the picture of peasant poverty in these prophetic texts. Even the passages with plausible claims to eighth-century composition *presume* and *allude to* the economic institutions and dynamics of their day, but nowhere describe them narratively or in full. The first audiences of these compositions had immediate knowledge of the social and cultural world presumed and addressed, and so had no need for such description. No modern reader, however, can simply presume such knowledge. Careful historical work is required for any twenty-first-century reader to understand the relevant context of this prophetic discourse on peasant poverty.

Recent interdisciplinary research into the dynamics of political economy in eighth-century Israel and Judah has begun to sketch the context that older passages in Amos, Hosea, Isaiah, and Micah all presume and address, but nowhere describe. The dynamics of change as a whole are often referred to as a process of "agricultural intensification." These changes include a number of elements that I will now undertake to discuss *seriatim*, but this organization into discrete factors is only for the sake of clarity in presentation. They are not independent variables, but rather *interdependent variables*, best understood as but facets of one integrated whole. Their interdependence is not only intrinsic to their reality; it is also a boon to historical research. Our sample of specific historical data is incomplete and skewed. Because so many facets of the institutional dynamics are closely intertwined, however, specific knowledge about the nature and direction of change in one dimension often allows us to posit what is going on in related dimensions with a high degree of probability.[1]

POLITICAL AND MILITARY CONTEXT

Biblical Israel and Judah were petty monarchies whose misfortune it was to inhabit the land bridge where the regional powers of their world, Egypt and Mesopotamia, met and clashed. For much of their history, Judah and Israel

---

1. I have previously addressed the dynamics of political economy in eighth-century Israel and Judah in a number of venues (Chaney 1989a, 1993, 1999, 2004a, 2004b, 2006, 2009). The present discussion presumes and often summarizes or mirrors those earlier articles. For many of my dialogue partners in that work, see Chaney 2004a:102 n12. Two recent sets of publication challenge the sketch presented here in whole or in part. I am convinced by neither set. Full engagement of their arguments here is impossible, since it would distort the shape and purpose of the present essay. Because both challenges are serious and learned, however, they should not be ignored. My less-than-satisfactory expedient, therefore, has been to summarize and critique each briefly in an Appendix to this essay, leaving fuller and more adequate response for future occasions. Please see that Appendix for more detail.

could only *react* geopolitically to initiatives taken by their larger and more powerful neighbors. In roughly the second quarter of the eighth century BCE, however, Israel and Judah enjoyed a significant, if relatively brief, respite from big-power domination. They were also at peace with one another, Judah having become a virtual vassal of the larger and more powerful Israel. Both expanded their territories and grew in military power during the long and mostly concurrent reigns of Jeroboam II of Israel (ca. 781–745 BCE) and Uzziah of Judah (ca. 781–747 BCE). The regional powers were either at low ebb or occupied with affairs closer to home. That relative security from powerful foreign enemies, coupled with their long tenure in office, gave these two kings an opportunity to initiate change in their political economies.

The situation changed just about the time they died. 745 BCE, the approximate year of Jeroboam II's death, was also the year of Tiglath-pileser III's accession to the Assyrian throne. That vigorous monarch quickly consolidated power at home, and then brought Assyrian might west to secure and expand its economic interests all the way from the Assyrian heartland to the port cities of the east Mediterranean littoral. In the wake of his powerful initiatives, Assyria would dominate affairs in Judah for more than a century and in Israel up to and including its demise. While Assyrian domination fundamentally altered the geopolitics of the region, Assyrian pressure, when it came, only intensified the initiatives that Jeroboam II and Uzziah had taken in their political economies. Military measures to resist Assyrian incursions and payment of tribute when these measures failed both tapped the same agrarian economic base.[2]

IMPORT/EXPORT TRADE: ITS NATURE, IMPLICATIONS, COSTS, AND BENEFITS

Jeroboam II and Uzziah had incentive as well as opportunity to change their political economies because of their active participation in international trade. The import/export trade of Israel and Judah in this period was mostly with and through the maritime city-states of Phoenicia, especially Tyre. Their seaborne transportation was much cheaper than any overland mode available (Nolan and Lenski 2009:181–83). Luxury goods, military *matériel*, and building materials for monumental architecture were the principal imports. Prominent among the latter were wooden timbers large enough

---

2. Readers unfamiliar with the political and military background presupposed can find a convenient summary with references in Miller and Hayes 2006:327–421; note, too, Parpola 2003.

to roof and panel temples, palaces, and other grand buildings. In the entire ancient Near East, such timber grew only in the Lebanon and Anti-Lebanon mountain ranges. Access to it was controlled by the Phoenicians (Liphshitz and Biger 1991; 1995). To pay for their imports, the courts of Jeroboam and Uzziah exported foodstuffs and fiber, above all the triad of wheat, olive oil, and wine (Geva 1982; J. S. Holladay 1995:380–82; Hopkins 1983, 1996; Noll 2013:265–70). A royal standardization of measures, and perhaps of weights as well, was instituted to expedite this seaborne trade in agricultural commodities (Kletter 1998).

Earlier, when the agricultural economies of Israel and Judah had functioned more at the subsistence level, storage jars had had no need to be exactly identical in volume. Since the foodstuffs they contained were stored and consumed near to where they were produced, the only constraints on the size of storage vessels were those of utility and practicality. Once significant interregional trade developed in the foodstuffs contained in such amphorae, however, economic efficiency dictated that they be made to a more uniform size. Archaeological remains witness such standardization in the Iron II period. Some of these amphorae are incised with the Hebrew letters *bt*, which spell the Hebrew name for the unit of volume they held (*bat*). Still others are incised with the Hebrew letters *bt lmlk*, spelling *bat lamélek*, "the *bat* of the king," or "the royal *bat*" (Avigad 1953; Inge 1941; Naveh 1992). Marine archaeology has discovered two Phoenician ships dating to this period, still laden with the standardized wine amphorae they were carrying to Egypt when they were sunk by a storm off the Philistine coast (Gore 2001:91–93).

Imports of luxury goods, military *matériel*, and the wherewithal of monumental architecture benefited the elite few, who constituted less than two percent of the total population. The foodstuffs and fiber exported to pay for these imports were produced by the peasant majority and competed directly with its subsistence.[3] Peasant producers could not consume what was exported; what they consumed, conversely, could not be exported. The supply of exportable commodities was finite and varied with erratic growing conditions, but the elite's appetite for luxury, military, and monumental imports was virtually limitless.

A simple cost/benefit analysis shows that the ruling elite bore few of the costs of the import/export trade, but enjoyed most of its benefits. The peasant majority, by contrast, bore most of the costs, but reaped few of the benefits (see the discussion below). As the situation developed, the ruling

3. Patterns of social stratification in agrarian societies are remarkably uniform (see the convenient graphic summary in Lenski 1966/1984:284–85; Nolan and Lenski 2009:170–71).

elite had a powerful economic incentive to increase production of the three preferred export crops. Olive oil and wine were particularly prized, since they were worth more per unit of weight or volume. The import/export trade of Israel and Judah in the eighth century BCE, therefore, widened the already gaping economic chasm between the wealthy urban elite and most peasants and artisans. It also pauperized portions of those already poor.

REGIONAL SPECIALIZATION OF AGRICULTURE AND HERDING

One way to increase production of the three preferred exports was through a regional specialization of agriculture under more centralized direction of the priorities and techniques of agricultural production. When the Hebrew text of 2 Chr 26:10 is read in congruence with current knowledge both of Hebrew syntax and of economic geography, it yields the following witness to such a process:

> He [Uzziah] built guard towers in the Steppe and hewed out many cisterns, for he had large herds; and in the Shephelah and in the Plain (he had) plowmen; and (he had) vineyard and orchard workers in the Hills and in the Carmel . . .

This verse suggests that herding was increased in the Negev under royal tutelage (see Rainey 1982:58; Chaney 1983:73–74; Hopkins 1983:200; Klein 2012:374). In this area, where normal rainfall was too sparse to permit much rain agriculture, the herding of sheep and goats exploited the seasonal grasses that sprang up during the winter rainy season. Guard towers that projected royal authority and offered protection from the raiding characteristic of pastoral activities now secured that herding (Faust 2012:180–89). Cisterns, hewed out at the direction of the crown, maximized the capacity of seasonal watering holes. Plowing—shorthand for the cultivation of cereal crops—was redoubled in the plain and piedmont regions best suited to grain agriculture. Perennial tree and vine crops, especially grapevines and olive orchards, were intensified in the uplands where they grew best. In each case, the economic exploitation of a given region was specialized to one or two crops by whose production that region could contribute maximally to the export trade and to the conspicuous consumption of the urban elites.

This one verse in the Chronicler is by no means the only evidence for the processes described. Archaeology adds multiple facets to the picture. Rock-cut oil- and grape-processing installations are almost as old as agriculture itself in Palestine. Archaeological surveys, however, suggest a proliferation of and innovations in such installations in the hill country in the eighth century BCE (Dar 1986:147–90; Eitam 1979; Walsh 2000:142–62). The *lmlk* seal impressions on stores that Hezekiah probably gathered in preparation for his defense against Sennacherib witness a system of royal vineyards in the hill country of Judah in the late eighth century BCE (R. Kessler 1992:144–48; Rainey 1982:57–61). Farther north and earlier in the same century, the Samaria ostraca document the flow of oil and wine to Israelite court officials from upland estates (Campbell 1991:109–12; I. T. Kaufman 1992; Premnath 2003:60–62, 81–83). These court records refer some dozen times to "washed oil," a superior grade of olive oil extracted by water from crushed olives without the use of presses. Subsequent processing of the pulp and the use of presses introduced impurities into the oil and reduced its quality. Since only a small fraction of the total output of oil could be produced by this method of "washing," Samaria's ruling elite are shown to have had luxurious tastes; note their use of the "finest oils" in Amos 6:6 (Stager 1983:241–45).

Archaeological surveys of total inhabited area, combined with comparatively normed coefficients of density, evidence a marked rise in the population of Israel and Judah during the Iron II period. While absolute growth occurred both in the lowlands and in the highlands, the hill country grew faster, for the first time in history accounting for more than half the total population of the region (Broshi and Finkelstein 1992; Herr 1997:137). One need not solve the old chicken-and-egg problem in social-scientific theory to know that rapid population growth and agricultural intensification almost always go hand in hand in agrarian societies (Boserup 1965; Grigg 1980; Netting 1993). In this case, the greater and more rapid growth occurred in the upland regions from which elite priorities demanded ever-increasing quantities of oil and wine.

Archaeology also shows that various marginal areas were inhabited in the eighth century, many for the first time. The badlands of western Samaria are a prime example. In most periods, they attracted more bandits than farmers. Such marginal areas tended to be cultivated only in periods of the greatest centralized control and intensification of agriculture. In this period, a number of settlements were built in these badlands, many on virgin sites. These latter were constructed according to the same or similar plans, occupied marginal niches in terms of water and resource availability, and included olive- and grape-processing installations (Dar 1986:147–90). At least one of the villages so witnessed also appears to be mentioned in the Samaria ostraca (assuming that Sefarin is the Sepher of the inscriptions; see Campbell 1991:110–11; Dar 1986:139; I. T. Kaufman 1992:925). Taken in sum, these data corroborate for Israel a picture of regional specialization and intensification under royal initiative similar to that conveyed by the Chronicler for Judah.

TECHNOLOGICAL INNOVATIONS

This agricultural specialization and intensification fostered the proliferation of technological innovation in order to increase production. An example is the beam press used in olive oil production. While the first such press appears in the archaeological record of the ninth century BCE, its use burgeoned in the eighth century (Eitam 1979; Stager and Wolff 1981:95-102). In that context, it helped to wring every last drop of oil from the annual olive crop, and to do so more efficiently than had previous methods. Technological innovations not infrequently wait upon incentives from the political economy to have their greatest historical impact. In this case, the demand of the urban elites for ever more olive oil drove the expanded use of the beam press.

"COMMAND" ECONOMIES

To a certain extent, at least, Israel and Judah developed in this period what economic historians call "command economies" (Chaney 1986:74; 1989a:20-21; Heilbroner 1975:7-46; Hopkins 1983:193; Nolan and Lenski 2009:154-55). Previously, the ruling elites had extracted as much "surplus" as possible from peasant production, but had left mostly to the peasants themselves decisions about what to grow and how to grow it. Now their desire for ever-increasing amounts of olive oil and wine led them to attenuate or even to usurp the decision-making functions of peasant households concerning the priorities and techniques of agricultural production.

Some recent archaeological priorities and techniques offer promise of more refined and documented analyses of the role of elites in economic decision-making. In older archaeological excavations, the bones and bone fragments from domesticated animals that had been butchered and eaten were not saved or examined when archaeologists unearthed them. They went straight to the excavation's dump. Today, reputable excavations of any size have an archaeozoologist on staff, or at least available for extensive consultation. The analysis of faunal remains by these specialists has discovered a number of interesting correlations, some of which witness "the degree of political centralization achieved by state and imperial regimes" (Wapnish and Hesse 2003:17).

> Thus, at points of low integration, herds were configured to service households and contained relatively more goats and pigs. As agricultural systems intensified and market engagement or taxation/tributary demands increased, cattle and sheep became more important components of a husbandry system now more focused on export. (ibid.:17–18)

While it is far too early to speak definitively, early returns seem to indicate greater centralization of economic decision-making in the southern Levant in the eighth century BCE.

Faunal remains from seventh-century Tell Jemmeh and Tell Miqne/Ekron, which have been conserved and analyzed carefully, point to the heavy intrusion of Assyrian imperial policy into local economies. "[Y]ounger animals up to three years of age were exported from the economy while the older stock was consumed at the site." This pattern "may reflect the export of live animals for tribute." "Assyrian policies dramatically increased the currency value of animals relative to their value as commodities and converted the pastoral sector to a 'colonial' economy" (Wapnish 1993:439). Evidence for this impact upon Levantine economies by Assyrian policies of tribute is less clear for the eighth century BCE, but similar results from other sites near grazing lands in the latter part of that century would scarcely surprise. Assyrian texts certainly witness Assyrian demands for animals as booty and tribute (ibid.:440). Skillfully managed, they transported themselves from tributary to master, whereas the overland transportation of grain, given the technology available, was prohibitively expensive. This extraction of animals as tribute only intensified the demands upon hill country peasants who were being pushed to produce more and more olive oil and wine for the conspicuous consumption of urban elites and for the much cheaper seaborne trade with and through the Phoenicians.

CONCENTRATION OF RISK AND EFFACEMENT OF TRADITIONAL RISK-SPREADING MEASURES

We can now place in a broader context how the elites' pressure to grow ever-increasing amounts of the few preferred crops concentrated risk and effaced the risk-spreading devices of traditional peasant agriculture. Historically, the Israelite heartland had been in the hill country. There Israelite peasants worked small plots of arable land in mixed subsistence. Family holdings were modest, with a high congruence between those who held the land and those who actually worked it. Such peasant tenure of small plots is typical of upland regions in agrarian societies across a broad geographic and chronological spectrum. The hill-country peasants of Israel and Judah before the eighth century BCE produced most of what they consumed and consumed most of what they produced. That included grain, whose production in the uplands was "inefficient" but necessary to the independent subsistence of peasant villagers there (Marfoe 1979:21–23; Stager 1985:24).

The situation in lowland Palestine had long been different, again in conformity with norms witnessed widely in agrarian societies. Landholdings in the lowlands were larger, on average, and concentrated in fewer hands. Most agricultural labor was done by tenant farmers, day-laborers, peasants under corvée or debt obligations, or other workers whose access to land, livelihood, and personal freedom were insecure, attenuated, or under threat. In short, land holdings and the labor necessary to bring them to production were often separated in the lowlands. Much agricultural labor was landless and at the mercy of large landlords for any access to a livelihood. Eighth-century urban elites therefore found it relatively easy to work their will for agricultural intensification in the lowlands (Chaney 1989a:21–22).

But what of the hill country? Had much of it remained in small plots, tilled by their holders according to the priorities of mixed subsistence, that system would have constituted a major impediment to the goals of the city-based elites. They sought maximal *efficiency* and regional specialization in the production of olive oil and wine from the hill country. Left to their own devices, however, hill country peasants sought to guarantee the *sufficiency* of their livelihood by spreading the risks inherent in rain agriculture as widely as possible. That risk-spreading included the growing of grain in the uplands (Hopkins 1983:187–88).

Even a sketch of their various risk-spreading mechanisms conveys something of the supple nuance of the methods and techniques involved. Fields that produced cereals in some years were not so used every year. To maintain fertility, they were periodically fallowed at some times and sown to legumes at others, at least in some rotations. As well as returning nitrogen to the soil, legumes also provided precious vegetable protein to the peasant diet (Borowski 1987:93–97). Fallowed fields supplemented uncultivable grazing land in providing pasture for the herding of sheep and goats. For subsistence farmers, such herding provided a hedge against the risk of purely agricultural pursuits. Animals so raised constituted a "disaster bank on the hoof" that stored surpluses from wet years to be drawn upon in dry years. Flocks were allowed to expand in wet years, when there was ample grass and water in the seasonal pastures. When the next dry year came, and pasturage and water were insufficient for the expanded flocks, culling both brought the flocks and their pasturage back into equilibrium and provided much needed protein in an otherwise lean year (Hopkins 1983:191).

The drying up of seasonal pastures and watering holes in the spring corresponded with the grain harvest. Much of the same labor necessary to move the flocks around the seasonal pastures during the rainy season now returned to the cereal fields to help with the all-important harvest. Once that grain harvest was secured, the flocks that had fed on the seasonal pastures in the wet season now grazed the stubble fields of the rainless summer, serving all the while as roving manure spreaders. Their bodily wastes, randomly distributed wherever they grazed, helped to replace the nutrients taken from the soil by the growing of grain. Herding nearer to the cereal-growing villages also made use of labor—the very young and the very old—that would not otherwise have been productive. In the process, the accumulated knowledge and wisdom of the grandparents' generation was readily passed to the young children of the village (Chaney 1989a:22).

Tree and vine crops rounded out the repertoire of village agriculture in the hills. Grown here and there in small stands where soil and climate were particularly favorable to them but not to grains, these perennials complemented cereal agriculture and herding. They required pruning and other hand labor over the wet winter season, when cereals grew with relatively little attention. Their harvest took place in the fall, just before plowing and sowing of the grain fields. The combination of cereal farming, rotation with legumes, the herding of sheep and goats, and the raising of tree and vine crops exploited synergistically both differentiated and overlapping ecological niches, while distributing and balancing various demands on much the same pool of village labor throughout the year. Because their processed fruit could be stored stably for extended periods, grapes, olives and other perennials made valuable contributions to the goal of spreading risk (Eitam and Heltzer 1996; Hopkins 1983:189; Walsh 2000).

The pressure from urban elites to produce ever-increasing quantities of olive oil and wine in the hills ran directly counter to the villagers' objective of spreading risk and optimizing labor through a diversity of subsistence means. This struggle between the values of *efficiency* and *sufficiency* was stark, if inadvertent. Sheep and goats maintained by households and their pastures, which were integral to village subsistence but not to the priorities of the urban elites, were probably the first element to be reduced. Meat for a few privileged urbanites was pastured in the steppe during the rainy season and then stall-fed in preparation for slaughter (cf. Amos 6:4). Stall-feeding also facilitated the collection and composting of wet manure that could be used to fertilize more intensively cropped perennials. Fallow and the grazing it had supported fell out of the mix (Chaney 1989a:23; Turkowski 1969:24). To the extent that livestock were raised for tribute, their herding constituted a specialized, pastoralist, economic activity, mostly in semi-arid regions, and no longer a part of village subsistence.

The intensified production of oil and wine in the hill country also shouldered aside the subsistence farming of grains there. Archaeology would seem to show that multi-purpose land, which had helped to spread risk, was gradually converted into terraces growing vineyards and olive trees (Edelstein and Kislev 1981; Faust 2012:166; Hopkins 1983:200; note Isa 5:1–7; Chaney 1999). Elite practices and policies may have given impetus to the process. That, at least, is a possible implication of Amos 5:11 as now read by most commentators (see Chaney 1999:108 and n2):

> Therefore, because you impose grain tax upon the poor one,
>   and exactions of wheat you take from him,
> you have built houses of hewn stone,
>   but you shall not dwell in them;
> you have planted desirable vineyards,
>   but you shall not drink their wine.

If these lines reflect a tax levied on grain grown "inefficiently" in the uplands, it would have added further incentive for the shift away from self-sufficiency among upland villagers. Even the intensified production of oil and wine in the hill country was somewhat at odds with elite demands on it. While demand tended to be steady or to increase, production itself was subject to the vicissitudes of the environment and, in the case of the olive, to a pattern of alternating yields.

SURVIVAL LOANS AND THEIR IMPLICATIONS

With risk-spreading diversification effaced and all "surpluses" extracted from hill country peasants even in good years, bad years spelled disaster. Peasant families faced a terrible calculus. They had too little grain to be able both to seed their fields and to sustain their lives until the next harvest in the spring. What they sowed, they could not eat; what they ate, they could not sow. Current hunger had to be measured against future starvation. This situation resulted in forced borrowing. The survival loans to which these peasants resorted out of stark necessity did not constitute "venture capital" in any sense, nor were the debt contracts entered into freely or without coercion (Chaney 1991:128–29; R. Kessler 2008:111–12; Lang 1983:117).

These survival loans also violated the social and cultural norms of the village. In periods of less centralized control and "surplus" extraction, peasants within certain village and/or kinship groups routinely gave each other survival loans free of interest. This system of loans was no more altruistic than modern insurance policies on automobiles or houses. It was, rather, a risk-spreading mechanism and insurance against catastrophic failure. Peasant households gave interest-free survival loans to neighboring families or kin who were experiencing a bad year in the sure knowledge that the vicissitudes of the environment would soon enough reverse the roles. Most agrarian societies, past and present, evidence some form of such loans (Chaney 1991:129; Critchfield 1983:345). As the situation developed in eighth-century Israel and Judah, however, most peasants were not able to make such loans. The only "surpluses" available were in the hands of the wealthy landlords or their agents.

The terms of the typical debt contract only exacerbated the peasants' plight. Most loans were made in silver bullion,[4] whose value relative to grain was the least when grain was scarcest. Relatively speaking, it took much silver to buy a little grain when grain was in short supply. The loans routinely came due at harvest, and were payable in kind at the very time when plentiful supply insured that grain was worth the least relative to silver. Simply granting the loan with silver as the medium of exchange and requiring that it be paid back in grain at harvest, therefore, imposed a crushing rate of interest in fact, if not in law (Chaney 2014b).

Surety for loans was the peasants' land holding, if they had managed to retain rights to any, and/or the indentured labor of one or more family members. Given the cycles of debt created in the situation, foreclosure was frequently at the discretion of the creditor. Wealthy landlords could first squeeze every last drop from a peasant family's labor, and then foreclose, thereby creating a growing pool of landless day-laborers and debt-slaves. Foreclosure on peasant land rights for non-payment of survival loans granted on impossible terms was also a mechanism of land consolidation. More and more land rights passed into fewer and fewer hands, as those few wealthy enough to grant survival loans foreclosed upon the desperate many who had no choice but to take them out. Land consolidation and an increase of landless day-laborers and debt-slaves walked hand in hand. The newly landless peasants often suffered still another indignity. They now labored part-time—at depressed wages and only at the landlord's good pleasure—on land to which their family had had secure rights for generations. Their loss of those rights meant not only severe economic insecurity, but a hiatus

---

4. Graeber says that bullion or coinage appears in transactions when patterns of communal trust break down. The transaction is thus depersonalized and reduced to a single, economic strand of relationship (2001:49–51, 211–22).

in cultural continuity and a diminution of social and legal status as well (Chaney 1989a:25–26; Lang 1983:117).

SOCIOECONOMIC SEGMENTATION AND ABSENTEE LANDLORDS

These changes in the political economies of Israel and Judah, particularly in the hill country, separated and segmented what previously had been integrated into one more organic social whole in the village. Not only were agricultural labor and land rights separated, but various factors of production—arable land, pasture, water, traction animals, tools, seed, manure, etc.—were segmented and subjected to separate rent. There was also a growth in absentee landlordism. With their promise of imported luxuries and greater access to political influence and social prestige, the capital cities of Samaria and Jerusalem drew landlords away from their country estates and their need for clientele support. Exchanges between landlords and peasants had never been a relationship of equals. When landlords lived on their country estates, however, they and their peasants attended many of the same ceremonial events. Their social relations were "multi-stranded," developed in a number of facets of life (Chaney 1989a:24–25; Lang 1983:119).

Removal of the landlords to the capital cities, where their advancement depended in no small part on their successful participation in the games of conspicuous consumption played at court, reduced their relationship to their peasants to a single strand of economic exploitation. What they wanted and needed from their lands and peasants was an ever-increasing flow of oil and wine. They cared less and less about the methods used to secure their bounty. That was the concern of the stewards they left in charge back in the country. The stewards, meantime, knew perfectly well that their own success depended on the metrics of the estate's output, not on the ethics of how they treated the agricultural labor that worked it.

COURT PROCEEDINGS

The foreclosures that played a crucial part in the dynamics of change described to this point came to court to be ratified. At the local level, "court" involved a largely consensus process in a meeting of the free males of the village at dawn before they dispersed to their fields for the workday. This "justice in the gate" had few procedural safeguards. As long as there were no overweening imbalances of power among its constituents, however, it could produce more than a modicum of justice. The changes already described, of course, produced an ever-greater differential in power. Landlords wealthy enough to provide survival loans could easily coerce or suborn the village court's decisions. Appeal was futile, since the king was literally the court of last resort (Chaney 1999:111–12; 2004b; Köhler 1956:127–50; Whitelam 1979).

One of the literary forms most common in the oldest material in the eighth-century prophets directly addressed this dilemma of the village courts. Rhetorically speaking, these prophetic oracles appealed the coerced and suborned decisions of the village courts, not to the king's court, but to the court of the King of kings. The authority the prophets claimed was not to speak in their own right, but to report the proceedings that they had overheard in God's law court in the sky. As auditors on God's processing and disposition of the case on appeal, they regularly declared a reversal of what happened in human courts, where the wealthy and powerful were found in the right and the powerless poor were adjudged guilty. According to the prophets, God had declared the poor debtors innocent and the powerful and rapacious landlords guilty. God's justice in these prophetic oracles was frequently poetic. The sentence pronounced corresponded to the indictment charged in a measure-for-measure fashion, thereby making the punishment fit the crime. In God's court, as the prophets reported it, the wealthy and powerful got to taste more than a bit of their own medicine (Blenkinsopp 1996:29–30; Ramsey 1977).

CHANGING GENDER ROLES WITH INCREASED MALE DOMINANCE

If one is to judge from widespread comparative work, there was also a significant change in gender roles in eighth-century Israel and Judah. Whether past or present, virtually all agrarian societies are patriarchal. Perhaps the most nuanced explanation that current social-scientific theory has to offer for this male dominance is that childbearing and the nursing and care of small children are incompatible with the circumstances and activities that surround plowing. Only women can bear and nurse children. Small children require frequent care and are not easily taken far from the safety of home in the village. Thus, the economic activities most compatible with the nursing and care of small children are those that can be performed in or close to home and that can tolerate frequent interruptions. Such activities include the processing, storage and preparation of foodstuffs and fiber, and the tending of "kitchen gardens" kept very near the houses in the village.

Plowing is the antithesis of such activities. It often takes place at significant distances from the village and involves large animals and plows whose movements are intrinsically dangerous to small children should they chance to get in the way. Given the relative cost of traction animals, they need to be used efficiently. Any significant interruption in their activities, therefore, is costly and counterproductive. Under such circumstances, a division of labor that locates female economic activities primarily in the "domestic domain," while assigning plowing and other field work mostly to males is efficient and rational. (During points of crisis in the agricultural year, such as harvest, when all available labor is needed in the fields, women work there as well, of course.) Coincident with this division of labor comes a dominance of males in the so-called "public domain," that part of society and culture that takes place outside the home. Gender roles, therefore, increasingly assign women to the domestic domain, men to the public domain (Bossen 1989; Nolan and Lenski 2009:167–68).

On a broadly comparative basis, social scientists can say that agricultural intensification usually exacerbates male dominance in agrarian societies. Predictably, as the percentage of field labor performed by females in intensified agriculture drops from the levels characteristic of subsistence agriculture, so, too, does the status of women. Women's activities—while no less arduous!—are increasingly restricted to the domestic domain (Bossen 1989; Meyers 1988:189–96). Meantime, as previously discussed, more and more of the decision-making regarding what to produce and how to produce it is removed to the public domain, where men have long dominated. Thus, it seems probable that an increase of male dominance was a concomitant of agricultural intensification in eighth-century Israel and Judah.[5] If so, some desperate peasant men, having watched their livelihoods, honor, and status debased and abused, would almost certainly have vented their anger and shame on their wives, mothers, daughters, and sisters. Elite males, doubly empowered by class and by gender, would have felt even fewer constraints in their treatment of lower class women.

These changes in gender roles are powerfully reflected in the book of Hosea, as it is read by a number of current scholars (Bird 1997b:219–36; Chaney 2004a; Keefe 2001). Their inter-disciplinary scholarship sees much of the rhetoric of Hosea as addressed specifically to elite males in such a way as to mock sarcastically their privileges and pretensions. The very term *ba'al*, which figures so prominently in Hosea, participates intrinsically in

---

5. MacDonald states that the relative height of male and female skeletal remains in Iron Age Israel and Judah suggests that women, on average, were less well-nourished than men as a result of "unfavorable social conditions discriminating against women" (2008:87).

hierarchies both of class and of gender. It is a title meaning "lord," both as the landlord is "lord" of his peasants, and as the husband is "lord" of his wife.

SOME IMPLICATIONS FOR CONSIDERING POVERTY TODAY

Many passages in the eighth-century prophets reflect and reflect upon the dynamics sketched above. Their explication must be left for other occasions. I conclude instead with a few brief remarks about contemporary implications (for much fuller and wider-ranging discussions, see Coomber 2010; Davis 2008). My remarks are brief for two reasons. First, when it comes to the complex ethical questions of modern economic systems and their dynamics, most readers of this essay are as expert as I—many far more so. I have neither standing nor wish to pontificate. As members of our own religious communities, we share the responsibility to grapple with contemporary questions of economic justice. Second, when we do our descriptive and analytical work on ancient texts and their contexts carefully enough, many of their implications are only too clear, sometimes uncomfortably so.

With those caveats, nevertheless, please allow me just a few concluding generalizations. Many texts from the eighth-century prophets—when read against the background here made more explicit—suggest to me that we must carefully examine the intermediate and long-term results of systemic economic changes. We must ask not only who benefits from such changes, but at whose expense? Do those injured suffer only temporary and partial loss, or are their losses permanent and irremediable? Does the new regime create compensating economic opportunities for those injured, or do the changes condemn them to being a permanent underclass, marginalized or even pauperized? Is the distance between the top and the bottom of the social pyramid increased or decreased? If the old economic order was reasonably well integrated and balanced, spreading risk and allowing various threats to be met nimbly and stably over long periods, how does the new order compare on these issues? Does it concentrate risk? Does that concentration increase the possibility of catastrophic failure? Does it concentrate economic decision making? If so, what knowledge about and experience of economic processes is denied those who make decisions that impact everyone? What are the likely results of a disconnect between such knowledge and such decision making? Are economic rewards received commensurate with economic risks taken, or do power dynamics dictate some other allocation?

What were the environmental costs of the old system? What are they in the new system? What is the sustainability of each?

When we juxtapose the world behind eighth-century prophetic texts with that currently in front of them, these and many similar questions about economic justice arise. How are we to "read" the "dynamic analogies?" I do not mean to suggest that conscientious adherents to "biblical faith" will, by good will and intelligence, come easily to clear or consensus answers. My experience suggests quite the contrary. But the presence of these texts in our Bibles suggests to me that sustained, in-depth, civil, and mutually respectful engagement of these questions in our communities of faith is incumbent upon us individually and corporately. We must, I believe, come to such questions not full of predetermined and self-serving "answers," but expectant of new perspectives, new insights, and new discoveries about others and ourselves. In that elusive pursuit of economic justice, the eighth-century prophets—read against the world they presume—can function powerfully as our mentors, not by providing us pat answers, but by pressing us for more probing, pertinent questions.

APPENDIX:
BRIEF SUMMARY AND CRITIQUE OF RECENT WORKS

Recently published works by three scholars—Philippe Guillaume (2012), Avraham Faust (2012), and Walter J. Houston (2004, 2006, 2008, 2010)—challenge, in whole or in part, the social description and analysis of eighth-century Israel and Judah that is presented in the essay above. Their challenge should not go unanswered, and so in the following pages I shall offer a preliminary critique of their works, primarily in regard to how their works challenge my own.

Philippe Guillaume

Guillaume's polemical and far-ranging book defies easy summary, but the following points are among his major emphases. 1) There are insuperable difficulties in dating the texts of the Hebrew Bible, including, most specifically, the "eighth-century" prophets. These texts can be related historically only to Persian Yehud, at the earliest, and to no earlier period. 2) Notions of "oppressed peasants" in Iron Age II Israel and Judah are "the myth of the helpless peasant," mere Marxist projections and figments of the romantic imaginations of liberal "Hebrew exegetes." Had the peasants of ancient

Israel been all that oppressed, they would have revolted, but there is no evidence for such revolts. 3) The biblical prophets were not champions of social justice. Instead, the "fulminations"—a favorite word—and "virulent denunciations of the rich" (2012:163) attributed to them "should be read as evidence of the power struggle between different elite groups rather than as clues of the actual economic situation on the ground" (248). 4) Attempts to understand the economic workings of ancient Israel should be focused, not on the prophetic literature, which is tendentious, but elsewhere in the Hebrew Bible. Guillaume offers numerous "rereadings" of those non-prophetic texts to prove his other points. 5) There was no struggle over land in ancient Israel, but rather an over-abundance of arable land combined with a chronic lack of labor and agricultural credit. 6) Loans were extended only to "creditworthy" peasants and were rarely oppressive. They were "an essential ingredient to a healthy economy" (192), serving to smooth out fluctuations in the allocation of available resources and labor. The primary creditors were "merchant-lenders" who operated in an active, developed grain market. 7) Notions of private ownership are useless in the analysis of ancient economies. It is better to speak of land allocation or possession and to find analogies for biblical practices in the land categories of the Ottoman Empire.

My critique of Guillaume's assertions proceeds in the same order as the summary above. 1) The literature referred to at the beginning of this essay (the works cited in Chaney 2006:145–46) is but the tip of the iceberg of a vast literature discussing the dating of various levels of composition and recomposition in the books of the "eighth-century" prophets, books that are widely viewed as literarily composite. The criteria for dating in much of that body of scholarship are specific and testable. They go far in clarifying the differing contexts that can account for the multiple perspectives and voices found in the same prophetic book. Guillaume may agree with critics of those analyses, but he owes his readers more than perfunctory citation of their criticisms (2012:44). Many serious students of the prophets still find that critique, which claims that nothing in the prophets can be related to anything historical before the Persian period, to be overly broad and lacking in specific engagement with previous scholarship. The constant repetition of dicta that "everybody knows" does not constitute an advance in scholarship.

2) Guillaume either ignores or is innocent of most of the social-scientific literature on peasant–landlord relations. Those exchanges almost always involve some element of exploitation. Not infrequently, the exploitation is extreme. Although Guillaume cites the work of Scott in support of his picture of the "empowered peasant" (63), Scott's larger body of work only makes clear the disadvantaged position of most peasants in most times and places. His exploration of *Weapons of the Weak: Everyday Forms of Peasant*

Resistance (1985) shows that peasants use covert means of resisting landlord exactions precisely because they are poor and not powerful enough to press their own interests more directly and openly. Guillaume acknowledges that Lenski's concept of "agrarian societies" (Lenski 1966/1984:189–296) "seems broad enough to encompass the reality reflected in biblical texts," but objects that "its very broadness reduces its heuristic value . . ." (2012:152). But Lenski's work demonstrates on a broadly comparative basis that agrarian societies, for all their variation in some respects, are remarkably consistent in patterns of social stratification that privilege an elite few—less than two percent of the population—and condemn a majority of the rest, predominantly peasants, to one or another level of poverty. Lenski's comparative work in historical sociology cannot by itself demonstrate anything specific about the status of peasants in ancient Israel's political economy. What it can and does demonstrate, however, is that the picture of peasant–landlord relations sketched in the present essay is consistent with what Lenski regularly finds to be true in agrarian societies as a generic type, whereas Guillaume's picture of ancient Israel is a glaring anomaly in a generic category defined by specific and testable criteria. I prefer the former odds to the latter. Guillaume protests on several occasions that if the peasants of ancient Israel had had that hard a life, they would have revolted, but they did not. This argument misses the point that successful peasant revolts—the kind that would leave historical evidence—are extremely rare in agrarian history. Those few that have made a mark on history share a number of conditions conducive to their success (Chaney 1983:61–67; Landsberger 1973; Wolf 1966, 1969). Few of those conditions were present in eighth-century Israel and Judah, leaving the lack of peasant rebellions scant evidence indeed for peasant wellbeing.

3) While Guillaume asserts repeatedly that the "fulminations" of the prophets are nothing more than the attack of one elite group upon another, he nowhere adduces a concrete context that would account plausibly for the content of the actual texts. He seems viscerally offended by charges that the rich and powerful are oppressing poor and lowly peasants, leaving his readers to ponder what has occasioned his own fierce heat. The nuanced account of the composition of the books of the "eighth-century" prophets preferred here, by contrast, posits plausible contexts and rhetorical vectors for each of the several perspectives contained in these prophetic books. It explains how and why a sharp critique of the ruling classes ends up in what are, in their final form, quite clearly elite documents.

4) In his quest for the economic relations reflected in the Hebrew Bible, Guillaume focuses upon fresh interpretations of a number of non-prophetic texts. Space does not permit discussion of his many "rereadings,"

but they frequently fail to inspire confidence. Most of these texts, too, are "tendentious," but the rhetorical vector of a text being "reread" is rarely clarified, and standard methodologies of philology and textual criticism are sometimes flouted. On more than one occasion, it is difficult to escape the feeling that the text is being rewritten to fit a paradigm more asserted by repetition than demonstrated.

5) Guillaume's claim of an over-abundance of arable land in ancient Israel can only be maintained by highly questionable generalizations and parallels. He takes the depopulated state of Persian Yehud as the demographic norm, whereas, in fact, it is the demographic anomaly, standing in marked contrast to all of Iron Age II in the southern Levant. Appeals to the availability of land in Mesopotamia ignore differences in natural environment and agricultural technology. In regard to arable land and the actual demographic situation in Iron Age II, Noll states "[T]he Cisjordan Highlands approached a point of full exploitation. That is to say, given ancient farming techniques, the Cisjordan Highlands achieved a population size that was taking advantage of all arable regions" (Noll 2013:262; cf. Faust 2012:260). Only Guillaume's chronological removal of the composition of all biblical texts to Persian Yehud can justify his "myth of an over-abundance of arable land."

6) Guillaume's treatment of credit consistently fails to make the distinction between what Boer calls "credit" and what he terms "debt" (2012; cf. Boer 2007). The former relies upon trust, not as a moral value, but "in terms of allocation, in which credit functions as one of the means for ensuring the mutual allocation and reallocation of all goods within the community. By contrast, debt operates mainly as an extractive economic device. That is, it extracts something—goods, labor, money, [I would add land]—from the debtor with the result that [the] lender's own wealth increases" (Boer 2012:2–3). Such debt ensures "that the flow of wealth runs from debtor to lender"; it "functions as a means of compulsion for labor"; and it "functions to ensure economic hierarchy" (ibid.:3–4). Guillaume treats all debt in ancient Israel as "credit," ignoring virtually all comparative (and biblical) evidence for the exploitive nature of "debt." His positing of an active international grain market and a large number of "merchant-lenders" in ancient Israel's economy flies in the face of the costs of overland transportation in the preindustrial world (Lenski 1966/1984:204–6). In the agricultural debt practices of Israel and Judah in Iron Age II, the primary lenders were landlords, not grain merchants (cf. R. Kessler 1989).

7) Guillaume's cautions against reading modern notions of land "ownership" into biblical texts are well taken. Concepts of "allocation" or "possession" are indeed more appropriate. The review of Ottoman land categories

and the suggestion of possible parallels in ancient Israel are suggestive and helpful. Some of Guillaume's applications probably press possible analogies too hard, however, even though he urges others not to do so. Notions and practices of land tenure in ancient Israel likely did not conform completely to any clear schematic that moderns can enunciate. Both concept and practice likely varied through time and place. Practice adhered sometimes more, sometimes less to theory. Multiple levels of claim upon the same plot of arable land and its produce were often the norm. Modern discussions should seek to avoid both anachronism and a level of precision that the sources do not allow. Whatever the concepts or practices of land tenure that obtained, however, the major differentials of power in society and the fact that access to land was, for much the greater part, access to the economic base virtually ensured that landlords would pressure peasants concerning the finite and all-important resource of arable land and the peasant labor necessary to bring it into production.

Avraham Faust and Walter J. Houston

The challenges that Faust and Houston pose to the picture offered in this essay are far less frontal than those laid down by Guillaume. For a time Houston (2004, 2006) was in basic agreement, with relatively minor nuances here and there, but then he began to encounter the work of Faust. That encounter prompted Houston to revise his previous work (2006) in a relatively major way (2008), and then to summarize his new position on the matters under discussion here (2010).

Faust's labors to collect and interpret archaeological data have been both encyclopedic and herculean. Happily, his findings, the publication of which had been spread broadly, are now brought to a focus in a single volume. While no summary can possibly do justice to his far-ranging work, his conclusions that bear upon the current discussion can be stated with surprising concision. Faust addresses the issue of social stratification in Iron II Israel and Judah by means of what he believes to be the only reliable archaeological indicator of relative wealth—house size and, secondarily, house quality. Using these rather narrowly focused criteria, Faust finds strong evidence for stark social stratification in the cities of Iron II Israel and Judah. In the villages and farmsteads, however, he finds a lack of significant social stratification and evidence for a peasant economy that was healthy and more than sufficient. "Thus, the processes of urbanization and specialization gradually caused major stratification [in the cities]" (Faust 2012:264).

"But this process was not pervasive: according to the archaeological record, this process did not apply in the rural sector..." (265).

Houston chides Faust for treating "urban and rural society quite separately, virtually as independent worlds which had little or nothing to do with each other" (2010:106). "None of Faust's evidence challenges the view that the villages, as well as the lower classes of the cities, were subject to the official class, and that the balance of redistribution did not favor them" (2010:106). Houston insists, however, "that the consequent inequality is more pronounced within the cities than between the cities and the villages, and evidence for it is more obtrusive in the cities" (ibid.). He examines numerous prophetic texts in light of that hypothesis and concludes

> that prophetic accusations of social injustice have a background primarily in the capital cities of Samaria and Jerusalem, and that both oppressors and victims mostly resided in those places, or nearby. These prophetic texts offer a moral evaluation, of course from a committed and some would say prejudiced viewpoint, of a process of rapid social change in the fortified cities of monarchical Israel and Judah. They cannot be used to challenge archaeological evidence that this process, during the monarchical era, touched rural areas only to a limited extent, except in the immediate hinterland of the capitals. (2010:113–14)

A number of factors cast doubt upon some of the conclusions of Faust and Houston and the certainty with which they are articulated. 1) As Faust admits repeatedly (2012:129, 206, 234, 272, etc.), "archaeological knowledge of rural settlement is very limited" (234). The severely limited archeological sample of villages contains very few larger villages—where greater evidence of social stratification might be expected—and may well not be particularly representative in other ways as well. The vast majority of the archaeological "evidence" is from "cities," but comparative sociology and anthropology indicate that the vast majority of the population would have been rural. Thus, archaeology in its current state can scarcely claim to trump all other evidence for the political economy of the peasantry in Iron II Israel and Judah.

2) Faust uses house size—and secondarily a somewhat subjective assessment of house quality—as the primary indicator of relative wealth. This one criterion is virtually the sole basis of his conclusion that the rural sector of Iron II Israel and Judah lacked significant social stratification. As Holladay observes on the basis of ethnographic analogy, however, "wealth distinctions (other than in storage capacity) may only poorly be reflected in domestic architecture" (1995:377). Houston concedes that "[s]ome social

differences could be hidden within houses built in happier days" (2010:105). Even Faust's treatment of the database for his sole archaeological indicator of relative wealth sometimes raises questions about his even-handedness. He "corrects" the principal excavator or site expert on several occasions, always to play down or explain away what those he corrects took as evidence for social stratification—thus, Campbell on Shechem (Faust 2012:63), Zorn on Mizpah (72–77), Dar on what he takes to be the house of a village leader or chief at Khirbet Jemein (136 and 169 n23), and Eitam on Beit Aryeh (137–38). On more than one occasion, Faust is forced to admit that the data he is reporting and analyzing point to greater social stratification—particularly in one of the very few large villages from which we currently have data—than his general conclusions would lead one to believe (141, 169–70, 175, 195). Faust is dismissive of serious attempts to find evidence of social stratification in small finds (41, 120–24). He may be correct about some or even many of the particulars that he disputes with other archaeological experts. All his "corrections" and disagreements, however, point uniformly toward the conclusion that there was no significant social stratification in the villages of Iron II Israel and Judah, leaving Faust's readers to wonder if some portion of that conclusion was foregone, and some portion of his arguments special pleading.

3) If a broader spectrum of archaeological evidence is examined, it reveals that urban elites had greater impact upon the political economy of the countryside than Faust and Houston wish to acknowledge. Faust himself describes and analyzes a series of "strongholds" and "fortresses" that represent a major projection of elite power into the hinterland (189, 192–93). Major taxes, corvée, and "extensive personnel and employment stratification" (193) are among the concomitants he admits. In his work in western Samaria, Dar finds roads that he dates to the Iron II period and interprets as built to move agricultural produce to market (137, 145). Faust readily admits that "[p]arts of western Samaria are an ecological fringe region that was not intensively settled in later periods" (176). It was, in fact, inhabited only when elite initiatives and population pressure pressed its marginal environment into agricultural production. Dar reports that many of the buildings in this area that date to the Iron II period, especially oil- and wine-processing installations, seem to have been built to quite similar plans, indicating a dimension of central planning.

A number of isolated "farmsteads," as opposed to villages, have been excavated from the period, mostly around Jerusalem and in western Samaria. Emphasizing those in the Jerusalem area, Houston quotes Hopkins (1997:307) that farmsteads reflect "the penetration of the countryside by the managerial arm of the city-based administration" (2010:112). When one includes the farmsteads of western Samaria in the mix, this phenomenon tells against the dictum of Faust and Houston that the economic penetration of urban elites into the countryside was minimal. In this regard, Hopkins' further comments, tutored as they are by a deep knowledge of the social sciences, are worth quoting:

> Surface dating has demonstrated the association of farmsteads with periods of high-density land use, a barometer of the growth of the urban sphere and its sway over the surrounding territory. Thus, the appearance of farmsteads is related to heightened security conditions and the burgeoning demand for specialized economic goods—that is, marketable commodities. (Hopkins 1997:306)

Farmsteads thus witness growing economic influence of urban elites both in the immediate environs of the capital city (Jerusalem) *and* in marginal lands some distance from the capital (Samaria). The latter were pressed into production only during periods of "high-density land use," when urban elites exercised maximal influence over the political economy of the rural hinterland.

4) Faust and Houston paint a picture of happy self-sufficiency for the rural peasantry of Iron II Israel and Judah based primarily on the domestic architecture of a few small villages. Their account finds the countryside touched but lightly by the stark social stratification and privation of the lower classes that characterized the cities. Using sophisticated interdisciplinary methods, broadly based in the sciences and social sciences, MacDonald renders a far less rosy account. After nuanced surveys of "Environment and Climate" (2008:50–56), "Food Shortage and Famine" (57–60), "The Consumption of Meat: Archaeological Evidence" (61–72), "The Consumption of Meat: Anthropological Evidence" (73–76), "Food Distribution" (77–79), and "Nutritional Deficiencies," which examines the evidence of human skeletal remains, he concludes:

> currently the evidence suggests that the population of ancient Israel did not enjoy good health. These demographic patterns are consistent with those from many other premodern agricultural communities. They suggest that most people had a short life, with a high level of infant mortality and few adults surviving beyond the age of fifty. This cannot be attributed to nutrition alone, but there are good grounds for thinking that poor nutrition played a contributory role. (86–87)

Life expectancy in the southern Levant appears to have been markedly lower in the Iron Age than in the preceding Bronze Age or the Hellenistic and Roman periods that followed (86). MacDonald's final words of conclusion are: "Our current state of knowledge suggests that the population of Iron Age Israel generally suffered from an inadequate diet, poor health, and low life expectancy. Their experience was little different from that of other premodern inhabitants of Palestine, and in some respects it may even have been worse" (87). MacDonald's conclusions are drawn after a judicious and methodological rigorous sifting of broad bodies of evidence, and deserve full credence unless and until the state of knowledge about such matters changes markedly.

5) Houston maintains "that the biblical text assumes that the characteristic relationship between rich and poor is that of patronage," and "that the most pervasive mechanism through which the poor were exploited was the abuse of this relationship" (2010:102; see also 2006:42–46). Since patronage involves a face-to-face relationship, Houston then asks, "How then can this mechanism be invoked to explain the exploitation of people in villages by people in cities, who would rarely meet?" (102). Houston finds his answer in the work of Faust—stratification exists only in the cities, so the poor of the prophetic critique are the urban poor, and not the peasantry of the countryside, who are the vast majority of the population. He then undertakes a survey of prophetic passages condemning the exploitation of the poor by the rich and argues that they all presume a locus in or near the capital cities of Samaria and Jerusalem.

While patron–client relations were undoubtedly important in ancient Israel, and work well to explain many phenomena alluded to in texts such as the narratives about Elijah and Elisha, Houston's reduction of all relationships between rich and poor to the patron–client paradigm is overly broad. The paradigm will not bear the weight he places upon it. Some landlord–peasant relationships fit the patron–client model, but surely not all. As for Houston's contention that prophetic oracles castigating the rich for oppressing the poor all presume a locus in or near the capital cities of Jerusalem and Samaria, the conclusion once again far exceeds the evidence and not infrequently involves special pleading to make it fit. A couple of examples must suffice. Despite Faust's special pleading (63), Campbell makes a very credible case for "rich oppressors" beyond Jerusalem and Samaria: "To me it seems probable that the domestic housing evidence from Shechem as well as Tirzah, Hazor, and other such sites points to the reality a prophet like Amos faced. It was not just the significantly wealthy at the court at Samaria but also people who lived only relatively better than their neighbors who may have been tempted to take advantage of others, to cheat them in trading, to live too comfortably for the well-being of the community" (1994:49–50).

Houston turns to Mic 2:1–5 and expresses the common judgment: "Here surely we have the oppression of the peasantry by the rich in order to enlarge landholdings" (2010:111). But then Houston rejects the commonly held view of commentators that Micah had events in and near his hometown of Moresheth-Gath in view. "We do not know whether Moresheth-Gath was a village or a city at this time. In fact, we do not even know where it was precisely, so there is little light available to shed on our question in this direction" (ibid.). He then argues that because Isaiah contains a similar passage (Isa 5:8–10), and Isaiah is linked to Jerusalem, "both the Isaiah and Micah texts, which are closely parallel, are set in Jerusalem" (112).

Most learned opinion places Moresheth-Gath at Tell ej-Judeideh, a 2.5 hectare site in the Shephelah, on the basis of Eusebius, Jerome, and the Medeba map (Broshi 1993; Roncace 2009). If that is correct, Moresheth was a large village or a small town. In any case, Moresheth-Gath was in the Shephelah, associated as it is with other towns and villages there in the punning lament in Mic 1:8–16. Lachish, which bears the brunt of blame in that lament (v. 13), was the large provincial "capital" of the Shephelah. It dominated the surrounding towns and villages and their burgeoning agricultural production in Iron II, and evidences stark social stratification (Faust 2012:78–82). Since the lament in Mic 1:8–16 immediately precedes the passage in Mic 2:1–5, Houston's restriction of the passage to Jerusalem alone seems wishful thinking, as does his restriction of the poor in prophetic oracles to the urban lower classes. Landlord–peasant relations defined the major axis of exploitation in eighth-century Israel and Judah. Some exploited peasants lived in cities, but the vast majority lived in villages. Many landlords had roots in the countryside, but moved to the cities, particularly the capital cities, to avail themselves there of imported luxuries and greater access to political influence and social prestige.

7

Bitter Bounty

The Dynamics of Political Economy Critiqued by the Eighth-Century Prophets

No segment of Christendom has emphasized the Old Testament as Christian Scripture more than the Reformed tradition. When one asks what so significant a portion of the Reformed heritage has to say about economics—particularly about economic justice—the Hebrew prophets come readily to mind. For many Reformed Christians, passages from the eighth-century prophets, Amos, Hosea, Isaiah, and Micah, give classical articulation to this prophetic view of economic realities.

The appropriation of these texts by the modern community of faith has often lacked clarity and effect, however, because of a lack of hermeneutical precision. A penchant for abstraction can sometimes be the culprit. The injunction of Amos 5:24 to "let justice roll down like waters," for example, is frequently quoted in tones which presuppose that everyone agrees about what economic justice is, but that certain people must be persuaded to be for it rather than against it. Such are not the terms of reality. People of faith in the vast majority favor economic justice as an abstraction, even as they can almost never agree about what it is or how to achieve it. The Almighty may create well enough *ex nihilo*, but mere mortals require data, especially when it comes to economics!

If abstraction is the Scylla of an adequate hermeneutic of prophetic economics, particularism is the Charybdis. Under the impress of the extreme individualism of American culture, many modern readers of the prophetic books assume that these texts excoriate a few venal individuals who deviated from norms otherwise observed in what was a healthy and just economic system.

Once again, little could be farther from the realities of ancient Israel and Judah. As a careful reading of the oracles concerning economic dynamics makes clear, the prophets critique certain changes in the political economy as an integrated whole. While these changes benefited the powerful and privileged few who initiated them *as a generic class*, the prophets insist that they did so at the expense of even meager subsistence for the impoverished majority, who are also understood *as a generic class*.

Dozens of oracles in the eighth-century prophets declare the judgment of Yahweh's court against the former because of their oppression of the latter. Although these texts allude to various aspects of the economic dynamics involved, they nowhere describe them in full. All parties to the ancient conflict were familiar with the operations of their economy—even though they valued them quite differently—and thus did not require that they be rehearsed. Modern readers of the prophets share no such preunderstanding, a fact that occasions this preliminary attempt to reconstruct those systemic dynamics for those not particpant in them.

Detailed exegesis of the pertinent prophetic texts would require a book far exceeding the bounds of this paper. Attention here will be focused instead on integrating data from disparate sources outside the prophetic books. Against the background thus sketched, it is hoped, many of the more obvious oracles will become self-explanatory.

My address to this task marks a return to matters previously treated far too briefly. In a paper first presented in December of 1981, I wrote as follows regarding the eighth century BCE:

> For historical reasons . . . most freeholding peasants in Israel and Judah were located in the highlands. As many small, subsistence plots in this hill country were foreclosed upon and joined together to form large estates, a change in the method of tillage also took place. Upland fields previously intercropped to provide a mixed subsistence for peasant families were combined into large and "efficient" vineyards and olive orchards producing a single crop for market. The increased production of wine and oil resulting from the formation of these plantations or latifundia played at least two roles in the new scheme of things. On the one hand, wine and oil were central to the increasingly

consumptive lifestyle of the local elite, epitomized in a sodality called the *marzēaḥ*. On the other, since wine and oil were more valuable than most agricultural commodities per unit of weight or volume, they made ideal exports to exchange for the luxury and strategic imports coveted by members of the ruling classes.

But the "efficiency" of these cash crops came at a brutal cost to the sufficiency of the livelihood which they afforded the peasants who actually produced them. The old system of freehold had provided this peasant majority secure access to a modest but adequate and integrated living. The new system saw them labor in the same fields, but only according to the cyclical demands of viticulture and orcharding and at wages for day-labor depressed by a sustained buyer's market. During lulls in the agricultural calendar, they were as unemployed as landless. Jobless or not, they were forced into the marketplace of which they had little or no experience to buy wheat and barley, the staples of their diet. They had previously produced these cereals sufficiently for themselves in their hillside plots, but now the same grains were grown "efficiently" on the large estates of the alluvial plains and piedmont region and shipped to market. In the marketplace, the meager and irregular wages of fieldhands bought even less sustenance than they should have because the vulnerable peasants were cheated with adulterated grain and dishonest weights and measures. Finally, the processes of foreclosure and expropriation which initiated these dynamics were accelerated by a wholesale suborning of the courts. Instead of stopping foreclosures based upon illegal forms of interest, these corrupted courts sanctioned the proceedings. (Chaney 1986:72–73; on the *marzēaḥ* in paragraph one of this quotation, see Coote 1981:36–39)

Although few today would accept without considerable nuance so bald a sketch of these dynamics as this offered in 1981 under the pressures of space and time, a remarkable diversity of scholars has since documented in greater detail many of the factors whose integration I sought then under a concept of latifundialization. The following attempt to delineate those factors necessarily moves seriatim, but its intent is to explore their systemic integration.

The political and military power and territorial expansion of Israel and Judah in the eighth century BCE—particularly during the long and mostly concurrent reigns of Jeroboam II and Uzziah—are beyond doubt. "By the mid-eighth century the dimensions of Israel and Judah together lacked but little of being as great as those of the empire of Solomon" (Bright 1981:258).

The particulars are well documented elsewhere (ibid., 255–59; Yeivin 1979; Aharoni 1982:251–54), and need not detain us here.

I would only highlight briefly two elements in this geopolitical situation. 1) Not since the "United Monarchy" of David and Solomon had Israel and Judah been so secure from immediate, external, military threat. This relative security, coupled with the lengthy tenure in office of both the allied kings, granted a greater than usual opportunity for royal administrations to rearrange their domestic furniture, including that of their economies. The accession of Tiglath-pileser III to the Assyrian throne in 745 BCE may serve conveniently to symbolize the closing of that window of opportunity. 2) That Jeroboam II and Uzziah had incentive, as well as opportunity, to effect change in the economies of their nations is suggested by the evidence for their active participation in international trade.

As David C. Hopkins recognizes, "the expansion of borders not only meant an increase in sources of income and produce for import/export trade, but also could lead, given propitious geopolitical conditions, to an expansion of transit trade" (Hopkins 1983:195). Morris Silver offers a concise, if maximalist, summary of the evidence for such propitious geopolitical conditions in eighth-century Israel and Judah (Silver 1983:49–52). Contra Silver, however, M. Elat is surely correct when he writes of this transit trade that "while it produced profits for the royal court and raised the standard of living of those close to it, it had only a limited influence on the local economy or on the occupational distribution of the country's inhabitants" (Elat 1979:186; cf. Lenski and Lenski 1987:183–85; and Hopkins 1983:195).

It was the import/export trade which heavily impacted the peasant majorities in Israel and Judah and tempted their rulers to become involved in changing the priorities, methods, and distribution of agricultural production. After a penetrating synopsis of the relevant data, Hopkins reaches the widely shared conclusion that "this literary, epigraphic, and artifactual evidence converges on oil, wine, and wheat as the commodities of choice in the monarchic economic network" (Hopkins 1983:196; cf. Silver 1983:24; and Lang 1983:123).

These commodities were exported mainly to and through the kingdom of Tyre (Elat 1979:225–28), a maritime society whose seaborne transportation was cheaper than the overland modes utilized of necessity by the transit trade in Israel and Judah (Lenski and Lenski 1987:216–19). This differential in transportation costs goes far to explain why a large proportion of Phoenicians could earn their living from transit trade, while most Israelites and Judahites could not. In return for their export of oil, wheat, and wine, Israel and Judah received luxury goods and military *matériel*. That such was the nature of the trade between Israel and Tyre can now be documented archaeologically as well as from written records, it would appear (Geva 1982:69–72).

The interface between this configuration of international trade and the pattern of social stratification in Israel and Judah is significant. Foodstuffs produced by the peasant majority were exported. Luxury goods and arms utilized by the elite minority were imported. While agricultural intensification probably raised the absolute amount of edible commodities produced, there were very finite limits to that increase, and exports competed directly with peasant sustenance. For all its erudition, Silver's "supply-side" analysis of the situation never comes to grips with these simple facts (Silver 1983:passim).

Faced with a finite supply of exportable commodities but possessed of an almost infinite appetite for imported luxuries, the elites in Israel and Judah had a powerful incentive to increase production of the three major export crops. One method used to gain this increase was a regional specialization of agriculture. At the Annual Meeting of the Society of Biblical Literature in 1981, Anson Rainey and I independently noted that 2 Chr 26:10—translated according to the known facts of Hebrew syntax and economic geography—records that Uzziah undertook just this process (Rainey 1982:58; Chaney 1986:73–74; Hopkins 1983:200).

> He built guard towers in the Steppe and hewed out many cisterns, for he had large herds; and in the Shephelah and in the Plain (he had) plowmen; and vineyard and orchard workers in the Hills and in the Carmel . . .

Here we learn that under royal tutelage, herding was increased in the steppe by means of guard towers and cisterns, plowing—the cultivation of cereal crops, the predominant of which was wheat—was intensified in the plain and piedmont region, and viticulture and orcharding were pressed in the uplands. In each case, the economic exploitation of a given region was specialized to the one or two products by whose production that region could contribute maximally to the export trade and/or to the conspicuous consumption of the local elite. Rainey has analyzed in some detail the exact nature and location of these districts in Judah (Rainey 1982:58–59).

Nor need this one verse in the Chronicler bear the whole burden of historical reconstruction. In light of the clarification of the stratigraphy at Lachish and taking this verse as a key, Rainey has been able to demonstrate that the much-discussed *lmlk* seal impressions from Judah witness a system of royal vineyards towards the end of the eighth century BCE (Rainey 1982:57–61). Farther north, the Samaria ostraca—despite all the controversies surrounding their exact dating and interpretation—"evidence the flow of oil and wine probably to officials of the royal court" (Hopkins 1983:199) sometime during the eighth century BCE. Perhaps the easiest reading of these documents is occasioned by the assumption that the existence of both private and royal vineyards and olive orchards is reflected therein (Premnath 1984:60–62). An ostracon from Tell Qasileh probably witnesses the export of oil in about this period (Silver 1983:17; Avigad 1979:33–34; and Maisler [Mazar] 1950:208–10). And epigraphic finds continue. Excavations in the City of David in 1978 produced a large stone plaque fragment from the latter part of the eighth century which may well refer to royal stores, either of grain or of treasure articles (Silver 1983:36–37; and Shiloh 1979:170).

Anepigraphic archaeology, too, provides further evidence, particularly on the processing of olive oil. While rock-cut olive and grape processing installations are probably almost as old as agriculture itself in Palestine, recent surveys suggest a proliferation of and innovation in such installations in the eighth century BCE (Eitam 1979:146–54). Of special interest is the evidence for use of the beam press to extract more oil from the olives. The earliest such press found is apparently from the ninth century BCE (Stager and Wolff 1981:95–102; and Stager 1983:244), but the device appears to have come into widespread use in the eighth century (Eitam 1979:146–54). As already indicated, the export trade was thirsty for every drop of olive oil it could get. Such intensification of the extraction process, in turn, probably led to different grades of oil. The finest resulted from crushing the olives and using water to extract the oil without presses. Subsequent processing of the pulp and the use of presses often introduced impurities into the oil and reduced its quality (Stager 1983:241–44). One may reasonably assume that certain of the demands of the export trade tended toward quantity—hence, the beam presses. The tastes of both local and foreign elites, on the other hand, preferred quality, an interpretation which appears to be borne out by the appearance of a term for the finer "washed oil" some dozen times in the Samaria ostraca (ibid.:241–45).

If the processing installations for oil and wine give little hint of who initiated their proliferation, 2 Chr 26:10, when corroborated by the inscriptional evidence for royal vineyards and olive orchards, strongly suggests elements of a "command economy" (Chaney 1986:74; Hopkins 1983:193 and 200 n71; Premnath 1984:56). Hopkins writes appositely, "the centralizing structure of the monarchy and its characteristic institutions bring about an attenuation of the decisionmaking functions of the primary productive units, perhaps a complete usurpation, in the creation of what has been called a 'command economy'" (Hopkins 1983:193). More than one distinguished social scientist has maintained that such "command economies" are characteristic of advanced agrarian societies as a generic class (Lenski and

Lenski 1987:183–85; Heilbronner 1975:7–46). Both the comparative data upon which these scholars base their general theories and the specific data adduced for ancient Judah and Israel should give pause to anyone inclined to follow Silver in his positing of largely private, free market economies in eighth-century Israel and Judah (Silver 1983:passim).

Even Silver agrees that many of the dynamics already discussed combined to consolidate more and more of the arable land into fewer and fewer hands (Silver 1983:73–77, 259–63). Once again, Hopkins has stated the matter with precision: "Besides demands to pay for its costs and the possibility of the loss of labor to the royal projects, the monarchical program of agricultural intensification cut into village-based agricultural systems most directly by its pursit of land" (Hopkins 1983:200; cf. Chaney 1986:72–73; and Dearman 1984:389–91).

The land consolidation reflected in the eighth-century prophets had historical roots. Prior to the founding of the Davidic state, Israel's secure holdings were concentrated in the hill country. "Landholdings in the hills were small in comparison with those in the plains" (Stager 1985:24), a pattern similar to that found in Leon Marfoe in southern Syria (Marfoe 1979:21–23). In premonarchic Israel, these small, hill country holdings typically supported a mixed, subsistence agriculture (Chaney 1983:50, 64–65).

This configuration changed with David.

> David not only defeated the Philistines, restricting them to their pentapolis and laying solid Israelite claim to the alluvial plains of Canaan for the first time, but succeeded in subjugating his neighbors on all sides. In that process of empire building, he incurred debts. His military retainers, many loyal to his person since his days as a social bandit, expected to be rewarded when he came into his glory. He had conquered an empire, and its administration necessitated the creation and importation of bureaucrats. In an agrarian context, these categories of obligation were payable in grants of land, that is, in patrimonial and prebendal estates.
>
> But what land did David have to grant? Certainly not most of the hill country, which supported his core constituency as peasant freehold. (The forces which led to the formation of the monarchy had produced some larger estates in the hill country [cf., e.g., 1 Sam 22:6–8], but these were as modest in number and importance as the military professionals whom they supported). But the richer plains had never been a secure part of premonarchic Israel, and were David's to grant by right of conquest. Accustomed to the typical agrarian combination of

patrimonial and prebendal domain, the estates of the lowlands simply received new overlords, in this case, newly created Israelite aristocrats and bureaucrats. (Chaney 1986:67–68; cf. Alt 1959:348–72; on the larger estates in the hill country supporting military professionals, see Halpern 1981:86–87 and passim; Ben-Barak 1981:73–91)

If this analysis is correct, the ruling elites of Israel had enjoyed primary control of the "breadbasket" areas of the plains long before the agricultural intensification of the eighth century BCE. For them to have implemented on their large, lowland estates measures designed to maximize the production of wheat would have been a relatively simple matter. But what of the hill country? If much of it remained in small plots, tilled by their holders according to the priorities of the village community, such a system would have constituted a major impediment to the goals of the city-based elite.

As already indicated, urban elites in Israel and Judah sought the maximally efficient production of wheat, oil, and wine for export and for their own consumption. Hill country peasants, left to their own devices in a village, would have sought to guaranteee the sufficiency of their livelihood by spreading the risks inherent in it as much as possible. "The crucial objective of village-based agriculture dictates the spreading of risk. The concentration of risk in a costly investment runs directly counter to this security-conscious objective" (Hopkins 1983:201).

While direct evidence is sparse, a combination of indirect evidence and broad-based comparisons allows the following sketch of risk spreading in Israelite upland agriculture to be offered with considerable confidence. Fields that produced cereals were not so used every year. To maintain fertility, they were periodically fallowed and probably also sown to legumes in at least some rotations. (Oded Borowski has collected the evidence from the Hebrew Bible and from archaeological remains for the cultivation of leguminous crops in ancient Israel [1987:93–97].) As well as returning nitrogen to the soil, these pulses would have been a significant source of protein in the diet. Fallow fields would have supplemented uncultivable grazing land in providing pasture for the herding of sheep, goats, and cattle—in varying numbers and proportions. For subsistence farmers, such herding provided "a hedge against the risk of purely agricultural pursuits" (Hopkins 1983:191).

Animals so raised constituted a "disaster bank on the hoof," which stored surpluses from good years to be drawn on in lean years. Their manure helped to fertilize the fallow fields where they grazed, though not so efficiently as if it had been composted. Herding also made use of labor in the village—the very young and the very old—which would not otherwise have been productive. Tree and vine crops would have rounded out the repertoire of village agriculture in the hills. Their labor demands were complementary to those of cereals, and their processed fruit could be stored stably for extended periods, making them valable contributors to the goal of spreading risk.

The demand or encouragement by the urban elite that only oil, wheat, and wine be produced and in ever increasing quanitites

> ran counter to the village's objective of spreading risk and optimizing labor through a diversity of subsistence means. Assuming a limitation on labor and land, a relative increase of production of these commodities meant a relative decrease in the production of others. The absolute increase in production if the agricultural village were to contribute a share of its produce to the state and also maintain its level of subsistence necessitated, at least along one likely pathway, an expansion of the percentage of village land given over to cultivation of the preferred commodities at the expense of grazing lands. Sheep and goats which were integral to the risk- and labor-spreading agriculture of the village were not integral to the taxation apparatus, and were pushed out of the village system. (Hopkins 1983:197).

When linked with the evidence in 2 Chr 26:10 for royal herding in the steppe, such considerations weigh heavily against Silver's statement that "it is not unreasonable to assume that land consolidation facilitated a transition from grain to stock farming to take advantage of the emergence of an affluent, meat-producing Israelite public" (Silver 1983:97–98). For reasons that are becoming increasingly apparent, we can hardly assume that the Israelite public at large was affluent. Lands in Judah that could support at least seasonal grazing but were too arid to be cultivable were scarcely sufficient to supply meat on a regular basis to the general public. All land that was cultivable was increasingly being pressed into producing one of the three preferred export crops.

A far more probably scenario would see animals headed for the tables of a few privileged urbanites pastured in the steppe during the wet season and then stall-fed in preparation for slaughter. Such stall-feeding would also have facilitated the collection and composting of manure, which in turn would have been in demand for fertility maintenance in the more intensively cropped fields. Lucian Turkowski, at least, reports just such a use of manure in the Judean hills when agriculture was intensified there in the last century: "From the nineteenth century new systems of increased agriculture spread to the Judean hills. This demanded that no part of the land should be left unproductive. The part formerly left fallow was now fertilized with manure..." (Turkowski 1969:24).

With the fallow went a significant part of village grazing land and its ability to sustain a "disaster bank on the hoof." In its place came hand weeding of cereal fields to provide fodder for stall-fed animals (ibid.:101). When this fodder proved insufficient to fatten the delicacies of the rich, precious cereals may well have been used. As Marvin Harris concedes, "it is true that the cost-benefits of intensification are not the same for peasants or workers as for members of the ruling class" (Harris 1979:103).

As part of this eighth-century intensification of agriculture in the hill country of Israel and Judah, multi-purpose land that had helped to spread risk was gradually converted into terraces growing vineyards and olive trees (Hopkins 1983:200; Edelstein and Kislev 1981:53–56). While elite demands on their production tended to be steady or to increase, that production itself was subject to the vicissitudes of the environment and, in the case of the olive, to a pattern of alternating yields (Hopkins 1983:197). Gone was the "inefficient" diversification that had spread the risk of such fluctuations in the past. Hopkins characterizes the changes and their implications as follows:

> A system-wide increase in crop specialization brings an increase in short-term production and efficiency, but also lowers resistance to catastrophe. The former relative self-sufficiency of the agricultural village gives way increasingly to a dependence upon the centralizing forces and the exchange network that they administer. Constant coordination and direction must emanate from this center, lest the whole structure collapse.
> ... The period [the eighth century] triggered a sharp jump of the needle that monitors movements on the continuum between autonomous village-based agriculture and an economy dominated by the central state. (ibid.:201)

Although quantitative data are difficult to secure, there is probably a high correlation generally in agrarian societies between such dynamics, on the one hand, and political stability, territorial expansion, growing import/export trade, and royal construction, on the other (ibid.)

These latter same factors are also correlated with an increase in what is sometimes called "rent capitalism" (Lang 1983a:167 n218). In such a system, not only are ownership of the land and labor separated (ibid.:118), but each of the factors of agricultural production is segmented from the others and subjected to separate rent (Wolf 1966:55–56; Coote 1981:29–32). While rural residence of the wealthy favors a multi-stranded patron-client relatioship with poor cultivators, a single-stranded relationship of economic exploitation is most often the result when the elite are urban-based (Lang 1983a:118–19). "This estrangement is favoured by the landlord's urban residence ('absentee landlordism') as well as by the situation of the upper classes which provides both for social prestige and political influence independent of any clientele support" (ibid.:119).

Inducements for rich landlords to live in the city include import trade in luxury items. "As soon as the market is able to provide luxury goods and gives rise to a corresponding urban life-style ... [,] then exploitation may be a consequence" (ibid.).

Under such circumstances, the contrast between the splendor of the cities and the misery of the countryside is stark and "can hardly be exaggerated" (ibid.:120). Recent studies indicate that this configuration characterized Neo-Assyrian society:

> Even under Esarhaddon more revenue was produced from internal provinces than was collected through conquest. Regardless of the wealth of the empire, the economic conditions of the peasant in the countryside never improved, but if anything became worse as the empire expanded. The question was not one of the supply of goods and services but of the demand of a central administration which claimed the right to acquire and redistribute them. (Dearman 1984:393-94; cf. Postgate 1974; and van Driel 1970)

While Israel and Judah were not empires in the sense that Assyria was, every other indication points to similar dynamics there in the eighth century BCE.

Such a system pressed the typical peasant cultivator hard even in good years, because there was incentive for the elite to extract every possible surplus, leaving only the barest subsistence necessary to continue production. In less than optimal years cultivators stripped of the insurance of diversification were forced to take out survival-loans. The social systems supported by diversified, subsistence agriculture had most probably included mutual obligations of interest-free survival loans within certain village and/or kinship groupings (Lang 1983a:120; Critchfield 1983:345). But the intensified system saw the only funds available increasingly in the hands of wealthy moneylenders bent onbecoming wealthier. "Taking a loan almost automatically leads to long-term or even permanent dependence because of the high interest rates ..." (Lang 1983a:117). In many cases, a cycle of encumbered harvests was created, each pledged to repay debts incurred in the prior porcurement of the factors of its production. Usurious interst rates—coupled with the nadir of the annual cycle of agricultural commodity values at harvesttime, when the debt contracts came due—insured the need for further, even larger loans. Foreclosure on collateral at the discretion of the lender often become a sword of Damocles hanging over the indebted peasant.

For historical reasons detailed above, the lowlands of Israel and Judah had, for the most part, probably been organized into large estates long before the eighth century BCE. Many cultivators there would have been landless tenants, most vulnerable to the dynamics of "rent capitalism." With intensified demand for wheat in the eighth century, these tenants would have been pressed even harder, leading to an increase in all forms of debt incurred for survival reasons, and producing growing numbers of debt-slaves.

The situation in the hill country had been different. Royal vineyards and olive orchards no doubt existed there from the emergence of the monarchy, but in much of the upland a tradition of small freeholders, working their own land in mixed subsistence, had struck deep root. But as seen above, each of the particulars of that system was under pressure to change in the eighth century. Urban elites could structure state taxation to induce, perhaps even force, increased production of oil and wine, with all the attendant losses in the spreading of risk. Bad years began to bring the necessity of loans from the rent capitalists of the cities, with upland plots offered as collateral.

Although the evidence is spotty and difficult and the secondary literature far too voluminous and controverted to be reviewed here, it seems likely that not all hill country plots were equally alienable. Those planted to vines and orchards were probably most often held in perpetuity by a given family, since such intensive cultivation of perennials takes many years to come to full fruition, and few cultivators will make such improvements on land that is periodically redistributed (Chaney 1983:50, 64–65). Evidence from later periods in Palestine (Turkowski 1969:23–32), as well as various comparisons and allusions (Chaney 1983:50, 64–65), combines to suggest that fields used to grow cereals were often held in common by the village as a whole and periodically reapportioned by lot to individual families.

It appears probable that the vineyards and olive orchards may have been the first lands to slip into the hands of the urban elites. They already controlled most of the best grain fields in the lowlands, and would at first have been primarily interested in oil and wine from the hills. Since vineyards and orchards "belonged" to individual families, they would have been less complicated to offer as collateral, even if they could not be sold outright. (First Kings 21 remains easiest to interpret, I believe, on the assumption that Israelite customary law forbade outright sale or trade of such property.) If the grain lands of the village were taxed in common, as evidence from later periods suggests (Turkowski 1969:23), heavy state taxes in kind would both have yielded wheat for the export trade and have supplied villagers a powerful incentive to terrace former grainfields and convert them to vines and trees. As Hopkins writes, "the alienation of land, usually the most productive, decreases the farming household's ability to control a variety of ecological niches and pushes the family, which must somehow provide for its subsistence, onto poorer and poorer lands at greater distances from its village (Hopkins 1983:201).

Unable to grow all their own grain, and in many cases forced off their lands altogether and relegated to agricultural wage labor, former freeholders went, of necessity, to grain traders to procure the staples of their diet.

The mortgaging of and foreclosure upon family lands, members, and property involved court action. While there was a long tradition of consensus justice in the village courts, state officials had long since enjoyed considerable success in limiting and subordinating local judicial functions in the name of the king (Dearman 1983:391-92; Whitelam 1979:passim). Given the priorities of royal policy in the eighth century BCE, there can be little astonishment that such courts did not and could not effectively block land consolidation and its concomitants. The bitterness of those whose dispossession was sanctioned by these courts should occasion even less surprise.

Such a sketch of the dynamics of political economy in eighth-century Israel and Judah can be rendered even more probable by close exegesis of the prophetic texts that both reflect and reflect upon these dynamics. That detailed study must await another occasion, as must any attempt to explicate the extended parallels between the world of these prophets and much of the so-called third world today. My only hope is that a slightly firmer foundation has been laid for both enterprises, for they are both intrinsic to any full dialogue between the Reformed faith and economics.

8

Whose Sour Grapes?

The Addressees of Isaiah 5:1–7 in the Light of Political Economy

Abstract

When the "Song of the Vineyard" is read in the context of the rapid agricultural intensification of Judah and Israel in the eighth century BCE—involving consolidation of small, subsistence plots into larger, market-oriented vineyards—previous interpretations of the pericope are rendered improbable. From Isaiah's perspective, the peasant majorities of Israel and Judah were the victims of viticultural injury, not its perpetrators. The vocatives and identifications of vv. 3 and 7 refer only to the top of the social pyramid in Israel and Judah. Social-scientific analysis of political economy in Isaiah's time, examination of other Isaianic oracles involving vineyards, genre analysis of the juridical parable, and lexicographical analysis of the terms designating the addressees of this particular parable all point independently to the same conclusion. Those trapped into self-condemnation by the parable were the ruling elites of Judah and Israel, led by the two dynastic houses, not the general populations of Jerusalem, Judah, and Israel.

∽

INTRODUCTION

Social-scientific methods and perspectives have contributed to the study of the Hebrew Bible in a variety of ways. In certain instances, wholly new questions have been asked. New universes of discourse are now at least in prospect as a result. In other cases, social-scientific perspectives prompt a fresh address to issues or problems already well-ensconced in the history of interpretation. The following essay falls into the latter category. For the most part, it uses methodological tools long standard in the workshop of historical-critical exegesis. What is new—and social scientific—is its attention to how radically readers' presuppositions about agrarian political economy condition the import of the literary unit in question.

Despite their disagreement about much else, previous interpretations of Isaiah's "Song of the Vineyard" seem all to have shared two presuppositions.[1] Mostly at a tacit level, they have assumed that the extended imagery of the vineyard refers to artifacts and activities that were routine in the experience of the ancient audience and thus of neutral valence in the rhetorical sensibilities of that audience. More explicitly, exegetes have argued that the יושב ירושלם and איש יהודה of v. 3 and בית ישראל and יהודה איש of v. 7, though all singular morphologically, are to be understood as collectives referring indiscriminately to the populations of Jerusalem, Judah, and Israel.

When this pericope is read in light of the rapid agricultural intensification of Judah and Israel in the eighth century BCE—a dynamic elsewhere witnessed by all four eighth-century prophets—both these assumptions are rendered improbable. The goals of this paper, then, are the demonstration of that improbability and the suggestion of alternate understandings that better accord with what is known or knowable.

"VINEYARD": A FIGHTING WORD

We may begin with the presumption that the preparation and cultivation of a new vineyard was a neutral topic in Isaiah's context. In this regard, Yehoshua Gitay's injunction is well repeated here, even if he himself fails to heed it fully:

> [W]e need to search for the condition, the polemic background against which the song has been recited. In this respect, it should be noted that a parable, a story, may be commonly known,

---

1. This analysis proceeds on the assumption that "Isaiah of Jerusalem" composed Isa 5:1–7. For a brief discussion of how subsequent levels of composition affected the reading of this unit, see the last paragraph.

but it must still be applied to a particular social moment . . .
[T]he point is to try to reconstruct the condition, the argumentative or rhetorical situation which caused the use of the parable. (1991:93–94)

Even a cursory look at the dynamics of political economy in Isaiah's time reveals a "social moment" that was polemical indeed, especially where the expansion of viticulture was concerned.

Strictures of space preclude here all but the briefest epitome of those dynamics of agricultural intensification. I have elsewhere given a somewhat fuller account of my understanding of that process (Chaney 1989a, 1993), an account that sought to integrate insights from a number of sources and perspectives (Chaney 1986; Coote 1981; Dearman 1988; Eitam; Elat; Geva; Hopkins 1983; Lang 1993a; Premnath 1984, 1988; Rainey 1982; Silver; Stager 1983, 1985). While individual details remain unclear or disputed, more recent studies (Broshi and Finkelstein; Herr; J. S. Holladay; Hopkins, 1996) have tended to confirm and nuance the salient features of the following sketch.

Eighth-century Israel and Judah saw an increase in international trade, in which their leaders imported luxury goods, military *matériel*, and the wherewithal of monumental architecture. To pay for these imports, foodstuffs—particularly the triad of wheat, olive oil, and wine—were exported. Imports mostly benefited an elite minority, while the exports necessary to procure them cut deeply into the sustenance of the peasant majority. Urban elites, whose priorities called for the maximally efficient production of the three preferred export commodities over the short term, pressed for a regional specialization of agriculture. Villagers' traditional priorities for the long-term sufficiency of mixed, subsistence agriculture and its penchant for risk spreading were overwhelmed by these pressures, and land consolidation proceeded apace. Not only were agricultural labor and land ownership increasingly separated, but the various other factors of production were segmented and each subjected to separate rent. Absentee landlordism proliferated. Many peasants were left no alternative to survival loans at de facto interest rates usurious by any standards. Foreclosure upon family land and family members pledged as collateral was often at the discretion of the creditor. The courts of law called upon to process such foreclosure proceedings came increasingly under the control of the urban elites who had initiated the agricultural intensification. These courts gave a façade of legality to foreclosures regarded as illegal by most peasants and their prophetic defenders. The prophets declared that actions by Yahweh's court of last resort had vindicated the poor peasants' cause and had found the urban elites guilty regarding the matters under adjudication.

Not all parts of the country were equally affected by these dynamics. The land best suited to wheat lay in the plains and the Shephelah, where most of it had long since been garnered into the large estates of the wealthiest and most powerful landlords. The conflict over agricultural priorities, techniques, and land took place primarily in the hill country, where the villagers' preferences for the sustainability and sufficiency of mixed, subsistence cropping constituted a major impediment to the urban elites' desire for the "efficient" production of ever greater quantities of wine and oil.

The conflict within the political economy of upland agriculture was not fought on equal terms. As noted above, survival loans with hill-country peasants' plots pledged as collateral gave urban elites a powerful tool to consolidate into their own hands lands from which they desired oil and wine, not mixed subsistence. This same small but powerful class also controlled state policies, including those of taxation. To further several of their goals at once, all they had to do was levy a heavy tax upon grain produced "inefficiently" by the subsistence farmers of the hill country. In the short term, such a tax secured them one of their three preferred commodities. But in the longer run, it also gave powerful incentive to convert into vineyards and olive orchards what had previously been multipurpose land. This conversion accomplished the increased production of wine and oil desired by the elite, both for domestic conspicuous consumption and for export. In the process, of course, many previously freeholding villagers lost their land and were ruined. Amos 5:11 most probably reflects this process and its causal linkages in its indictment and futility curses:

> Therefore, because you impose cereal tax[2] upon the poor one,
>   and exactions of grain you take from him,
> you have built houses of hewn stone,
>   but you shall not live in them;
> you have planted delightful vineyards,
>   but you shall not drink their wine.

Nor is archaeological evidence lacking for the intensification of wine and oil production in the hills. While rock-cut olive and grape processing

---

2. This translation of the *hapax legomenon*, בשׁס, is supported both by the parallel line and by a probable Akkadian cognate, *šabāšu/šabāsu*, as seen already by Harry Torczyner (6–7). Numerous commentators, translators, and lexicographers have since adopted this reading (Paul 1991:172–73). Whether or not the Hebrew term here involves a wordplay on בוס, "tread down, trample," must remain a matter of conjecture, though the suggestion is thoroughly plausible.

installations are probably almost as old as agriculture itself in Palestine, archaeological surveys (Eitam 1979; Dar 1986:147–90; Campbell 1991:109–12) suggest a proliferation of and innovation in such installations in the eighth century BCE. Some ancient terracing can probably also be traced to this time (Edelstein and Kislev), though such installations are notoriously difficult to date with certainty. Anson F. Rainey argues strongly that the much-discussed *lmlk* seal impressions from Judah witness a system of royal vineyards toward the end of the eighth century. Farther north, the Samaria ostraca—despite all the controversies surrounding their exact dating and interpretation—"evidence the flow of oil and wine probably to officials of the royal court" (Premnath 1984:62) sometime during that same century. A survey of west Samaria by Shimon Dar reports, not only the founding of new villages on virgin sites in Iron II, but the presence in and near them of wine and oil processing installations. While the best exemplars date from later periods, massive and well-constructed "towers" are frequently associated with these installations. Dar traces the antecedents of these towers to Iron II and interprets them as centers for the fermentation and storage of wine. Only wine's need for darkness and moderately low, constant temperatures, he argues, can explain the unique features of these "towers," whose construction required an enormous expenditure of labor.[3] If one joins its excavators (Aharoni 1993) in identifying Ramat Raḥel with biblical Beth-HaKerem, this "house of the vineyard" was founded, probably in the eighth century BCE, as a royal stronghold surrounded by vineyards, gardens, and farmhouses.

Taken as a whole and in context, such evidence implies more than a simple boom in viticulture in Isaiah's time. The vineyards being constructed and planted by the processes described in Isa 5:2 were at the vortex of a battle that convulsed Judahite and Israelite society. To the urban elite who had them built on the lands recently acquired by the processes sketched above, these vineyards were the proud symbols of economic progress and prosperity. To the peasants whose subsistence plots had been expropriated and combined to yield the sites for these new vineyards, matters looked different. The injustice of their loss of hereditary lands and livelihood was aggravated by a cruel irony—many now worked land that had been in their families for generations, but they worked it as landless day-laborers. That gnawing memory could only add to the bitterness of wages below

---

3. Walsh (1998:49) has recently reiterated a more general interpretation of "field towers" as providing security against intruders and pests. While only a few Iron Age "field towers" have been found (ibid.), they might not all have shared the same function. Some may be interpreted plausibly as defensive structures, but Dar reasons that the placement and construction of others preclude security as their main purpose.

subsistence for the backbreaking labor of vineyard construction. In such a context, "vineyard" was not a neutral word, nor was Isaiah's choice of material for his parable a bucolic happenstance.

Analysis of the sharp conflict provoked by the terms and conditions of this vineyard construction also calls into severe question the assumption that Isaiah's parable condemns indiscriminately the entire populations of Jerusalem, Judah, and Israel. Only a tiny percentage of those populations initiated, benefited from, and favored the process, but they held the reins of power. The vast majority were the victims of a process they hated, not its perpetrators, but the workings of political economy rendered them helpless to ameliorate their own plight. Under those circumstances, one would expect a prophetic parable about a vineyard to condemn those responsible for the process, not to blame its victims.

VICTIMS AND PERPETRATORS ELSEWHERE IN ISAIAH

But we need not speculate. Other Isaianic texts in the immediate literary and historical context make the matter clear. If the consonantal text of Isa 3:12 is read according to most of the ancient versions and a growing consensus of modern commentators and translators (Kaiser 1983:74–78; Wildberger 1991:137–39; NJB; NEB), Isa 3:12–15 yields the following:

> My people—every one of their exactors is a gleaner,
>   and creditors rule over them.
> My people, your leaders mislead you,
>   and the course of your paths they confuse.
> Yahweh has taken his stand to litigate;
>   he stands to vindicate his people.[4]
> Yahweh comes in judgment
>   against the elders of his people and their officials.
> "It is you who devour the vineyard;
>   the spoil of the poor is in your houses!
> What do you mean by crushing my people,
>   by grinding the face of the poor?"

---

4. I read עמו ("his people") with LXX and Syr for MT's עמים ("the peoples"). MT represents a later orientation to Israel among the nations. Here the focus is on Yahweh's people as the poor whose vineyards are expropriated. For לדין עמו as "to vindicate his people," see the clear contexts in Deut 32:36; Pss 50:4; and 135:14.

As is widely recognized, other elements of the same process are evinced by the "woe oracle" immediately following the parable of the vineyard in Isa 5:8–10.

> Alas for those who join house to house,
>> who add field to field,
>
> until there is no place left,
>> and you are made to dwell alone in the midst of the land!
>
> Yahweh of Hosts in my hearing:
> "I swear that the great houses shall be desolate,
>> large and fine ones without lordly inhabitant!
>
> For ten acres of vineyard shall produce but one bath,
>> and a homer of seed shall produce only an ephah!"

Commentators frequently remark upon the land consolidation reflected in v. 8 and its similarity to the concerns expressed in Mic 2:2. The niceties of the "futility curses" in v. 10 have received less attention, though they are germane to the issues under discussion. The word translated "acre" is צמד, which means literally "yoke" or "span." By extension, it also signifies the amount of land a plowman can plow in a day with a yoked team of traction animals (BDB: 855; HALAT: 967). Like its counterparts in the native languages of many other traditional agrarian societies, it is basically a unit of peasant labor, not a mathematically exact quantity of land treated as a commercial entity. In Isaiah's carefully crafted language, however, the futilely low yield of formerly subsistence land now planted to vineyard is expressed in terms of a wine amphora of standardized capacity, designed to facilitate trade in wine as a commodity. Archaeology has now recovered several exemplars of this royally standardized eighth-century amphora inscribed with either בת or בת למלך (Avigad 1953; Inge; Mittmann; Naveh). Isaiah's parallel line continues the contrast between a positive valence for vocabulary rooted in the world of village subsistence and a negative tenor for terms that epitomize the innovations pressed by the urban elite in their program of agricultural intensification. The חמר is an "ass-load," an inexact measurement pertinent to the work realities of peasants (HALAT: 317). The איפה, approximately one tenth of a חמר, is the dry measure equivalent of the בת (BDB: 35; HALAT: 41), and like it, is a standardized unit intended to expedite commercial transactions—this time, in grain. As is so often the case with prophetic language, Isaiah's words have both a concretely precise denotation and emotionally charged connotations that assist rhetorically in driving home the judgment rendered.

Neither Isa 3:12–15 nor Isa 5:8–10 leaves any doubt about the identity of those guilty of crimes concerning vineyards. Even John H. Hayes and Stuart A. Irvine, who prefer to read the vast majority of Isaiah as addressing matters of international politics, see the obvious implications. Apropos Isa 5:8 they write:

> The verse appears to denounce those whose ambition is to acquire property, house after house and field after field, "until there is no more space and you (pl.) dwell alone in the midst of the land." If the people being condemned here are the same as those in 3:14–15, then Isaiah is denouncing the government officials and social leaders who, through money-lending, land foreclosures, and their status as political administrators, are amassing enormous wealth from the peasant and small land-owning classes. (1987:103)

If both these passages clearly castigate the ruling classes for their aggressive activity in viticulture, how can the parable of the vineyard blame all the people, most of whom are victims? How indeed? Although he does not see how to resolve it, Hans Wildberger feels the incongruity surfaced by this question. He writes: "And yet, one ought to note the ambivalence between 3:14 and 5:7: In the first passage, the leaders of the people are accused of having grazed the vineyard bare; in this verse [5:7], the people themselves must acknowledge that "being grazed bare" is certainly deserved" (1991:185).

FORM-CRITICAL CONSIDERATIONS

A quick glance at the form criticism of Isa 5:1–7 only heightens the incongruity. After the work of John T. Willis, Adrian Graffy, and Gale A. Yee, there can be little doubt that our passage is a juridical parable, the other three unambiguous examples of which in the Hebrew Bible occur in 2 Sam 12:1–14; 14:5–17; and 1 Kgs 20:35–43. As Yee notes repeatedly (1981:33, 35, 36, 37, 39), all instances other than Isaiah's parable of the vineyard concern a royal figure. Nor is the peculiar applicability of this genre to kings difficult to explicate. As quite literally the court of last resort, Judahite and Israelite monarchs were well accustomed to the role of judge. But who could pass judgment on the supreme judge of the land? Given his power, who was foolhardy enough to try? The juridical parable, or, as Graffy (1979:408) prefers, the "self-condemnation parable," addressed both these questions. If justice were poetic enough to fool the king, he could be tricked into self-judgment. Viewed from such a perspective, form criticism corroborates and amplifies the query already raised by our other analyses—can the terms in vv. 3 and 7

168   PEASANTS, PROPHETS, AND POLITICAL ECONOMY

designating the addressees of Isaiah's parable of the vineyard be understood as referring to royal and/or elite figures?

LEXICOGRAPHICAL EVIDENCE

While I believe that lexicography allows an unambiguously affirmative answer to the question thus urged to the fore, I want to be careful not to overstate the evidence. The morphologically singular יושב, איש, and בית can all carry a collective sense, as a glance at any of the full-dress lexica will demonstrate. The terms' collective meanings in certain other passages have allowed to go unchallenged their being so understood in Isaiah's parable. But perusal of the more recent lexica reveals another, equally significant fact—each of the terms in question can and does refer to royal and/or elite figures. The briefest summary of the evidence must suffice here.

That regarding יושב is perhaps the most complicated. A heterogeneous group of distinguished scholars including Albrecht Alt (1941:246), Frank Moore Cross and David Noel Freedman (248–49), Norman K. Gottwald (1979:512–34), and Wilfred G. E. Watson has argued persuasively that יושב not infrequently refers to one who "sits on a throne" or "in judgment," one who "rules," who is "lord," or who "presides in adjudication." It may be added that a formulaic expression utilizing a cognate term in Ugaritic suggests that יושב can also include the sense of "besitting" a major landed estate. The formula (KTU 1.1:3.1; 1.3:6.15–16; 1.4:8.12–14; 1.5:2.15–16) reads, "GN, the throne of his sitting (ksu ṯbt), GN, the land of his ancestral inheritance (arṣ nḥl)." Agrarian political economy makes ready sense of this cluster of meanings. It is precisely the wealthy landlords who occupy thrones of power, where they sit in judgment on their social inferiors. In all of these senses, the king is the יושב par excellence.

A survey of the uses of יושב in the singular in Biblical Hebrew heightens the probability that יושב ירושלים in Isa 5:3 refers to the ruling elite of Jerusalem and/or to the Davidic king. Some 72 of the 178[5] occurrences in the MT must be regarded as singular in meaning because they have a singular subject of the "sitting" expressed as a noun or pronoun.[6] Of these

---

5. This enumeration does not include 2 Sam 23:8, where MT's inclusion of ישב in a personal name apparently involves textual corruption (McCarter 1984:489).

6. The 40 of these occurrences not involving a king are Gen 14:12; 18:1; 19:1; 23:10; 24:3, 37, 62; Exod 18:14; Judg 3:20; 4:2; 10:1; 16:9, 12; 1 Sam 1:9; 4:13; 2 Sam 7:2; 1 Kgs 13:11, 14, 25; 17:19; 2 Kgs 1:9; 2:18; 6:32; Isa 6:5; Jer 29:32; 49:31; Ezek 2:6; 8:1; 12:2; Zech 7:7; Ps 17:12; Prov 3:29; Job 2:8; Esth 2:19, 21; 5:13; 6:10; Ezra 9:4; 1 Chr 5:8; 9:16. Two of these texts (1 Sam 1:9; 4:13) involve Eli's "sitting" upon the "throne" or "seat of honor" (הכסא).

72, 32 witness a king doing the "sitting" or "ruling."⁷ Among the remaining occurrences, another 16 refer to God as "enthroned" upon the cherubim or in other regal postures.⁸ יושב also occurs as an unambiguously singular substantive 15 times.⁹ Nine of these 15 involve a "throne sitter."¹⁰ One of these, Jer 33:17, evidences a significant concatenation of the terms under discussion in the parable of the vineyard: "David shall never lack a man (איש) sitting (ישב) upon the throne of the (dynastic) house of Israel (בית ישראל)." Another 20 occurrences of יושב involve a formula of destruction and/ or desolation that gains rhetorical power from its singularity—"without (even a single) inhabitant" or similar expressions.¹¹

How, then, did the collective sense of the singular form, יושב as "inhabitants," "population," or "people" take its rise? The simplest answer probably lies in some 25 instances where it is immediately associated with a morphologically singular gentilic such as "the dweller of the land, the Canaanite."¹² Nine occurrences of יושב הארץ ("inhabitant[s] of the land/ earth")—or יושב בה, in which ארץ is the antecedent of the suffix—are readily understood as an extension of this usage.¹³ So, too, are one mention each of the "inhabitant(s)" (יושב) of "this coastland" (Isa 20:6), and of the יושב מואב, Jer 48:43; usually translated, "inhabitants of Moab"), if the latter is not to be understood with William L. Holladay (1989:364) as "enthroned Moab." "Tent dweller(s)" (יושב אהלים) (Gen 4:20; 25:27), is only a slight further extension. In a use of ישב that is semantically related but syntactically unique, Isa 49:19 assures a destroyed Zion, "surely now you will be too cramped for (your) inhabitant(s)" (מיושב). Closely related to these uses of singular יושב to designate the "dweller(s), inhabitant(s)," or "population" in a given region or mode of existence is its occurrence with the collective noun, עם ("people"), as its subject, for example, "the people who dwell/ live . . ."¹⁴

7. Exod 11:5; 12:29; Num 21:1, 34; 33:40; Deut 1:4 [2x]; 3:2; 4:46; Josh 12:2, 4; 1 Sam 14:2; 19:9; 22:6; 26:3; 2 Sam 7:2; 9:13; 11:1; 16:3; 18:24; 19:9; 1 Kgs 15:18; Jer 22:2; 29:16; 36:22; 38:7; 40:10; Prov 20:8; Esth 5:1; 1 Chr 17:1; 20:1; 2 Chr 16:2.

8. 1 Sam 4:4; 2 Sam 6:2; 1 Kgs 22:19; 2 Kgs 19:15; Isa 6:1; 37:16; 40:22; Pss 2:4; 9:12; 22:4; 55:20; 80:2; 99:1; 123:1; 1 Chr 13:6; 2 Chr 18:18.

9. In addition to the citations in the following note, Lev 15:6; 1 Sam 30:24; Isa 28:6; Jer 21:9; 38:2; Ps 91:1. Note that Isa 28:6 involves "the one who sits in judgment."

10. 1 Kgs 1:48; 3:6; 8:25; Jer 22:30; 33:17; 36:30; Amos 1:5, 8; 2 Chr 6:16.

11. Isa 5:9; 6:11; Jer 2:15; 4:7, 29; 9:10; 26:9; 33:10; 34:22; 44:2, 22; 46:19; 48:9; 50:3; 51:29, 37, 62; Zeph 2:5; 3:6; Ps 69:26.

12. Gen 13:7; 14:7; 34:30; 50:11; Num 13:29 [3x]; 14:25, 45; Deut 1:44; 11:30; Josh 9:7; 16:10; 17:16; 24:8, 18; Judg 1:9, 10, 17, 21, 29; 3:3; 11:21; 2 Sam 5:6; 1 Kgs 9:16.

13. Exod 34:12, 15: Num 14:14; Isa 24:17; 26:21; Jer 47:2; Ezek 7:7; Hos 4:3; Amos 8:8.

14. Num 13:18, 19 [2x], 28; 22:5; Isa 10:24; 33:24; Jer 29:16.

This enumeration leaves only eight occurrences of יושב in the singular to be accounted for, including Isa 5:3, and all eight, significantly, involve the יושב of a city. יושב דור in Judg 1:27 should probably be emended to יושבי דור on the basis of parallels within the verse, multiple Hebrew manuscripts, the versions, and the *Qere*. (The verse may involve more extensive textual corruption as well.) Norman K. Gottwald has already argued cogently that יושב שמרון in Isa 9:8 should be translated as "the ruling class of Samaria" (1979:515). All other instances involve the יושב ירושלים—usually translated "inhabitants of Jerusalem"—and thus, like Isa 9:8, the יושב of a capital city.

Three of those occurrences of יושב ירושלים appear in Zech 12:7, 8, and 10. While the context is far from certain in a number of particulars, all three verses find יושב ירושלים parallel to בית דוד ("house of David"). In light of the evidence summarized here, emendation of these singulars to the plural, following several Hebrew manuscripts and the versions (Meyers and Meyers 1993:307) is probably not mandated. The more difficult reading, when fully comprehensible and closely paralleled, is to be preferred. The Meyerses are surely on the right track, however, when—following the lead of Gottwald—they translate and interpret the term:

> "Leaders of Jerusalem" is probably an inclusive term for the royal bureaucracy, with its authority extending not just in the city of Jerusalem itself but over all the territory for which Jerusalem is the capital. Thus, although "leaders" is coupled with "Jerusalem," the extent of the leaders' rule goes beyond the capital city. The term applies to the period of monarchic rule before the Exile but not to the exilic and postexilic periods, when kingship and its associated governance structures ceased to exist. Hence the use of "leaders of Jerusalem" and "house of David" in this context involves language of past political organization being projected upon the eschatological future. (323–24)

The usage in Zechariah 12 thus strengthens the conclusion that the יושב of a capital city is probably that city's ruling class of royal officials—absent conclusive contextual evidence to the contrary.

Isaiah 8:14 presents a strikingly similar picture from a literary and historical context much nearer the "Song of the Vineyard." A translation of vv. 12–14 is perhaps the quickest way to convey its significance.

> 12 Do not call conspiracy all that this people calls conspiracy, and what it fears, neither fear nor dread. 13 Yahweh of Hosts, *him* you shall regard as a conspirator;[15] *he* shall be your fear, *he*

---

15. This translation follows many commentators (Kaiser 1983:190; Watts 1985:119; Wildberger 1991:354–58) in reading תקשירו for MT's תקדישו. While this emendation

shall be your dread. 14 For he will become a conspiracy[16] and a tripping rock and a stumbling stone to both (dynastic) houses of Israel (לשני בתי ישראל), a trap and a snare to the ruler(s) of Jerusalem (ליושב ירושלים).

Can there be any real doubt that this passage speaks of dynastic houses and court elites, who routinely engage in conspiracies, and not of the general populace?

Isaiah 22:21 is still more explicit. The context involves a critique of Shebna, the one על-הבית or "official in charge of the royal household" (v. 15), who is declared guilty of great presumption. He is called a disgrace to his master's house and told that he will be pulled down from his post. The narrative continues, beginning in v. 20, with this address to Shebna:

> 20 On that day I will call my servant Eliakim son of Hilkiah, 21 and I will clothe him with your robe, and your sash I will bind on him. Your authority I will commit to his hand, and he shall be a father (לאב) to the ruler of Jerusalem (ליושב ירושלים) and to the (dynastic) house of Judah (לבית יהודה). 22 I will place the key of the house of David (בית דוד) on his shoulder; he shall open, and no one shall shut; he shall shut, and no one shall open.

The context and parallel phrases make clear that the new master of the royal household derives his authority from and owes his allegiance to the Davidic dynast, variously referred to as the ירושלים יושב, the בית יהודה, and the בית דוד. Any lingering doubt can be removed by Gen 45:8, where Joseph, in the capacity of the vizier of Egypt, speaks as follows: "So it was not you who sent me here, but God; he has made me a father (לאב) to Pharaoh, and lord of all his house and ruler over all the land of Egypt." In the parlance of biblical Hebrew, then, the official over the palace is "father" to the king, "lord" of the royal household, and "ruler" to the general populace. The implications for the meaning of יושב ירושלים in Isa 22:21 could scarcely be clearer.

In light of this lexicographical evidence and the issues raised by the preceding discussions of the political economy of viticulture, of literary genre, and of other Isaianic passages regarding vineyards, the phrase יושב ירושלים of Isa 5:3 is far more readily viewed as referring to the ruling dynast and/or ruling classes of Jerusalem than to the city's general population. The plural imperative (שפטו-נא) of v. 3 is no impediment to the most restrictive and

---

perhaps enhances the larger case being made here, the retention of MT's reading in no way impedes it.

16. This translation follows Wildberger (1991:354–56) and Watts (1985:119) in reading מקשר for MT's מקדש.

singular sense of "ruling dynast." It can be understood as deferential address to the monarch. Note the comparable, plural forms addressed to Ahaz in Isa 7:13, where they, like the title, "House of David" (בית דוד), are dripping with sarcasm.

A situation similar to that with יושב ירושלים exists with the איש יהודה ("man/men of Judah") in Isa 5:3, 7. Although the discussion must be severely limited, it is important once again to admit the complexity of the database. איש יהודה and its counterpart, איש ישראל, clearly can have a collective meaning, but it occurs most often in military or quasi-military contexts referring to the body of Judahite or Israelite troops in much the sense of German *Mannschaft* (Moore 1895:207).[17] By Isaiah's time, the militarily significant איש יהודה was a relatively small body of large and powerful landholders. On the other hand, A. Jirku (1950:319) and A. D. Crown (1974:110–12) have argued independently that איש in biblical Hebrew can have the same sense as *amīlu* in peripheral Akkadian. The latter is used routinely, especially in the Amarna letters, to refer to a local dynast as "the man" of the political entity over which he ruled. Jirku finds his examples in 2 Sam 10:6, 8, while Crown argues cogently from Exod 2:14 and 1 Kgs 2:2; 8:25. I have already noted 1 Kgs 8:25 above for its use of יושב. Crown does not mention other texts previously treated here under יושב, (Jer 22:30; 33:17; 2 Chr 6:16) that also use איש to designate a member of a dynastic line. Quite apart from these lines of reasoning, Ps 49:3 has commonly been understood to pose בני-איש and בני-אדם as a contrasting pair. The former are the highborn, the latter the lowly. Hans-Joachim Kraus argues that the בני-איש of Ps 4:3 carry this same elite connotation (1988:144, 148, 481).

Given these patterns in the lexicographical data and the broader analysis developed here, איש יהודה in Isa 5:3 and 7 is most easily read as referring either to the ruling dynast of Judah or to its military aristocracy. As with the term יושב ירושלים, in fact, the use of איש יהודה may finesse the distinction between the king and the other members of the ruling classes. Both initiated and benefited economically from the activities condemned by the prophet.

Finally, the בית ישראל ("house of Israel") of Isa 5:7 almost certainly has reference to the northern kingdom. Within the context of the juridical parable, however, does it connote the general population of that kingdom or its ruling, dynastic "house"? Examples of the former meaning are too numerous to require documentation, but the latter is unambiguously attested as well. Since a frequent sense of בית is "household," and since the state in agrarian societies is most often the extended "household" of the

---

17. Examples with איש יהודה include Judg 15:10; 1 Sam 11:8; 15:4; 2 Sam 19:15, 17, 42, 43, 44; 20:4; 2 Kgs 23:2. For איש ישראל, one could cite, e.g., Josh 9:6, 7; Judg 7:23; 8:22; 9:55; 20:20, 36; 2 Sam 19:44.

king, בית can carry the meaning of "dynasty," "dynastic house," or even ruling "dynast." Instances with בית דוד ("house of David"), for example, include 1 Sam 20:16; 2 Sam 3:1, 6; 1 Kgs 12:19, 20, 26; 13:2; 14:8; 2 Kgs 17:21; Isa 7:2, 13; 22:22; Jer 21:12; Zech 12:7, 8, 10, 12; 13:1; Ps 122:5; 2 Chr 10:19; 21:7 (cf. *HALAT*: 120). The same sense of בית occurs with Saul (2 Sam 3:1, 6; 1 Chr 12:30), Jeroboam (1 Kgs 13:34; 14:10 [2x], 13, 14; 15:29; 16:3, 7; 21:22; 2 Kgs 9:9; 13:6; Amos 7:9), Baasha (1 Kgs 16:11, 12; 2 Kgs 9:9), Ahab (2 Kgs 8:18, 27 [3x]; 9:7, 8, 9; 10:10, 11, 30; 21:13; Mic 6:16; 2 Chr 21:6, 13; 22:3, 4, 7, 8), Jehu (Hos 1:4), and Hazael (Amos 1:4). בעל בת in the sense of "lord of the dynasty" occurs in Phoenician and Punic (Gevirtz 1961:142 n1).

Regarding the phrase בית ישראל itself, several passages, including two already cited, are germane. Jeremiah 33:17, quoted above in the discussion of יושב, reads, "David shall never lack a man (איש) sitting (ישב) upon the throne of the dynastic house of Israel (אל-כסאי בית ישראל)." Similarly, Isa 8:14 parallels "the two dynastic houses of Israel" (שני בתי ישראל) with the ruler(s) of Jerusalem (יושב ירושלים). Hosea 1:4 is equally instructive: "And the LORD said to him, 'name him Jezreel, for in a little while, I will visit the blood of Jezreel upon the dynasty of Jehu (בית יהוא), and I will put an end to the reign (ממלכות) of the dynastic house of Israel (בית ישראל).'" Other contexts where this meaning of בית ישראל seems likely include 2 Sam 12:8; 1 Kgs 20:31; Jer 2:26; Hos 1:6; 5:1; Amos 6:1; Mic 3:1, 9. Note, too, the parallel use of בית יהודה in texts such as Isa 22:21—already cited in the discussion of other terms—and 2 Chr 22:10. Clear lexicographical possibility thus allows what previous analysis has rendered probable—the בית ישראל of Isa 5:7 is the "dynastic house" or even the "ruling dynast" of Israel.

CONCLUSIONS

Several different modes of analysis and bodies of evidence point independently to the same conclusions about the addressees of Isaiah's "Song of the Vineyard." Study of the political economy of viticulture in Isaiah's time reveals sharp conflict over a process of agricultural intensification that enriched the powerful few but dispossessed and impoverished many peasants. Form-critical analysis of juridical parables shows Isa 5:1–7 to be an exemplar of a genre uniquely applicable to an elite or—most particularly—a royal audience. Other Isaianic oracles with vineyards as a major theme specifically castigate the wealthy and powerful pinnacle of society, not the population of the nation as a whole. Lexicographical analysis of the terms designating the addressees of the "Song of the Vineyard" demonstrates that all can and do elsewhere refer to elite and/or royal figures. Thus, Isaiah's choice of vineyard construction as the topic of his parable was most probably a polemical critique, not a neutral happenstance. Those trapped into self-condemnation by the parable were the ruling elites of Judah and Israel, led by the two dynastic houses and their sitting dynasts, not the general populations of Jerusalem, Judah, and Israel.

These conclusions apply to Isa 5:1–7 as a separate unit. The unit was preserved, however, by a complex process of incorporation into a series of larger literary contexts in the growing book of Isaiah, each stage of which had its own sociohistorical context (Sweeney 1996:31–62). Two of the most significant of those contexts were the royal "reforms" of the late Judahite monarchy and the anticipation by Jewish exiles in Babylon of their return to Jerusalem to build the Second Temple. In both instances, the polemical focus of the text's (re)composition in the face of strong, countervailing forces was upon national identity and unity. Under such circumstances, earlier prophetic judgments were understood to presage and explain the fall of the monarchic nation-states of Israel and Judah. Since the several terms designating the addressees of Isaiah's "Song of the Vineyard" were intrinsically multivalent and context-dependent in their meaning, they came—in those literary and historical contexts—to be understood as referring to the nations and their populace as a whole. The dominance of the nation-state in much of modern history has rendered this shift in meaning only too congenial to subsequent readers representing a broad spectrum of perspectives. Historical interpretation, particularly when focused through the lens of the social sciences, reveals behind the later reuses a much more specific critique of those who ruled the political economies of ancient Judah and Israel.

9

Accusing Whom of What?

Hosea's Rhetoric of Promiscuity

INTRODUCTION

Reading the text of Hosea is a bit like looking into a kaleidoscope. One image tumbles into the next, often with little or no boundary or transition. Trope is layered upon trope, leaving to the reader's discernment the many complexities of preunderstanding and interdependence. Such material demands of its interpreter both a sharp eye and a light hand—not to mention a healthy dose of humility. Failure to focus sharply enough the myriad analogues of Hosea's metaphors and similes will rob them of both analytical and evocative power. Too literal or heavy-handed a treatment risks killing the rich symbols outright.

Social-scientific tools can render an important service in effecting the desired balance, because the vast majority of Hosea's metaphors and similes involve social institutions. The clearer our understanding of the institutional structures and dynamics to which allusion is made in the text, the sharper the focus of our reading and the defter our discernment of the polyvalent and interactive tropes. The text of Hosea, however, most often excoriates by metaphoric allusion rather than by direct description. In the interpretation of such a text, overarching presuppositions about the social world addressed tend to be controlling. Commentators find in the complexities and difficulties of this most complex and difficult text what their presuppositions lead them to expect.

For many decades the primary *Gestalt* presupposed was some version of a "Canaanite fertility cult" in which "sacred" or "cultic" prostitution figured prominently (Albright 1956:68–94; Andersen and Freedman 1980; Balz-Cochois 1982; Davies 1993:38–51; King 1988:97–101; Mays 1969:25–26; Wolff 1974:14). More generally, interpreters understood Hosea to be exercised about the adulteration of Israelite "religion" through the "syncretistic" influences of "debased, Canaanite" beliefs and practices. This focus upon "religious" institutions and dynamics in Hosea was further shaped by a frequent heuristic contrast between Hosea and Amos. As recently as late 2002 this definition-by-contrast finds reiteration by David L. Petersen in what promises to be a widely used introduction to the prophetic literature. "Amos and Hosea try to explain to those in Israel why they are to suffer such a dire fate. Interestingly, the reasons they offer are diverse. Amos inveighs against social and economic practices in the northern kingdom, whereas Hosea focuses on religious and political misdeeds" (2002:10). Read through this lens, Hosea's metaphors and similes—many of which are less than self-evident—are unlikely to be understood as involving "social and economic practices." Moreover, this perspective tacitly separates "economic" and "political" institutions and dynamics into different realms.

Recent scholarship has subjected the aptness of this *Gestalt* for interpreting Hosea and the accuracy of its several presuppositions to increasingly sharp criticism. I find that critique compelling and wish to build upon its alternative presuppositions. Space precludes all but the briefest review here. Readers unfamiliar with the growing discussion may consult the details of the literature cited in the following summary.

CRITIQUE OF A GESTALT OF "CULTIC PROSTITUTION"

1. There is little or no unambiguous evidence for "sacred" or "cultic" prostitution in biblical Israel. While long a fixture of Hosea studies, notions of "sacred prostitution" in biblical Israel and its *Umwelt* today appear to be largely a figment of scholars' imaginations, nourished by brief but sensationalist accounts in Herodotus. Later accounts in Greek and Latin authors frequently cited in this regard now appear to be derived from Herodotus, whose narrative of Babylonian practices has long been viewed with skepticism by scholars specializing in the study of his writings. In their stricter definition, so-called "sacred marriage" texts from Mesopotamia come only from the limited periods of Ur III and Isin. Upon closer examination they

are viewed by many cuneiformists as concerned to present the king as a son of the gods and hence divine. Cultic prostitution is nowhere in view in these texts. In short, "sacred prostitution" is not at all the constant it was once presented as being in the ancient Near East (Adler 1989; Bird 1989, 1997; Bucher 1988; Cooper 1975; Fisher 1976; Gruber 1986; Hooks 1985; Keefe 1995, 2001; Oden 1981; Renger 1975; Westenholz 1989).

2. Phyllis Bird has argued persuasively that Hosea's identification of Israelite cults with prostitution was polemical, symbolic, and innovative (1989). In linking prostitution with the cultus Hosea more likely presents us with an interpretive *novum* than with an allusion to a ubiquitous cultural artifact. The Deuteronomistic Historian, Jeremiah, and Ezekiel probably amplify what Hosea began. They should be read in light of Hosea's innovation rather than Hosea's being read in light of their "evidence." Conversely, virtually all agrarian religion—including ancient Yahwism—is much concerned with the fertility of fields, flocks, herds, and the human community. Were it not, it would be truly irrelevant to the agrarian context.

3. Hosea 4:11–14, long considered bedrock for the "cultic prostitution" model because of its mention of qĕdēšôt, has been demonstrated instead to be a parade example of Hosea's polemical and innovative "intercourse" between prostitution and cult. A qĕdēšāh was a "hierodule" or "female cult functionary," not a "cult prostitute" (Bird 1997b:229–36; Gruber 1986; Keefe 2001:54–55, 100–101; Zevit 2001:462–63 and nn52 and 53).

4. The "cultic prostitution" paradigm has made far too facile and simplistic an equation of female cultic personages, female deities, and sacralized sexuality in Canaanite religion in specific and ancient Near Eastern religion in general (Keefe 2001:60–61). The database, epigraphic and anepigraphic, and more recent research into dimensions of gender in ancient Near Eastern religion do not support this generalizing conflation.

5. The "religious syncretism" believed by the older *Gestalt* to be rampant in eighth-century Israel finds scant support in the extra-biblical, epigraphic record, as the studies of Jeffrey H. Tigay (1986) and Jeaneane D. Fowler (1988) have made clear. The notable absence of anthropomorphic idols from the archaeological excavations of Israelite shrines of the period seems to point in the same direction (Keefe 2001:121).

6. The separation of ancient Israel into religious, social, economic, and political dimensions more or less discrete from one another flies in the face of everything known by sociology and anthropology about agrarian societies as a generic type on the basis of comparative study. Even to speak of their "integration" may be a dangerous anachronism. The far more probable assumption is that they were quite incompletely differentiated in Hosea's Israel. If, as seems patent, all three of Hosea's prophetic contemporaries decry

what they regard as abuses in the political economy, should not the default position be to ask if Hosea in any way reflects the same conditions and how his critique of Israel's "religion" is related thereto?

7. Critics of the older set of assumptions in Hosea studies have offered a compelling sociology-of-knowledge analysis of how the model arose, why it persisted for so long unchallenged, and why challenges have now surfaced when and how they have (ibid.:62–65, 140–89; Sherwood 1996).

Even this all-too-brief summary suggests why the once-dominant *Gestalt* of "cultic prostitution" and its concomitants can no longer be regarded as probable, though it continues to have distinguished proponents and is likely to endure in certain quarters for some time into the future. But destruction by critique is proverbially easier than the construction of a new interpretive paradigm. That is particularly true in a field like Hosea studies, where so many issues are interdependent, and changing assumptions about one element changes what it is possible to assume about others. My tentative proposal of an alternative interpretive paradigm is therefore, of necessity, multifaceted, though in essence relatively simple.

AN ALTERNATIVE HYPOTHESIS

Building on the work of Phyllis Bird and Alice Keefe, though differing from both in ways I shall try to specify, I propose that "promiscuity" in the book of Hosea is primarily a figure for dynamics in the political economy of Israel, most particularly for the dynamics of agricultural intensification (Bird 1989, 1997b; Keefe 1995, 2001). To the extent that "religious" institutions and practices come within the purview of that figure they involve the sacral legitimation of agricultural intensification, its architects, and short-term beneficiaries. Viewed through this lens, Hosea's "wife of promiscuity" becomes a sarcastic trope for the male urban warrior elite of Israel and for the land whose agricultural priorities and techniques they increasingly dictated. The bastard children, whose illegitimacy is a function of the "promiscuity" of this "mother," are primarily a metaphor for the Israelite lower classes. Just as illegitimate children in agrarian, patriarchal societies share their mother's ill-treatment while being innocent of her guilt, so these Israelite peasants suffer innocently from the various results and punishments occasioned by the elite's "promiscuous" pursuit of agricultural intensification.

Presuppositions of the Alternative Paradigm

The reasoning that supports this thesis presupposes several vectors in previous scholarship. While each is the subject of ongoing research, strictures of space prohibit all but a brief epitome here. Please note, however, that they are systemically interdependent. If one changes the pre-understanding of any one of them, what is possible or impossible for several of the others tends to shift accordingly.

1. I have argued elsewhere (Chaney 1986, 1989a, 1993, 1999) in concert with many others (Coote and Coote 1989:45–51; Dearman 1987; Elat 1979; Geva 1982; Gottwald 2001; Herr 1997; J. S. Holladay 1995; Hopkins 1983, 1996: Lang 1983b); Premnath 1984, 1988, 2003; Stager 1983, 1985; Bender 1997; McNutt 1999:148–81; Schloen 2001) that agricultural intensification and its concomitants were stark facts in eighth-century Israel and Judah, and are clearly reflected and reflected upon in the books of Amos, Isaiah, and Micah. As a policy, agricultural intensification was initiated and engineered by the urban-based ruling elite of both nations in close coordination with one another. While it greatly enhanced the wealth and power of the pinnacle of the social pyramid in the short term, it impoverished the burgeoning peasant masses and destroyed both the web of their social relations and their risk-spreading, subsistence agriculture. Nor was it sustainable in the longer term.

Eighth-century Israel and Judah saw an increase in international trade, in which their leaders imported luxury goods, military *matériel*, and the wherewithal of monumental architecture. To pay for these imports, foodstuffs—particularly the triad of wheat, olive oil, and wine—were exported. Imports benefited mostly an elite minority, while exports necessary to procure them cut deeply into the sustenance of the peasant majority. Urban elites, whose priorities called for the maximally efficient production of the three preferred export commodities over the short term, pressed for a regional specialization of agriculture. Villagers' traditional priorities for the long-term sufficiency of mixed, subsistence agriculture and its penchant for risk-spreading were overwhelmed by these pressures, and land consolidation proceeded apace. Not only were agricultural labor and land ownership increasingly separated, but the various other factors of production were segmented and each subjected to separate rent. Absentee landlordism proliferated. Many peasants were left no alternative to survival loans at de facto interest rates usurious by any standards. Foreclosure on family land and family members pledged as collateral was often at the discretion of the creditor. The courts of law called upon to process such foreclosure proceedings came increasingly under the control of the urban elites who had initiated the agricultural intensification. These courts gave a façade of legality to foreclosures regarded as illegal by most peasants and their prophetic defenders. The prophets declared that actions by YHWH's court of last resort had vindicated the poor peasants' cause and had found the urban elites guilty regarding the matters under adjudication.

Not all parts of the country were equally affected by these dynamics. The land best suited to wheat lay in the plains and the Shephelah, where most of it had long since been garnered into the large estates of the wealthiest and most powerful landlords. The conflict over agricultural priorities, techniques, and land took place primarily in the hill country, where the villagers' preference for the sustainability and sufficiency of mixed, subsistence cropping constituted a major impediment to the urban elites' desire for the "efficient" production of ever-greater quantities of wine and oil.

The conflict within the political economy of upland agriculture was not fought on equal terms. As noted above, survival loans with hill-country peasants' plots pledged as collateral gave urban elites a powerful tool to consolidate into their own hands lands from which they desired oil and wine, not mixed subsistence. This same small but powerful class also controlled state policies, including those of taxation. To further several of their goals at once, all they had to do was to levy a heavy tax on grain produced "inefficiently" by the subsistence farmers of the hill country. In the short term such a tax secured them one of their three preferred commodities, but in the longer run it also gave powerful incentive to convert into vineyards and olive orchards what had previously been multipurpose land. This conversion accomplished the increased production of wine and oil desired by the elite, both for domestic conspicuous consumption and for export. In the process, of course, many previously freeholding villagers lost their land and were ruined. Amos 5:11 probably reflects this process and its causal linkages in its indictment and futility curses:

> Therefore, because you impose cereal tax[1] upon the poor one,
>   And exactions of grain you take from him,
> You have built houses of hewn stone,
>   But you shall not dwell in them as lord,
> You have planted delightful vineyards,
>   But you shall not drink their wine.

1. This translation of the hapax legomenon *bšs* is supported both by the parallel line and by a probable Akkadian cognate, *šabāšu/šabāsa*, as seen already by Torczyner (Tur-Sinai) 1936:6–7). Numerous commentators, translators, and lexicographers have since adopted this reading (Paul 1991:172–73). Whether or not the Hebrew term then involves a wordplay on *bws*, "tread down, trample," must main a matter of conjecture, though the suggestion is thoroughly plausible.

Nor is archaeological evidence lacking for the intensification of wine and oil production in the hills. While rock-cut olive- and grape-processing installations are probably almost as old as agriculture itself in Palestine, archaeological surveys suggest a proliferation of and innovation in such installations in the eighth century BCE (Campbell 1991:109–12; Dar 1986:147–90; Eitam 1979; Walsh 2000:142–62). Some ancient terracing can probably also be traced to this time (Edelstein and Kislev 1981), though such installations are notoriously difficult to date with certainty. The Samaria ostraca—despite all the controversies surrounding their exact dating and interpretation—"evidence the flow of oil and wine, probably to officials of the royal court" in the eighth century (Premnath 1984:62). A survey of west Samaria by Shimon Dar reports not only the founding of new villages on virgin sites in Iron II but the presence in and near them of wine- and oil-processing installations (Dar 1986).

While the best exemplars date from later periods, massive and well-constructed "towers" are frequently associated with these installations. Dar traces the antecedents of these towers to Iron II and interprets them as centers for the fermentation and storage of wine. Only wine's need for darkness and moderately low, constant temperature, he argues, can explain the unique features of these towers, whose construction required an enomorous expenditure of labor. Carey Ellen Walsh now appears to agree with this interpretation (2000:128–36), after earlier seeing the towers as primarily defensive (1999:49). Towers in Jordan dating to the Iron II period, not discussed by Dar and Walsh, seem easiest to interpret as agricultural in function, though some role in defense cannot at present be excluded (H. O. Thompson 2000; Younker 1989, 1990, 1996).

The population estimates of Magen Broshi and Israel Finkelstein (1992) for Iron II Palestine, based on archaeological surveys and anthropologically standardized coefficients of density, offer striking evidence for rapid population growth in eighth-century Israel and Judah. Even more significant, perhaps, they document such rapid growth in the population of the hill country that for the first time in history it exceeded that of the lowlands. One need not solve the old chicken-and-egg debate in demographic and economic theory about population growth and agricultural intensification (Boserup 1965; Grigg 1980; Netting 1993) to note that one usually witnesses the other.

To reiterate, then, agricultural intensification was a stark fact in eighth-century Israel and Judah. It is clearly a major issue addressed by all Hosea's prophetic contemporaries. Is it sound method to assume, a priori, that Hosea ignored it or that the religious realities he addressed in no way interfaced with it?

2. Agricultural intensification exacerbated male dominance in Israel, as it has and does in most traditional agrarian societies. By agrarian society I mean a human society in which the economic base is provided by a tillage of fields that knows the plow and traction animals in some form, but not the extensive use of inanimate energy sources associated with the industrial revolution (Lenski 1984:190–296). Virtually all agrarian societies known to history are patriarchal. A major perspective in current economic anthropology sees the primary cause for this correlation in the incompatibility of the activities associated with plowing and those associated with the care of infants and small children. Protracted warfare also exacerbates gender inequities. Drafting and rewarding only men for state undertakings that are distant and dangerous offers less chance that agricultural production and human reproductive levels will be disrupted. The rewarding of men with control over family land and labor promotes their loyalty to the state and maintains their incentive to serve in its levies. Experience in such activities gives men more leverage in negotiating with the state. Once ensconced for these reasons, male dominance tends to reproduce itself socially and to create elaborate ideological justifications for its being how things "ought" to be (Bossen 1989; Meyers 1989:189–96).

3. The Hebrew verb *zānāh*, and particularly the plural abstract noun, *zĕnûnîm*, favored by Hosea, refer to sexual activity that is "promiscuous," as Francis I. Andersen and David Noel Freedman (1980:157–69), and Phyllis Bird (1989:80–82) have shown. In a patriarchal agrarian context the primary concern about such behavior is that it places in doubt the *paternity*, and hence the *legitimacy* of any children born to a "promiscuous woman." Because her focus is elsewhere when treating this term, Keefe—in an otherwise trenchant discussion—misses the importance of paternity and legitimacy in Hosea's rhetoric (1995, 2001).

4. The rhetorical vector of much of the book of Hosea presumes a male audience. To quote Bird, "By appealing to the common stereotypes and interests of a primarily male audience, Hosea turns their accusation against them" (1989:89). This technique has marked affinities with the juridical parable, a genre that I have elsewhere argued is applied exclusively in the Hebrew Bible to elite addressees (Chaney 1999). The obvious example in eighth-century prophecy is Isa 5:1–7. Hosea's dense literary allusiveness—much remarked upon by commentators—also requires a formally educated, and therefore probably upperclass, male audience. Bird has emphasized the gender dimension of the audience that Hosea's rhetoric presumes (1989), Keefe the class dimension (1995, 2001). Only when the two are combined in discerning the foil of Hosea's polemic can a major vector of his rhetoric be discerned with clarity.

5. While redaction criticism has, in my opinion, proved highly efficacious in the study of Amos, Isaiah, and Micah, I cannot term successful any of the full-scale redaction-critical analyses of Hosea. I say this despite the great learning of several studies and their obvious contributions on individual points (Emmerson 1984; Yee 1987). To be sure, the book bears clear signs of Judahite editorial activity that took place after the fall of Samaria. Although I would not argue that material in the book apparently antecedent to this Judahite editorializing gives direct access to the historical prophet, I do believe that the basic metaphors it preserves refer to institutional dynamics in roughly the third quarter of the eighth century BCE and that these metaphors derive from the named prophet.

6. The Judahite circles in which Hosea was preserved were intensely nationalistic. Certainly from Josiah on, the critique of all the eighth-century prophets was understood as applying to the nation as a whole, with little or no distinction of various classes of inhabitants. But just as obviously materials in Amos, Isaiah, and Micah that were preserved in this nationalist guise express quite a different perspective. Much of the critique is addressed exclusively to members of the ruling urban elite. Far from being their perpetrators, the peasant and lower-class majority are seen as the innocent victims of the activities excoriated (Coote 1981; Mays 1976; Sweeney 1996). Given the history of composition and interpretation of the book of Hosea, is it not likely that it, too, has seen critiques that earlier applied only to elite classes broadened to include the whole of Israel?

7. Older scholarship tended to view the much-noted obscurities of the book of Hosea as occasions for text-critical or philological operations—or some combination of the two—to vouchsafe the true, *singular* meaning of the text. More recent literary studies, particularly when pursued in conversation with the conceptual matrix sketched here, suggest a different initial approach to such obscurities. Commentators should first ask, I believe, if the received Hebrew text witnesses a coining of words or phrases, a bending of forms beyond their usual malleability, an audacious paronomasia, and/or a jarring juxtaposition of universes of discourse elsewhere deemed to be mutually exclusive. All these phenomena can evoke several realities simultaneously, such that they interpret one another in language that is intrinsically multivalent. This is not at all to posit a completely inerrant received text, but rather to argue that "difficult" passages should be scrutinized for exemplars of the devices just noted before the "difficulties" are emended or explained away to achieve a single, referential meaning.

The anomalous form *'ĕhî* in Hos 13:7, 10, 14, for example, is likely a play between and among *'ehyeh*, "I am, I shall be, I shall become," *'ayyēh*, "where?" and *'Ehyeh*, the form of the divine name in Hos 1:9 and Exod

3:14 (Andersen and Freedman 1980:635; Landy 1995:160–67). Thus, for instance, v. 14b would read "I am /*'Ehyeh* is / where are your plagues, O Death, I am / *'Ehyeh* is / where is your destruction, O Sheol?" If this reading is cogent, its "meaning" inheres in the "semantic innovation" elicited by the "tension" between and among the several semantic fields involved. Resolving that tension, either by textual emendation or morphological explanation, destroys the essence of the text.

8. Ronald Hendel's analysis of the aniconic tradition in early Israel argues that its rejection of sacral kingship as a fundamental orienting structure demanded also a rejection of the divine images that symbolized the authority of the king (1988). Building upon that analysis, Keefe reasons that Hosea's repeated invectives against idols, bull icons, priests, and sanctuaries may be read convincingly as an attack upon a whole complex of ritual activity that legitimated and collaborated with structures of political and economic power (2001:95–96, 118–30). His attacks upon the "promiscuities" of these cults thus concern their role in the dynamics of political economy, and do not constitute a pervasive critique of a putative "fertility religion."

While each of these presuppositions begs for fuller discussion, I now turn to the analysis of several problems occasioned when the "promiscuous wife" of Hosea is understood primarily as a trope for the nation of Israel as a whole.

Problems with Understanding "Gomer" as the Whole of Israel and Alternatives Thereto

1. Such interpretation tends to forget about the children. They are emphasized by the biblical text, both in chs. 1–2 where the promiscuity metaphor is prominent, and in chs. 4–14 where it moves in and out of view. In a number of Hosean texts the children are clearly a metaphor for Israel.

Keefe surfaces this problem only to dismiss it. Early in her study she writes,

> There have been all manner of theories broached which hope to make sense of these children as symbolic presences within the extended metaphor. The perceived problem revolves around a confusion regarding the allegorical correspondence intended here: if the mother symbolizes Israel, then what of the children, whose names indicate that they also symbolize Israel?
>
> The search for a clear set of allegorical correspondences to assign to the parts of the metaphor ends in frustration as it is based

upon the faulty premise that the trope is an allegory, rather than a complex metaphor, which draws upon a set of symbolic associations tied up with the intertwining images of woman, children, land and nation. (Keefe 2001:22)

She continues to distinguish—à la I. A. Richards (1971) and Paul Ricoeur (1976)—between "tropes of substitution" and "tropes of invention," ". . . where the 'tension' between semantic fields elicits a 'semantic innovation' which does not simply clothe an idea in a new image, but reveals 'something new about the reality'" (Ricoeur 1976:53). "Thus the vehicle is not dispensable, and the meaning of the metaphor may not be resolved by neatly assigning the correct tenor to it. This is the case only in allegory or analogy, where a resemblance serves to illustrate the point in a new manner, but the point remains essentially the same. But unlike allegories, 'real metaphors are not translatable'" (ibid.:52; Keefe 2001:23 n14).

I agree with Keefe on the theoretical level, but believe that she misapplies metaphor theory to the point at issue in Hosea's rhetoric. Hosea's "wife of promiscuity" and her "children of promiscuity" are indeed—I hope to show—not simply allegories or analogies, but parade examples of "tropes of invention." They are complex and interactive metaphors by the most stringent definitions of the term. But for the "tension" between semantic fields to elicit the brilliant "semantic innovations" that all but the most ham-handed of commentators know to be Hosea's signature, it must "work" without undue confusion. The ambiguities articulated by the "tropes of invention" must reveal new richness and clarity, not merely obfuscate all semantic fields involved. I suspect that Keefe's failure to see paternity and legitimacy as important dimensions of these metaphors has been detrimental to her discernment on this particular point.

2. Viewed through the lens of modern marriage customs and morality, the principle valence of the promiscuity metaphor is often understood as adultery and fidelity. But as we have already seen, Hosea's parlance clearly emphasizes promiscuity over adultery. The verb *zānāh* and its related nouns occur twenty-one times in the book (1:2, 2, 2, 2; 2:4, 6, 7; 3:3; 4:10, 11, 12, 12, 13, 14, 15, 18, 18; 5:3, 4; 6:10; 9:1), *nā'ap* and its cognate noun only six (2:4; 3:1; 4:2, 13, 14; 7:4). When the two "roots" occur together (2:4; 4:13, 14), *zānāh* always enjoys priority in their poetic pairing. For the male Israelites of Hosea's time, particularly those of the upper classes, the issue highlighted by this language is that of *paternity*.

In the days before *in vitro* fertilization, the *maternity* of a child was never in question. The mother was always present at birth. The ancient Near East, in fact, lacked a modern understanding of reproductive physiology.

The entire fetus was thought to derive from the father's semen, the mother's womb providing only the nurturing "matrix." But the *paternity* of a child could be insured only when the mother's sexuality had been the exclusive domain of one man. Female promiscuity placed paternity in doubt. To guarantee paternity, strict sanctions were laid against female promiscuity, thereby creating a double standard between the sexes for sexual behavior.

But why was paternity such an issue for men, particularly those of the ruling elite, and what had it to do with agricultural intensification? Paternity was the nexus where the two most basic functions of any agrarian society—production and reproduction—came together. Arable land, the means of production, passed from generation to generation patralineally. Inheritance went only to "legitimate" sons, those whose paternity was beyond question.

For the elite latifundializers such legitimacy became a virtual obsession. No stricture on their women was too great if it insured that their inherited and accumulated land and wealth, their political and military power, and their social prestige passed only to sons guaranteed to be born of their own seed. In the elite male sodality known as the *marzēaḥ*—mentioned in Amos (6:7) and Jeremiah (16:5) and mirrored in Isaiah and Hosea (Coote 1981:36–39; McLaughlin 2001; Woo 1998)—both the boundaries of this elite class and the continuities between and among its generations, living and dead, were celebrated and reinforced by the voluptuous consumption of the preferred commodities of agricultural intensification.

3. I have already hinted at another problem with understanding Hosea's "promiscuous wife" principally as a metaphor for the whole nation of Israel. Such interpretation ignores class divisions and their importance in Hosea's world and in the oracles of his prophetic contemporaries.

Class and gender, moreover, intersected powerfully as salient categories in eighth-century Israel's patterns of stratification. The language of elite male virility in Hosea's world and diction was the language of power and privilege in the political economy. Status sex was a potent symbol of authority and prestige, as Absalom and Ahithophel understood when, in the process of Absalom's attempted usurpation of David, they made a public display of his assumption of his father's harem (2 Sam 16:20–23). Conversely, when the aging David flunked the virility test administered by "Miss Israel," Abishag the Shunammite, it was yet another sign that the struggle for succession was on in earnest (1 Kgs 1:1–4).

Military institutions added an important dimension to this mix of class and gender stratification. The urban elite males were also a military elite. Much of their identity was wound up in their role as warriors, a role for which they practiced long hours. This identity as elite male warriors spawned a culture of *machismo* that fed back into their obsession with guaranteeing the paternity of their offspring. The more completely they controlled and dominated their women's sexuality, the more they not only insured the paternity of their childen, but the more status and honor they gained in their macho fraternity. Failure to control their women's sexuality, on the other hand, led to dishonor and humiliation. For members of Israel's urban male warrior elite, therefore, few things could be more abhorrent than for one of *their* women to be sexually promiscuous. When they defeated other warrior elites, however, one of the major ways of humiliating their vanquished enemies was through the violation of their women (Gilmore 1990; Keefe 1993; Stone 1996).

Each of the several facets of urban male warrior elite identity that I have discussed is part of the semantic field of one word in biblical Hebrew, *ba'al*. Whatever the exact identity and content of the divinity or divinities and cults evoked by this title in Hosea's parlance, they served to grant sacral legitimation to one class of elite men and their activities. In religious terms, *ba'al* was the "lord" of land, women, and political, military, economic, judicial, and social power and privilege writ large. *Ba'al* was the urban male warrior elite projected to infinity, and all attempts to understand "baalism" in Hosea must reckon with that fact. "Baalism" sanctioned agricultural intensification and the powerful few who instigated it and benefited from it.

Numerous details in the text of Hosea 1 and 2 and beyond confirm this analysis or can be viewed with greater nuance because of it. Space permits mention of only a few. The text itself interprets the trope of the promiscuous wife in 1:2: "Go, take for yourself a wife of promiscuity and children of promiscuity, for *the land* commits great promiscuity from after YHWH." The "gifts" the promiscuous wife seeks from her lovers are the preferred products of agricultural intensification, headed by the triad of grain, new wine, and new oil. As Bird has rightly argued, Hosea links the trope of promiscuity polemically with that of prostitution to castigate the greed of this agricultural intensification (Bird 1989). Vines and fig trees are called *'eṭnāh* "(harlot's) hire." The term occurs only in Hos 2:14 and was probably coined as a pun with *tĕ'ēnāh*, "fig (tree)," and perhaps with *ta'ănāh*, "rutting time." Elsewhere, including Hos 9:1, the form is *'eṭnān*.

In the context of chap. 9, "Israel" is accused of having loved a "harlot's hire" on all the threshing floors of grain. As commonly recognized by students of the subject (Matthews 1987) and evidenced in detail in Assyrian sources (*CAD*, vol. 1, A, part 1, 129–30 under *adru*; Payne Smith 1903:4, for cognate Syriac sources), activities at the threshing floor constituted a climax and point of control in cereal production. Payment of peasants' survival loans and rents was most often due in grain delivered at harvest time to the threshing floor. Even the threshing floors themselves were sometimes pledged and foreclosed upon in the process of agricultural loans.

With regard to the gender dimension of the class–gender nexus under discussion, Gomer's name in Hosea probably deserves a second look. In the genealogies of Gen 10:2, 3 and 1 Chr 1:5, 6, as well as in Samaria ostracon 50:1, Gomer is a *male* name. Whatever its etymology and meaning—and both are disputed (Andersen and Freedman 1980:171)—can its gender in Hosea's rhetoric really be regarded as either neutral or irrelevant (Macintosh 1997:11–12), particularly when that rhetoric is so stridently polemical with regard to gender, and male gendering of the name is witnessed by a source as proximate geographically and chronologically as the Samaria ostraca? At least the alternative paradigm being developed here permits a new and rhetorically potent perception of Gomer's gender.

4. My final problem with the usual understanding of Gomer as a trope for all Israel regards modern obsession with personality and interpersonal relations. As long recognized by some students of the book, the text of Hosea grants almost no access to the persons of the prophet, his wife, or her children. These characters serve rather as tropes to convey the prophet's message. Thus the primary task of exegesis is not to speculate about personal details that are inaccessible but to elucidate Hosea's tropes in the socio-historical context of his time.

The male urban warrior elite of Hosea's time, if confronted with wives guilty of sexual promiscuity, would have reacted by meting out some combination of beating, confinement, public stripping, humiliation, divorce, exile, injury, deprivation of food and water, induced illness, and death. In Hosea's parlance each of these actions becomes a figure for what the Assyrian army was doing to Israel's elite male warriors and to the land and agricultural production they dominated. Rhetorically they are hoist with their own petard, their fate interpreted to them as being that which their macho culture knew only too well was what a "promiscuous woman" richly deserved. This bitterly sarcastic inversion shares much with the self-condemnation into which the juridical parable tricked powerful men, long accustomed to passing judgment on women and their social inferiors. It loses most of its punch if Gomer is a figure for all Israel or even for all male Israelites.

Focusing the trope of the promiscuous wife more sharply facilitates a concomitant clarification of the identity and significance of the illegitimate children. In patriarchal agrarian contexts bastard children are routinely marginalized and abused. They are innocent of their mother's guilt, but they share her fate and punishment. Thus the peasants and other members of the lower classes are innocent of responsibility for agricultural intensification; they are instead its victims. But they share their "mother's" punishment in the form of Assyrian military activity and ecological degradation. The trope works at another level as well. Bastards cannot inherit; they are landless. That was precisely the state into which the promiscuity of agricultural intensification forced growing numbers of peasants in Hosea's Israel, as they were dispossessed by foreclosure and land consolidation proceeded apace.

This interpretation of Hosea's promiscuous wife and children whose legitimacy is in question grants the tropes a power and nuance they otherwise lack, not only in the texts that pronounce judgment but also in those that proclaim salvation. In a reversal unthinkable in the macho culture of the warrior latifundializers, Hosea says these bastard children will be granted legitimacy and inheritance in a world where the depredations of the warring classes are abolished and the earth yields its bounty in the subsistence village agriculture that YHWH intended all along. In such a world, where *grace* requires as its *prerequisite* that the presuppositions of patriarchy and hierarchy be overthrown, even the male urban warrior elite can be redeemed. They can become the faithful wife, free of the promiscuity of agricultural intensification, who knows that her divine husband is not her *baʿal* but her *'îš* (2:18). Changes in social systems are usually accompanied by concomitant changes in their legitimating religious symbol systems.

The names of the bastard children figure as well in the dialectic between judgment and salvation. Jezreel is the firstborn son (1:4), and his name also serves as the punchline in Hosea's verbal picture of healing and restoration (2:24). A name more pregnant with meaning or more multivalent can scarcely be imagined. It is, of course, a pun on Israel and thus an added indication that the children, not the promiscuous mother, are the more frequent figure for most of the nation's population. But Jezreel also evokes Jehu's bloody usurpation of the Omrids (1:4), a bloodbath pitched by its legitimating apology as necessary to end the Omrids' oppressive drive for agricultural intensification and the "baalism" that sanctioned it (1 Kings 21; 2 Kings 9–10; White 1997). Hosea and his audience knew, however, that Jehu's dynasty, still on the throne in Hosea's early years in the person of Jeroboam II, had outdone the dynasty it usurped in both offences. The literal sense of Jezreel, "God sows/inseminates," evoked understandings of both agriculture and paternity that the prophet regarded as "legitimate," but could also carry the double entendre of God's sowing destruction.

CONCLUSIONS

Thus the literary figures of Hosea's text, salvific as well as judgmental, provide a sweeping critique of agrarian Israel's systemic integration—those who rule it, "benefit" from it and legitimate it. Hosea says the urban male military elite are "promiscuous women" who achieve just the opposite of what they purport: instability, not stability; infertility, not fertility; illegitimacy, not legitimacy; infidelity, not fidelity; insecurity, not security; impotence, not potency; dishonor, not honor; sickness, not health; want, not prosperity; defeat, not victory; frenetic titillation on the way to destruction, not intimate understanding and loyal relationship.

10

Producing Peasant Poverty

Debt Instruments in Amos 2:6–8, 13–16 *

ASSUMPTIONS ABOUT THE COMPOSITIONAL HISTORY OF THE BOOK OF AMOS

Regarding the larger literary context of the text in question, I make a number of assumptions that can only be acknowledged. Space does not allow their justification here, and most scholarly readers could document for themselves, no doubt, the arguments for and against each of these suppositions. (1) I assume that the book of Amos, in its received form, is a product of the Persian period. (2) The book also evidences previous levels of composition congruent in detail with the language and interests of the Deuteronomistic History. In my view, one may still speak cogently of a Deuteronomistic History, the "first edition" of which—along with much of the

---

* I am delighted to dedicate this article to Bob Coote, my esteemed colleague and friend for most of our professional lives. During our decades in common at San Francisco Theological Seminary and the Graduate Theological Union, we repeatedly taught courses together on the so-called eighth-century prophets. The best of what I know about the subject I learned from and with Bob Coote. The oracle treated here figured importantly in his first book. We have discussed it many times over the years. I offer this treatment not in any sense as a culmination of that discussion but merely as the latest chapter in an ongoing dialogue.

"Deuteronomistic" composition in several of the prophetic books—finds its most probable social matrix in the royal "reforms" of the late Judahite monarchy. Although this strain of composition undoubtedly continued into the exile and beyond, the late monarchy has greater explanatory power as its initiating social context. (3) Anterior to this "Deuteronomistic" level of composition in Amos lies material that was recomposed according to the needs and interests of later periods. This earlier level of composition is characterized by a relative handful of self-contained literary forms and content subjects. Though I make no claim that this material gives direct access to the person of Amos, its concerns and emphases comport well with what is known about the socioeconomic dynamics of eighth-century Israel. Once again, these concerns are generic enough to be of interest in many later periods, but systemic changes particular to the eighth century BCE seem the most likely impetus for the generation of these prophetic oracles in the first place.[1]

THE POLITICAL ECONOMIES OF ISRAEL AND JUDAH IN THE EIGHTH CENTURY BCE

I have outlined my understanding of the socioeconomic dynamics of Israel and Judah in the eighth century BCE in several previously published articles that focus especially on the dynamics of political economy. Summarized far too briefly, that understanding includes the following points. (1) The elites of Israel and Judah—who were in league—participated actively in international trade. Mostly via the city-states of Phoenicia, they imported luxury goods, military *matériel*, and the wherewithal of monumental architecture. To pay for these imports, which benefited primarily the elite few, they exported foodstuffs and fiber. Wheat, olive oil, and wine, the triad of Palestinian agriculture, headed the list of exports and featured prominently in the increasingly consumptive lifestyle of the domestic elites. This diversion of staple commodities away from their producers cut deeply into the sustenance of the peasant majority. (2) The situation gave court elites incentive to extract through taxation the largest possible "surplus" of these commodities. (3) Pressure to grow ever-increasing amounts of the few preferred crops concentrated risk and effaced the risk-spreading mechanisms

---

1. Coote himself (1981) still gives one of the most cogent accounts available for the compositional history of the book of Amos. This work has never received the scholarly attention it deserves, at least in part because he sought to make it accessible to a wider readership. For just a hint of the analyses that underlie the generalization of this first paragraph, see, further, Chaney 2006:146–49, and the works there cited.

of the peasants' more traditional subsistence agriculture. (4) Attenuation of risk-spreading measures rendered peasants ever more vulnerable to the vicissitudes of an erratic climate. When natural disaster struck, they were left no alternative but survival loans from the elite on terms dictated by the creditors. Foreclosure on family land rights and/or the labor of family members pledged as collateral was often at the discretion of the wealthy urban creditors. Debt instruments thus accomplished a second round of "surplus" extraction that often resulted in the pauperization of the peasantry, greater land consolidation and debt-slavery. (5) Traditional village courts had few procedural safeguards when processing foreclosures. Increased social stratification gave urban elites the power to coerce or suborn their decisions. Thus perverted, these courts gave a façade of legality to foreclosures deemed illegal by most peasants. Against that background, the rhetoric of the eighth-century prophets appeals these cases to YHWH's law court in the sky. As auditors on the proceedings in God's court, the prophets report the vindication there of the peasants' cause and declare that YHWH has found the ruling elites guilty with regard to the matters under adjudication. YHWH's disposition of a case, as reported by the prophets, often "makes the punishment fit the crime" through a "measure-for-measure" correlation between indicttment and sentence.[2]

ASSUMPTIONS ABOUT THE "ISRAEL ORACLE" IN AMOS 2:6–16

I make the following further assumptions about the "Israel oracle" in Amos 2:6–16. (1) The older oracle that relates to the eighth century is found only in those portions of vv. 6–8, 13–16 that are translated below. Portions of the received text not translated are understood to represent later, "Deuteronomistic" recomposition. (2) This recomposition is also responsible for placing the oracle as the culmination of oracles against foreign nations in Amos. Such recomposition presumed the oracle to be typical of Amos (see Coote 1981:1–109; cf. Wolff 1977:106–13, 133–35, 164–73). (3) In addition to the meaning of the text in its received literary context, the eight-century oracle has structural and semantic integrity relative to the context of its composition. (4) The significant parallel to v. 6c in Amos 8:6 occurs in a literary unit (8:4–6) more heavily recomposed than the "Israel oracle" in chap. 2. (5) As is true of most of the self-contained units in the eighth-century prophets,

---

2. See Chaney 2014a and the literature there cited. In an appendix to that work (46–53), the criticisms of Faust 2012; Guillaume 2012; and Houston 2008, and 2010, are examined and themselves critiqued (see 136–47 above).

the language of Amos 2:6–8, 13–16 is full of ironic and sarcastic double entendre. Discernment of such paronomasia at modern scholars' distance from the text calls for humility and tentativeness in the readings offered. By the nature of such material, however, the greater risk is of underinterpretation, not overinterpretation.[3]

TRANSLATION OF AMOS 2:6–8, 13–16[4]

6 Thus YHWH has said:
   Because of their selling the innocent by means of the silver,
      and the indigent {by means of the pledged harvest}—
            {because of pledges/contracts [lit.: "sandals"]}
7 The ones that {trample upon the dust of the earth,}
         {pant after the soil of the earth,}
      {(that trample) against the head of the poor;}
      {(that pant after) the choicest produce of the poor;}
      and they {shunt aside the legal cause of the afflicted;}
         {push the afflicted out of the way;}
   A man and his father they bring to foreclosure [lit.: "shaking out"]
      "in order to" profane my holy name;
8 Furthermore, upon garments taken in distraint they stretch out,
      and the wine of those fined they drink;
13 Look here, I am about to place an impediment under you,
      as a cart lurches to a stop
      when it is full to overflowing with harvested grain.
14 Flight shall vanish from the swift,
      the strong shall not regain his strength,
   The warrior shall not rescue his life,
   15   the bowman shall not stand fast,
   The swift of foot shall not escape,
      he who drives the horse shall not save his life,
16 The strongest-willed among the warriors
      will flee naked on that day—oracle of YHWH.

---

3. The present study is not an isolate. For previous, related works, see Chaney 1986, 1989a, 1993, 1999, 2004a, 2004b, 2006.

4. The brackets in the following translation indicate my belief that the text so treated means not one or the other of the bracketed renderings, but both.

AMOS 2:6c

Few passages in prophecy have evoked more commentary than the last line of v. 6 and its parallel in Amos 8:6. The NRSV represents the tradition followed by most modern English translations: "because they sell the righteous for silver, and the needy for a pair of sandals." Speiser stated the problem with this rendering concisely in 1940: "The ordinary interpretation of this saying that the poor could be enslaved for so trifling a thing as a pair of shoes is unconvincing . . . and economically improbable" (1940:18). Kessler has more recently cast doubt on the existence of a developed slave market in the eighth century BCE (1989). In his search for a more adequate understanding of *nʿlym*, Speiser looked first to Ruth 4:7: "Now this was the custom formerly in Israel with reference to redemption and exchange transactions: to confirm any such matter, a man would draw off his sandal and give it to his counterpart. This was the process of attestation in Israel" (1940:16).

Speiser next turned to Samuel's self-justification in 1 Sam 12:3, which harks back in contrast to the "way of the king" in 1 Samuel 8. The MT reads: "Here I am: testify against me before YHWH and before his anointed. Whose ox have I taken? Or whose ass have I taken? Whom have I oppressed by extortion? Whom have I crushed? Or from whose hand have I taken a bribe to blind my eyes with it, and I will repay you." The Hebrew of MT for the clumsy latter part reads *kpr wʾʿlym ʿyny bw*. The LXX, confirmed by the summary of this passage in Sir 46:19 (in both Greek and Hebrew),[5] presumes instead *kpr wnʿlym ʿnw by*: "Or from whose hand have I taken a bribe or sandals? Testify against me, and I will repay you" (Speiser 1940:17). This reading is text-critically superior (McCarter 1980:208–10; and less clearly Auld 2011:126–27), obviates MT's clumsiness and seems to presuppose "sandals" in the symbolic meaning of "pledges, obligations for debt," or the like, perhaps in the sense of what is "bound" or "made fast" (cf. the meaning of the verb *nʿl*). Other passages that involve the use of sandals as a probative instrument include Deut 25:9 and Pss 60:8; 108:9. With respect to the usage of "sandals" in Amos 2:6 and 8:6, Speiser concluded, "We have here a proverbial saying which refers to the oppression of the poor by means which may be legal but do not conform to the spirit of the law" (1940:18).

A decade after Speiser wrote, Gordis agreed that the passage dealt with questionable practices in a court of law but on the basis of quite a different understanding of the philology: "The usage in Amos 'for the sake of' *baʿăbhûr naʿălayim* (for which read *naʿălam*) militates against such an

---

5. For the Hebrew text, see now, conveniently, Beentjes (2003:83).

interpretation [i.e. Speiser's], as it clearly indicates that *nʿlm*, like its parallel *ksp*, is the object of the corrupt practice, not the means" (1950:45 n6). Gordis then proposes that *nʿlym* be emended to a noun derived from *ʿlm*, "probably *naʿălam*," meaning "bribe." This critique of Speiser is cogent in its insistence that *bʿbwr*, "for the sake of, on account of, because of," is not a natural parallel for the preposition *b-* when used to indicate instrument or means (ibid.:45; Paul 1991:163–64 follows Gordis). Whatever one makes of the other occurrences of *naʿălam* proposed by Gordis, however, his emendation of Amos 2:6 to carry this meaning falls to the ground the moment one reads v. 6 with v. 7, which seems clearly to presuppose MT's reading in the sense of "sandals."

Lang has treated this problem somewhat more recently, appropriately placing it within the context of peasant debt (Lang 1981). On the basis of Ruth 4:7, already quoted, Lang reasons that *nʿlym*, "a pair of sandals," came to mean "pledge, bond, contract."[6] Arguing from Akkadian parallels that *bksp* can mean "because of silver," he translates this verse, "selling the innocent because of silver (i.e., debts of money) and the poor because of a pair of sandals" (Lang 1983b:126). A survey of biblical passages having to do with borrowing and lending certainly indicates that silver was the most frequent medium in which loans were made (cf. Exod 22:24 [Eng., v. 25]; Lev 25:37; Deut 23:20 [Eng., v. 19]; Ezek 18:8 [cf. LXX]; Ps 15:5; and Neh 5:4, 10, 11). "A pair of sandals" in the sense of "pledge, bond" or "obligation for debt" makes a more than adequate parallel for silver in that context and seems quite likely in light of Ruth 4:7 and 1 Sam 12:3 as understood by LXX and Sir 46:19.

Lang's reading of "because of silver," however, faces insurmountable philological problems. Whatever *ina kaspi* may mean in Akkadian, *mkr b-* in biblical Hebrew means to "sell for/with/at" (cf. Gen 37:28; Deut 21:14; Joel 4:3 [Eng., 3:3]; Nah 3:4; Ps 44:13), except when it occurs in the idiom "sell into the hand of." If the parallel in Amos 8:6, which uses *qnh*, to "buy" or "acquire," is invoked, the case is even stronger. Used with *b-*, *qnh* clearly means to "buy for/with/by means of" a given medium of exchange (cf. Gen 33:19; 47:19; Josh 24:32; 2 Sam 24:24 [2x]; 1 Kgs 16:24; Isa 43:24; Jer 32:25, 44; 1 Chr 21:24). To put the matter a bit differently, the history of the philological interpretation of Amos 2:6c and 8:6 indicates that readings that have translated *mkr/qnh b-* according to known Hebrew idiom have had trouble making sense of *bʿbwr nʿlym*, whereas straightforward translation of the latter clause violates idiomatic usage attested uniformly for the former.

---

6. Ibid., 483; Lang 1983b:125. For this basic understanding, see also, e.g., Andersen and Freedman 1989:312–13; Premnath 2003:163–64.

PRODUCING PEASANT POVERTY 197

Faced with that impasse, I propose to cut the Gordian knot by analyzing *bʿbwr* as a second occurrence of the preposition *b-* plus the noun *ʿbwr*, meaning "produce, yield, harvest, crop, grain." This noun occurs elsewhere in biblical Hebrew twice (Josh 5:11, 12) and at least twice—perhaps more in abbreviation—in inscriptional Hebrew (*DCH* 6:232). Cognates with the same meaning abound in Akkadian and several dialects of Aramaic (Payne Smith 1903:398a; Hoftijzer and Jongeling 1995:822–23). Akkadian *ebūru* is particularly significant, for it is frequently used in contracts and other documents to refer to harvest as the time when loans come due (*CAD* 4:16–20; *AHw* 1:83–84).

Such a reading escapes the philological difficulties of Lang's analysis while fitting even more precisely the context of peasant debt that he adduces. Loans to poor peasants by wealthy landlords would typically have been made in silver before the new crop came in, when grain was scarce and expensive in terms of its price in silver. At harvest time, the loan would have been due in kind—a "pledged" or "contracted" crop—when grain was plentiful and thus worth less relative to silver. The creditors' simple manipulation of the terms according to which the loan was given and repaid involved de facto interest that was crushing, in addition to whatever de jure "interest" the loan may have borne. The debtor was *'bywn*, "indigent, one who begs" (Humbert 1952), meaning that his indebtedness was not for a commercial loan but for survival.

The text uses aphoristic language to capture the crucial beginning and ending of this desperate transaction. "By means of the silver" in which the survival loan to the indigent one is paid out and "by means of the pledged harvest," the form in which repayment is required, wealthy landlords are able to "buy and sell" vulnerable peasants. The reference is not to a developed slave market but rather to a cycle of encumbered harvests that allowed creditors to bleed debtors white and then, at their discretion, to foreclose upon peasant land rights and peasant labor pledged as collateral. Such foreclosures resulted in further land consolidation by landlords already land-rich and in a growth of debt-slavery.

The elite-dominated human courts in the time of Amos routinely sanctioned such transactions. According to the prophetic text, however, YHWH's court has declared the ruined debtor *ṣdyq*, "innocent" (see Wolff 1977:165; Coote 1981:35; Paul 1991:77; Sweeney 2000:214), regarding the debt and foreclosure under adjudication. In everyday Hebrew, of course, *bʿbwr* meant "because of, for the sake of," so *bʿbwr nʿlym* inevitably meant both "because of the sandals/pledges/loan contracts" and "by means of the pledged/contracted harvest." As noted above, the brackets at this point and elsewhere in my translation indicate my belief that the text means not one or the other of the bracketed renderings but both, in a pithy wordplay that concentrates the irony and evokes a whole dynamic of debt in just a few memorable words.

AMOS 2:7

Verse 7a, I believe, confronts us with more of this paronomasia, as indicated in the translation. Though the etymology of *š'p* presents problems that have not been solved definitively, most commentators, translators, and lexicographers find here a meaning of "trample." In other passages, *š'p* can clearly mean "gasp, pant, pant after" and "long for" (see BDB 983; *HALOT* 4:1375, 1446-47; *DCH* 8:217-18). At one level, the antecedent of the *hš'pym* found here is almost certainly to be understood as the "sandals" that end v. 6. They "trample upon the dust of the earth" and "against the head of the poor." But with the other meaning of *š'p*, it is the *n'lym* in the sense of "pledges, debt contracts," and those who wield them, that "pant after the soil of the earth." (For *'pr* as "soil," cf. Job 5:6 and 14:8.) This meaning of "pant after" also works well with *r'š* in its sense of the "choicest produce" (cf. Deut 33:15 and Sir 11:3). Exodus 22:4 (Eng., v. 5) evidences legal liability, in certain instances, for a defendant to provide from "the best of his field." The "pledges/debt contracts" and the crreditors that dictated their terms certainly "panted after" all they could extract from their poor debtors, and that could easily have involved quality as well as quantity.

As is widely recognized, "[t]he phrase 'to turn aside the way of the afflicted' in 2:7b is a metaphor signifying the failure of the administrative/judicial system to mitigate the circumstances of property loss" (Dearman 1984:384). The "pledges/debt contracts" certainly accomplished such loss of property. In their more literal sense, the "sandals" of wealthy creditors could also "push the afflicted out of the way." The language of vv. 6c and 7a seems carefully constructed to maintain this double entendre throughout. Does *n'lym* in this double sense continue as the subject in v. 7b, and can it solve outstanding problems there?

The NRSV is once again representative of most modern translations of this line: "father and son go in to the same girl, so that my holy name is profaned." In most instances, such translations presume a violation of the law in Exod 21:7-11, which provides that when a daughter is sold into debt-slavery, she may become the sexual partner of the father or the son in the household that has acquired her, but not both (cf., e.g., Sweeney 2000:215-16). Though abuse of this situation would fit well enough in the prophet's roll call of debt-related oppression, serious philological problems attend this reading, as long recognized. Biblical Hebrew routinely uses *bw'* as the verb in contexts where sexual relations are involved. Most lexica are forced to create a separate, unlikely category of meaning for this passage alone for *hlk* to have such sexual connotations. The entries refer the reader back to *bw'*, which the text of Amos does not use, for the meaning (BDB 231; *HALOT* 1:247; cf. *DCH* 2:547, 551). Most translations supply the "same" girl/maiden/prostitute, even though nothing in the Hebrew text requires or even suggests this sense. Nor does *nʿrh* mean either "female debt-slave" or "prostitute," both roles for which biblical Hebrew knows precise terms.

The analysis of the passage to this point suggests an alternative that keeps *nʿlym* as the subject of the verb in this line as well and that involves none of the problems of the usual reading. I propose that in Amos 2:7, *nʿrh* means not "young woman" but "foreclosure, shaking out." The evidence comes from Neh 5:13, which is better understood in the larger context of Neh 5:1–13:

> There was a great outcry from the people and from their wives against their Jewish brothers. For there were those who said, "Our sons and our daughters we are giving in pledge[7] that we may secure grain, eat it, and stay alive." And there were those who said, "Our fields, our vineyards, and our houses we are giving in pledge that we may secure grain during the famine." And there were those who said, "We have borrowed money [*ksp*] for the king's tax upon our fields and our vineyards. Now our flesh is like the flesh of our brothers, our children are like their children; and yet we have to force our sons and our daughters to be slaves—some of our daughters have already been enslaved! But we are powerless because the nobles[8] have our fields and our vineyards."
>
> I was very angry when I heard their outcry and these words. I took counsel with myself, and I brought charges against the nobles and officials. I said to them, "You are exacting interest, each from his brother." And I held a great convocation against them, and I said to them, "So far as we were able, we have bought back [*qnynw*] our Jewish brothers who had been sold/sold themselves [*hnmkrym*] to the nations; but you even sell [*tmkrw*] your brothers in order that they may be sold [*wnmkrw*] to us!" They were silent, and could not find a word to say. So I said, "The thing you are doing is not good. Should you not walk in the fear of our God because of the reproach of

---

7. Reading *ʿrbym* for MT's *rbym*; cf. v. 3.
8. Reading *lḥrym* with LXX and Old Latin for MT's *lʾḥrym*; cf. v. 7]

the nations, our enemies? Moreover, I and my brothers and my retainers are lending them money (*ksp*) and grain. Now let us leave off this interest! Return to them immediately their fields, their vineyards, their olive orchards, and their houses, and the exaction[9] of money [*hksp*], grain, new wine, and oil that you have been taking from them as creditors." Then they said, "We will return these and demand nothing more from them; we will do just as you say."

But I called the priests and made them swear to fulfill this promise. Moreover, I shook out [*nʿrty*] the lap of my garment and said, "So may God shake out [*ynʿr*] from his house and his acquired property every man who does not fulfill this promise; just so may he become shaken out [*nʿwr*] and emptied!' And all the convocation said, "Amen!" And they praised YHWH. And the people did as they had promised.

Several things are apparent once this passage is juxtaposed to the oracle in Amos 2:6–8, 13–16. Both the subject matter and the vocabulary of the two passages echo each other. In Neh 5:13, a powerful concentration of the root *nʿr* occurs. It is used in the qal to describe Nehemiah's symbolic action with the lap of his garment. The Masoretes point it as a piel in the occurrence that calls upon God to "shake out from his house [*byt*] and his acquired possessions [*ygyʿ*]" every man who does not keep his promise to stop taking interest, to return interest already taken, and to restore all prior foreclosures. The image is surely one of measure-for-measure: "If you do not stop the practices that lead to foreclosure and restore all previous foreclosures, may God foreclose on all you have, both inherited [*byt*] and acquired [*ygyʿ*]." The one having been thus foreclosed upon is described with the qal passive participle of *nʿr*, which in turn is linked to the term "emptied" [*rq*], that is, "foreclosed upon and without property."

The use of the root *nʿr* in so many different conjugations in this one verse, where its meaning and context are patent, demonstrates its ability to spawn technical vocabulary dealing with foreclosure. It is plausible, therefore, that one such word was a feminine noun, *nʿrh*, meaning "foreclosure." Why the word is used in this context in Amos is as easy to understand as why subsequent generations confused this technical term for its more common and general homophone. Linked with this misperception was another—the reading of the consonants *ylkw* as a qal, *yēlěkû*, "they go," rather than a hiphil, *yōlîkû*, "they bring," as proposed in the translation given here. Such a reading not only unifies the subject of the oracle but also continues

---

9. Reading *wmšʾt* for MT's *wmʾt*.

the wordplay on the literal and symbolic meanings of *nʿlym*. Sandaled footsteps literally bring a man and his aged father to the foreclosure proceedings upon their family land rights, but it is far more significantly the "pledges/loan contracts" and their wealthy beneficiaries that bring the family to ruin. On this understanding, the line evokes the horror of a family being stripped at one fell swoop—by means of debt instruments—of their land rights, their livelihood, their home, their place in the social fabric and the free status of their labor. If we may judge from Neh 5:13, *nrʿh* would have been a charged term in prophetic speech, able to conjure up without embellishment scenes of unspeakable pathos.

The last clause of v. 7, "'in order to' profane my holy name," may have influenced the misreading of what immediately precedes it. Though this language is frequent in the Holiness Code and Ezekiel, Jer 34:16 demonstrates that it is not restricted to that literature and that it is elsewhere applied to contexts dealing explicitly with debt and its consequences. The conjunction *lmʿn* is ironic. As BDB notes pertinently of its use, "in rhetorical passages, the issue of a line of action, though really undesigned, is represented by it ironically as if it were designed" (BDB 775). According to prophetic speech, the foreclosures that are the stock-in-trade of human courts profane the sanctity of the proceedings in God's court.

AMOS 2:8

In v. 8 the wordplay with *nʿlym* finally comes to an end. The subject of the third-person-plural verbs is the same "they" with whom the indictment begins in v. 6: "because of their selling." Even when the *n'lym* remain in play, of course, it is really the creditors who dictate their ruinous terms who are the indicted "they." Verse 8 specifies two other means creditors use to pressure debtors. Paul, following Milgrom, argues strongly that the *bgdym ḥblym* are not the familiar "garments taken in pledge" but rather "garments taken in distraint" (Paul 1991:83–95; Milgrom 1975; cf. Premnath 2007). Such seizure of personal property takes place only when the loan falls due and the debt is defaulted. It layers another dimension of harassment on the already desperate debtor. "Fines" or "compensations" were levied by the same small but powerful class of landlords who were able to make loans and shaded quickly into simply another excuse to extract preferred commodities, in this case wine.

AMOS 2:13-16

The "Deuteronomistic" recomposition in vv. 9–12 may have deleted references to other ills pertaining to peasant debt. About that currently available data tell us nothing. What is clear is that *hnh 'nky* in v. 13 accomplishes a deft pivot from indictment to sentence. As stated above, prophetic oracles frequently evidence a discernible measure-for-measure correspondence between indictment and sentence in order "to make the punishment fit the crime." No previous interpretation of this passage known to me, however, has been able to show convincingly how this indictment and this sentence are related to each other.

Much of the obscurity resides in the verb *ʿwq/ʿyq*, which occurs only in v. 13 in all of biblical Hebrew. Two facts can illustrate the state of discussion concerning its meaning and significance. (1) the range of possible etymologies and meanings listed by Harper in 1905 is virtually the same as that given by *HALOT* in 1995 and *DCH* in 2007 (Harper 1905:62–63; *HALOT* 2:802; *DCH* 6:314). (2) Fully aware of that range of possibilities, Coote chose to leave the word untranslated as hopelessly obscure (1981:11). A lengthy rehearsal of previous scholarship would avail nothing here and hence will be foregone.

As background for my proposed solution, I offer rather the following more general remarks on the solutions previously proposed. (1) All attempts to read *ʿwq* appeal, of necessity, to context and to the cognate languages, mostly Arabic. (2) Many take their point of departure from the presumption that something relative to the cart becomes a figure for an earthquake, a presumption that is both unnecessary and unsubstantiated by any other words in the oracle. (3) Many involve irregular phonological or morphological correspondences between languages or capricious emendations of the text, all of which are to be rejected out of hand. (4) None has attempted to integrate the imagery of the cart into the whole scene of punishment that it initiates. (5) Many proposed solutions assume that the predominant characteristic of a cart full of harvested grain is its weight. Such is not the case, as time spent in the Two-Thirds World—particularly in semiarid southern India—has impressed upon me. Carts filled with water tanks, stone, bricks, wet earth, or other materials of high density are noteworthy for their weight. Those filled with low density materials such as harvested grain or straw are characterized rather by their bulk. The load overflows the cart on all sides, rendering it precarious indeed should the cart strike too large an impediment while in motion.

The etymology that I prefer has long been a contender. Its basis is Arabic *ʿwq*, which in the first and fourth stems means to "hinder, prevent, impede, withhold, retard, turn someone back, divert from a course" and in the fifth and eighth stems to "become hindered, prevented, withheld, turned back or away, retarded, restrained, diverted (Lane 1863–93 5:2198–200). Such a sense allows the hiphil participle, *mʿyq*, to be understood uncontrivedly as "impede, place an impediment in the way of." The translation of *tʿyq*, whose subject is obviously the cart, presumes a meaning of "being restrained, impeded, stopping quickly, abruptly."[10] The image evoked is that of a moving cart—overflowing with harvested grain—that strikes an unexpected impediment. The obstacle not only stops the cart in its tracks but also, owing to inertia, scatters much of its precious cargo. Such an image of hindrance and ruin comports well with the remainder of the judgment.

Though clearly attested elsewhere in biblical Hebrew, *ʿglh*, "cart," is not frequent in its occurrence. The sparseness of this attestation corresponds with the evidence drawn by ethnographic analogy from traditional agricultural practices in later periods in Palestine. Although Wellhausen overstates the matter when he denies any use of farm carts in either ancient or modern Palestine (1963:74), harvested grain was far more often transported to the threshing floor on the backs of various beasts of burden, using special frames (Dalman 1933:53–60; Turkowski 1969:103; Hopkins 2007:158–59). Dalman quotes figures indicating that typically a cart could carry six times as much as an ass and three times as much as a camel (1933:59). Carts would obviously have been of greater utility in the breadbaskets of the lowlands than in the marginal grain fields of the hill country.

Was greater use of carts to transport unthreshed grain from the harvest field to the threshing floor an element in the intensification of wheat cultivation in the plains in the eighth century? If so, the overflowing cart made an appropriate symbol for the whole process that the prophet castigated. Hungry for more grain to export as payment for imported luxuries and strategic goods, the urban elite pressed for ever more efficient means to hurry the grain away from its producers. Just as a cart full to overflowing with harvested grain could thus symbolize the pathos of forced exchange, the cart's sudden and ruinous encounter with an unexpected impediment could stand as a figure for the punishment of those responsible. Sentence can be understood to correspond with indictment at last.

The full significance of the wrecked cart is brought home in vv. 14–16 with a rapid series of sledgehammer blows. The elite who devise and profit from the indicted system of debt instruments that accomplish secondary surplus extraction are also the political and military elite, accustomed to

---

10. On the possibility of this meaning in the Targum, see Cathcart and Gordon 1989:80 and n21.

the power and speed that make them invincible. But like the wrecked cart, they will be impeded in place, stripped of their strength and glory, ruined before they know what has happened. According to the prophetic text, the principle of measure for measure dictates the judgment already passed in YHWH's court on the wealthy creditors who are enriching themselves through debt instruments that effect the pauperization of large parts of the peasantry.

CONCLUSIONS

Most of the conclusions regarding new solutions to old philological problems have been drawn in the body of the paper. A few additional remarks may be hazarded here, nevertheless. The proposed readings of *bʿbwr nʿlym* in Amos 2:6, *hnʿrh* in v. 7, and *mʿyq* and *tʿyq* in v. 13 are not offered in isolation. They unify both the literary structure and the subject matter of the oldest form of the "Israel oracle" in Amos 2. The interpretation of the "sandals" advanced here reveals a delicious double entendre that increases the irony and sarcasm of vv. 6c–7. Abuse of debt instruments, made more fully visible in the oracle's indictment, and the discernment of their place in the wider dynamics of political economy in eighth-century Israel and Judah fit well the historical picture of those dynamics derived from other sources. If the "sound-bite" language of Amos 2:6c—and 8:6—has been correctly understood, it evidences an insidious convention in survival loans to poor peasants. The loans were routinely granted with silver as the medium of exchange but were due at harvest in new crop. The difference in the relative value of silver and grain when the loans were taken out and when they came due imposed a ruinous de facto interest on such loans, even if the de jure interest charged was modest or even null. As all these matters illustrate, detailed interpretation of specific prophetic texts and synthetic, historical delineation of the contexts in and for which they were composed walk hand in hand. Each can contribute to a clearer understanding of the other in a process that is intrinsically dialogical.

11

Micah—Models Matter

Political Economy and Micah 6:9–15

Abstract
Recent studies illumine the political economies of Israel and Judah in the eighth century BCE. The intricate textual and philological problems of Mic 6:9–15 yield fresh solutions when current knowlege of these dynamics informs their analysis. Beyond the clarification of individual cruxes, the literary structure of the passage is unified in a measure-for-measure correspondence between indictment and sentence. More precise attention to the systemic dynamics castigated also enhances detection and appreciation of the frequent paronomasia that heightens the irony and sarcasm of the unit. Taken in sum, the analysis strengthens the suggestion that Mic 6:9–15 is closely associated in context and compositioin with most of Micah 1–3.

∽

At the outset, I need to acknowledge a number of assumptions I make in the study that follows. Strictures of space preclude any significant attempt justifying these assumptions, though I shall try to reference literature that argues in greater detail for what I can only presume here.

With regard to the history of composition of the so-called eighth-century prophets, I assume that the books of Amos, Hosea, Isaiah, and Micah are, in something close to their received form, products of the Persian period. All four books also evidence levels of composition congruent in detail with the language and interests of the Deuteronomistic History (See, e.g., Coote 1981; Mays 1976; Sweeney 1996; Yee 1987). In my view, the most probable social matrix for the composition of this material is the royal "reforms" of the late Judahite monarchy (See, e.g., Cross 1973:274–89; Knoppers 1993, 1994; Nelson 1981; Sweeney 2001). While this strain of composition undoubtedly continued into the exile and beyond, the late monarchy has greater explanatory power as its initiating social context. Anterior to this "Deuteronomistic" level of composition in the four eighth-century prophets lies material that was recomposed according to the needs and interests of the later periods. This earlier level of composition is characterized by a relative handful of self-contained literary forms and content subjects. While I make no claim that this material gives direct access to the named prophets, its concerns and emphases comport well with what is known about the socioeconomic dynamics of eighth-century Israel and Judah (see Coote 1981). Once again, these concerns are generic enough to be of interest in many later periods, but systemic changes particular to the eighth century BCE seem the most likely impetus for the generation of these prophetic oracles in the first place.

DYNAMICS OF EIGHTH-CENTURY POLITICAL ECONOMY

I have published previously in several articles my understanding of the social world of Israel and Judah in the eighth century BCE, focusing especially on the dynamics of political economy (Chaney 1986, 1989a, 1993, 1999, 2004a). Many other scholars have contributed to that interpretation and continue to do so (see the works cited in Chaney 2004a:102 n12). A brief epitome of that ongoing work may be articulated in the following points:

1. Geopolitically, Israel and Judah occupied the land bridge where the regional superpowers met and clashed. As a result, stimulus for change in their political economies often came from beyond their borders. During the long and mostly concurrent reigns of Jerohoam II of Israel (ca. 781–745 BCE) and Uzziah of Judah (ca. 781–747 BCE), however, the two small kingdoms were relatively free from external military threat. They were in league, with the smaller Judah probably functioning as

a virtual vassal of the stronger Northern Kingdom. Coupled with the lengthy tenure in office of both kings, this situation gave the elites of the two states an unusual freedom to initiate change in their political economies. By the time foreign imperial power reasserted itself upon Israel and Judah in the person of Tiglath-pileser III, it served mostly to intensify the dynamics of political economy initiated earlier in the eighth century.

2. Israelite and Judahite elites had incentive as well as opportunity to change their politicai economies because of their active participation in international trade. Their import/export trade was mostly with and through the maritime city-states of Phoenicia. Luxury goods, military *matériel*, and the wherewithal of monumental architecture were imported. To pay for these imports, foodstuffs and fiber were exported. Wheat, olive oil, and wine, the triad of Palestinian agriculture, headed the list of exports. The costs and benefits of this trade were grossly disproportionate by class. Imports benefitted the elite few, but their cost in exported foodstuffs cut deeply into the sustenance of the peasant majority.

3. Prior to this time, wine and oil amphorae varied in capacity. The storage needs of subsistence agriculture required only utility, not uniformity, in the size of these vessels. Since wine and olive oil were the preferred exports in the greatly increased import/export trade of the eighth-century BCE, however, incentive for uniform units to expedite that trade resulted in a royal standardization of the *bt* ("bath"; see Chaney 1999:110–11, and the works there cited).

4. One way to increase production of the three preferred agricultural commodities was through a regional specialization of agriculture. Second Chronicles 26:10 witnesses such a process for Uzziah's Judah. Archaeological surveys show a marked proliferation of rock-cut olive and grape processing installations in the hill country in the eighth century BCE. The *lmlk*, ("for the king") seal impressions from Judah point to a system of royal vineyards in the uplands, while the Samaria ostraca document the flow of oil and wine to officials of the northern royal court from both private and royal vineyards and orchards (see Chaney 2004a:104, and the works there cited).

5. When integrated with comparatively normed coefficients of density, archaeological surveys of the total inhabited area evidence a marked rise in the population of Israel and Judah in the Iron II period. While absolute growth occurred in both the lowlands and the highlands, the

hill country grew faster, for the first time accounting for over half the total. One need not solve the old chicken-and-egg problem in social-scientific theory to know that rapid population growth and agricultural intensificntion are almost always correlated in agrarian societies. Archaeology also shows that various marginal areas, tilled only during periods of greatest central control and agricultural intensification, were inhabited in the eighth century BCE, many for the first time (see ibid.:105, and the works there cited).

6. Agricultural specialization and intensification fostered the proliferation of technological innovations. While scantly attested in the previous century, the beam press came into its own in the eighth century as an instrument for increasing the volume and efficiency of oil production.

7. In the eighth century, Israel and Judah increasingly developed "command economies," in which urban elites reduced or usurped villagers' power to make their own decisions regarding the priorities and techniques of agricultural production.

8. Pressure to grow ever-increasing amounts of the few preferred crops concentrated risk and effaced the risk-spreading mechanisms of the peasants' more traditional subsistence agriculture.

9. Land consolidation proceeded apace, aided and abetted by tax policy that discouraged the subsistence farming of cereals in the hill country, and thereby incentivized the raising of olives and grapes there instead.

10. Not only were agricultural labor and land ownership separated, but the various factors of production were segmented and subjected to separate rent.

11. There was a growth in absentee landlordism. With their promise of imported luxuries and greater access to political influence and social prestige, the capital cities drew landlords away from their country estates and their need for clientele support. What had previously been multi-stranded relations with their peasants were reduced to a single strand of economic exploitation.

12. Attenuation of risk-spreading measures rendered peasants ever more vulnerable to the vicissitudes of an erratic climate. When natural disaster struck, they were left no alternative to survival loans at de facto interest rates usurious by any standards. Foreclosure on family land and/or the indentured labor of family members pledged as collateral was often at the discretion of the wealthy urban creditors. Debt

instruments thus served as a major means of accomplishing both land consolidation and the pauperization of the peasantry.

13. Traditional village courts had few procedural safeguards. Increased socioeconomic stratification gave urban elites the power to coerce or suborn their decisions. Thus perverted, these courts gave a façade of legality to foreclosures deemed illegal by most pensants and other members of the lower classes. Against this background, the rhetoric of the eighth-century prophets appeals these cases to YHWH's divine law court in the sky. As auditors on the proceedings in God's court, the prophets report the vindication there of the peasants' cause, and declare that YHWH has found the urban elites guilty with regard to the matters under adjudication.

Can knowledge of these systemic dynamics inform and enhance the textual exegesis of oracles belonging to the earliest level of composition in the eighth-century prophets? Only a book-length treatment of the many oracles of these prophets whose subject is political economy could fully address that question. This far briefer venue allows only limited explication of one representative example.

MICAH 6:9–15 AS AN EXAMPLE

I have chosen to use Mic 6:9–15 for that purpose. Micah 6:9–16 is widely regarded as constituting a discrete unit (see Andersen and Freedman 2000:539–60; Ben Zvi 2000:153–65; McKane 1998:193–206; Runions 2001:169–72; and the works they cite). Elements of both form and content demarcate it from what precedes. Verse 16, which ends the unit in its canonical form, is virtually self-contained. Its vocabulary and rhetorical vector seem to echo the Deuteronomistic Historian's appropriation of Jehuid apology in 1 and 2 Kings, and likely mark it as an addition to the older unit (Mays 1976:148–49; McKane 1998:203–6; Wolff 1990:186, 197–98; see White 1997).

Of all the materials in the book of Micah after chapter 3, moreover, the unit in 6:9–15 is that most frequently associated by historical scholars with the dynamics of the prophet's own time. The unambiguous lines of this pericope seem to evince the same processes of political economy reflected elsewhere in the eighth-century prophets—including, quite notably, Micah 1–3. The passage so bristles with textual and/or philological difficulties, however, that both its literary stircture and its relation to any known set of socioeconomic dynamics have been in doubt. Proposed "solutions" to

210 PEASANTS, PROPHETS, AND POLITICAL ECONOMY

these problems have most often proceeded piecemeal, leaving both text and context in a focus decidedly blurred. The more extreme of these "solutions" have simply rewritten the text. Can insights from political economy help to illumine any of these issues?

Critically Established Text of Micah 6:9–15

9 קול יהוה לעיר יקרא[a] שמע[b] מטה[c] ומי יעדהו[d]
10 האשא[e] בת[f] רשע ואיפת רזון[g] זעומה
11 האזכה במאזני רשע ובכיס אבני מרמה
12 אצרות רשע אצרו[h] עשיריה[i] מלאו חמס
ישביה[j] דברו שקר לשונם רמיה בפיהם
13 גם אני החליתי הכותך[k] השמם על חטאתך
14 אתה תאכל ולא תשבע[l] וישחך[m] בקרבך
תסג[n] ולא תפליט[o] תפלט[p] לחרב אתן
15 אתה תזרע ולא תקצור
אתה תדרך זית ולא תסוך שמן
ותירוש[q] ולא תשתה יין

Translation of the Critically Established Text

The voice of YHWH calls the city (to account)—
Pay heed, O "tribe" that perverts (justice),
 for who can summon *him* (to court)?!
"Can I bear the wicked *bath* measure,
Or the accursed *ephah* of (leanness)   ?
  {the "potentate"}
Can I be clear with balances of wickedness,
Or with a bag of deceitful weight-stones?
Stores of wickedness they lay up,
Its [the city's] rich are full with wrong-doing.
Its lords speak lies;
As for their tongues—treachery is in their mouths!
For my part, *I* shall make sore your smiting,
Devastating (you) for your sins!
You will eat, but not be satisfied,
For you will be bent double with regard to your insides!
Should you {overtake} (something),
  {encroach upon}
  {fence}

you will not secure (it),
Should you "deliver" (someone),
    I shall give (them) to the sword!
You will sow, but not reap;
You will tread olives, but not pour oil (in anointing),
And (you will tread/dispossess) must, but not drink wine."

    a. In view of the poetic parallel and literary structure to be discussed below, יקרא is best understood in the well-attested sense of "call to account, summon" (C. L. Miller 1996:331–40).

    b. Read שמע, with LXX and Syriac, for MT's שמעו. MT's plural probably reflects the influence of Mic 6:1–2. ותושיה יראה שמך is a later addition, as seen by many commentators (see, e.g., Allen 1976:375; Mays 1976:143, 146; McKane 1998:193, 205; Shaw 1993:162; Wolff 1990:185, 191; and the works they cite).

    c. מטה probably involves paronomasia. As "tribe," it is kinship language used sarcastically of the urban elite, whose policies in Micah's time tended to efface such affiliations and their concomitants. Note a similarly sarcastic use of משפחה in Mic 2:3. But מטה is also the Hiphil participle of נטה. Used in the Hiphil, נטה often refers to "thrusting aside," "perverting," or "wresting" justice, even when the object is only implied, but not expressed (BDB 641a; *HALOT* 2:693b). Thus מטה can mean simultaneously "tribe" and "perverter of (justice)."

    d. ומי יעדה עוד, MT's much-discussed crux, has never received convincing interpretation. Many moderns since Wellhausen have followed LXX in preferring עיר (πόλιν) to MT's עוד, and then redividing and emending the resulting text to read ומועד העיר, "and assembly of the city."[1] Offered with Wellhausen's characteristic brevity and reserve—"vielleicht darf man, zum Teil nach der Septuaginta, ומועד העיר, lesen" (Wellhausen 1963:148)—this solution is ingenious, but suffers major liabilities. Lexicographically, מועד elsewhere means the "appointed time or place of meeting," not "assembly (of citizens)." The presumed sense of מועד in the reconstructed text of Mic 6:9 is unparalleled elsewhere, even though attestation is quite broad (BDB 417–18; *HALOT* 2:557–58).

    Once social history and the social perspective of the remainder of the unit are invoked, moreover, this emendation becomes even less plausible. No citizen assembly is evidenced for Jerusalem in Micah's time, nor is one likely according to any credible model for his society and its dynamics.

---

    1. See McKane 1998:193–94, and Runions 2001:169–70, for citation of earlier scholars who variously follow Wellhausen or propose even less felicitous "solutions."

212   PEASANTS, PROPHETS, AND POLITICAL ECONOMY

Other lines in the oracle castigate the ruling elite of the capital and their activities. Given the known parameters of change in eighth-century Judahite society, social-scientific models would predict increased social stratification and centralization of power, not citizen assemblies. On the other hand, "the city" in Micah's parlance is Jerusalem, the capital.[2] Its population had grown substantially in his lifetime, but in the rank order of cites and towns, its power had grown even more significantly, and at the expense of other sites, save, perhaps, Lachish. In that social and rhetorical context, "the city" in v. 9a refers far more probably to the few whose power is symbolized and made manifest in the monumental architecture of Jerusalem than to the city's total population, understood without differentiation.

Wide acceptance of Wellhausen's tentative emendation of v. 9c has probably obscured evidence for the line's elucidation that lies close to hand. Micah's text should probably be read in light of Jer 49:19; 50:44; and Job 9:19, the certain occurrences in MT of the Hiphil of יעד. The meaning of these Hiphils is, unambiguously, "to summon" or "to arraign." Jer 49:19b reads, with YHWH speaking, "For who is like me? Who can summon/arraign me (ומי יעידני)? Who is the shepherd who can stand before me!" Jeremiah 50:44b reads, again with YHWH speaking, "For who is like me? Who can summon/arraign me (ומי יועדני)? Who is the shepherd who can stand before me?" Job 9:19 reads: אם-לכח אמיץ הנה ואם-למשפט מי יועידני. In the first half of this verse, הנהו should probably be read for MT's הנה. With most moderns, I read the last word of the verse as יועידנו instead of MT's יועידני; cf. LXX and Syriac.[3] The tradition behind MT likely made the change to remove even the slightest suggestion that a human being might call God to account. The texts in Jeremiah might also have influenced this passage in Job. In any case, the slightly emended text may be translated, "If it is a matter of power, *he* is the strong one; if it is a matter of justice, who can summon/arraign *him*?" In each of these three passages, then, this use of מי with the Hiphil of יעד clearly involves a rhetorical question expressing God's incomparable power to summon any human being to arraignment. What could be more at home in a judgment oracle by a prophet named מיכה?

Since all three occurrences of מי plus the Hiphil of יעד appear to have God as the object of the rhetorical question, it is probably easiest in Mic 6:9 to read ומי יועדהו "for who can summon/arraign *him*?" with YHWH in v. 9a taken as the antecedent of the pronominal suffix. Read thus, v. 9c is a brief

2. A majority of commentators identifies "the city" as Jerusalem. For a partial list, along with citation and critique of a minority opinion that Samaria is involved, see Ben Zvi 2000:158, 162–64.

3. See, e.g., Pope 1973:72; somewhat differently, but to the same effect, Habel 1985:182–83.

and disputatious ejaculation addressed to the urban elite, who are indicted and judged in the remainder of the oracle. As a class, they were accustomed to summoning others and passing judgment upon them. They were also Micah's opponents who repeatetily tried to silence him. In this impassioned parenthesis, the prophet warns them to listen up, for it is *YHWH* who is calling the city and those who rule it to account. They cannot summon him up the way they do the peasants, whom they cheat and dispossess. Quite the reverse. In his call to the city, YHWH is summoning *them* for judgment. Micah's use of the rhetorical question may also be a defense of the source and authority of his judgment oracle. He does not speak in his own right, he insists, but only as an auditor on YHWH's court. No mere mortal summons YHWH to court for arraignment!

The עוד that follows יעדה in MT probably took its rise as עיר, a gloss suggesting that the suffix be read as third feminine singular rather than third masculine singular, with the city of v. 9a rather than YHWH as the antecedent. Such a reading is witnessed by LXX's πόλιν, which does not have the article. The tradents who originated this gloss might have had the same pious concerns as those in Job 9:29—to remove any hint that a human being could call God to account. Once the tradition behind MT lost the Hiphil inflection of יעד, however, עיר was easily corrupted into עוד.

e. After the ardent interjection of v. 9c, and as promised in v. 9a, YHWH here in v. 10 begins to speak directly in the first person. Of the two minor emendations standardly proposed for the first word of v. 10,[4] I prefer האשא "can I bear," to האשה "can I forget," for two reasons. The loss of the א from the form seems the more likely of the two haplographies. נשא in the sense of "bear, endure, permit" seems the closer parallel to (ב) זכה, "be clear (with)."

f. If אצרות רשע is understood as intrusive in v. 10—as will be argued below in the discussion of v. 12—the reading of בת for בית allows vv. 10 and 11 to be read as a poetic unit, clearly integrated in structure and content, and dealing exclusively with the dishonest use of weights and measures in exchange transactions to cheat those already vulnerable.

> Can I bear the wicked *bath* measure,
>   Or the accursed *ephah* of leanness?
>
> Can I be clear with balances of wickedness,
>   Or with a bag of deceitful weight-stones?

---

4. For a summary of scholars choosing each option, see McKane 1998:194–95.

בת and איפה also occur paired, and in the same order, in the futility curse of Isa 5:10:

> For ten acres of vineyard shall produce but one *bath*,
> And a *homer* of seed shall produce only an *ephah*!

This curse is part of a sentence issued in God's court for the crime of unscrupulous land consolidation. I have sought elsewhere to explicate its social location and rhetorical vector.

> The word translated "acre" is צמד, which means literally "yoke" or "span." By extension, it also signifies the amount of land a plowman can plow in a day with a yoked team of traction animals (BDB: 855; *HALAT*: 967). Like its counterparts in the native languages of many other traditional agrarian societies, it is basically a unit of peasant labor, not a mathematically exact quantity of land treated as a commercial entity. In Isaiah's carefully crafted language, however, the futilely low yield of formerly subsistence land now planted to vineyard is expressed in terms of a wine amphora of standardized capacity, designed to facilitate trade in wine as a commodity. Archaeology has now recovered several exemplars of this royally standardized eighth-century amphora inscribed with either בת or בת למלך (Avigad 1953; Inge; Mittmann; Naveh). Isaiah's parallel line continues the contrast between a positive valence for vocabulary rooted in the world of village subsistence and a negative tenor for terms that epitomize the innovations pressed by the urban elite in their program of agricultural intensification. The חמר is an "ass-load," an inexact measurement pertinent to the work realities of peasants (*HALAT*: 317). The איפה, approximately one-tenth of a חמר, is the dry measure equivalent of the בת (BDB: 35; *HALAT*: 41), and like it, is a standardized unit intended to expedite commercial transactions—this time, in grain. As is so often the case with prophetic language, Isaiah's words have both a concretely precise denotation and emotionally charged connotations that assist rhetorically in driving home the judgment rendered (Chaney 1999:110–11).

These same connotations for בת and איפה are as likely for Micah's usage as for Isaiah's, since both critique the same generic context.

    g. Is there a sarcastic pun here between רזון, "leanness, wasting, scantness," and רזן, "potentate," a title that appears parallel to מלך in Prov 14:28? Certainty is impossible, but several lines of reasoning render such paronomasia plausible. As seen above, the איפה was the dry-measure counterpart of the בת, which is known to have undergone royal standardization in the eighth-century BCE. Because this standardized liquid measure was ceramic, numerous exemplars of the eighth-century בת have survived, several with identifying inscriptions. As a dry-measure, on the other hand, the איפה would have been constructed of organic materials that decompose without leaving evidence for the archaeological record. Social-scientific study of agrarian societies regarding exchange transactions in grain may go far to make good this lack of more concrete evidence.

The function of units of dry measure for cereals in such societies is complex. When grain is involved in commerce among agrarian elites, accurate, standardized units are of the essence to expedite large-scale trade between relative equals. When transactions entailing grain take place between landlord and peasant or grain merchants and the poor, however, the exact size of baskets or other devices used to measure cereals is characteristically malleable, almost always to the disadvantage of the weaker party to the transaction. Amos 8:5 famously witnesses the situation in which grain is scarce and dear, and the poor must buy it in the market for survival. The איפה is smaller than standard, the counterweight in the balances used to weigh the payment in silver is heavier than standard, and the balances themselves are rigged to exacerbate the overpayment.

When a tenant's rent is due to his landlord at harvest time in kind, however, grain measures tend to expand. James Scott analyzes a typical example from Burma and its impact within peasant culture:

> The most transparent and despised method of circumventing local traditions was to devise a "landlord's basket" that held more. The ingenuity of landowners and their agents in the design of such baskets was seemingly inexhaustible. Some baskets were constructed so as to balloon out as they received rice, others were shaped to prevent leveling and ensure a heaping basket, certain methods of pouring increased the basket's capacity, and if it were shaken vigorously several times as it was filled, it would hold more ... The capacity of absentee landlords to adapt a special "rent-basket" that was always larger than the "village basket" came to be a galling symbol of their power to impose their will. (Scott 1976:71; cited partially by Hillers 1984:82)

Couper reports that the peasants affected by such practices often named the offending instrument, blaming it for their plight.

> But the light in which the villagers regard these baskets may be seen from the names which they give to them; for example the basket of a Letpadan landlord is known as "the cart-breaker,"

this basket is said to equal 150 milk tins as compared with the village basket of 136.

Tenants resent bitterly this right of enlarging the basket which the landlords have arrogated to themselves and many ascribe [to it] their present distress. (Cited in Scott 1976:71)

In Micah's generic counterpart to that world, then, it is not a far reach to suggest that poor peasants would protest bitterly that "the potentate's איפה"—whether as a standard unit for the grain that was rushed from their fields into international trade, as scant measure for the poor at the grain merchant's stall, or as the enlarged landlord's unit that alienated more and more of the crop from those who produced it—was, for them, "an איפה of leanness, wasting, and scantness." The Burmese example, and those like it from virtually every agrarian society from which there is sufficient evidence, at the very least grant verisimilitude to the conjecture that the language of Micah's oracle involves a bitterly ironic play between the two meanings of רזון in biblical Hebrew.

h. The reconstruction of this half-line presumes the following history of textual transmission: אצרות רשע was first lost by haplography, the basis of which is patent. The parent of MT later added it back, perhaps from a marginal gloss, but misplaced it into v. 10. This misplacement was probably influenced by the frequent association of בית and אוצר and the occurrence of רשע in both expressions. Thus, this same process of transmission accounts for the reading of בת as בית in v. 10. This change, in turn, would have influenced the reading of האש for האשא, since without the reading of בת, האשא was no longer intelligible. Some version of the full half-line reconstructed here as v. 12a may have occurred in the Hebrew *Vorlage* of the LXX in v. 10. LXX reads: θησαυρίζων θησαυροὺς ἀνόμους as a part of v. 10.

The loss of אצרות רשע in v. 12 by hapiography left אצרו orphaned at the beginning of v. 12, where it was subsequently read as אשר, a particle often in evidence in the book of Micah. Possible influences include the עשיריה, which follows immediately, and, perhaps, the smudging of the tail on the צ. If the reading of ואשר in v. 14 already existed, it too could have been such an influence. Alternatively, the reading of a secondary אשר in v. 12 might have been the source or the pattern for the reading of ואשר in v. 14. While the reading of אשר in v. 12 was intelligible and transmittable, it is hardly poetic, as most commentators have seen. The secondary אשר, however, might have seemed to assist in bridging the gap between the עיר of v. 9 and the third feminine singular suffixes of v. 12. Such a function might have helped to solidify its place in the text.

The form אצרו, reconstructed as a part of v. 12a, bridges between the divine first-person address of vv. 10 and 11 and the third-person indictment of v. 12. It is congruent with the plural perfects, מלאו and דברו that follow. The "they" that "lay up stores of wickedness" are both the unjust weights and measures that are the subject of YHWH's first-person speech in his own voice and the "rich" men and "lords" of the city who are castigated in the third-person indictment that follows immediately. Micah says that wicked and deceitful weights and measures have increased the "surplus" extracted by the urban elite from the peasants of the countryside. Thus the storehouses of the capital city lay up "stores of wickedness."

i. Content and context require that the antecedent of the third feminine singular suffixes of v. 12 be the עיר addressed in the beginning in v. 9a. This construction is bold, but it is no license to reorder the verses. The overweening supremacy of Jerusalem and its ruling elite in eighth-century Judah allowed such elliptical syntax to remain unambiguous.

j. As I have argued at length elsewhere (Chaney 1999:112–16), the participle ישב in this and other contexts where the urban elite are clearly the addressees, is not to be read as an undifferentiated indication of the "inhabitants, citizens, townsmen," or "people." In such contexts, the ישבים are those who "besit" large estates and seats of judgment and power. The ישב par excellence is the king who "besits" the throne.

k. גם-אני signals the hinge between indictment and sentence. It marks the sharpest possible disjunction between the human criminals and their divine prosecutor. YHWH, the judge who summoned the ruling elite of Jerusalem for trial in v. 9, and then prosecuted their crimes, now announces their sentence and serves as its executor. That the heavenly judge at this point personalizes the sentence by addressing each perpetrator in the second masculine singular should occasion no surprise. This rhetorical device for heightening the specificity of address is common in the prophets. The exalted social position of those so addressed had effectively placed them beyond the justice of human courts. How the worm turns when the prophet's rhetoric takes the case on appeal to the heavenly court of last resort!

l. The sentence proper now begins with this first in a series of futility curses.

m. After all the discussion (Ehrman 1973:103–5; Cathcart and Jeppesen 1987:110–15; McKane 1998:196–98), MT's consonants are most easily read as a Hiphal imperfect third masculine singular from שחח or שחה plus the second masculine singular suffix. A literal translation would be, "For it will bend you down with respect to your insides." Most forms once thought to be Hithpalel from שחה are, of course, in the light of the Ugaritic evidence, Hishtaphel from חוה. But Prov 12:25 seems to witness a Hiphil form from שחה with a use of the preposition ב- not unlike that here. Two forms in Isa 25:12 and 26:5, both parallel to השפיל, are standardly read as Hiphil from

שחח. In our text, I read the third masculine singular form as expressing an indefinite subject (GKC §144d) and the -ב of בקרבך as meaning "with regard to, respecting," much as in Prov 12:25. The image thus conveyed is that the haughty rich, who are overly full of food wrested from the starving poor, will become victims of their own gluttony. They will be humbled, bowed down, and brought low by severe nausea and/or diarrhea. Such an understanding of the line seems to be supported by both Syriac and Targum.

n. תסג is a second masculine singular Hiphil jussive, but from what "root"? Wordplay seems likely among נשׂג "overtake," as what a predator does to its prey, סוג I, which in the Hiphil usually refers to "displacing" or "moving back" a boundary marker, and סוג II, which seems to deal with "fencing about." From Micah's perspective, the urban elites of his time were guilty of all three actions against the persons or fields of the poor peasants. Knowledge of the systemic dynamics of the political economies of Judah and Israel once again provides the background against which sarcastic paronomasia can be explored.

o. In its other occurrence in the Hiphil, Isa 5:29, פלט is used in figurative speech of a lion carrying off its prey to secure it. That image works well here, too. The rapacious elite may "overtake" the persons and fields of their peasant prey, they may gain more land by "displacing" boundary markers, they may even "fence about" the land they have taken, but they will not be able to "drag off into security" the prey upon which they have pounced. Fields cannot be carried into exile.

p. As discussed above, ואשר is probably secondary. Its occurrence at this point may be related to the secondary אשר in v. 12. In a delicious play on פלט in two different conjugations, the predator has become the prey. The urban elite, unable to secure their kill in the first half of the bicolon, have, by its second half, themselves become the kill!

q. As seen by Pope (1972:178–79) and Loretz (1977), among others, ותירוש involves wordplay. The form can be heard both as a noun, meaning "must, new wine," and as a second masculine singular imperfect verb, meaning, variously, "you shall tread, take possession of, dispossess, drive out, impoverish." In the prophet's sarcastic paronomasia, it probably means all of the above simultaneously and in concert.

r. As here reconstructed, the oracle proceeds in regular bicola, save only for the single tricolon that marks its conclusion. Recognition of such a terminating device confirms the judgment of many scholars, noted above, that v. 16 derives from a later recomposition of the book of Micah that is reminiscent of the language and concerns of the Deuteronomistic Historian's incorporation and reorientation of Jehu's apology. This tripartite capstone of the series of futility curses, of course, reprises the triad of Palestine's agricultural economy and the terms of its production and distribution. The architects and beneficiaries of agricultural intensification will reap none of the fruits of all the labor they worked so hard to commandeer!

CONCLUSIONS

1. When combined with the textual, linguistic, and literary tools standardly in use in exegesis, attention to the dynamics of agrarian political economy facilitates fresh and intrinsic interpretation of several of the cruxes in Mic 6:9–15.

2. The results unify the oracle rhetorically and clarify its literary structure. It opens with a summons to judgment in v. 9 expressed in the prophet's voice. In vv. 10 and 11, the קול יהוה (voice of YHWH) asks in the first person a dramatic series of rhetorical questions that begin the indictment. Verse 12 continues the indictment in the third person. The divine first person reappears in v. 13 to initiate the sentence. Thereafter, the judgment is personalized to each of those guilty of the crimes indicted by use of the second-person singular. A measure-for-measure correspondence between the indictment and the sentence makes the punishment fit the crime. A version of this measure-for-measure dynamic also operates within the futility curses that express most of the sentence.

3. As interpreted here, the oracle more clearly and consistently reflects systemic processes well known from numerous other passages in the eighth-century prophets, including most of Micah 1–3. This congruence strengthens the suggestion that it is closely associated in context and composition with those earlier chapters in the book.

4. When the dynamics of political economy castigated by the eighth-century prophets are brought into sharper focus, modern interpreters are better positioned to detect and appreciate the frequent paronomasia that heightens the irony and sarcasm of prophetic judgment oracles.

5. If I am correct in my assessment of one such pun in v. 10—if איפת רזון identifies both "an איפה of leanness" and "an איפה of the potentate"—the reading adds allusive witness to a growing body of archaeological and textual evidence for change and conflict in the configuration and function of weights and measures in eighth-century Israel and Judah.

6. Adding the perspectives of political economy to the exegetical toolbox has proved fruitful enough in the interpretation of Mic 6:9–15 to invite similar study of other pericopes in the eighth-century prophets that presume and address the same systemic dynamics.

12

Korea and Israel

Historical Analogy and Old Testament Interpretation[1]

Abstract

This conceptual essay seeks a disciplined comparison of Korea and Israel as monarchic societies, a comparison that explores differences as well as similarities. Methodological control is sought in comparative sociology and anthropology, particularly in Gerhard Lenski's delineation of "agrarian societies." Other similarities between Israel and Korea—not common to all agrarian societies as defined by Lenski—are investigated. 1) The arable land in both occurred in small regional units that differed from one another in a number of variables. 2) Both evolved monarchic nation-states as a result of secondary state

---

1. It was an honor and privilege to read a version of this paper at the International Conference in Celebration of the Jubilee Year of the Korean Society of Old Testament Studies. I am most grateful for the warm welcome accorded me on that occasion and for the responses there to my essay. I congratulate the Society most heartily for having achieved this impressive milestone in its distinguished history.

Most of this essay was written during the spring term of 2010, while I was a Visiting Professor at The United Graduate School of Theology of Yonsei University. A version of the paper was delivered there on May 17, 2010. I hereby acknowledge with deep gratitude the generous hospitality of the administration, faculty and students at Yonsei.

formation. 3) Regionally based centers of power in both vied with one another for political control. "National unification" involved one of these regions' domination of the others through a combination of military and diplomatic means. 4) Whenever central control weakened in either of the resulting monarchic states, however, regional loyalties produced rival candidates for national leadership. 5) Regionalism and factionalism were intrinsic to the process of state formation both in Korea and in Israel. 6) Rival narratives of state formation express this regionalism and factionalism repeatedly in the agrarian histories of both societies, as well as in modern historiography regarding both. 7) This regionally initiated factionalism—particularly among elites—was exacerbated both in Korea and in Israel by their larger geopolitical position. Both were caught between more populous and powerful neighbors whose major-power interests met and clashed in Israel and Korea, respectively. Links between particular elite factions in Korea and Israel and specific "superpowers" often proved ephemeral, but the generic pattern of such alliances describes a powerful constant in the monarchic histories of both Korea and Israel. The "superpowers" routinely sought their own vested interests in these relations, while the factionalized elites of the two smaller states just as routinely sought to leverage powerful international connections to their own advantage domestically. 8) In both Korea and Israel, religious ideology was wielded by rival elites as a major medium to express and conduct regional and factional conflicts. 9) As a result, the official articulation of religious ideology in both societies was more often than not polemical. 10) Influence from herders, though impacting the two societies by different means, probably heightened male dominance in both. Summary examples illustrating these generalizations are then offered from the Hebrew Bible, beginning with "The Apology of David" in 1 and 2 Samuel and ending with the circumstances and actors of "The Division of the Kingdoms." These examples include frequent allusions to Korean analogs.

A series of hermeneutical suggestions and questions concludes the essay. What would be the result if Korean Old Testament scholars owned and honed their unique knowledge of and access to Korean history and culture as an intentional and distinctive part of their contribution to scholarship on the Hebrew Bible? Can comparative study of factionalism and sectionalism in biblical Israel and preindustrial Korea gain us some critical distance on the polemical articulation of religious ideology in both? What are the implications of understanding that both the biblical canon and Korean religious history include many voices that are "partial" in both senses of the English word—and for similar reasons?

~

INTRODUCTION

Any attempt to compare preindustrial Korea with biblical Israel must seem a strange project for an American professor of Old Testament who does not speak or read Korean. Add that my knowledge of Korean history is mostly self-taught and gained, of necessity, from sources available in western languages, and a topic nearer the center of one of my research interests in Hebrew Bible would seem a far more obvious choice of subject for this occasion. My genuine interest since the 1980s in the comparison of Korea and Israel hardly compensates for a lack of firsthand access to much that is intrinsically and essentially Korean. One brief written foray into this topic several years ago (Chaney 2001) probably would have ended my seemingly quixotic quest were it not for repeated experiences epitomized in a conversation that I had a number of years ago with a Korean colleague in theological education.

He had obtained his doctoral education in the United States and visited there often. On one such trip, he asked me to share with him what my Korean-American colleague, Dr. Warren Wonkyeng Lee, and I were doing in a course we were co-teaching that compared Israel and Korea. I replied that while I would be happy to share with him, he could learn nothing from me about Korea, because I had learned much of the little I knew from him. I have never forgotten his reply. He told me that, while of course I knew the history and culture of the United States in far more detail than he, he could show me things about them that I did not see because I was too close to them. In that regard, his "outsider" status gave him a perspective that was difficult or impossible for me to gain unaided. Conversely, he said, I occupied an analogous perspective regarding Korean history and culture. He promised to correct my errors of fact and of naïve misinterpretation, but urged that he was actively interested in what my outsider's eyes saw. We pledged to each other that day continuing and candid sharing of what we thought we saw when we looked at the other's homelands and their histories.[2]

---

2. This difference in perspective between "insiders" and "outsiders" is formalized in anthropological theory in the epistemological distinction between "emic" and "etic."

It is in the posture and spirit taught me that day—and on many other days by many other Korean and Korean-American colleagues—that I come to this subject. I do not in any way presume to interpret the Old Testament *for* Korean Christians and their churches nor to tell them how they should interpret it for themselves.[3] I have neither standing nor desire to assume such a posture. What I will try to offer is a very preliminary sketch of some of what I *think* I see when I juxtapose my work as a professional student of the Hebrew Bible with my interested beginner's knowledge of matters Korean. I hope and expect to be corrected on subjects large and small.

SOME ELEMENTS OF COMPARISON

The theoretical basis for my comparison of Korea and Israel during their monarchic periods lies in the fields of historical and comparative sociology and anthropology. More specifically, I refer to Gerhard Lenski's delineation of a limited number of generic types of human societies that have existed in the world (Lenski 1984:90–93; Lenski 2005:81–109; and Nolan and Lenski 2009:63–75.). Many of the societies about which we have the most historical information, including both Korea and Israel during their lengthy periods as monarchies, are what Lenski calls *agrarian* societies. In his theoretical framework, agrarian societies have as their principal economic base peasant agriculture that uses the plow and traction animals in some form, but does not make the extensive use of inanimate energy sources associated with the industrial revolution. For all their variation in the *specifics* of history and culture, societies meeting Lenski's definition of "agrarian" manifest striking similarities to one another at the *generic* level (Lenski 1984:189–296; Lenski 2005:96–99; and Nolan and Lenski 2009:137–75).

Agrarian societies, for example, are almost always monarchic in political organization, and evidence a remarkable consistency in their patterns of social stratification. A ruling elite of slightly less than two percent of the population controls more than half of the total goods and services produced by society. A peasant majority of from seventy to ninety percent of the population produces most of society's goods and services, but routinely gives up more than half its production to a variety of rents, taxes, and fees. Together

---

See, classically, Harris 1968:568–604.

3. On the other hand, I know from personal experience that I learn much when Korean Christians embrace their national experience and cultural heritage as a part of their disciplined interpretation of Old Testament texts. Several Korean scholars whose doctoral work I have been privileged to supervise have found historical analogies between Korea and Israel useful in voicing their own perspective on Old Testament interpretation; see Cho 2002; Hong 2006; S.-J. Kim 1996; and Woo 1998.

these exactions extract an economic "surplus" that is then redistributed based on priorities that the ruling elites set.[4] According to the historical indications we have, such was the situation both in Korea and in Israel from the time each evolved into a monarchic state.

Preindustrial Korea and biblical Israel shared a number of other characteristics, however, not evidenced by all agrarian societies.[5] The arable land in both occurred in relatively small regional units. Separated from one another by various natural impediments, these cantons were characterized by certain differences in climate, topography, soil, size and configuration of fields, and mix of crops and goods produced.[6] In both cases, this situation contrasted with the oldest, larger, near neighbor—Egypt in the case of Israel, China with regard to Korea. Major riverine systems in Egypt and China facilitated communication and transportation over far more extensive inland areas. They simultaneously provided incentive for the centralized control of the political economy necessary to bring large river valleys to their full potential for preindustrial agricultural production.[7] Egypt and China also present social scientists with major examples of "primary state formation," instances where the state arose without significant outside influence.

Israel and Korea, on the other hand, provide textbook illustrations of "secondary state formation." (For the comparative study of state formation, see, classically, Fried 1967 and Service 1975.) That is where a state is formed under the considerable influence of an older, neighboring state. The earlier chapters of the political history both of Syro-Palestine and of Korea are dominated by Bronze Age walled towns under the impress of the larger and older neighbors. Regional centers of power emerged early in the Iron Age in both areas, and these regions contested rule where their fluid borders met and crossed. National unification in both societies—David's kingdom in Israel and the so-called Silla unification in Korea—involved one of these regions' dominating the others through a combination of military and diplomatic means. Whenever central control weakened in either of the resulting monarchic nation-states, however, regional identities and loyalties

---

4. Note the convenient graphic summary in Lenski 1984:284–85; cf. Nolan and Lenski 2009:170–71.

5. The following discussion partially reprises an analysis that I first sketched in my essay, Chaney 1991:326 n6; Some wording is repeated here with permission.

6. For Korea, see, conveniently, Y.-H. Park et al., eds., 2008:2–13; and S. H. Kim et al., 2008. Most atlases of biblical Israel continue to be dependent for technical data upon the classical *Atlas of Israel*, 1985. Among older Bible atlases, that of Baly and Tushingham (1971) contains an unusually full treatment of matters relevant to this essay.

7. This is not at all to embrace the widely criticized theories of Karl Wittfogel (1981), but only to posit this factor as one among many.

born of the geographic environment produced a fractious gaggle of rival candidates for national leadership.[8]

Regionalism and factionalism were thus intrinsic to the process of state formation both in Korea and in Israel.[9] They were and are also intrinsic to the task of conceptualizing state formation in both societies. Critics of the "Silla Unification" version of state formation in Korea point out that proponents of the view have lived and worked in a modern South Korean state dominated during a formative period by leaders from the southeast of the country, the home territory of Silla. Some of these critics seek to find the mainstream of Korean national origins in Goguryeo and its successor states of Balhae and "Later Goguryeo." Though its rulers ranged far and wide, its territorial center of gravity was in what are today parts of North Korea and Manchuria—areas of particular interest to the proponents of this historical view (cf. Cumings 2005b:22–45; Han 2010a:56–64, 87–271; J. B. Kim 2004:27–35; K. Lee 1984:9–109; Noh 2004:3–25; and Song 2004:133–58). I have neither the knowledge nor the standing to evaluate independently these rival narratives of state formation in Korea. I note only that both the processes themselves and their historical interpretation were and are contested in ways that have deep regional and factional roots. Historical events on the ground were almost certainly more complicated and crosscut than any of the competing historical narratives, left to themselves, would make plain.

A parallel characterization is equally true for biblical Israel. From a Jerusalemite perspective, influenced heavily by the Deuteronomistic History and Deuteronomistic editing in a number of other Old Testament books, a true monarchic state began only with David. Texts in the Hebrew Bible

---

8. For Syro-Palestine and Israel, see, conveniently, Miller and Hayes (2006:1–85), and the literature there cited. For Korea, cf., variously, Cumings (2005:19–57); Han (2010a:75–304); and K. Lee (1984:9–138).

9. The discussion of *factionalism* has been far more explicit among historians of Korea, though Cho, 2002:105–334, begins comparative work. K. Lee (1984) controversially takes factionalized elites as the most salient factor in Korean history. In the Korean original, a concluding chapter, "The Ruling Elite and the Course of Korean History," not translated in the English version of the book (see p. vi), develops the theoretical point at some length. Cumings (2005b:22) comments briefly but trenchantly on the powerful role of *regionalism* in Korean history.

Discussions of Korean factionalism usually focus on the Joseon dynasty, particularly its latter portion. For a useful collection of writings about factionalism from within Joseon-dynasty Korea itself, see, Ch'oe, Lee, and de Bary, eds. (2000:12–33). Cf., further, Deuchler (1992:93, 299–300); Haboush and Deuchler, eds. (1999:5–6, 47–48, 123–24, 129); Jin (2005:407–12, 458); S. H. Kim et al. (2008:124–27); B. Lee (2008:109–12); Palais (1996:7, 19, 63–64, 92–93, 96–98, 101–2, 113, 457, 459; 539–40); and, Palais (1975:15–16, 291–92 n30).

of a more northerly provenance, where they have survived Jerusalemite editing, take a somewhat different tack. Certain Assyrian texts suggest to some that an Israel they could recognize as a monarchic state arose with the Omrids. Contemporary disputes among minimalist, maximalist, and moderate historians of ancient Israel routinely privilege one or another of these regionally and factionally rooted perspectives (see the convenient summary in Miller and Hayes 2006:119–326 and the literature there cited). Such historiographic battles are rarely lacking connections with regional conflicts in the modern Middle East, whether or not their contestants are fully conscious of those connections. Once again my concern here is to note this regionally and factionally based contestation and its longevity, not to resolve it.

The larger geopolitical location, moreover, reinforced this topographical proclivity for factionalized elites both in Korea and in Israel. Biblical Israel was flanked by societies more populous and powerful than itself. A significant role for these superpowers in the political economies of Palestine did not begin with the defeat and exile of the national leaders of Israel and Judah. Long before the superpowers dominated these petty states outright, they rarely ceased to meddle in the affairs of their smaller neighbors, who occupied the land bridge where superpower interests met and clashed. Egyptian, Mesopotamian, and other foreign diplomats sought influence with various factions of the Israelite and Judahite elites toward their own superpower ends. The latter, just as obviously, sought to strengthen their own hands domestically through powerful international connections, while at the same time retaining as much autonomy as possible from their foreign allies. Specific alignments were as intrinsically unstable as the generic dynamic was constant over extended periods.

Similarly, the factionalization of the elites of agrarian Korea was exacerbated by its geopolitical position in northeast Asia as "a shrimp among whales." Korea occupied the "turf" where the regional superpowers—China and, later, Japan (to whom Korea had mediated much in Chinese culture),[10]

---

10. The geopolitical position of Korea differed from that of Israel in at least one significant regard. Israel was caught between the two, ancient, primary, riverine civilizations of Egypt and Mesopotamia, both far larger and older than Israel. China was in an analogous role for Korea. Japan, by contrast, was a secondary state, dependent in many ways upon cultural antecedents in and initiatives from Korea. Japan was long the more populous of the two, however. McEvedy and Jones (1978:177, 181) offer the following estimates for the populations of Korea and Japan, respectively: in 800 CE, 2 million vs. 4 million; in 1500, 4 million vs. 17 million; in 1700, 6.25 million vs. 29 million; and in 1850, 9 million vs. 32 million. That difference in the size of the two societies frequently translated into differences in political and military power. Japan's nineteenth-century embrace of industrial technology exacerbated, but did not initiate, its power to pressure

and later still, Russia, the powers of western Europe and the United States of America—all contested claims and influence. Specific links between any given Korean elite faction and one of the larger, foreign powers often proved ephemeral, but the generic pattern of such alliances describes a powerful constant in Korean history.[11]

To be cogent and honest, of course, any socio-historical comparison such as that being sketched here between Korea and Israel as monarchies must look at significant differences as well as similarities. The two climates were quite different. Israel had a relatively mild, rainy winter and a mostly dry summer, both typical of its Mediterranean climate. Rainfall varied markedly, not only in its annual total, but also in its timing within the rainy season. Wheat was the staple grain, produced by rain agriculture. Because of the high risks inherent in rain agriculture in such a climate, the herding of sheep and goats and the raising of perennial tree and vine crops were important mechanisms of spreading risk. With its temperate climate and year-round precipitation, Korea was not quite as risky an agricultural environment. Irrigated, wet-paddy production of rice provided the staple grain. While both drought and flood could cause periodic devastation, neither was as omnipresent a threat as was drought in Israel. Long, severe winters in most of Korea helped to control agricultural pests in a manner not true for Israel's milder winter climate, but were themselves the source of much suffering.[12]

Korea was significantly larger than Israel both in territory and in population. The boundaries of both were fluid and fluctuated historically. For comparative purposes, however, it suffices to note that the Korean peninsula, south of the Yalu-Dumen border, is slightly over 220,000 km^2, while modern Israel plus the West Bank and Gaza cover approximately 27,000 km^2 (McEvedy and Jones 1978:142, 176). McEvedy and Jones estimate the population of Israel to have averaged less than 1 million throughout the Old Testament period, and often less than half that (ibid.:141–44). In Korea,

---

its Korean neighbor.

11. In addition to the controversial theories of K. Lee (1984) and the materials listed in n9 above, note, too, the perspectives of Yong-sop Kim and his students on late Joseon, now represented in English by Pang and Shin, eds. (2005).

12. According to modern measurements and assuming climatic variations within a relatively limited range in historical times, we can assume that a large majority of the territory of ancient Israel received between 300 and 800 mm. mean annual rainfall, with areas to the south and east receiving far less, and only mountainous regions near Lebanon receiving more; see *Atlas of Israel* (1985:12). By similar measure, a large majority of historical Korea received between 800 and 1400 mm. mean annual rainfall, with areas still wetter in the south and east and under 800 mm. only in the northeast; see Y.-H. Park et al. (2008:12).

they estimate a population of 1 million in 600 CE to have climbed to about 7.5 million by 1800 and to 12 million by 1900 (ibid.: 176–78). Using more recent data, Broshi and Finkelstein estimate a peak population for Israel and Judah combined to have reached ca. 460,000 in Iron Age II (1992:47–60), though Herr warns that their estimates for Transjordon are too high (1997:137). Estimates for Korea in the *Atlas of Korean History* agree in range with those of McEvedy and Jones, and vary internally for an eighteenth century peak in the population of Joseon from "over ten million" to a graphic depiction of over 18 million (S. H. Kim et al. 2008; cf. 132 with 108).

A population of 400,000 for ancient Israel would yield a population density of approximately 14.8 per km². A Korean population of 4 million, the estimate of McEvedy and Jones for both 1200 and 1500 and the average of all their estimates for the intervals from 600 to 1800 (1978:177), yields a population density of 18.2 per km². While such figures obviously should not be pressed—based, as they are, upon estimates—they tentatively confirm the rough comparability of agrarian technology in the Iron Age monarchies of Israel and Korea during most of their life. The numbers, of course, mask the markedly uneven distribution of population in the territories of both societies. The higher figure in Korea can be interpreted plausibly as the result, at least in part, of the higher average precipitation there. The much higher population figures for later Joseon probably reflect advances in agrarian technology and influences from industrializing societies, among other factors, and belie certain stereotypes of later Joseon as a moribund "hermit kingdom."

Korea and Israel also varied markedly in their access to the sea and their intercourse with other societies across it. Israel and Judah lacked significant harbors during monarchic times.[13] Their access to the sea was mostly through the Phoenician city-states. Korea, by contrast, was rich in natural ports. From an early period these ports supported fishing, seaborne trade, and international political and military relations. Whereas Israel occupied the land bridge where the regional superpowers met and clashed, Korea's interactions with China were by sea as well as by land, and with Japan, of necessity, by sea. Were any of Korea's episodes of technological innovation, such as that experienced during Sejong's time, related in any way to the maritime component in its advanced agrarian society?[14]

---

13. Only in Herod's time did his massive construction of an artificial harbor at Caesarea Maritima fundamentally change that situation. See, conveniently, Hohlfelder (1992:798–803).

14. For a review of innovations in early Joseon, see, conveniently, Y. W. Han (2010b:83–123). Lenski (2005: 99–101) and Nolan and Lenski (2009:181–83) note that the rate of technological innovation was faster, on balance, in maritime societies than

The agrarian monarchies of Israel and Korea were both related to herding societies, but in somewhat different ways. Regions too arid to support cultivation bounded Israel on the south and east. Between cropland and true desert, however, lay significant territories with sufficient precipitation during the rainy winter to support seasonal grasses and water holes. These areas served as winter pastures for flocks of sheep and goats. This use not only allowed economic exploitation of land too dry to cultivate, but also provided a "disaster bank on the hoof" that stored surpluses from wet years to be utilized in dry years when crops were sparse. The same flocks found summer pasture on the stubble of the harvested grain fields, fertilizing them with their bodily wastes as they grazed. Such herding was thus symbiotic with cereal agriculture in biblical Israel, and was incorporated into its agrarian society as an integral part (see Hopkins 1985:245–50; cf. Chaney 1989a:22–23).

Agrarian Korea had no such integral relationship with herding. It was a significant economic activity only in the relatively dry northeastern corner. But the vast grasslands of Central Asia were home to horse-riding herders who, in various configurations, were a major political factor in Manchuria and along what eventually became Korea's northern border. Such herders had a major impact in Goguryeo and its successor states, on Goryeo in the form of the Mongol invasions of the thirteenth century, and on Joseon in the form of the Manchu invasions, to name only the most famous instances. Many other periods of Korean history witnessed pressure and raids from the north by herders hungry to share the more abundant food supply of Korean agriculturalists. Notwithstanding that major and repeated political role, the generalizations of Nolan and Lenski about herding societies as a class also seem to fit the specifics of Korean history: "Despite their many military victories, herding peoples were never able to destroy the agrarian social order.

---

in the advanced agrarian societies to which they were most often related. The latter period of Goryeo saw an active maritime trade through the harbor near the capital on the Yeseong River estuary; see Han (2010a:265–67). Early Joseon saw an emphasis on naval forces to suppress Japanese piracy and to convert the relationship from raiding to trading; see Han (2010b:45–48). While Korea's trading partners in this period ranged from as far away as Arabia, Song China was the major such partner. Cumings writes of this period (2005b:42),

> Scholars have long pondered the rapid commercial and industrial development of the Song period, and the wide trading network that culminated in Admiral Cheng Ho's seven seafaring expeditions to the Persian Gulf and the African coast in the period of Yi Sŏng-gye and Sejong, that is, 1405–33. The question is, Why did this fruitful period come to an end?

That is, indeed, an important historical question. Another is whether an increased maritime component in Korea's agrarian society helped to spark technological innovation there.

In the end, it was always they, not agrarian peoples, who changed their mode of life" (Nolan and Lenski 2009:181; cf. Lenski 2005:101-3).

The analysis of herding societies by Nolan and Lenski may suggest one influence that they exercised in Israel and Korea both, though, as seen above, through rather different mechanisms. Even though virtually all agrarian societies are patriarchal in their gender relations,[15] herding societies appear even more male-dominant. Nolan and Lenski posit a principal reason for these tendencies. "Above all, they reflect the often militant nature of pastoral life. Raiding and warfare are frequent activities, and as we have noted before, these activities stimulate the growth of political authority" (Nolan and Lenski 2008:180). Does the ongoing influence of herding life upon monarchic Israel and Korea—even if by different means— help to account for the often-virulent patriarchalism in both? If so, that influence was compounded by the fact that their geopolitical positions guaranteed that they saw more than their share of agrarian warfare. Periods of protracted warfare and of agricultural intensification both tend to exacerbate male dominance (Bossen 1989:330-50; Chaney 2004a:106; and Meyers 1989:189-96.). Such technological, geopolitical and economic factors in the heightening of patriarchalism deserve to be investigated alongside the ideological influences of Neo-Confucianism more usually discussed by historians of Korea (cf. Cumings 2005b:47; Deuchler 1992:231-81; B. Lee 2008:5-6, 15-81; Palais 1996:27).

Other similarities between Israel and Korea suggest themselves. Barley was a secondary crop in both. Typically grown on land that was more marginal because of less availability of water, relatively higher altitude, soil that was alkaline, saline, or nutrient-poor, or some combination of these factors, it often served as the food of the poor in both societies (cf. Borowski 1987:91-92; Hopkins 2006:398; and Palais 1996:110). Arable land occurred in both in a patchwork of relatively small fields, interrupted by mountains in Korea, and both by mountains and by desert badlands in Israel. The topography of both produced many relatively small rivers and streams, though some of Korea's rivers were relatively larger and notably more navigable. But no huge valleys in either concentrated food production and social control, as was the case in China, Mesopotamia, and Egypt. Areas that could produce the most grain in both—Cholla in the case of Korea, areas in and near the Esdraelon and coastal plains in the case of Israel—tended to send more grain to their political capitals than they received commensurate goods and services from their national governments. Regional resentment was

---

15. Nolan and Lenski 2009:167-68. For a cogent explanation of the patriarchalism of agrarian societies, see Bossen 1989:318-50.

endemic in the areas thus exploited, and could be fanned into the flames of open rebellion when other factors proved conducive to it. Earlier tribal and/ or regional identities frequently resurfaced in these rebellions. Relatively slight differences in regional dialects also took on added significance in such conflicts.

The sources of regionalism and factionalism both in Korea and in Israel were thus multiple and similar. In addition, and most significantly, religious ideology in both societies served as a major medium to express and conduct regional and factional struggles. Rival elites often appealed to the same or similar religious traditions, but leveraged them to their own advantage and to their opponents' detriment. As a result, the articulation of religious ideology in both societies was frequently quite polemical. This disputatiousness of religious expression, in fact, recurred in Israel and Korea both across extended periods of time and wide variations in other factors. In my previous article, I surveyed the role of religious ideology in a whole series of regional and factional struggles in Korea. I also discussed briefly the genre and purpose of the Yahwist, Elohist, Deuteronomistic History, and the Priestly Writing in this same, comparative framework.[16] Chungshin Park has recently treated the first century of Protestantism in Korea from a similar perspective (2003). Strictures of space prevent repetition of any of that material here. Instead, as time permits, I wish to look at other examples.

REGIONALISM AND FACTIONALISM IN THE ESTABLISHMENT OF DAVID'S THRONE AND DYNASTY[17]

One obvious place to begin is with a brief discussion of the nature and function of what is often called "The Apology of David" in 1 Sam 16:14 through 2 Sam 5:10. These chapters present David's emergence over against the failures and purported crimes of Saul, whom he usurped. An insightful study of this material by McCarter judges it to be a royal apology (McCarter 1980;

---

16. Chaney 2001. On the role of religious ideology in Korean factionalism and sectionalism, note particularly the summarizing quotations in "Pluralism" from Eckert et al., 1990). On factionalism and religious ideology in biblical Israel and beyond, see, conveniently, Coote and Coote 1990.

17. Many contemporary scholars of the Hebrew Bible doubt, of course, any access to a "historical David." By writing this section of the current essay and those that follow, I reveal that I am neither minimalist nor maximalist. For convenient discussion of the historical issues regarding David and a representative sample of the literature, see Halpern 2001; McKenzie 2000; and Miller and Hayes 2006:148–85.

cf. Dick 2004). Following Hoffner's study of similar Hittite texts (1975b), McCarter characterize such an "apology" as "a document composed for a king who had usurped the throne, composed in order to defend or justify his assumption of the kingship by force" (Hoffner 1975b:49, quoted by McCarter 1980:495–96). Documents written in this genre routinely present the king or leader usurped as inept, corrupt, unpopular, and having lost the mandate of heaven. His usurper is just as routinely pictured as arising from obscurity through merit and being of spotless integrity, though frequently slandered. "Convenient" deaths that helped to pave his way to the throne, for instance, are "explained" as neither his doing nor intent. He also enjoys both popular acclaim and divine mandate.

Saul and David, respectively, as portrayed in 1 Sam 16:14 through 2 Sam 5:10, certainly fit this pattern. Sectional as well as personal rivalries were involved. Saul was a Benjaminite, David a Judahite. The winner of a regionally based power struggle thus framed the perspectives and categories that have dominated perceptions of the period. If Saul or his apologist could speak from the grave, how might the historical picture be changed or nuanced? As we have already seen, accounts of national origins in general, and in Israel and Korea in specific, are rarely "neutral" or "objective." "History" is always a mediation between what is known or knowable about the past and the concerns, viewpoints, vested interests and meaning making of the historian and his or her constituency.

The founders of the Goryeo and Joseon dynasties in Korea both produced documents that—while not identical in literary genre—struck many of the same notes as David's apology, and for similar reasons. Both regional and factional factors played a role in the chaos and disintegration that preceded and led to the founding of Goryeo (cf. Han 2010a:238–48; and K. Lee 1984:97–105).

> All three rebel leaders of the Later Three Kingdoms period hoisted the banners of their independence in former Paekche and Koguryo territories. To rally support behind them, they exploited, with apparent success, the residual anti-Silla sentiment in these areas by invoking memories of long-vanquished kingdoms. That such sentiments could be exploited some two and a half centuries after the first attempt at unified rule in the peninsula is suggestive of a less than complete success in that original endeavor. Perhaps even more revealing is the fact that those who exploited it were persons with no known Paekche or Korguryo lineage in their background. (Lee and de Bary, eds. 1997:145)

Various of the proclamations of Wang Geon, Goryeo's dynastic founder known also by his posthumous title, Taejo, emphasize the failings and cruelty of Gungye, whom he usurped, faults that are seen as leading to the loss both of popular support and of divine mandate. He, by contrast, is portrayed as enjoying "hearty support" and the mandate of heaven, as learning from his predecessors' mistakes, working for the good of the whole country, and exhibiting widely acknowledged merit and integrity (ibid.:151–56). Yi Seonggye issued similar documents to justify his usurpation that brought the chaos and rivalries of the last years of Goryeo to an end (ibid.:272–76; cf. Han 2010b:25–30; and K. Lee 1984:162–65).

In biblical Israel, sectionalism and factionalism did not end with the "Davidic Unification." Numerous factors point to regional and factional conflicts throughout David's rule and far beyond (Chaney 1986:67–74). He became "king" of his home tribe of Judah first. Only years later and separately did he assume the throne of the "northern tribes," and even then the North was grudging. Leaders in the remnant of the Saulid camp sensed that their hand had played out. With no viable heir to the throne, they apparently saw David as a lesser evil than the Philistines. Sensitive to these tensions, David took measures to address certain of the regional and factional rivalries inherent in his so-called "United Monarchy" (see Miller and Hayes [2006:167–69] and the literature there cited).

Choice of a capital city loomed large amidst these tensions. The natural capital of his home tribe of Judah was Hebron, an old Bronze Age city-state. Shechem was in many ways the counterpart in the northern hill country. Had David chosen Hebron as his national capital, he would have alienated further the already suspicious North. A choice of Shechem, however, would have separated him from his base of power and left his most stalwart supporters feeling betrayed. Rather than either of these costly choices, then, David opted to move the national capital to Jerusalem, an old Jebusite city on the border between North and South, but not previously part of either. It had become David's possession through right of conquest by his personal troops.[18] David also sought religious legitimation for his new capital by

---

18. Miller and Hayes 2006:169–72. Like David, the founders of the Goryeo and Joseon dynasties both chose to emphasize their break with the immediate past by moving their capitals. Geopolitical concerns were involved in both cases. Han (2010a:241) says Wang Geon "moved the capital back from Cheorwon to his power base of Songak (Gaeseong)." Cf. Lee 1984:111–12. The decadence of Goryeo's final years encouraged the new Joseon dynasty to symbolize a fresh start by moving the capital from Gaeseong to Hanyang (Seoul).

> While Baekje had been able to build a strong kingdom with Hanyang as its capital for over 500 years, the city was thereafter intermittently occupied by both Goguryeo and Silla. In this regard, as Hanyang incorporated cultural

bringing the ark there after its return by the Philistines. He hoped thereby to link his regime to the religious traditions and rituals previously focused in Samuel, Shiloh and its priesthood. Shiloh was in the territory of Ephraim, a major northern tribe (Miller and Hayes 2006:176–77). The northern tribes, however, never "owned" Jerusalem, "the city of David," as their capital the way David's home tribe of Judah did.

Other elements point to continuing tensions within his regime. The national sanctuary that he established in Jerusalem had a dual high priesthood. Abiathar traced his line back to Shiloh and represented its tradition. Zadok, whose origins scholars have traced variously to Jerusalem or Hebron, was more identified with the innovations of the Davidic monarchy than with the North's religious past. David's military command was similarly divided. Joab, his kinsman, was in charge of the tribal levies—citizen soldiers with roots firmly in the soil of premonarchic Israel. Benaiah son of Jehoiada, on the other hand, was over "the Cherethites and Pelethites," Cretan and Philistine mercenary shock troops who were related to David much as he and his band of irregulars had once been related to Achish, the Philistine ruler of Gath (Chaney 1986:70; and Miller and Hayes 2006:177–79).

REGIONALISM AND FACTIONALISM IN SOLOMON'S SUCCESSION AND ADMINISTRATION[19]

The factional tensions witnessed in these dual administrative structures became only too apparent when David grew old and his sons and retainers struggled with one another over the succession to his throne. (Absalom's earlier attempt to usurp his father had surfaced—in the persons of Mephiboseth (Merib-baal) and Shemei son of Gera—old animosities regarding David's usurpation of Saul; Miller and Hayes 2006:172–76). The final struggle to succeed David involved Adonijah, David's fourth son by his wife Haggith in Hebron, and Solomon, the tenth of David's sons, born after David was long ensconced in Jerusalem. Among the party that supported Adonijah were Joab and Abiathar. Their respective counterparts, Benaiah and Zadok, conversely, supported Solomon (Chaney 1986:70).

---

elements of all three kingdoms, it was in many ways the least affected by regional sentiment. (Han 2010b:32–33)

Cf. K. Lee (1984:165) and P. H. Lee and de Bary, eds. (1997:277–78). Both Gaeseong and Hanyang were in the region where the Silla and Goguryeo spheres of influence and centers of gravity met and overlapped; cf., conveniently, S. H. Kim et al. 2008:68–69.

19. For the many historical issues regarding Solomon and his administration, see Miller and Hayes (2006:186–220) and Handy, ed. (1997).

As a much younger son, Solomon was by no means the obvious choice to succeed his father. When he at last surmounted this factional struggle for power, however, his actions regarding those of his father's officials who had supported his rival are informative. He instructed Benaiah to violate the sanctuary of the altar to which Joab had fled. Benaiah unceremoniously dragged Joab from the altar and dispatched him forthwith. Abiathar's treatment was a bit different. As a priest, he might have been more powerful in death than in life if Solomon had martyred him. Instead, he removed him from office and the center of power in Jerusalem by exiling him to his country estate at Anathoth (Ibid.; cf. Halpern 2001:391–406).

Both dynamics find numerous parallels in the factional power struggles of the Joseon dynasty in Korea. Many a high official paid with his life for being on the wrong side of a succession struggle. Others, whose lives were spared, were nevertheless rendered relatively powerless by being banished from Seoul and its court intrigues to live in exile "under the grass roof" on their family estates. Sectional and clan rivalries were frequently involved.

Another element of sectional and factional conflict manifests similarities between Israel and Korea. Royal and elite marriages in both these monarchic states involved complex diplomatic ties (for Korea, see B. Lee 2008:48–52, 109–84). David's rise to power was replete with multiple marriages designed to forge alliances and to neutralize or overcome rivals (Levenson and Halpern 1980). Just as David's sons by these wives were rivals to succeed to their father's throne, their mothers were rivals, both for David's favor and on behalf of their sons' dynastic ambitions. Bathsheba's role in the final contest of David's sons for his throne was only the first of many such episodes. Any royal wife whose son succeeded to the throne would probably enjoy an influential position at court (see Bowen 2001 and the literature there cited). Solomon, if one is to credit a historical kernel in the tendentious biblical descriptions, took the convention of diplomatic marriages to new heights, thereby forming marriage alliances with a number of foreign rulers.

Most royal wives remained in active contact with their fathers, uncles, brothers, and male cousins. They could thus serve as two-way conduits between affairs at court and the interests of their home clan or country. That is why, in the books of Kings, the formulary summarizing the reign of a king of Judah usually mentions his mother by name and often by affiliation (ibid.:616–17 provides a convenient table with references). These data are not biblical trivia. They are important indications of powerful connections and influences impacting the king in question and his rule. The matters at issue far transcended merely personal considerations.

Another tension fractured the elites of the Israelite and Korean monarchies. Aristocracies in both were supported by agricultural production on landed estates that they often held in perpetuity and passed on from father to son in so-called patrimonial domain. The more secure an aristocrat's hold on the tenure and income of his land, the greater his de facto independence from the crown. The bureaucracies necessary to administer both of these monarchies formed the other pole of this tension. Deployed at least partially on models from Egypt and China, respectively, bureaucrats in Israel and Korea usually enjoyed much of their power and privilege only as long as they retained royal favor and office. When the income of a particular estate supported the holder of a given bureaucratic office only while he was incumbent in that office, so-called prebendal domain obtained. Such arrangements gave the crown greater power. (For a description and analysis of "patrimonial" and "prebendal" domains, see, classically, Wolf 1966:50–59.)

Patrimonial and prebendal domains are ideal types, with the histories both of Israel and of Korea witnessing many mixtures and combinations. Tensions between landed aristocrats, on the one hand, and the crown and its royal bureaucrats, on the other, however, constituted an important source of fractioning (for Korea, see the well-informed generalizations of Cumings 2005b:40). In Korea's Joseon dynasty, for instance, particularly in its latter period, the yangban aristocracy was markedly successful in resisting royal taxation. That configuration of power left an enfeebled national government to face the aggressive incursions of Japan and the West in the late nineteenth and early twentieth centuries (Han 2010b:269–72 and 2010c:25–120; and K. Lee 1984:224–327).

When powers and jurisdictions between the aristocracy and the royal bureaucracy were not clearly defined, peasantries usually suffered. Peasant agriculture was the economic base, both of the aristocracy and of the royal court. Both sets of overlords had incentive to extract as much "surplus" as possible. If not restrained by clear jurisdictional lines, the combined demands of local aristocrats and royal bureaucrats could easily bring vulnerable peasants to ruin, thereby killing the goose that laid the golden egg. Under such circumstances, peasants longed for redress from a "good king," who could and would understand, balance, and modulate the multiple pressures on peasant production, and restrain both aristocratic and bureaucratic rapaciousness. Understanding these complex tensions goes far to illumine both the iconic status of King Sejong in Korean history and culture and the rise of so-called "messianic expectation" in biblical Israel. (On Sejong, see Kim-Renaud 1997; for "messianic expectation" in Israel, see Day, ed. 1998 and the literature there cited.)

Solomon's administrative structures concentrated power in the royal court and drove the peasantry, particularly that of north Israel, to the brink. While details remain unclear and disputed, it seems probable that Solomon's tax regime favored his home region and power base in Judah and bore heavily on the North. Corvée duty on royal building projects and royal land constituted a direct tax on peasant labor and added to the already heavy burden of taxes in kind (see, conveniently, Miller and Hayes 2006:212–14, and the literature they cite). One is reminded of the role of the Cholla region in most of Korean history. It was the "rice bowl," much of whose production was exported to feed others, but it received few commensurate goods or services in return. It is small wonder that many of its citizens through the years have cast longing glances back to the days of Baekje's power.

REGIONALISM, FACTIONALISM, AND NATIONAL DIVISION

Royal dynasties deemed oppressive by significant sections of their realm are particularly vulnerable when an old king dies and his son and successor has not yet consolidated his reign. That was the case when Solomon died and his son and designated heir, Rehoboam, sought to succeed him. Many of the elements of sectionalism and factionalism already reviewed were involved in the ensuing events that ultimately divided the South and the North into the separate monarchies of Judah and Israel. David, it should be remembered, had come to rule the two regions separately.[20] Solomonic consolidation of royal power had removed the checks and balances of David's regime and had consistently favored Judah over northern Israel. That northern hostility

---

20. Partial parallels in Korea deserve thoughtful, nuanced exploration. National division in Korea is so traumatic a topic that it is often difficult to discuss it historically. Any historical account of the division has powerful ethical and political implications in the present. As an American, I am painfully aware of the role my government played. Probably this can be said, however, with wide agreement among historians—in Korea, as in Israel, regional identities and differences, broadly correlated with the two divided nations, *preceded* the particular national state that was divided. K. Lee (1984:71) writes that "Unified Silla and Parhae confronted each other hostilely much like the southern and northern halves of a partitioned nation . . ." While Cumings (2005b:35) cautions that Lee's characterization may risk some retrojection, he does so in the context of making precisely the point about regionalism being pressed here. Elsewhere (2005a:405–6), Cumings summarizes what he regards to be the surest conclusion of Yong-sop Kim's detailed and voluminous scholarship: "the root cause of the national division is to be found in the history of lord and peasant, and the remedies that both Koreas took (or did not take) to deal with the fundamental problems that arose from those longstanding relationships." As we are about to see, elite-peasant relations were also of the essence in the division of ancient Israel.

to Solomon's oppressive policies had left his son in a weakened position is evidenced by Rehoboam's traveling to Shechem—the "natural" capital of the North—to meet with the assembly of Israel (1 Kgs 12:1). Had he been playing a stronger hand, representatives of the North would undoubtedly have come to the court in Jerusalem to do obeisance.

There are several indications that oppressive taxation of the North was a major bone of contention. Corvée duty seems to have been particularly hated. Rehoboam was asked, "Now therefore lighten the hard service of your father and his heavy yoke that he placed on us, and we will serve you" (1 Kgs 12:4). The older men who counseled Rehoboam advised that he heed the people's request. His younger advisors, however, like him born to the purple, counseled a harsh and contemptuous show of authority: ". . . thus you should say to them, 'My little finger is thicker than my father's loins. Now, whereas my father laid on you a heavy yoke, I will add to your yoke. My father disciplined you with whips, but I will discipline you with scorpions'" (1 Kgs 12:10–11). When Rehoboam took the advice of his young contemporaries, the people of the North seceded from the rule of the Davidic dynasty: "What share do we have in David? We have no inheritance in the son of Jesse. To your tents, O Israel! Look now to your own (dynastic) house, O David" (1 Kgs 12:16).

Three public personages who figure prominently in these events of national division also point up the fact that sectional animosities, fueled in part by Jerusalem's abuse of corvée service in the North, were at the heart of the dispute. Rehoboam sent Adoram—also called Adoniram—to quell the rebellion of the Northerners. When corvée had been instituted later in David's reign, Adoram was the officer placed in charge. He had functioned as chief of corvée throughout Solomon's rule. He thus epitomized what northern peasants who had suffered under the corvée of the Davidic dynasty so hated, and they responded corporately by judging him guilty of capital crimes and stoning him to death (see, conveniently, McMillion 1992:76).

In its break with the Davidids, the North was led by Jeroboam. His background is instructive. A man of humble beginnings, he had impressed Solomon with his ability. As a result, the king had placed him over the corvée of "the house of Joseph," that is, of the two large and powerful northern tribes of Ephraim and Manasseh. As is frequently the case for such officials in agrarian monarchies, Jeroboam had "played both ends against the middle." While he had been ingratiating himself to Solomon, he had also been playing on northern grievances that he knew only too closely. When Solomon found him out, he fled to Egypt. Egypt's geopolitical strategy in Syro-Palestine had for centuries been the policy of "divide and conquer." The kingdom on the Nile routinely harbored dissident leaders from the petty states of western Asia. Jeroboam undoubtedly enjoyed Egyptian encouragement in sundering the realm of the Davidids. Small-power factional and sectional politics were inseparably linked to large-power geopolitical manipulation in Israel as in Korea. (On Jeroboam, see, conveniently, Toews 2008:241–45.)

Because Jeroboam was the son of a nobody, an upstart and a secessionist, he needed religious legitimation even worse than most agrarian kings. We should note carefully where he found it. The prophet Ahijah, called "the Shilonite," sanctioned Jeroboam's secession with an acted prophecy (1 Kgs 11:29–38). Ahijah's title, "the Shilonite," links him with the same religious tradition represented by Abiathar. David had, of course, welcomed Abiathar as one half of his dual high priesthood, but Solomon had deposed him and exiled him to his family estate in Anathoth for supporting Solomon's rival, Adonijah. That faction of northern religious tradition now came back to bite Solomon's son in the person of Ahijah. Three centuries later, Jeremiah, who was "from among the priests who are in Anathoth in the land of Benjamin" (Jer 1:1) and who had a special interest in the traditions of Shiloh, probably served as an heir of that same, continuing tradition.

Even after Jeroboam had made good on the political establishment of a separate northern state of Israel with the help of Ahijah's religious legitimation, he still had a problem of religion. The ark—at one time the chief icon of the Shilonite religious tradition in which Samuel, Abiathar, and Ahijah all stood—now resided in the inter sanctum of the Davidic dynastic temple built by Solomon in Jerusalem. Jeroboam could scarcely stabilize his fledgling secessionist state if his subjects trooped back to Jerusalem to worship in a temple controlled by and legitimating his enemy, Rehoboam. Jeroboam desperately needed state shrines of his own.

His solution to this problem was to reconstitute the old patriarchal shrines at Bethel and Dan as royal sanctuaries that legitimated his rule. Bethel proved to be of particular significance. It sat just north of his border with Rehoboam's Judah on the ridge road that ran south to Jerusalem. There it could intercept any of his subjects who might be tempted to travel to Jerusalem to worship. By increasing travel to and jurisdiction in Bethel, Jeroboam also increased his subjects' "ownership" of this site and their willingness to defend the nearby border against Judahite incursions. (Dan, his other royal sanctuary, was in the far north, where it could serve similar functions in helping to defend Jeroboam's border against growing Aramaean power.)

Bethel's pedigree was impeccable. It was none other than the place where Israel's eponymous ancestor, Jacob/Israel had experienced a theophany promising future greatness, both to Jacob's descendants and to the site itself. One analysis plausibly views the much-discussed Elohistic strand in the Tetrateuch as a polemical recomposition of the Yahwist, designed to legitimate Jeroboam's breakaway regime. If that is, in fact, the case, the particular combination of J and E in the biblical account of this theophany (Gen 28:10–22) receives detailed illumination.[21]

As we have seen, Jereboam's shrines required an iconographic alternative to the ark in order to symbolize and mediate God's presence. In Jerusalem, as in Shiloh before it, the ark was understood as a pedestal upon which Yahweh was invisibly enthroned. Jeroboam chose a parallel iconography that claimed patriarchal roots even older than the ark's. The "Bull" or "Mighty One of Jacob/Israel" is a divine epithet designating Israel's God in Gen 49:24; Isa 1:24; 49:26; 60:16; and Ps 132:2, 5. In the Northwest Semitic material culture outside of Israel and Judah, the bull frequently served as a symbol of strength with various deities represented as sitting astride it, enthroned on its back. Many historians of religions understand Jeroboam's "golden calves" at Bethel and Dan as standing solidly in this tradition of iconography. In 1 Kings 12–13, the Deuteronomistic Historian, eager to legitimate the Josianic Reform, clearly understands these "golden calves" as idolatrous and apostate. If Yahweh was conceived as enthroned invisibly upon their backs, however, they were no more idolatrous or apostate than the ark. The matter was rather one of two rival sections and factions making alternative use of religious traditions to legitimate their particular vested interests. (On Jeroboam's religious institutions, see Toews 1993 and the literature there cited.)

CONCLUSIONS AND IMPLICATIONS

If occasion permitted, many further examples of socio-historical parallels between agrarian Korea and biblical Israel could be adduced, along with significant and clarifying differences. Those further examples, I believe, would bolster the analysis I have offered, as well as nuancing it. The space available, however, allows only some brief conclusions and hints of where such an analysis may lead if pursued. In all of this, my concern is to open discussion and dialogue, not to effect any premature or dogmatic closure.

---

21. See Coote 1991. If Coote is correct in reading the Elohist as an apologist for Jeroboam I, E's mandate for administrative hierarchy in Exod 18:13–27 (see Coote 1991:121–22), may be compared readily with Taejo's proclamation on the formation of government from the first year of the Goryeo dynasty (see P. H. Lee and de Bary 1997:153). Secessionists and usurpers most often find it easier to unite popular resentment against the old regime than to legitimate their new regime, while at the same time enforcing control and discipline within it.

If there is any cogency in the comparison of Korea and Israel that I have sketched, then what significance may we find in it? I shall simply offer some brief suggestions to stimulate your further thoughts and analysis.

If Korea and Israel are as similar at a generic level as I believe, knowledge of Korean history and culture can help to tutor scholars of biblical Israel about what questions to ask their fragmentary and skewed data base, and how to conceptualize the possible relationships within it. On the whole, the Korean side of the comparison is far more fully documented and understood than is ancient Israel. Comparative suggestions can never substitute for specific data, but they can and should inform how partial data are processed and evaluated. In this regard, I believe that Korean Old Testament scholars have an inbuilt tool denied those of us in the field whose nations have experienced histories far less like that of biblical Israel. Korean biblical scholarship has reached a kind of critical mass in the present generation of persons trained to an internationally recognized level. My plea to my Korean colleagues would be to follow their own research agenda wherever they lead, to be sure, but to consider owning and honing their knowledge of and access to Korean history and culture as an intentional and distinctive part of their contribution to scholarship on the Hebrew Bible. I, for one, would love to hear more from them in this guise.

Though the history of agrarian Korea is, as stated, known in greater detail than the history of monarchic Israel, methodologically disciplined comparison of the two can benefit the interpretation of both histories. Theoretical dimensions of the comparison have called attention to a significant maritime component in Korea's agrarian society—a component fundamentally lacking in Israel during the Old Testament period. Can attention to maritime influences help to explain certain periods of rapid technological innovation in Korean history? Israel and Korea have both been shown to have sustained significant influence from herding societies, though by different means. Does that influence help to explain the strength of male dominance in both societies? Examining the environmental, technological, political, economic, and social dimensions of patriarchy in both societies can provide an important supplement to discussions of gender that focus on the ideological.

I have argued that elite factionalism and sectionalism were deeply intrinsic to the socio-historical dynamics both of biblical Israel and of preindustrial Korea. That analysis could be extended readily into all the later periods of the Israelite and Judahite monarchies, and on more certain historical footing than the early period that I have hazarded to survey. I have understood the articulation of religious ideology in both societies as more often than not polemical, at least in part as a result of that pervasive factionalism and sectionalism. Can such an analysis help to gain us critical distance on the disputatious expression of religious ideology both in Israel and in Korea? What are the implications of understanding that both the biblical canon and Korean religious history include many voices that are "partial" in both senses of the English word—and for similar reasons? In churches, nations and a world increasingly drawn close and interdependent by technological advances in transportation, communication and economic activity, can any of us afford the polemical parochialism born of the factions and regions of a past now definitively and irrevocably changed? If trying to force all players to produce one single melody is no longer viable or faithful, how do we learn together to produce a symphony?

13

Some Choreographic Notes on the Dance of Theory with Data

A Response to Roland Boer,
The Sacred Economy of Ancient Israel

Abstract

This volume is a tour de force that exceeds any predecessor in its theoretical scope. Even more important than its intriguing syntheses are its probing questions, its analytical categories and tools, and its challenges to easy assumptions. Boer's pursuit of theoretical integration, however, sometimes leads him to overgeneralize. He staunchly maintains, for example, that arable land was plentiful in all times and places in ancient Southwest Asia. Comprehensive archaeological surveys of the southern Levant tell a different story. The Iron II population was more than double that of the Bronze Age or of Iron I. The highlands particularly witnessed the occupation of marginal niches. Population pressure on arable land was a reality in Iron II Palestine. Similarly, the many standardized wine amphorae recovered from two eighth-century BCE Phoenician ships sunk off the Philistine coast contradict Boer's repeated insistence that there is no evidence for long-distance trade in bulk goods.

As a genre, book jacket blurbs are prone to hyperbole. Roland Boer's new book is a happy exception to that norm. Exaggerating the significance of this tour de force would be difficult indeed. It exceeds any predecessor in its theoretical scope, cohesion, and integration. The body of scholarship that it compasses has to be impressive even to its most learned critics. Today's out-sized review panel is tacit recognition of the scope of Boer's erudition, however much strictures of time prevent our doing it justice. To his readers' delight and relief, moreover, Boer's erudition is not infrequently punctuated with tongue-in-cheek humor.

The greatest significance of this book lies, not so much in the tentative synthesis that it proposes—important as that is—but in the probing questions that it raises, the analytical categories and tools that it offers, and in its challenges to easy assumptions. It is a bone that when gnawed will nourish us for a long time. With our digestion so incomplete, a review seems almost premature. But the courage of Boer's offering and his willingness to open himself to response and critique on so many fronts must kindle a corresponding courage in his reviewers. Boer assures his readers that while "my narrative may give the impression of deft confidence, my specific arguments should always be understood in terms of 'possibly' and 'maybe'" (4). That goes double for this reviewer.

Since Boer's book has been available for some months and has already been the subject of one review panel in this Society, I shall attempt no summary of its rich complexity. I turn, rather, to a random and very partial list of insights in Boer's analysis that particularly sparked my interest. 1) His expert exposition of the rich and contentious heritage of *Régulation* Theory and his systematic application of its strategies to the analysis of ancient Southwest Asia is a signal contribution. 2) Boer turns the usual *political* discussions of crisis and stability on their head. What is a crisis for the extractive economics of states and empires allows village agriculture to recapture its complex and subtle equilibrium. The fundamental contradiction of states practicing extractive economic policies is that they kill the goose that lays the golden egg. 3) Boer's analysis makes a penetrating distinction between credit and debt. The former applies to the dynamics of allocative regimes, the latter to those that are extractive. 4) When debt easement occurs in extractive regimes, it is partial and selective in its application and serves as a barometer of economic instability. 5) The predominant military institutions in a situation are a reliable guide to the type of regime involved. Allocative regimes witness militias, extractive regimes standing armies.[1] 6) In his brief

---

1. From a different theoretical perspective, Lenski articulated much the same insight long ago regarding "agrarian societies": "[T]he greater the military importance of the peasant farmer, the better his economic and political situation tended to be, and

conclusion (217–22), Boer explores the possibility of a subsistence regime's being normative for today. After enunciating the advantages of subsistence regimes, he candidly admits their shortcomings regarding gender and age. If this book were read in isolation, its conclusion might seem a bit thin. Read in the context of his other prolific publications and his life choices, it deserves respect and attention.

The remainder of my time could easily be dedicated to sincere praise for other aspects of Boer's book. To do so, however, would be to squander much of its value. It is often questioning and polemical, designed to elicit response and critique. Although I would love to engage Boer on many fronts, time allows only comments that cluster around two topics: 1) his assumption that arable land was plentiful in all periods throughout ancient Southwest Asia; and 2) his understanding of the nature and history of interregional economic exchange. I shall focus particularly on the Iron II period in the southern Levant, since that is where most of my recent research has concentrated.

Throughout his work, Boer staunchly maintains that land was plentiful in all times and places in ancient Southwest Asia, and that to assume otherwise is to "impose assumptions from our own era" (70). I find this conclusion unconvincing for several reasons. In a book that finds room for discussions of bestiality (91–94) and professional flatulence (105)—both germane to the conversation, to be sure—Boer's discussion neglects any serious address to historical demography. He speaks only of the small size of individual towns and villages with little reference to time or place (87), and refers only in passing to "some population increase," especially in Iron Age II.

This absence of a treatment of population is significant. Only a few decades ago, "estimates" of populations in ancient Southwest Asia were guesses, with the figures of one "expert" varying exponentially from another. That is no longer the case. In the southern Levant, comprehensive archaeological surveys of total inhabited area, when combined with comparatively normed coefficients of density, give estimates of human population in major archaeological periods that involve only a relatively small margin of error. The Iron II population in Palestine was more than double that of the Bronze Age or of Iron I. The highlands grew much faster than the lowlands and for the first time included half or more of the total population (Broshi and Finkelstein 1992, as corrected by Herr 1997:137). The conclusion that Noll draws for Iron II seems highly probable: "[T]he Cisjordan Highlands approached a point of full exploitation. That is to say, given ancient farming

---

conversely, the less his military importance, the poorer his economic and political situation" (Lenski 1984:275).

techniques, the Cisjordan Highlands achieved a population size that was taking advantage of all arable regions" (2013:262). Archaeology evidences for this period the population of several peripheral areas, a number for the first time. Settlements built in the badlands, many on virgin sites, occupied marginal niches in terms of water and resource availability (Chaney 2014a:38, and the literature there cited). Population pressure on arable land was a reality in Iron II Palestine.

Why does Boer's analysis miss such demographic phenomena? Several reasons suggest themselves. Much of his discussion of arable land speaks of ancient Southwest Asia as a whole with little attention to regional differences. Although Boer alludes more than once to "the analytic fiction of distinguishing between synchronic and diachronic" (193 n2), his analysis here fails to address the inherent problematic successfully. Human populations vary significantly over time, a fact that a mostly synchronic analysis obscures. In both spatial and temporal terms, then, a focus on theory has led to overgeneralization. Population pressure on land in agrarian contexts usually walks hand in hand with the dynamics of agricultural intensification. Failure to detect that pressure leads one to miss many of its concomitants. Recent scholarly focus on the Persian period may also have tempted Boer to regard severely depopulated Yehud as a demographic norm, rather than the stark demographic anomaly it is.[2]

Boer insists repeatedly that long-distance economic exchange in ancient Southwest Asia was only in preciosities—high-value, luxury items. The Amarna correspondence can be read as consonant with this view. But was it generally true of ancient Southwest Asia? Both Diakonoff and Liverani, Boer's frequent mentors, answer in the negative (175 n83; 204 n26). Boer suggests that in this position they are uncharacteristically haunted by the ghost of Adam Smith, a specter he is zealous to exorcize from ancient Southwest Asia. I suspect, rather, that Boer's analysis has fallen victim to a hardening of the categories, to a hermetically sealed dichotomy between "preciosities" and "bulk goods." Part of the solution to this puzzle inheres, I believe, in the difference in preindustrial transportation costs between overland and seaborne exchange. Overland costs were high and soon exceeded the value of all but the most precious goods. Seaborne costs were much lower, a difference that Boer recognizes but then seeks to blur.

The problematic can be illustrated by the situation of eighth-century Israel—and I use the term advisedly. On my understanding, the Israelite ruling class imported preciosities from and through their Phoenician

---

2. That is almost certainly the case with Guillaume (2012), who agrees with Boer about the ready availability of arable land.

neighbors. But how were they to pay for those imports? Boer raises the question in general (185), but fails to offer answers that fit the Israelite situation. The Israelite ruling class had preciously few locally produced preciosities to offer. Instead, I believe that they exported high quality wine and olive oil to the Phoenicians and through them elsewhere by sea, particularly to Egypt (cf. Hos 12:1 [Heb. 12:2]: "and oil is borne to Egypt"). The short distances between Israel and Phoenicia also allowed some transfer of grain from Israel to feed Phoenicians, a critical mass of whom were sailors, not farmers.[3]

Boer's account repeatedly insists that there is a telling absence of evidence for long-distance trade in any bulk goods. The eighth century has produced several collections of artifacts that contradict that argument from silence. Marine archaeology has discovered two Phoenician ships dating to the mid-eight century—dubbed *Tanit* and *Elissa* by their discoverers—still laden with rows of the standardized wine amphorae they were carrying to Egypt when they were sunk by a storm off the Philistine coast.[4] Back on land, excavations of earlier periods in the southern Levant have produced oil and wine amphorae of irregular size that were instead suited to their terrestrial environment. They were limited in capacity only by the requirements of utility for subsistence storage. The eighth century BCE, by contrast, saw a standardization of the volume of these amphorae to facilitate broader exchange of high-value bulk goods, particularly fine oil and wine. Some are incised in Hebrew, *bt*, "*bat* (measure)" or *bt lmlk*, "the *bat* of the king" or "the royal *bat*."[5]

---

3. For a much fuller explication of this understanding, see Chaney 2014a:36–44.

4. See Ballard et al. 2002; Finkelstein et al. 2011; Finkelstein 2013. Boer argues that these amphorae—which he does not discuss in the book—and those in other, earlier shipwrecks (Boer 181–82) were found empty and therefore are not evidence for exchange of wine or oil. In the light of current evidence, such argumentation appears to be special pleading. All of the amphorae in the significant sample raised by the archaeologists from *Tanit* and *Elissa* had resin linings. Tartaric acid, an organic acid that occurs mainly in grapes or grape products, such as wine, was found in the pine pitch that lined one amphora (Ballard et al. 2002). These "torpedo" amphorae were highly standardized to Egyptian units of measurement (Finkelstein et al. 2011), were specialized to fit and be secured in the ships' holds, constituted the vast majority of the ships' cargoes, and find counterparts in excavations on land only near seaports or other sites intimately associated with seaborne exchange (Ballard et al. 2002:157–61). If these amphorae had contained mere ballast water, as Boer suggests, the ships' primary cargo would have been ballast water and none of the care and expense evidenced in the resin linings, standardization and specialization would make sense. Simple ballast stones, six of which were, in fact, found on *Elissa* (Ballard 2002:159 table 2), would have served the function of ballast far more probably and cheaply.

5. For fuller discussion and reference to other sources, see Chaney 2014a:36; and Zapassky et al. 2009.

Note the asymmetry of the exchange envisioned—the elite benefited, the peasants paid. The imports were preciosities that benefited only the Israelite ruling class. The exports were primarily fine oil and wine, which the rulers extracted from the subsistence of their peasant producers. There is no question here of entrepreneurial farmers producing a surplus for profit. Amos 6:1–7 portrays the ruling class in Samaria and Jerusalem conspicuously consuming both imported luxuries and the finest of domestic wines, oils, and meats in what the text (v. 7) refers to as a *marzēaḥ*. Boer's discussion of beer and wine makes no reference to this text and misses the gender and class dimensions of the sodality involved: "This type of group [the *marziḫu*] seems to have been ubiquitous across the ruling class, town groups, and subsistence village groups" (68 n45). The dominant opinion of scholarship on this institution sees instead in most of its far-flung iterations a sodality of upper-class males. The class dimensions in Amos 6:1–7 are blatant.

In all of this, the Phoenicians are a problem for Boer's analysis. His closest scholarly allies dissent from his view and embrace the evidence for seaborne exchange in more than preciosities in the first millennium BCE. No amount of critical theory applied to Ezekiel 27–28 can erase from history the maritime exchange carried by the Phoenicians. Lenski's more eclectic general theory, which owes much to Marx but is dismissed by Boer as lacking "the richness and complexity" (122 n33) of Marxist theory, can accommodate the Phoenicians readily. They are a "maritime society," a relatively small form seen as adjunct to "agrarian societies" and usually subsumed by them in the end (see Lenski 1984:91–93, 191–92, 203, 436, 445; and Nolan and Lenski 2009:181–83). One such society in Lenski's analysis was the Netherlands in the sixteenth century, by Boer's analysis the first capitalist power (80 n91; 177). My point is not to make the Phoenicians capitalists. They clearly were not in Lenski's view or mine. It is rather to argue that the complex concatenation that Boer sees in the sixteenth-century Dutch was not a complete novum. That society was in some aspects adumbrated by the Phoenicians and other maritime societies. One of those adumbrations was that Phoenician ships carried high-value bulk goods as well as preciosities.

When I began this review, I had hoped to engage Boer on subsistence agriculture in Israelite villages, particularly with regard to land tenure, allocation of labor, and pressures from the monarchic state and its ruling class. Although I have recently addressed such issues (Chaney 2014a), Boer's book has caused me to refine some of my concepts and terminology. By the same token, I find his rich treatment of these topics on certain points somewhat overgeneralized, e.g., his failure to distinguish village land in extensive annual cultivation from that in intensive perennial cultivation. That distinction has important implications for periodic reallocation of village land.

I eagerly anticipate Boer's separate publication of longer sections of biblical interpretation excised from this volume for reasons of length (cf. 51 n118). As stated at the outset, the quality and scope of this volume put us greatly in Boer's debt and encourage high hopes for that future publication. I thank him again for the myriad contributions of this landmark work, even as I express the judgment that his brilliant application of *Régulation* Theory has solved some but not all of the difficulties of that most problematic of all Marxist categories, the Asiatic Mode of Production.

Acknowlegments

The author and publisher gratefully acknowlege the journals and books where these essays were published in earlier forms:

Chapter 1: "Ancient Palestinian Peasant Movements and the Formation of Premonarchic Israel" was first published in *Palestine in Transition: The Emergence of Ancient Israel*, edited by David Noel Freedman and David F. Graf, 39–90. SWBA 2. Sheffield: Almond Press, 1983. Used with permission.

Chapter 2: "Joshua and the Deuteronomistic History" was first published as "Joshua," in *Books of the Bible*, edited by Bernhard W. Anderson, 1:103–12. 2 vols. New York: Scribner, 1989. Used with permission.

Chapter 3: "Coveting Your Neighbor's House in Social Context" was first published in *Pacific Theological Review*, and a revised version was published in *The Ten Commandments: The Reciprocity of Faithfulness*, edited by William P. Brown, 302–17. Louisville: Westminster John Knox, 2004. Used with permission.

Chapter 4: "Systemic Study of the Israelite Monarchy" was first published in *Semeia* 37 (1986) 53–76. Used with permission.

Chapter 5: "Debt Easement in Israelite History and Tradition" was first published in *The Bible and the Politics of Exegesis: Essays in Honor of Norman K. Gottwald on His Sixty-fifth Birthday*, edited by David Jobling et al., 127–39, 325–29. Cleveland: Pilgrim Press, 1991. Used with permission.

Chapter 6: "The Political Economy of Peasant Poverty" was first published as "The Political Economy of Peasant Poverty: What the Eighth-Century Prophets Presumed but Did not State." In *The Bible, the Economy, and the Poor*, edited by Ronald Simkins and Thomas Kelly, 34–60. Journal of Religion and Society Supplement Series 10. Omaha, NE: Creighton University, 2014. Used with permission.

Chapter 7: "Bitter Bounty: The Dynamics of Political Economy Critiqued by the Eighth-Century Prophets" was first published in *Reformed Faith and Economics*, edited by Robert L. Stivers, 15–30. Lanham, MD: University Press of America, 1989; and a slightly abridged version was published in *The Bible and Liberation: Political and Social Hermeneutics*, edited by Norman K. Gottwald and Richard A. Horsley, 250–63. Maryknoll, NY: Orbis Press, 1993.

Chapter 8: "Whose Sour Grapes? The Addressees of Isaiah 5:1–7" was first published in *Semeia* 87 (1999) 105–22. Used with permission.

Chapter 9: "Accusing Whom of What? Hosea's Rhetoric of Promiscuity" was first published in *Distant Voices Drawing Near: Essays in Honor of Antoinette Clark Wire*, edited by Holly E. Hearon, 97–115. Collegeville, MN: Liturgical Press, 2004. Used with permission.

Chapter 10: "Producing Peasant Poverty: Debt Instruments in Amos 2:6b–8, 13–16" was first published in *Reading a Tendentious Bible: Essays in Honor of Robert B. Coote*, edited by Marvin L. Chaney et al., 19–34. HBM 66. Sheffield: Sheffield Phoenix Press, 2014. Used with permission.

Chapter 11: "Micah—Models Matter: Political Economy and Micah 6:9–15" was first published in *Ancient Israel: The Old Testament in Its Social Context*, edited by Philip F. Esler, 145–60, 329–30. Minneapolis: Fortress Press, 2006. Used with permission.

Chapter 12: "Korea and Israel: Historical Analogy and Old Testament Interpretation" was first published in *The Korean Journal of Old Testament Studies* 16 (2010) 87–120. Used with permission.

Chapter 13: "Some Choreographic Notes on the Dance of Theory with Data: A Response to Roland Boer, *The Sacred Economy of Ancient Israel*" was first published in *Horizons in Biblical Theology* 38/2 (2016) 137–44. Used with permission.

Bibliography

Adler, Elaine June. 1989. "The Background for the Metaphor of Covenant as Marriage in the Hebrew Bible." PhD diss., University of California Berkeley.
Aharoni, Yohanan. 1967. *The Land of the Bible: A Historical Geography*. Translated by Anson F. Rainey. Philadelphia: Westminster.
———. 1976. "Nothing Early and Nothing Late: Re-writing Israel's Conquest." *BA* 39:55–76.
———. 1982. *The Archaeology of the Land of Israel*. Edited by Miriam Aharoni. Translated by Anson F. Rainey. Philadelphia: Westminster.
———. 1993. "Ramat Raḥel." In *The New Encyclopedia of Archaeological Excavations in the Holy Land*, edited by Ephraim Stern, 1261–67. New York: Simon & Schuster.
Albright, W. F. 1932. *The Excavations of Tell Beit Mirsim*. Annual of the American Schools of Oriental Research 12. New Haven: American Schools of Oriental Research.
———. 1938. *The Excavations of Tell Beit Mirsim*, Vol. 2. Annual of the American Schools of Oriental Research 17. New Haven: American Schools of Oriental Research.
———. 1943. *The Excavations of Tell Beit Mirsim*, Vol. 3. Annual of the American Schools of Oriental Research 21–22. New Haven: American Schools of Oriental Research.
———. 1956. *Archaeology and the Religion of Israel*. 4th ed. Baltimore: Johns Hopkins University Press.
———. 1960. *The Archaeology of Palestine*. Rev. ed. Baltimore: Penguin.
———. 1975. "The Amarna Letters from Palestine." In *The Cambridge Ancient History*, 3rd ed., eds. I. E. S. Edwards et al., II/2:98–119. Cambridge: Cambridge University Press.
Allen, Leslie C. 1976. *The Books of Joel, Obadiah, Jonah, and Micah*. New International Commentary on the Old Testament. Grand Rapids: Eerdmans.
Alt, Albrecht. 1936. "Josua." In *Werden und Wesen des Alten Testaments: Vorträge gehalten auf der Internationalen Tagung Alttestamentlicher Forscher zu Göttingen vom 4.–10. September 1935*, edited by P. Volz et al., 13–29. BZAW 66. Berlin: Töpelmann. Reprinted in *Kleine Schriften zur Geschichte des Volkes Israels*, 1:176–92. Munich: Beck, 1953.
———. 1939. "Erwägungen für die Landnahme der Israeliten in Palestina." *Palästinajahrbuch des Deutschen evangelischen Instituts für Altertumswissenschaft des Heiligen Landes zu Jerusalem* 35:8–63. Reprinted in *Kleine Schriften zur Geschichte des Volkes Israel*, 1:126–75. Munich: Beck, 1953.

———. 1941. "Meros." *ZAW* 58:244–47. Reprinted in *Kleine Schriften zur Geschichte des Volkes Israel*, 1:274–77. Munich: Beck, 1959.

———. 1949. "Die phönikischen Inschriften von Karetepe." *Die Welt des Orients* 1:272–87.

———. 1953. "Das Verbot des Diebstahls im Dekalog." In *Kleine Schriften*, 1:333–40. Munich: Beck.

———. 1955. "Micha 2, 1–5, *GÊS ANADASMOS* in Juda." In *Interpretationes ad Vetus Testamentum pertinentes Sigmundo Mowinckel septuagenario missae*, 13–23. Oslo: Forlaget Land og Kirke. Reprinted in *Kleine Schriften zur Geschichte des Volkes Israels*, edited by Martin Noth, 3:373–81. Munich: Beck, 1959.

———. 1959. "Der Anteil des Königtums an der sozialen Entwicklung in der Reichen Israel und Juda." In *Kleine Schriften zur Geschichte des Volkes Israel*, edited by Martin Noth, 3:348–72. Munich: Beck.

———. 1966a. "The Origins of Israelite Law." In *Essays on Old Testament History and Religion*, 79–132. Translated by R. A. Wilson. Oxford: Blackwell, 1966. German orig. 1934.

———. 1966b. "The Settlement of the Israelites in Palestine." In *Essays on Old Testament History and Religion*, 135–69. Translated by R. A. Wilson. Oxford: Blackwell.

Andersen, Francis I., and David Noel Freedman. 1980. *Hosea*. AB 24. Garden City, NY: Doubleday.

———. 1989. *Amos*. AB 24A. Garden City, NY: Doubleday.

———. 2000. *Micah*. AB 24E. New York: Doubleday.

Artzi, P. 1964. "'Vox Populi' in the el-Amarna Tablets." *Revue d'assyriologie et d'archeologie orientale* 58:159–66.

Astour, M. C. 1964. "The Amarna Age Forerunners of Biblical Anti-Royalism." In *For Max Weinreich on His Seventieth Birthday*, 6–17. The Hague: Mouton.

———. 1976. "Habiru." In *IDBSup* 382–85.

Atlas of Israel: Cartography, Physical and Human Geography. 1985. 3rd ed. New York: Macmillan.

Auld, A. Graeme. 2011. *I and II Samuel: A Commentary*. OTL. Louisville: Westminster John Knox.

Austin, M. M., and P. Vidal-Naquet. 1977. *Economic and Social History of Ancient Greece: An Introduction*. Translated by M. M. Austin. Berkeley: University of California Press.

Avigad, Nahman. 1953. "Another *bat le-melekh* Inscription." *IEJ* 3:121–22.

———. 1979. "Hebrew Epigraphic Sources." In *The Age of the Monarchies: Political History*, edited by Abraham Malamat, 20–43. The World History of the Jewish People IV/1. Jerusalem: Massada.

Bagnall, Roger S. 1976. *The Administration of the Ptolemaic Possessions Outside Egypt*. Columbia Studies in the Classical Tradition 4. Leiden: Brill.

Ballard, Robert D. et al. 2002. "Iron Age Shipwrecks in Deep Water off Ashkelon, Israel." *American Journal of Archaeology* 106:151–68.

Baltzer, Klaus. 1987. "Liberation from Debt Slavery after the Exile in Second Isaiah and Nehemiah." In *Ancient Israelite Religion: Essays in Honor of Frank Moore Cross*, edited by Patrick D. Miller et al., 477–84. Philadelphia: Fortress.

Baly, Dennis. 1963. *Geographical Companion to the Bible*. New York: McGraw-Hill.

Baly, Denis, and A. D. Tushingham. 1971. *Atlas of the Biblical World*. New York: World.

Balz-Cochois, Helgard. 1982. *Gomer: Der Höhenkult Israels im Selbstverständnis der Volksfrömmigkeit: Untersuchungen zu Hosea 4.1—5.7*. Europäische Hochschulschriften XXIII/191. Frankfurt: Lang.
Beentjes, Pancratius C. 2003. *The Book of Ben Sira in Hebrew*. VTSup 68. Leiden: Brill.
Ben-Barak, Zafrira. 1981. "Meribaal and the System of Land Grants in Ancient Israel." *Bib* 62:73–91.
Bender, S. 1997. *Social Structure of Ancient Israel*. Jerusalem Biblical Studies 7. Jerusalem: Simor.
Ben Zvi, Ehud. 2000. *Micah*. FOTL 21B. Grand Rapids: Eerdmans.
Bess, S. Herbert. 1963. "Systems of Land Tenure in Ancient Israel." Ph.D. diss., University of Michigan.
Bird, Phyllis A. 1989. "'To Play the Harlot': An Inquiry into an Old Testament Metaphor." In *Gender and Difference in Ancient Israel*, edited by Peggy L. Day, 75–94. Minneapolis: Fortress.
———. 1997a. "The End of the Male Cult Prostitute: A Literary-Historical and Sociological Analysis of Hebrew *qedesh-qedeshim*." In *Congress Volume: Cambridge, 1995*, edited by John A. Emerton, 37–80. VTSup 66. Leiden: Brill.
———. 1997b. *Missing Persons and Mistaken Identities: Women and Gender in Ancient Israel*. OBT. Fortress.
Blenkinsopp, Joseph. 1996. *A History of Prophecy in Israel*. Rev. ed. Louisville: Westminster John Knox.
Blum, Jerome. 1961. *Lord and Peasant in Russia: From the Ninth to the Nineteenth Century*. Princeton: Princeton University Press.
Boecker, Hans Jochen. 1980. *Law and Administration of Justice in the Old Testament and Ancient Near East*. Translated by Jeremy Moiser. Minneapolis: Augsburg.
Boer, Roland. 2007. "The Sacred Economy of Ancient 'Israel.'" *SJOT* 21:29–48.
———. 2012. "Credit and Debt." Paper presented at the annual meeting of the Society of Biblical Literature, Chicago, November 17, 2012.
———. 2015. *The Sacred Economy of Ancient Israel*. LAI. Louisville: Westminster John Knox.
Boling, Robert G. 1982. *Joshua*. AB 6. Garden City, NY: Doubleday.
Boren, Henry C. 1977. *Roman Society: A Social, Economic, and Cultural History*. Lexington, MA: Heath.
———. 1992. *Roman Society: A Social, Economic, and Cultural History*. 2nd ed. Lexington, MA: Heath.
Borowski, Oded. 1987. *Agriculture in Iron Age Israel*. Winona Lake, IN: Eisenbrauns.
Boserup, Ester. 1965. *The Conditions of Agricultural Growth*. London: Allen & Unwin.
Bossen, Laurel. 1989. "Women and Economic Institutions." In *Economic Anthropology*, edited by Stuart Plattner, 318–50. Stanford: Stanford University Press.
Bottéro, Jean. 1961. "Désordre économique et annullation des dettes en Mésopotamie à l'époque paléo-babylonienne." *JESHO* 4:113–64.
Bowen, Nancy R. 2001. "The Quest for the Historical *Gĕbîrâ*." *CBQ* 64:597–618.
Bright, John. 1953. "The Book of Joshua: Introduction and Exegesis." In *Interpreter's Bible*, edited by George Arthur Buttrick, 2:541–673. Nashville: Abingdon.
———. 1965. *Jeremiah*. AB 21. Garden City, NY: Doubleday.
———. 1972. *A History of Israel*. 2nd ed. Philadelphia: Westminster.
———. 1981. *A History of Israel*. 3rd ed. Philadelphia: Westminster.

Broshi, Magen. 1993. "Judeideh, Tell." In *The New Encyclopedia of Archaeological Excavations in the Holy Land*, edited by Ephraim Stern, 3:837-38. Jerusalem: Israel Exploration Society and Carta.

Broshi, Magen, and Israel Finkelstein. 1992. "The Population of Palestine in Iron Age II." *BASOR* 287:47-60.

Brueggemann, Walter. 1994. "The Book of Exodus: Introduction, Commentary, and Reflections." In *NIB*, 1:675-981.

Brunt, P. A. 1971. *Social Conflicts in the Roman Republic*. Ancient Culture and Society Series. New York: Norton.

Bucher, Christina. 1988. "The Origin and Meaning of *ZNH* Terminology in the Book of Hosea." Ph.D. diss., Claremont Graduate School.

Bury, J. B. 1959. *A History of Greece*. 3rd ed. London: Macmillan.

Butler, Trent C. 1983. *Joshua*. WBC 7. Waco, TX: Word.

Callaway, J. 1976. "Excavating Ai (et-Tell): 1964-72." *BA* 39:18-30.

Campbell, Edward F., Jr. 1960. "The Amarna Letters and the Amarna Period." *BA* 23:2-22. Reprinted in *The Biblical Archaeologist Reader*, edited by Edward F. Campbell and David Noel Freedman, 3:54-75. Garden City, NY: Doubleday, 1970.

———. 1975. "Moses and the Foundations of Israel." *Interpretation* 29:141-54.

———. 1976. "Two Amarna Notes: The Shechem City-State and Amarna Administrative Terminology." In *Magnolia Dei: The Mighty Acts of God: Essays on the Bible and Archaeology in Memory of G. Ernest Wright*, edited by Frank M. Cross et al., 39-54. New York: Doubleday.

———. 1991. *Shechem II: Portrait of a Hill Country Vale. The Shechem Regional Survey*. American Schools of Oriental Research Archaeological Reports 2. Atlanta: Scholars.

———. 1994. "Archaeological Reflections on Amos's Targets." In *Scripture and Other Artifacts: Essays on the Bible and Archaeology in Honor of Philip J. King*, edited by Michael D. Coogan et al., 32-52. Louisville: Westminster John Knox.

Carney, T. F. 1975. *The Shape of the Past: Models and Antiquity*. Lawrence, KS: Coronado.

Carroll, Robert P. 1986. *Jeremiah: A Commentary*. OTL. Philadelphia: Westminster.

Cary, M. 1960. *A History of Rome down to the Reign of Constantine*. 2nd ed. London: Macmillan.

Cary, M., and H. H. Scullard. 1975. *A History of Rome Down to the Reign of Constantine*. 3rd ed. London: Macmillan.

Cassuto, Umberto. 1967. *A Commentary on the Book of Exodus*. Translated by I. Abrahams. Jerusalem: Magnes. Hebrew orig., 1951.

Cathcart, Kevin J., and Robert P. Gordon. 1989. *The Targum of the Minor Prophets*. Aramaic Bible 14. Wilmington, DE: Glazier.

Cathcart, Kevin J., and Knud Jeppesen. 1987. "More Suggestions on Mic 6,14." *SJOT* 1:110-15.

Chaney, Marvin L. 1976. "ḤDL-II and the 'Song of Deborah': Textual, Philological, and Sociological Studies in Judges 5, with Special Reference to the Verbal Occurrences of ḤDL in Biblical Hebrew." PhD diss., Harvard University.

———. 1982. "You Shall not Covet Your Neighbor's House." *Pacific Theological Review* 15:2-13.

———. 1983. "Ancient Palestinian Peasant Movements and the Formation of Premonarchic Israel." In *Palestine in Transition: The Emergence of Ancient Israel*, edited by David Noel Freedman and David F. Graf, 39–90. SWBA 2. Sheffield: Almond. [Chapter 1 in this volume]

———. 1986. "Systemic Study of the Israelite Monarchy." *Semeia* 37:53–76. [Chapter 4 in this volume]

———. 1989a. "Bitter Bounty: The Dynamics of Political Economy Critiqued by the Eighth-Century Prophets." In *Reformed Faith and Economics*, edited by Robert L. Stivers, 15–30. Lanham, MD: Univesity Press of America. [Chapter 7 in this volume]

———. 1989b. "Joshua." In *The Books of the Bible*, edited by Bernhard W. Anderson, 1:103–12. New York: Scribners. [Chapter 2 in this volume]

———. 1991. "Debt Easement in Israelite History and Tradition." In *The Bible and the Politics of Exegesis: Essays in Honor of Norman K. Gottwald on His Sixty-fifth Birthday*, edited by David Jobling et al., 127–39, 325–29. [Chapter 5 in this volume]

———. 1993. "Bitter Bounty: The Dynamics of Political Economy Critiqued by the Eighth-Century Prophets." In *The Bible and Liberation: Political and Social Hermeneutics*, edited by Norman K. Gottwald and Richard A. Horsley, 250–63. Maryknoll, NY: Orbis.

———. 1999. "Whose Sour Grapes? The Addressees of Isaiah 5:1–7 in the Light of Political Economy." *Semeia* 87:105–22. [Chapter 8 in this volume]

———. 2001. "Pluralism in Text and Context: Some Reflections on a Hermeneutic of Dynamic Analogy between Biblical Israel and Historical Korea." Korean translation by Cho Eun Suk. *Christian Thought* 513:198–219. Reprinted in *Biblical Israel through an Agrarian Lens: Essays on Religion and Society in Old Testament History, Literature and Interpretation*, 271–93. Edited by Taek Joo Woo. Translated by Samuel Cheon, Eun Suk Cho, Seong Hyuk Hong, Tae Hun Kim, Young-Hye Kim, Chong Hun Pae, and Taek Joo Woo. Seoul: Handl, 2007. [Korean]

———. 2004a. "Accusing Whom of What? Hosea's Rhetoric of Promiscuity." In *Distant Voices Drawing Near: Essays in Honor of Antoinette Clark Wire*, edited by Holly E. Hearon, 97–115. Collegeville, MN: Liturgical. [Chapter 9 in this volume]

———. 2004b. "'Coveting Your Neighbor's House' in Social Context." In *The Ten Commandments: The Reciprocity of Faithfulness*, edited by William P. Brown, 302–17. Louisville: Westminster John Knox. [Chapter 3 in this volume]

———. 2006. "Micah—Models Matter: Political Economy and Micah 6:9–15." In *Ancient Israel: The Old Testament in Its Social Context*, edited by Philip F. Esler, 145–60, 329–30. Minneapolis: Fortress. [Chapter 11 in this volume]

———. 2007. *Biblical Israel through an Agrarian Lens: Essays on Religion and Society in Old Testament History, Literature and Interpretation* [Korean]. Edited by Taek Joo Woo. Translated by Samuel Cheon, Eun Suk Cho, Seong Hyuk Hong, Tae Hun Kim, Young-Hye Kim, Chong Hun Pae, and Taek Joo Woo. Seoul: Handl.

———. 2009. "Micah, Book of." In *The New Interpreter's Dictionary of the Bible*, edited by Katharine Doob Sakenfeld, 4:73–76. Nashville: Abingdon.

———. 2014a. "The Political Economy of Peasant Poverty." In *The Bible, the Economy, and the Poor*, edited by Ronald Simkins and Thomas Kelly, 34–60. Journal of Religion and Society Supplement Series 10. Omaha, NE: Creighton University. http://moses.creighton.edu/JRS/toc/SS10.html. [Chapter 6 in this volume]

———. 2014b. "Producing Peasant Poverty: Debt Instruments in Amos 2:6b–8, 13–16." In *Reading a Tendentious Bible: Essays in Honor of Robert B. Coote*, edited by

Marvin L. Chaney et al., 19–34. Hebrew Bible Monographs 66. Sheffield: Sheffield Phoenix. [Chapter 10 in this volume]

Childe, V. Gordon. 1951. *Man Makes Himself*. New York: New American Library.

———. 1964. *What Happened in History*. Baltimore: Penguin.

Childs, Brevard S. 1963. "A Study of the Formula, 'Until This Day.'" *JBL* 82:279–92.

———. 1974a. *The Book of Exodus*. OTL. Philadelphia: Westminster.

———. 1974b. "The Etiological Tale Re-examined." *VT* 24:387–97.

Cho, Eun Suk. 2002. "Josianic Reform in the Deuteronomistic History Reconstructed in the Light of Factionalism and Use of Royal Apology." Ph.D. diss., Graduate Theological Union.

Ch'oe, Yŏng-ho, Peter H. Lee, and Wm. Theodore de Bary, eds. 2000. *From the Sixteenth to the Twentieth Centuries*. Vol. 2 of *Sources of Korean Tradition*. New York: Columbia University Press.

Claburn, W. Eugene. 1973. "The Fiscal Basis of Josiah's Reforms." *JBL* 92:11–22.

Coomber, Matthew J. M. 2010. *Re-Reading the Prophets through Corporate Globalization: A Cultural-Evolutionary Approach to Economic Injustice in the Hebrew Bible*. Biblical Intersections 4. Piscataway, NJ: Gorgias.

Cooper, Jerrold S. 1975. "Heilige Hochzeit. B. Archäologisch." In *Reallexikon der Assyriologie* V/4:259–69. Berlin: de Gruyter.

Coote, Robert B. 1981. *Amos among the Prophets: Composition and Theology*. Reprint, Eugene, OR: Wipf & Stock, 2005.

———. 1991. *In Defense of Revolution: The Elohist's History*. Minneapolis: Fortress.

Coote, Robert B., and Mary P. Coote. 1990. *Power, Politics, and the Making of the Bible: An Introduction*. Minneapolis: Fortress.

Coote, Robert B., and Norman K. Gottwald, eds. 2007. *To Break Every Yoke: Essays in Honor of Marvin L. Chaney*. SWBA 2/3. Sheffield: Sheffield Phoenix.

Coote, Robert B., and David Robert Ord. 1991. *In the Beginning: Creation and the Priestly History*. Minneapolis: Fortress.

Coote, Robert B., and Keith W. Whitelam. 1987. *The Emergence of Early Israel in Historical Perspective*. SWBA 5. Sheffield: Almond.

Critchfield, Richard. 1983. *Villages*. Garden City, NY: Doubleday.

Cross, Frank Moore. 1973. *Canaanite Myth and Hebrew Epic: Essays in the History of the Religion of Israel*. Cambridge: Harvard University Press.

Cross, Frank Moore, Jr., and David Noel Freedman. 1955. "The Song of Miriam." *JNES* 13:237–50.

Crown, A. D. 1974. "An Alternative Meaning for איש in the Old Testament." *VT* 24:110–12.

Crüsemann, Frank. 1983. *Bewahrung der Freihezt: Das Thema des Dekalogs im sozialgeschichtlicher Perspektive*. Kaiser Traktate 78. Munich: Kaiser.

———. 1988. "Das Bundesbuch—historischer Ort und institutioneller Hintergrund." In *Congress Volume: Jerusalem, 1986*, edited by J. A. Emerton, 27–41. VTSup 40. Leiden: Brill.

Cumings, Bruce. 2005a. "Afterword." In *Landlords, Peasants and Intellectuals in Modern Korea*, edited by Kie-chung Pang and Michael D. Shin, 399–406. Cornell East Asia Series 128. Ithaca, NY: Cornell University East Asia Program.

———. 2005b. *Korea's Place in the Sun: A Modern History*. Updated ed. New York: Norton.

Dalman, Gustav H. 1933. *Arbeit und Sitte in Palästina*, Vol. 3: *Von der Ernte zum Mehl.* Gütersloh: Bertelsmann.

Dar, Shimon. 1986. *Landscape and Pattern: An Archaeological Survey of Samaria 800 B.C.E.—636 C.E.* British Archeological Report 308. Oxford: British Archaeological Report.

David, M. 1948. "The Manumission of Slaves under Zedekiah: A Contribution to the Laws about Hebrew Slaves." *Oudtestamentische Studiën* 5:63–79.

Davies, Graham I. 1993. *Hosea.* Old Testament Guides. Sheffield: Sheffield Academic.

Davis, Ellen F. 2008. *Scripture, Culture, and Agriculture: An Agrarian Reading of the Bible.* Cambridge: Cambridge University Press.

Day, John, ed. 1998. *King and Messiah in Israel and the Ancient Near East: Proceedings of the Oxford Old Testament Seminar.* JSOTSup 270. Sheffield: Sheffield Academic.

Dearman, J. Andrew. 1984. "Prophecy, Property and Politics." In *Society of Biblical Literature 1984 Seminar Papers*, edited by Kent H. Richards, 383–97. Chico, CA: Scholars.

———. 1988. *Property Rights in the Eighth-Century Prophets: The Conflict and Its Background.* SBLDS 106. Atlanta: Scholars.

Deuchler, Martina. 1992. *The Confucian Transformation of Korea: A Study of Society and Ideology.* Harvard-Yenching Institute Monograph Series 36. Cambridge: Harvard University Press.

Dever, William G. 1974. *Archaeology and Biblical Studies: Retrospects and Prospects.* Evanston.

———. 1977. "The Patriarchal Traditions." In *Israelite and Judaean History*, edited by John H. Hayes and J. Maxwell Miller, 70–120. OTL. Philadelphia: Westminster.

———. 1995. "Social Structure in Palestine in the Iron II Period on the Eve of Destruction." In *The Archaeology of Society of the Holy Land*, edited by Thomas E. Levy, 416–30. New York: Facts on File.

———. 2003. *Who Were the Early Israelites, and Where Did They Come From?* Grand Rapids: Eerdmans.

Diakonoff, I. M. 1975. "The Rural Community in the Ancient Near East." *JESHO* 17:121–33.

Dick, Michael B. 2004. "The 'History of David's Rise to Power' and the Neo-Babylonian Succession Apologies." In *David and Zion: Biblical Studies in Honor of J. J. M. Roberts*, edited by Bernard Batto and Kathryn Roberts, 3–19. Winona Lake, IN: Eisenbrauns.

Dietrich, Manfred, Oswald Loretz, and Jaoquin Sanmartin. 1974. "Zur ugaritischen Lexikographie (XI)." *UF* 6:19–38.

———, eds. 1995. *The Cuneiform Alphabetic Texts from Ugarit, Ras Ibn Hani and Other Places.* 2nd ed. Münster: Ugarit.

Driel, G. van. 1970. "Land and People in Assyria." *Bibliotheca Orientalis* 27:168–75.

Eckert, Carter J. et al. 1990. *Korea Old and New: A History.* Seoul: Ilchokak.

Edelstein, Gershon, and Mordechai Kislev. 1981. "Mevasseret Yerushalayim: The Ancient Settlement and Its Agricultural Terraces." *BA* 44:53–56.

Edzard, Dietz Otto. 1965. "The Old Babylonian Period." *The Near East: The Early Civilizations*, edited by Jean Bottéro et al., 177–231. Translated by R. F. Tannenbaum. Delacorte World History 2. New York: Delacorte.

Ehrman, A. 1973. "A Note on Micah 6:14." *VT* 23:103–5.

Eitam, David. 1979. "Olive Presses of the Israelite Period." *Tel Aviv* 4:146–54.

Eitam, David, and Michael Heltzer, eds. 1996. *Olive Oil in Antiquity: Israel and Neighbouring Countries from the Neolithic to the Early Arab Period*. History of the Ancient Near East / Studies 7. Padua: Sargon.

Elat, Moshe. 1979. "Trade and Commerce." In *The Age of the Monarchies: Culture and Society*, edited by Abraham Malamat, 173–86. World History of the Jewish People IV/2. Jerusalem: Massada.

Emerton, J. A. 1992. "The Translation of Isaiah 5,1." In *The Scripture and the Scrolls: Studies in Honour of A. S. van der Woude on the Occasion of His 65th Birthday*, edited by F. García Martínez et al., 18–30. VTSup 49. Leiden: Brill.

Emmerson, Grace I. 1984. *Hosea: An Israelite Prophet in Judean Perspective*. JSOTSup 28. Sheffield: JSOT Press.

Faust, Avraham. 2012. *The Archaeology of Israelite Society in Iron Age II*. Translated by Ruth Ludlum. Winona Lake, IN: Eisenbrauns.

Finkelstein, Israel. 1995. "The Great Transformation: The 'Conquest' of the Highlands Frontiers and the Rise of Territorial States." In *The Archaeology of Society of the Holy Land*, edited by Thomas E. Levy, 349–65. New York: Facts on File.

———. 2013. *The Forgotten Kingdom: The Archaeology and History of Northern Israel*. ANEM 5. Atlanta: Society of Biblical Literature.

Finkelstein, Israel et al. 2011. "Phoenician 'Torpedo' Amphoras and Egypt: Standardization of Volume Based in Linear Dimensions." *Ägypten und Levant* 21:249–59.

Finkelstein, J. J. 1961. "Ammiṣaduqa's Edict and the Babylonian 'Law Codes.'" *Journal of Cuneiform Studies* 15:91–104.

———. 1965. "Some New *Misharum* Material and Its Implications." In *Studies in Honor of Benno Landsberger on His Seventy-Fifth Birthday*, edited by Hans G. Göterbock and Thorkild Jacobsen, 233–46. Assyriological Studies 16. Chicago: University of Chicago Press.

Fisher, Eugene J. 1976. "Cultic Prostitution in the Ancient Near East? A Reassessment." *Biblical Theology Bulletin* 6:225–36.

Flanagan, James W. 1981. "Chiefs in Israel." *JSOT* 20:47–73.

Forbes, R. J. 1972. *Studies in Ancient Technology*. Vol. 9. 2nd ed. Leiden: Brill.

Fowler, Jeaneane D. 1988. *Theophoric Personal Names in Ancient Hebrew: A Comparative Study*. JSOTSup 49. Sheffield: JSOT Press.

Freedman, David Noel. 1976. "Deuteronomic History." In *IDBSup*, 226–28.

———. 1989. "The Nine Commandments: The Secret Progress of Israel's Sins." *Bible Review* 5/6:28–37, 42.

———. 2000. *The Nine Commandments: Uncovering a Hidden Pattern of Crime and Punishment in the Hebrew Bible*. New York: Doubleday.

Frick, Frank S. 1971. "The Rechabites Reconsidered." *JBL* 90:279–87.

Fried, Morton H. 1967. *The Evolution of Political Society: An Essay in Political Anthropology*. New York: Random House.

Fritz, Volkmar. 1969. "Die sogenannte Liste der besiegten Könige in Joshua 12." *Zeitschrift des deutschen Palästina-Vereins* 85:136–61.

Gadd, C. J. 1971. "The Cities of Babylonia." In *Cambridge Ancient History*, edited by I. E. S. Edwards et al., 1/2:141–42. Cambridge: Cambridge University Press

———. 1973. "Hammurabi and the End of His Dynasty." In *Cambridge Ancient History*, edited by I. E. S. Edwards et al., 2/1:176–227. Cambridge: Cambridge University Press.

Gamoran, Hillel. 1971. "The Biblical Law against Loans on Interest." *JNES* 30:127–34.

Gerstenberger, Erhard S. 1965. *Wesen und Herkunft des "apodiktischen Rechts."* Wissenschaftliche Monographien zum Alten und Neuen Testament 20. Reprint, Eugene, OR: Wipf & Stock, 2009.

Geus, C. H. J. de. 1975. "The Importance of Agricultural Terraces, with an Excursus on the Hebrew Word *gbl*." *PEQ* 107:65–74.

———. 1976. *The Tribes of Israel.* Studia semitica Neerlandica 18. Assen. Van Gorcum.

Geva, Shulamit. 1982. "Archaeological Evidence for the Trade between Israel and Tyre." *BASOR* 248:69–72.

Gevirtz, Stanley. 1961. "West-Semitic Curses and the Problem of the Origins of Hebrew Law." *VT* 11:137–58.

Gilmore, David D. 1990. *Manhood in the Making: Cultural Concepts of Masculinity.* New Haven: Yale University Press.

Gitay, Yehoshua. 1991. *Isaiah and His Audience: The Structure and Meaning of Isaiah 1–12.* Studia Semitica Neerlandica 30. Assen: VanGorcum.

Gnuse, Robert. 1985. *You Shall not Steal: Community and Property in the Biblical Tradition.* Maryknoll, NY: Orbis.

Gordis, Robert, 1950. "'*Na'ălam*' and Other Observations on the Ain Feshka Scrolls." *JNES* 9:44–47.

Gore, Rick. 2001. "Ancient Ashkelon." *National Geographic* 199:66–93.

Gottwald, Norman K. 1974. "Were the Early Israelites Pastoral Nomads?" In *Rhetorical Criticism: Essays in Honor of James Muilenburg,* edited by J. J. Jackson and Martin Kessler, 223–55. Pittsburgh Theological Monograph Series 1. Pittsburgh: Pickwick.

———. 1975. "Domain Assumptions and Societal Models in the Study of Pre-Monarchic Israel." In *Congress Volume: Edinburgh 1974,* 89–100. VTSup 28. Leiden: Brill.

———. 1976a. "Israel, Social and Economic Development of." In *IDBSup*, 465–68.

———. 1976b. "Nomadism." In *IDBSup*, 629–31.

———. 1978a. "The Hypothesis of the Revolutionary Origins of Ancient Israel: A Response to Hauser and Thompson." *JSOT* 7:37–52.

———. 1978b "Were the Early Israelites Pastoral Nomads?" *Biblical Archaeology Review* 4:2–7.

———. 1979. *The Tribes of Yahweh: A Sociology of the Religion of Liberated Israel, 1250–1050 B.C.E.* Maryknoll, NY: Orbis. 2nd ed. with corrections, 1981. Reprint, Biblical Seminar 66. Sheffield: Almond, 1999.

———. 1986. "Political Economy and Religion in Biblical Societies: Seeking the Connections." Unpublished paper presented to the AAR Liberation Theology Group, Atlanta, November.

———. 2001. *Politics in Ancient Israel.* LAI. Louisville: Westminster John Knox.

Graeber, David. 2011. *Debt: The First 5,000 Years.* Brooklyn: Melville House.

Graffy, Adrian. 1979. "The Literary Genre of Isaiah 5,1–7." *Bib* 60:400–409.

Greenberg, Moshe. 1955. *The Hab/piru.* American Oriental Series 39. New Haven: American Oriental Society.

———. 1962. "Crimes and Punishments." In *IDB*, 1:733–44.

Grigg, David B. 1980. *Population Growth and Agrarian Change: An Historical Perspective.* Cambridge Geographical Studies 13. Cambridge: Cambridge University Press.

Gruber, Mayer I. 1986. "Hebrew *qĕdēshāh* and Her Canaanite and Akkadian Cognates." *UF* 18:133–48.

Guillaume, Philippe. 2012. *Land, Credit and Crisis: Agrarian Finance in the Hebrew Bible*. BibleWorld. Sheffield: Equinox.

Habel, Norman. 1985. *The Book of Job: A Commentary*. OTL. Philadelphia: Westminster.

Haboush, Jayyun Kim, and Martina Deuchler, eds. 1999. *Culture and the State in Late Chosŏn Korea*. Harvard East Asian Monographs 182. Cambridge: Harvard University Press.

Halpern, Baruch. 1975. "Gibeon: Israelite Diplomacy in the Conquest Era." *CBQ* 37:303–16.

———. 1981. "The Uneasy Compromise: Israel between League and Monarchy." In *Traditions in Transformation: Turning Points in Biblical Faith*, edited by Baruch Halpern and Jon D. Levenson, 59–96. Winona Lake: Eisenbrauns.

———. 2001. *David's Secret Demons: Messiah, Murderer, Traitor, King*. Grand Rapids: Eerdmans.

Han, Young Woo. 2010a. *Ancient/Goryeo*. Vol. 1 of *A Review of Korean History*. Translated by Chaibong Hahm. Paju Book City: Kyongsaewon.

———. 2010b. *Joseon Era*. Vol. 2 of *A Review of Korean History*. Translated by Chaibong Hahm. Paju Book City: Kyongsaewon.

———. 2010c. *Modern/Contemporary Era*. Vol. 3 of *A Review of Korean History*. Translated by Chaibong Hahm. Paju Book City: Kyongsaewon.

Handy, Lowell K., ed. 1997. *The Age of Solomon: Scholarship at the Turn of the Millennium*. Studies in the History and Culture of the Ancient Near East 11. Leiden: Brill.

Harper, William Rainey. 1905. *A Critical and Exegetical Commentary on Amos and Hosea*. ICC. Edinburgh: T. & T. Clark.

Harrelson, Walter. 1997. *The Ten Commandments and Human Rights*. Rev. ed. Macon, GA: Mercer Unlversity Press.

Harris, Marvin. 1968. *The Rise of Anthropological Theory: A History of Theories of Culture*. New York: Crowell.

———. 1979. *Cultural Materialism: The Struggle for a Science of Culture*. New York: Random House.

———. 1980. *Culture, People, Nature: An Introduction to General Anthropology*. 3rd ed. New York: Harper & Row.

Hauer, Chris, Jr. 1980. "The Economics of National Security in Solomonic Israel." *JSOT* 18:63–73.

Hauser, Alan J. 1978a. "Israel's Conquest of Palestine: A Peasants' Rebellion?" *JSOT* 7:2–19.

———. 1978b. "Response to Thompson and Mendenhall." *JSOT* 7:35–36.

Hayes, John H., and Stuart A. Irvine. 1987. *Isaiah, the Eighth-Century Prophet: His Times and Preaching*. Nashville: Abingdon.

Helck, Wolfgang. 1962. *Die Beziehungen Ägyptens zur Vorderasien im 3. und 2. Jahrtausend v. Chr.* Ägyptologische Abhandlungen 5. Wiesbaden: Harrassowitz.

Heilbroner, Robert L. 1975. *The Making of Economic Society*. 5th ed. Englewood Cliffs, NJ: Prentice-Hall.

Heltzer, Michael. 1976. *The Rural Community in Ancient Ugarit*. Wiesbaden: Reichert.

Hendel, Ronald. 1988. "The Social Origins of the Aniconic Tradition in Early Israel." *CBQ* 50:113–48.

Herr, Larry G. 1997. "The Iron Age II Period: Emerging Nations." *BA* 60:114–83.

Herrmann, J. 1927. "Das zehnte Gebot." In *Sellin-Festschrift: Beiträge zur Religionsgeschichte und Archäologie Palästinas: Ernst Sellin zum 60. Geburtstage dargebracht*, edited by A. Jirku, 69–82. Leipzig: Deichert.

Hillers, Delbert R. 1984. *Micah: A Commentary on the Book of the Prophet Micah*. Hermeneia. Philadelphia: Fortress.

Hobsbawm, Eric J. 1965. *Primitive Rebels: Studies in Archaic Forms of Social Movement in the 19th and 20th Centuries*. New York: Norton.

———. 1969. *Bandits*. New York: Delacorte.

———. 1973. "Social Banditry." In *Rural Protest: Peasant Movements and Social Change*, edited by H. A. Landsberger, 142–57. New York: Barnes & Noble.

Hoenig, Sidney B. 1969. "Sabbatical Years and the Year of Jubilee." *Jewish Quarterly Review* 59:222–36.

Hoffner, Harry A., Jr. 1975a. "*Bayit*." In *Theological Dictionary of the Old Testament*, edited by G. Johannes Botterweck and Helmer Ringgren, 2:107–16. Grand Rapids: Eerdmans.

———. 1975b. "Propaganda and Political Justification in Hittite Historiography." In *Unity and Diversity: Essays in the History, Literature, and Religion of the Ancient Near East*, edited by Hans Goedicke and J. J. M. Roberts, 49–62. Johns Hopkins Near Eastern Studies. Baltimore: Johns Hopkins University Press.

Hoftijzer, J., and K. Jongeling. 1995. *Dictionary of the North-West Semitic Inscriptions*. 2 vols. Handbuch der Orientalistik 20, 21. Leiden: Brill.

Hohlfelder, Robert L. 1992. "Caesarea." In *ABD*, 1:798–803.

Holladay, John S., Jr. 1995. "The Kingdoms of Israel and Judah: Political and Economic Centralization in the Iron IIA–B (ca. 1000–750 BCE)." In *The Archaeology of Society of the Holy Land*, edited by Thomas E. Levy, 368–98. New York: Facts on File.

Holladay, William L. 1973. "The Kingdom of Yahweh." *Interpretation* 27:269–74.

———. 1989. *Jeremiah 2: A Commentary on the Book of Jeremiah, Chapters 26–52*. Hermeneia. Minneapolis: Fortress.

Hong, Seong-Hyuk. 2006. *The Metaphor of Illness and Healing in Hosea and Its Significance in the Socio-Economic Context of Eighth-Century Israel and Judah*. Studies in Biblical Literature 95. New York: Lang.

Hooks, Stephen. 1985. "Sacred Prostitution in Israel and the Ancient Near East." Ph.D. diss, Hebrew Union College.

Hopkins, David C. 1983. "The Dynamics of Agriculture in Monarchical Israel." In *Society of Biblical Literature 1983 Seminar Papers*, edited by Kent H. Richards, 177–202. Chico, CA: Scholars.

———. 1985. *The Highlands of Canaan: Agricultural Life in the Early Iron Age*. SWBA 1/3. Sheffield: JSOT Press.

———. 1996. "Bare Bones: Putting Flesh on the Economics of Ancient Israel." In *The Origins of the Ancient Israelite States*, edited by Volkmar Fritz and Philip R. Davies, 121–39. JSOTSup 228. Sheffield: Sheffield Academic.

———. 1997. "Farmsteads." In *The Oxford Encyclopedia of Archaeology in the Near East*, edited by Eric M. Meyers, 2:306–7. New York: Oxford University Press.

———. 2006. "Barley." In *The New Interpreter's Dictionary of the Bible*, edited by Katharine Doob Sakenfeld, 1:398. Nashville: Abingdon.

———. 2007. "'All Sorts of Field Work': Agricultural Labor in Ancient Palestine." In *To Break Every Yoke: Essays in Honor of Marvin L. Chaney*, edited by Robert B. Coote and Norman K. Gottwald, 149–72. SWBA 2/3. Sheffield: Sheffield Phoenix.

Hossfeld, Frank-Lothar. 1982. *Der Dekalog: Seine späten Fassungen, die orignale Komposition und seine Vorstufen*. Orbis Biblicus et Orientalis 45. Göttingen: Vandenhoeck & Ruprecht.

Houston, Walter J. 2004. "Was There a Social Crisis in the Eighth Century?" In *In Search of Pre-Exilic Israel*, edited by John Day, 130–49. JSOTSup 406. London: T. & T. Clark.

———. 2006. *Contending for Justice: Ideologies and Theologies of Social Justice in the Old Testament*. LHBOTS 428. London: T. & T. Clark.

———. 2008. *Contending for Justice: Ideologies and Theologies of Social Justice in the Old Testament*. 2nd ed. London: T. & T. Clark.

———. 2010. "Exit the Oppressed Peasant? Rethinking the Background of Social Criticism in The Prophets." In *Prophecy and the Prophets in Ancient Israel: Proceedings of the Oxford Old Testament Seminar*, edited by John Day, 101–16. LHBOTS 561. London: T. & T. Clark.

Humbert, Paul. 1952. "Le mot biblique 'ebyon.'" *Revue d'histoire et l'philosophie religieuse* 32:1–6.

Inge, Charles. 1941. "Post-Scriptum." *PEQ* 73:106–9.

Jackson, Bernard S. 1975. "Liability for Mere Intention in Early Jewish Law." In *Essays in Jewish and Comparative Legal History*, 202–34. Studies in Judaism in Late Antiquity 10. Leiden: Brill.

Janzen, J. Gerald. 1997. *Exodus*. Westminster Bible Companion. Louisville: Westminster John Knox.

Jin, Duk-kyu. 2005. *Historical Origins of Korean Politics*. Translated by Jei-min Kim. Seoul: Jisik-sanup.

Jirku, A. 1950. "Der 'Mann von Tob' (II. Sam 10:6.8)." *ZAW* 62:319.

Kaiser, Otto. 1983. *Isaiah 1–12: A Commentary*. 2nd ed. Translated by John Bowden. OTL. Philadelphia: Westminster.

Kaufman Ivan T. 1992. "Samaria Ostraca." In *ABD* 5:921–26.

Kaufman, Stephen A. 1987. "The Second Table of the Decalogue and the Implicit Categories of Ancient Near Eastern Law." In *Love and Death in the Ancient Near East: Essays in Honor of Marvin H. Pope*, edited by J. H. Marks and Robert M. Good, 111–16. Gilford, CT: Four Quarters.

Kautsky, John H. 1982. *The Politics of Aristocratic Empires*. Chapel Hill: University of North Carolina Press.

Keefe, Alice A. 1993. "Rapes of Women/Wars of Men." *Semeia* 61:79–97.

———. 1995. "The Female Body, the Body Politic and the Land: A Sociopolitical Reading of Hosea 1–7." In *Feminist Companion to the Latter Prophets*, edited by Athalya Brenner, 70–100. FemCB 8. Sheffield: Sheffield Academic.

———. 2001. *Woman's Body and the Social Body in Hosea*. Gender, Culture, Theory 10. JSOTSup 338. London: Shefficld Academic.

Kessler, Martin. 1971. "The Law of Manumission in Jer 34." *Biblische Zeitschrift* 15:105–8.

Kessler, Rainer. 1989. "Die angeblichen Kornhändler von Amos VIII 4–7." *VT* 39:13–22.

———. 1992. *Staat und Gesellschaft im vorexilischen Juda: Vom 8. Jahhundert bis zum Exil*. VTSup 47. Leiden: Brill.

———. 2008. *The Social History of Ancient Israel: An Introduction*. Translated by Linda M. Maloney. Minneapolis: Fortress.

Kim, Jung Bae. 2004. "Formation of the Ethnic Korean Nation and the Emergence of Its Ancient Kingdom States." In *Korean History: Discovery of Its Characteristics and Developments*, edited by the Korean National Commission for UNESCO, 27–35. Vol. 5 of Anthology of Korean Studies. Seoul: Hollym. Reprinted from *Korea Journal* 27 (1997).

Kim, Seong Hwan et al. 2008. *Atlas of Korean History*. Translated by Whanyung Kim and Jeong-hyeon Yi. Singapore: Stallion.

Kim, Sung-Jae. 1996. "The Ger and the Identity of Ancient Israel." Th.D. diss., Graduate Theological Union.

Kim-Renaud, Young-Key. 1997. *King Sejong the Great: The Light of Fifteenth Century Korea*. Rev. ed. Washington, DC: International Circle of Korean Linguistics.

King, Philip J. 1988. *Amos, Hosea, Micah: An Archaeological Commentary*. Philadelphia: Westminster.

Klein, Ralph W. 2012. *2 Chronicles: A Commentary*. Hermeneia. Minneapolis: Fortress.

Klem, H. 1976. "Verbot des Menschendiebstahls im Dekalog? Prüfung eine These Albrecht Alts." *VT* 26 (1976) 161–69.

Kletter, Raz. 1998. *Economic Keystones: The Weight System of the Kingdom of Judah*. JSOTSup 276. Sheffield: Sheffield Academic.

Knoppers, Gary. 1993. *Two Nations under God: The Deuteronomistic History of Solomon and the Dual Monarchies*. Vol. 1, *The Reign of Solomon and the Rise of Jeroboam*. HSM 52. Atlanta: Scholars.

———. 1994. *Two Nations under God: The Deuteronomistic History of Solomon and the Dual Monarchies*. Vol. 2, *The Reign of Jeroboam, the Fall of Israel, and the Reign of Josiah*. HSM 53. Atlanta: Scholars.

Knudtzon, J. A. 1915. *Die El-Amarna-Tafeln*. 2 vols. Reprinted, Aalen: Zeller, 1964.

Köhler, L. 1956. *Hebrew Man*. Translated by Peter R. Ackroyd. Nashville: Abingdon.

Kramer, Samuel Noah. 1963. *The Sumerians: Their History, Culture, and Character*. Chicago: University of Chicago Press.

Kraus, F. R. 1958. *Ein Edikt des Königs Ammi-saduqu von Babylon*. Studia et Documenta ad Iura Orientis Antiqui Pertinentia 5. Leiden: Brill.

———. 1965. "Ein Edikt des Königs Samsu-Iluna von Babylon." In *Studies in Honor of Benno Landsberger on His Seventy-Fifth Birthday*, edited by Hans G. Göterbock and Thorkild Jacobsen, 225–31. Assyriological Studies 16. Chicago: University of Chicago Press.

———. 1984. *Königliche Verfügungen in altbabylonischer Zeit*. Studia et documenta ad iura Orientis antiqui pertinentia 11. Leiden: Brill.

Kraus, Hans-Joachim. 1988. *Psalms 1–59*. Translated by Hilton C. Oswald. Continental Commentaries. Minneapolis: Augsburg.

Kupper, J.-R. 1957. *Les nomades en Mesopotamie au temps des rois de Mari*. Bibliotbeque de Ia Faculte de Philosophic et Lettres de l'Universite de Liege 142. Paris: Les Belles Lettres.

LaBianca, Øystein S., and Randall W. Younker. 1995. "The Kingdoms of Ammon, Moab and Edom: The Archaeology of Society in Late Bronze/Iron Age Transjordan (ca.

1400–500 BCE)." In *The Archaeology of Society of the Holy Land*, edited by Thomas E. Levy, 399–414. New York: Facts on File.

Landsberger, Betty H., and Henry A. Landsberger. 1973. "The English Peasant Revolt of 1381." In *Rural Protest: Peasant Movements and Social Change*, edited by H. A. Landsberger, 95–141. New York: Barnes & Noble.

Landsberger, Henry A. 1969. "The Role of Peasant Movements and Revolts in Development." In *Latin American Peasant Movements*, edited by Henry A. Landsberger, 1–61. Ithaca: Cornell University Press.

———. 1973. "Peasant Unrest: Themes and Variations." In *Rural Protest: Peasant Movements and Social Change*, ed. Henry A. Landsberger, 1–64. New York: Barnes & Noble.

Landy, Francis. 1995. *Hosea*. Readings: A New Biblical Commentary. Sheffield: Sheffield Academic.

Lane, Edward W. 1863–93. *An Arabic–English Lexicon*. 8 vols. London: Williams & Norgate.

Lang, Bernhard. 1981. "Sklaven und Unfreie im Buch Amos (II 6, VIII 6)." *VT* 31:482–88.

———. 1983a. *Monotheism and the Prophetic Minority: An Essay in Biblical History and Sociology*. SWBA 1. Sheffield: Almond.

———. 1983b. "The Social Organization of Peasant Poverty in Biblical Israel." In *Monotheism and the Prophetic Minority: An Essay in Biblical History and Sociology*, 114–27. SWBA 1. Sheffield: Almond.

Lapp, Paul W. 1967. "The Conquest of Palestine in the Light of Archaeology." *Concordia Theological Monthly* 38:283–300.

———. 1969a. *Biblical Arahaeology and History*. New York: World.

———. 1969b. "The 1968 Excavations at Tell Ta'annek." *BASOR* 195:2–49.

Latron, André. 1936. *La vie rurale en Syrie et au Liban: etude d'economie sociale*. Mémoires de l'Institut français de Damas. Beirut: Imprimerie Catholique.

Lee, Bae-yong. 2008. *Women in Korean History*. Translated by Kyong-hee Lee. Seoul: Ewha Woman's University Press.

Lee, Ki-baik. 1984. *A New History of Korea*. Translated by Edward W. Wagner, with Edward J. Shultz. Cambridge: Harvard University Press.

Lee, Peter H., and Wm. Theodore de Bary, eds. 1997. *From Early Times through the Sixteenth Century*. Vol. 1 of *Sources of Korean Tradition*. New York: Columbia University Press.

Lemche, Niels Peter. 1975. "The 'Hebrew Slave': Comments on the Slave Law Ex. xxi 2–11." *VT* 25:129–44.

———. 1976. "The Manumission of Slaves—The Fallow Year—The Sabbatical Year—The Yobel Year." *VT* 26:38–59.

———. 1979. "*Andurārum* and *Mīšarum*: Comments on the Problem of Social Edicts and Their Application in the Ancient Near East." *JNES* 38:11–22.

Lenski, Gerhard E. 1966. *Power and Privilege: A Theory of Social Stratification*. New York: McGraw-Hill.

———. 1976. "History and Social Change." *American Journal of Sociology* 82:548–64.

———. 1984. *Power and Privilege: A Theory of Social Stratification*. 2nd ed. Chapel Hill: University of North Carolina Press.

———. 2005. *Ecological-Evolutionary Theory: Principles and Applications*. Boulder: Paradigm.

Lenski, Gerhard, and Jean Lenski. 1978. *Human Societies: An Introduction to Macrosociology*. 3rd ed. New York: McGraw-Hill.

———. 1987. *Human Societies: An Introduction to Macrosociology*. 5th ed. New York: McGraw-Hill.

Levenson, Jon D., and Baruch Halpern. 1980. "The Political Import of David's Marriages." *JBL* 99:507–18.

Levy, Thomas E., ed. 1995. *The Archaeology of Society in the Holy Land*. New York: Facts on File.

Lewy, Julius. 1958. "The Biblical Institution of *Dĕrôr* in the Light of Akkadian Documents." *Eretz Israel* 5:21–31.

Liphshitz, Nili, and Gideon Biger. 1991. "Cedar of Lebanon (*Cedrus Libani*) in Israel during Antiquity." *IEJ* 41:167–74.

———. 1995 "The Timber Trade in Ancient Palestine." *Tel Aviv* 22:121–27.

Liverani, Mario. 1965. "Implicazioni sociali nella politica di Abdi-Ashirta di Amurru." *Rivista degli Studi Orientali* 40:267–77.

———. 1974. "La royauté syrienne de l'âge du bronze recent." *Le palais et la royauté, archéologie et civilisation*, edited by Paul Garelli, 329–56. XIX Recontre assyriologique internationale. Paris: Geuthner.

Long, Burke O. 1968. *The Problem of Etiological Narrative in the Old Testament*. BZAW 108. Berlin: Töpelmann.

Loretz, Oswald. 1977. "Hebräisch *tjrwš* and *jrš* in Mi 6,15 und Hi 20,15." *UF* 9:353–54.

Lorton, David. 1974. *The Juridical Terminology of International Relations in Egyptian Texts through Dyn. XVIII*. Johns Hopkins Near Eastern Studies. Baltimore: Johns Hopkins University Press.

Luke, J. T. 1965. "Pastoralism and Politics in the Mari Period: A Re-Examination of the Character and Political Significance of the Major West Semitic Tribal Groups of the Middle Euphrates." Ph.D. diss., University of Michigan.

Lys, Daniel. 1974. "La vigne et le double je: Exercice de style sur Esaie V 1–7." In *Studies on Prophecy: A Collection of Twelve Papers*, 1–16. VTSup 26. Leiden: Brill.

MacDonald, Nathan. 2008. *What Did the Ancient Israelites Eat? Diet in Biblical Times*. Grand Rapids: Eerdmans.

Macintosh, A. A. 1997. *Hosea*. ICC. Edinburgh: T. & T. Clark.

Maddin, Robert et al. 1977. "How the Iron Age Began." *Scientific American* 237:122–31.

Maier, Johann. 1985. *The Temple Scroll: An Introduction, Translation and Commentary*. JSOTSup 34. Sheffield: JSOT Press.

Maisler (Mazar), Benjamin. 1950. "The Excavations at Tell Qasileh: Preliminary Report." *IEJ* 1:61–76, 125–40, 194–218.

Maloney, Robert P. 1974. "Usury and Restrictions on Interest-Taking in the Ancient Near East." *CBQ* 36:1–20.

Marfoe, Leon. 1979. "The Integrative Transformation: Patterns of Sociopolitical Organization in Southern Syria." *BASOR* 234:1–42.

Matthews, Victor H. 1987. "Entrance Ways and Threshing Floors: Legally Significant Sites in the Ancient Near East." *Fides et Historia* 19:25–40.

Mayes, A. D. H. 1983. *The Story of Israel between Settlement and Exile: A Redactional Study of the Deuteronomistic History*. London: SCM.

Mays, James Luther. 1969. *Hosea: A Commentary*. OTL. Philadelphia: Westminster.

———. 1976. *Micah: A Commentary*. OTL. Philadelphia: Westminster.

McCarter, P. Kyle, Jr. 1973. "Rib-Adda's Appeal to Aziru (*EA* 162, 1–21)." *Oriens Antiquus* 12:15–18.

———. 1980a. "The Apology of David." *JBL* 99:489–504.

———. 1980b. *I Samuel*. AB 8. New York: Doubleday.

———. 1984. *II Samuel*. AB 9. Garden City, NY: Doubleday.

McEvedy, Colin, and Richard Jones. 1978. *Atlas of World Population History*. New York: Penguin.

McKane, William. 1998. *The Book of Micah: Introduction and Commentary*. Edinburgh: T. & T. Clark.

McKenzie, Steven L. 2000. *King David: A Biography*. Oxford: Oxford University Press.

McLaughlin, John L. 2001. *The marzēaḥ in the Prophetic Literature: References and Allusions in Light of the Extra-Biblical Evidence*. VTSup 86. Leiden: Brill.

McMillion, Phillip E. 1992. "Adoniram." In *ABD*, 1:76.

McNutt, Paula M. 1999. *Reconstructing the Society of Ancient Israel*. LAI. Louisville: Westminster John Knox.

Mendenhall, George E. 1947. "The Message of Abdi-Ashirta to the Warriors. *EA* 74." *JNES* 6:123–24.

———. 1954. "Ancient Oriental and Biblical Law." *BA* 17:26–46. Reprinted in *The Biblical Archaeologist Reader*, edited by Edward F. Campbell and David Noel Freedman, vol. 3, 3–24. Garden City, NY: Doubleday, 1970.

———. 1962. "The Hebrew Conquest of Palestine." *BA* 25:66–87.

———. 1970. "The Hebrew Conquest of Palestine." In *The Biblical Archaeologist Reader*, edited by Edward F. Campbell and David Noel Freedman, vol. 3, 100–120. (Slight revision of 1962).

———. 1973. *The Tenth Generation: The Origins of the Biblical Tradition*. Baltimore: Johns Hopkins University Press.

———. 1975a. "The Conflict between Value Systems and Social Control." In *Unity and Diversity: Essays in the History, Literature, and Religion of the Ancient Near East*, edited by Hans Goedicke and J. J. M. Roberts, 169–80. Johns Hopkins Near Eastern Studies. Baltimore: Johns Hopkins University.

———. 1975b. "The Monarchy." *Interpretation* 29:155–70.

———. 1976a. "'Change and Decay in All Around I See': Conquest, Covenant, and *The Tenth Generation*." *BA* 39:152–57.

———. 1976b. "Social Organization in Early Israel." In *Magnalia Dei: The Mighty Acts of God: Essays on the Bible and Archaeology in Memory of G. Ernest Wright*, edited by Frank Moore Cross et al., 132–51. Garden City, NY: Doubleday.

———. 1978. "Between Theology and Archaeology." *JSOT* 7:28–34.

Meyers, Carol. 1988. *Discovering Eve: Ancient Israelite Women in Context*. New York: Oxford University Press.

Meyers, Carol L., and Eric M. Meyers. 1993. *Zechariah 9–14*. AB 25C. Garden City, NY: Doubleday.

Milgrom, Jacob. 1975. "The Missing Thief in Leviticus 5:20ff." *Revue international des droits de l'antiquité* 3.22:71–85.

Miller, Cynthia L. 1996. *The Representation of Speech in Biblical Hebrew Narrative*. HSM 55. Atlanta: Scholars.

Miller, J. Maxwell. 1977. "The Israelite Occupation of Canaan." In *Israelite and Judaean History*, edited by John H. Hayes and J. Maxwell Miller, 213–84. OTL. Philadelphia: Westminster.

Miller, J. Maxwell, and John H. Hayes. 2006. *A History of Ancient Israel and Judah*. 2nd ed. Louisville: Westminster John Knox.

Mittmann, Siegfried. 1992. "'Königliches *bat*' und '*tet*-Symbol': Mit einem Beitrag zu Micha 1,14b und 1 Chronik 4,21–23." *Zeitschrift des deutschen Palästina-Vereins* 107:59–76.

Moore, Barrington, Jr. 1966. *Social Origins of Dictatorship and Democracy: Lord and Peasant in the Making of the Modern World*. Boston: Beacon.

Moore, George F. 1895. *A Critical and Exegetical Commentary on Judges*. ICC. Edinburgh: T. & T. Clark.

Moran, William L. 1953. "Amarna *šumma* in Main Clauses." *Journal of Cuneiform Studies* 7:78–80.

———. 1967a. "The Conclusion of the Decalogue (Ex 20,17=Dt 5,21)." *CBQ* 29:543–54.

———. 1967b. "Habiru (Habiri)." In *New Catholic Encyclopedia*, 6:878b–80b. Washington, DC: Catholic University.

———. 1969. "The Death of 'Abdi-Asirta." *Eretz-Israel* 9:94*–99*.

———. 1975. "The Syrian Scribe of the Jerusalem Amarna Letters." In *Unity and Diversity: Essays in the History, Literature, and Religion of the Ancient Near East*, edited by Hans Goedicke and J. J. M. Roberts, 146–66. Johns Hopkins Near Eastern Studies. Baltimore: Johns Hopkins University Press.

Na'aman, Nadav. 1986. "Habiru and Hebrews: The Transfer of a Social Term to the Literary Sphere." *JNES* 45:271–88.

Naveh, Joseph. 1992. "The Numbers of *Bat* in the Arad Ostraca." *IEJ* 42:52–54.

Nelson, Richard D. 1981a. *The Double Redaction of the Deuteronomistic History*. JSOTSup 18. Sheffield: JSOT Press.

———. 1981b. "Josiah in the Book of Joshua." *JBL* 100 (1981) 531–40.

———. 2002. *Deuteronomy: A Commentary*. OTL. Louisville: Westminster John Knox.

Netting, Robert McC. 1993. *Smallholders, Householders: Farm Families and the Ecology of Intensive, Sustainable Agriculture*. Stanford: Stanford University Press.

Neufeld, E. 1955. "The Prohibitions against Loans at Interest in Ancient Hebrew Law." *HUCA* 26:355–412.

———. 1958. "Socio-Economic Background of *Yōbēl* and *Šĕmiṭṭā*." *Rivista degli studi orientali* 33:53–124.

———. 1961. "*Jus redemptionis* in Ancient Heberew Law." *Revue internationale des droits de l'antiquité* 8:30–40.

———. 1962. "Inalienability of Mobile and Immobile Pledges in the Laws of the Bible." *Revue internationale des droits de l'antiquité* 9:33–44.

Nicholson, E. W. 1973. *Exodus and Sinai in History and Tradition*. Growing Points in Theology. Richmond: John Knox.

Nielsen, Eduard. 1968. *The Ten Commandments in New Perspective: A Traditio-historical Approach*. Translated by D. J. Bourke. SBT 2/7. Naperville, IL: Allenson.

Noh, Tae Don. 2004. "Theories of the Formation of the Korean Minjok." In *Korean History: Discovery of Its Characteristics and Developments*, edited by the Korean National Commission for UNESCO, 3–25. Vol. 5 of Anthology of Korean Studies. Seoul: Hollym. Reprinted from *Korea Journal* 37 (1997).

Nolan, Patrick, and Gerhard Lenski. 2009. *Human Societies: An Introduction to Macrosociology*. 11th ed. Boulder: Paradigm.

Noll, K. L. 2013. *Canaan and Israel in Antiquity: A Textbook on History and Religion.* 2nd ed. London: Bloomsbury.

North, Robert. 1954. *Sociology of the Biblical Jubilee.* Analecta Biblica 4. Rome: Pontifical Biblical Institute Press.

Noth, Martin. 1953. *Das Buch Josua.* 2nd ed. Handbuch zum Alten Testament 7. Tübingen: Mohr/Siebeck.

———. 1960. *The History of Israel.* 2nd ed. Translated by P. R. Ackroyd. New York: Harper & Row.

———. 1966. *Laws in the Pentateuch and Other Essays.* Translated by D. R. Ap-Thomas. Philadelphia: Fortress.

———. 1981. *The Deuteronomistic History.* 2nd ed. JSOTSup 15. Sheffield: JSOT Press. [A partial translation of Noth's *Überlieferungsgeschichtliche Studien*, 1943.]

Oden, Robert. 1981. *The Bible without Theology: The Theological Tradition and Alternatives to It.* San Francisco: Harper & Row.

Oppenheim, A. Leo. 1963. *Ancient Mesopotamia: Portrait of a Dead Civilzation.* Chicago: University of Chicago Press.

Oppenheim, A. Leo et al., eds. 1964. *The Assyrian Dictionary of the Oriental Institute of the University of Chicago*, vol. 1, A, part 1. Chicago: Oriental Institute.

Palais, James B. 1975. *Politics and Policy in Traditional Korea.* Harvard East Asian Series 82. Cambridge: Harvard University Press.

———. 1996. *Confucian Statecraft and Korean Institutions: Yu Hyŏngwŏn and the Late Chosŏn Dynasty.* Korean Studies of the Henry M. Jackson School of International Studies. Seattle: University of Washington Press.

Pang, Kie-chung, and Michael D. Shin, eds. 2005. *Landlords, Peasants and Intellectuals in Modern Korea.* Cornell East Asia Series 128. Ithaca, NY: Cornell University East Asia Program.

Park, Chung-shin. 2003. *Protestantism and Politics in Korea.* Seattle: University of Washington Press.

Park, Young-Han et al., eds. 2008. *Atlas of Korea.* Seoul: Sung Ji Mun Hwa.

Parpola, Simo. 2003. "Assyria's Expansion in the 8th and 7th Centuries and Its Long-Term Repercussions in the West." In *Symbiosis, Symbolism, and the Power of the Past: Canaan, Ancient Israel, and Their Neighbors from the Late Bronze Age through Roman Palaestina*, edited by William G. Dever and Seymour Gitin, 99–111. Winona Lake, IN: Eisenbrauns.

Parsons, Talcott. 1977. *The Evolution of Societies.* Edited by Jackson Toby. Prentice-Hall Foundations of Modern Sociology Series. Englewood Cliffs, NJ: Prentice-Hall.

Paul, Shalom M. 1970. *Studies in the Book of the Covenant in the Light of Cuneiform and Biblical Law.* VTSup 18. Reprint, Eugene, OR: Wipf & Stock, 2005.

———. 1991. *Amos: A Commentary on the Book of Amos.* Hermeneia. Minneapolis: Fortress.

Paul, Shalom M., and William G. Dever. 1973. *Biblical Archaeology.* New York Times Library of Jewish Knowledge. New York: Quadrangle.

Payne Smith, J. (Mrs. Margoliouth). 1903. *A Compendious Syriac Dictionary: Founded upon the Thesaurus Syriacus of R. Payne Smith.* Reprint, Ancient Language Resources. Eugene, OR: Wipf & Stock, 1999.

Peckham, Brian. 1985. *The Composition of the Deuteronomistic History.* HSM 35. Atlanta: Scholars.

Perdue, Leo G. et al. 1997. *Families in Ancient Israel. Family, Religion, and Culture.* Louisville: Westminster John Knox.

Petersen, David L. 2002. *The Prophetic Literature: An Introduction.* Louisville: Westminster John Knox.

Phillips, A. 1970. *Ancient Israel's Criminal Code: A New Approach to the Decalogue.* New York: Schocken.

Pintore, F. 1972. "Transiti di truppe e schemi epistolari nella Siria egiziana dell'età di el-Amarna." *Oriens Antiquus* 11:101–31.

———. 1973. "La prassi della marcia armata nella Siria egiziana dell'età di el-Amarna." *Oriens Antiquus* 12:299–318.

Polzin, Robert. 1980. *Moses and the Deuteronomist: Deuteronomy, Joshua, Judges. A Literary Study of the Deuteronomistic History, Part 1.* New York: Seabury. Reprint, Indiana Studies in Biblical Literature. Bloomington: Indiana University Press, 1993.

Pope, Marvin H. 1973. *Job.* 3rd ed. AB 15. Garden City, NY: Doubleday.

Postgate, J. N. 1974. "Some Remarks on Conditions in the Assyrian Countryside." *JESHO* 17:225–43.

Premnath, D. N. 1984. "The Process of Latifundialization Mirrored in the Oracles Pertaining to Eighth Century B.C.E. in the Books of Amos, Hosea, Isaiah and Micah." Ph.D. diss., Graduate Theological Union.

———. 1988. "Latifundialization and Isaiah 5.8–10." *JSOT* 40:49–60.

———. 2003. *Eighth-Century Prophets: A Social Analysis.* St. Louis: Chalice.

———. 2007. "Loan Practices in the Hebrew Bible." In *To Break Every Yoke: Essays in Honor of Marvin L. Chaney*, edited by Robert B. Coote and Norman K. Gottwald, 173–85. SWBA 2/3. Sheffield: Sheffield Phoenix, 2007.

Rainey, Anson F. 1970. *El Amarna Tablets 359–379: Supplement to J. A. Knudtzon, Die El-AmarnaTafeln.* Alter Orient und Altes Testament 8. Neukirchen-Vluyn: Neukirchener.

———. 1982. "Wine from the Royal Vineyards." *BASOR* 245:57–62.

Ramsey, George W. 1977. "Speech-Forms in Hebrew Law and Prophetic Oracles." *JBL* 96:45–58.

Renger, Johannes M. 1975. "Heilige Hochzeit. A. Philologisch." In *Reallexikon der Assyriologie* V/4:350–59. Berlin: de Gruyter.

Richards, Ivor A. 1971. *The Philosophy of Rhetoric.* 1936. Reprint, Oxford: Oxford University Press.

Ricoeur, Paul. 1976. "Metaphor and Symbol." In *Interpretation Theory: Discourse and the Surplus of Meaning.* Fort Worth: Texas Christian University Press.

Riemann, Paul Alfonso. 1963. "Desert and Return to Desert in the Pre-exilic Prophets." PhD diss., Harvard University.

Rofé, Alexander. 1990. "The Tenth Commandment in the Light of Four Deuteronomic Laws." In *The Ten Commandments in History and Tradition*, edited by Ben-Zion Segal and Gershon Levi, 45–65. Publications of the Perry Foundation for Biblical Research, the Hebrew University of Jerusalem. Jerusalem: Magnes.

Roncace, Mark. 2009. "Moresheth." In *The New Interpreter's Dictionary of the Bible*, edited by Katharine Doob Sakenfeld, 4:140. Nashville: Abingdon.

Rosenbaum, Jonathan. 1979. "Hezekiah's Reform and the Deuteronomistic Tradition." *HTR* 72:23–43.

Rowton, Michael B. 1965. "The Topological Factor in the 'apiru Problem." In *Studies in Honor of Benno Landsberger on His Seventy-fifth Birthday, April 21, 1965*, edited by Hans G. Güterbock and Thorkild Jacobsen, 375–87. Assyriological Studies 16. Chicago: University of Chicago Press.

———. 1976a. "Dimorphic Structure and the Problem of the 'Apiru–'Ibrim." *JNES* 35:13–20.

———. 1976b. "Dimorphic Structure and Tribal Elite." In *Al-Bahit: Festschrift Joseph Henninger zum 70. Geburtstag am 12. Mai 1976*, 219–57. Studia Instituti Anthropos 28. St. Augustin bei Bonn: Anthropos-Instituts.

———. 1976c. "Dimorphic Structure and Topology." *Oriens Antiquus* 15:17–31.

———. 1977. "Dimorphic Structure and the Parasocial Element. *JNES* 36:181–98.

Runions, Erin. 2001. *Changing Subjects: Gender, Nation and Future in Micah*. Playing the Texts 7. London: Sheffield Academic.

Sarna, Nahum. 1973. "Zedekiah's Emancipation of Slaves and the Sabbatical Year." In *Orient and Occident: Essays Presented to Cyrus H. Gordon on the Occasion of His Sixty-Fifth Birthday*, edited by Harry A. Hoffner, 143–49. Altes Orient und Altes Testament 22. Neukirchen-Vluyn: Neukirchener.

———. 1979. "The Biblical Sources for the History of the Monarchy." In *The Age of the Monarchies: Political History*, edited by Avraham Malamat, 3–19. The World History of the Jewish People IV/1. Jerusalem: Massada.

Sasson, Jack M. 1974. Review of *The Tenth Generation: The Origins of the Biblical Tradition*, by George E. Mendenhall. *JBL* 93:294–96.

Schloen, J. David. 2001. *The House of the Father as Fact and Symbol: Patrimonialism in Ugarit and the Ancient Near East*. Studies in the Archaeology and History of the Levant 2. Winona Lake, IN: Eisenbrauns.

Schottroff, Willy. 1970. "Das Weinberglied Jesajas (Jes 5 1–7): Ein Beitrag zur Geschichte der Parabel." *ZAW* 82:68–91.

Schwienhorst-Schönberger, Ludger. 1990. *Das Bundesbuch (Ex 20,22—23,33): Studien zu seiner Entstehung und Theologie*. BZAW 188. Berlin: de Gruyter.

Scott, James C. 1976. *The Moral Economy of the Peasant: Rebellion and Subsistence in Southeast Asia*. New Haven: Yale University Press.

———. 1985. *Weapons of the Weak: Everyday Forms of Peasant Resistance*. New Haven: Yale University Press.

Seeligmann, I. L. 1961. "Aetiological Elements in Biblical Historiography." *Zion* 26:141–69 (Hebrew).

Service, Elman R. 1975. *Origins of the State and Civilization: The Process of Cultural Evolution*. New York: Norton.

Shaw, Charles S. 1993. *The Speeches of Micah: A Rhetorical-Historical Analysis*. JSOTSup 145. Sheffield: JSOT Press.

Sheppard, Gerald T. 1982. "More on Isaiah 5:1–7 as a Juridical Parable." *CBQ* 44:45–47.

Sherwood, Yvonne. 1996. *The Prostitute and the Prophet: Hosea's Marriage in Literary-Historical Perspective*. Gender, Culture, Theory 2. JSOTSup 212. Sheffield: Sheffield Academic.

Shiloh, Yigal. 1979. "City of David: Excavation 1978." *BA* 42:165–71.

Silver, Morris. 1983. *Prophets and Markets: The Political Economy of Ancient Israel*. Social Dimensions of Economics. Boston: Kluwer-Nijhoff.

Sjoberg, Gideon. 1960. *The Preindustrial City: Past and Present*. New York: Free Press.

Soden, W. von. 1965. *Akkadisches Handwörterbuch*. Wiesbaden: Harrassowitz.

Soggin, J. Alberto. 1972. *Joshua: A Commentary*. Translated by R. A. Wilson. OTL. Philadelphia: Westminster.

Song, Kiho. 2004. "Several Questions in Historical Studies of Balhae." In *Korean History: Discovery of Its Characteristics and Developments*, edited by the Korean National Commission for UNESCO, 133–58. Vol. 5 of Anthology of Korean Studies. Seoul: Hollym. Reprinted from *Korea Journal* 30 (1990).

Speiser, E. A. 1940. "Of Shoes and Shekels." *BASOR* 77:15–20.

Stager, Lawrence E. 1976. "Agriculture." In *IDBSup*, 11–13.

———. 1983. "The Finest Olive Oil in Samaria." *Journal of Semitic Studies* 28:241–45.

———. 1985. "The Archaeology of the Family in Ancient Israel." *BASOR* 260:1–35.

Stager, Lawrence E., and Samuel R. Wolff. 1981. "Production and Commerce in Temple Courtyards: An Olive Press in the Sacred Precinct at Tel Dan." *BASOR* 243:95–102.

Stamm, J. J. 1967. *The Ten Commandments in Recent Research*. Translated by M. E. Andrew. SBT 2/2. London: SCM.

Stech-Wheeler, Tamara et al. 1981. "Iron at Taanach and Early Iron Metallurgy in the Eastern Mediterranean." *American Journal of Archaeology* 85:245–68.

Ste. Croix, G. E. M. de. 1981. *The Class Struggle in the Ancient Greek World from the Archaic Age to the Arab Conquests*. London: Duckworth. [2nd corr. ed., 1983]

Stein, Siegfried. 1953. "The Laws on Interest in the Old Testament." *Journal of Theological Studies* 4:161–70.

Stone, Ken. 1996. *Sex, Honor, and Power in the Deutemnomistic History*. JSOTSup 234. Sheffield: Sheffield Academic.

Sweeney, Marvin A. 1996. *Isaiah 1–39, with an Introduction to Prophetic Literature*. FOTL 16. Grand Rapids: Eerdmans.

———. 2000. *The Twelve Prophets*: Vol. 1, *Hosea, Joel, Amos, Obadiah, Jonah*. Berit Olam. Collegeville, MN: Liturgical.

Talmon, Shemaryahu. 1966. "The 'Desert Motif' in the Bible and in Qumran Literature." In *Biblical Motifs: Origins and Transformations*, edited by A. Altmann, 31–63. Cambridge: Harvard University Press.

Tcherikover, Victor. 1959. *Hellenistic Civilization and the Jews*. Translated by S. Applebaum. New York: Jewish Publication Society. Reprinted, New York: Atheneum, 1970.

Thompson, Harry O. 2000. "Some Towers in Jordan." In *The Archaeology of Jordan and Beyond: Essays in Honor of James A. Sauer*, edited by Lawrence E. Stager et al., 482–89. Studies in the Archaeology and History of the Levant 1. Winona Lake, IN: Eisenbrauns.

Thompson, Thomas L. 1978. "Historical Notes on 'Israel's Conquest of Palestine': A Peasants' Rebellion?" *JSOT* 7:20–27.

Tigay, Jeffrey H. 1986. *You Shall Have No Other Gods: Israelite Religion in the Light of Hebrew Inscriptions*. Harvard Semitic Studies 31. Atlanta: Scholars.

Toews, Wesley I. 1993. *Monarchy' and Religious Institution in Israel under Jeroboam I*. Society of Biblical Literature Monograph Series 47. Atlanta: Scholars.

———. 2008. "Jeroboam." In *The New Interpreter's Dictionary of the Bible*, edited by Katharine Doob Sakenfeld, 3:241–45. Nashville: Abingdon.

Torczyner (Tur-Sinai), Harry. 1936. "Presidential Address." *Journal of the Palestine Oriental Society* 16:6–7.

Tsevat, Matitiahu. 1979. "The Emergence of the Israelite Monarchy." In *The Age of the Monarchies: Political History*, edited by Avraham Malamat, 61–99. The World History of the Jewish People IV/1. Jerusalem: Massada.

Tucker, Gene M. 1972. "The Rahab Saga (Joshua 2): Some Form-Critical and Traditio-Historical Observations." In *The Use of the Old Testament in the New and Other Essays: Studies in Honor of William Franklin Stinespring*, edited by J. M. Efird, 66–86. Durham: Duke University Press.

Turkowski, Lucian. 1969. "Peasant Agriculture in the Judaean Hills." *PEQ* 101:21–33, 101–12.

Turnham, T. J. 1987. "Male and Female Slaves in the Sabbath Year Laws of Exodus 21:1–11." In *Society of Biblical Literature 1987 Seminar Papers*, edited by Kent H. Richards, 545–49. Atlanta: Scholars.

Vaux, Roland de. 1967. "Tirzah." In *Archaeology and Old Testament Study*, edited by D. W. Thomas, 371–83. Oxford: Oxford University Press.

Wacholder, Ben Zion. 1973. "The Calendar of Sabbatical Cycles during the Second Temple and the Early Rabbinic Period." *HUCA* 44:153–96.

———. 1975. "Chronomessianism: The Timing of Messianic Movements and the Calendar of Sabbatical Cycles." *HUCA* 46:201–18.

Waldbaum, Jane C. 1978. *From Bronze to Iron: The Transition from the Bronze Age to the Iron Age in the Eastern Mediterranean*. Studies in Mediterranean Archaeology 54. Göteborg: Aström.

Walsh, Carey Ellen. 1999. "God's Vineyard: Isaiah's Prophecy as Vintner's Textbook." *Bible Review* 14/4:43–49, 52–53.

———. 2000. *Fruit of the Vine: Viticulture in Ancient Israel*. HSM 60. Winona Lake, IN: Eisenbrauns.

Wapnish, Paula. 1993. "Archaeozoology: The Integration of Faunal Data with Biblical Archaeology." In *Biblical Archaeology Today, 1990*, edited by Avraham Biran and Joseph Aviram, 426–42. Jerusalem: Israel Exploration Society.

Wapnish, Paula, and Brian Hesse. 2003. "Archaeozoology." In *Near Eastern Archaeology: A Reader*, edited by Suzanne Richard, 17–26. Winona Lake, IN: Eisenebrauns.

Watson, Wilfred G. E. 1970. "David Ousts the City Ruler of Jebus." *VT* 20:501–2.

Watts, John D. W. 1985. *Isaiah 1–33*. WBC 24. Waco, TX: Word.

Weber, Max. 1952. *Ancient Judaism*. Translated and edited by Hans H. Gerth and Don Martindale. Glencoe, IL: Free Press.

Weill, H. M. 1938. "Gage et cautionnement dans la Bible." *Archives d'histoire du droit orientale* 2:171–241.

Weinfeld, Moshe. 1972. *Deuteronomy and the Deuteronomic School*. Reprint, Winona Lake, IN: Eisenbrauns, 1992.

———. 1991. *Deuteronomy 1–11*. AB 5. New York: Doubleday.

Weippert, Manfred. 1971. *The Settlement of the Israelite Tribes in Palestine: A Critical Survey of Recent Scholarly Debate*. Translated by James D. Martin. SBT 2/21. London: SCM.

———. 1974. "Semitische Nomaden des zweiten Jahrtausends: Ober die S3sw der Aegyptischen Quellen." *Bib* 55:265–80, 427–33.

———. 1976. "Canaan, Conquest and Settlement of." In *IDBSup*, 125–30.

Wellhausen, Julius. 1963. *Die kleinen Propheten übersetzt und erklärt*. 4th ed. Berlin: de Gruyter.

Wertime, Theodore A., and James D. Muhly, eds. 1980. *The Coming of the Age of Iron.* New Haven: Yale University Press.
Westbrook, R. 1985. "Biblical and Cuneiform Law Codes." *Revue biblique* 92:247–64.
Westenholz, Joan Godnick. 1989. "Tamar, Qĕdēshā, Qadishtu, and Sacred Prostitution in Mesopotamia." *HTR* 82:245–65.
White, Marsha C. 1997. *The Elijah Legends and Jehu's Coup.* Brown Judaic Studies 311. Atlanta: Scholars.
Whitelam, Keith W. 1979. *The Just King: Monarchic Judicial Authority in Ancient Israel.* JSOTSup 12. Sheffield: JSOT Press.
Wildberger, Hans. 1991. *Isaiah 1–12: A Commentary.* Translated by Thomas H. Trapp. Continental Commentaries. Minneapolis: Fortress.
Williams, Gary Roye. 1985. "Frustrated Expectations in Isaiah V 1–7: A Literary Interpretation." *VT* 35:459–65.
Willis, John T. 1977. "The Genre of Isaiah 5:1–7." *JBL* 96:337–62.
Wilson, Robert R. 1980. *Prophecy and Society in Ancient Israel.* Philadelphia: Fortress.
Wise, Michael O. 1990. *A Critical Study of the Temple Scroll from Qumran Cave 11.* Studies in Ancient Oriental Civilization. Chicago: Oriental Institute.
Wiseman, D. J. 1953. *The Alalakh Tablets.* London: British Institute of Archaeology at Ankara.
Wittfogel, Karl. 1981. *Oriental Despotism: A Comparative Study of Total Power.* New York: Vintage.
Wolf, Eric R. 1966. *Peasants.* Foundations of Modern Anthropology Series. Englewood Cliffs, NJ: Prentice-Hall.
———. 1969. *Peasant Wars of the Twentieth Century.* New York: Harper & Row.
Wolff, Hans Walter. 1974. *Hosea: A Commentary on the Book of the Prophet Hosea.* Hermeneia. Translated by Gary Stansell. Philadelphia: Fortress.
———. 1977. *Joel and Amos: A Commentary on the Books of the Prophets Joel and Amos.* Translated by Waldemar Janzen et al. Hermeneia. Philadelphia: Fortress.
———. 1990. *Micah: A Commentary.* Translated by Gary Stansell. Continental Commentaries. Minneapolis: Augsburg.
Woo, Taek Joo. 1998. "The *Marzēaḥ* Institution and Rites for the Dead: A Comparative and Systemic Study with Special Attention to the Eighth-Century Prophets." Ph.D. diss., Graduate Theological Union.
Wright, Christopher J. H. 1984. "What Happened Every Seven Years in Israel?" *Evangelical Quarterly* 56:129–38.
———. 1990. *God's People in God's Land: Family, Land and Property in the Old Testament.* Grand Rapids: Eerdmans.
Wright, G. Ernest. 1962. *Biblical Archaeology.* Rev. ed. Philadelphia: Westminster.
———. 1967. "The Provinces of Solomon (I Kings 4:7–19)." *Eretz Israel* 8:58*–68*.
Yadin, Yigael. 1963. *The Art of Warfare in Biblical Lands: In the Light of Archaeological Study.* 2 vols. New York: McGraw-Hill.
———, ed. and trans. 1983. *The Temple Scroll.* Jerusalem: Israel Exploration Society.
Yee, Gale A. 1981. "The Form-Critical Study of Isaiah 5:1–7." *CBQ* 43:30–40.
———. 1987. *Composition and Tradition in the Book of Hosea: A Redaction-Critical Investigation.* SBLDS 102. Atlanta: Scholars.
Yeiven, S. 1979. "The Divided Kingdom: Rehoboam–Ahaz / Jeroboam–Pekah." In *The Age of the Monarchies: Political History*, edited by Abraham Malamat, IV/1:161–72. Jerusalem: Massada.

Younker, Randall W. 1989. "Towers in the Region Surrounding Tell 'Umeiri." In *The Madaba Plains Project: The 1984 Season at Tell el-'Umeiri and Vicinity and Subsequent Studies*, edited by Lawrence T. Gerraty et al., 195–98. Madaba Plains Project Series 1. Berrien Springs, MI: Andrews University Press.

———. 1990. "Architectural Remains from the Hinterland Survey." In *Madaba Plains Project: The 1987 Season at Tell el-'Umeiri and Vicinity and Subsequent Studies*, edited by Larry G. Herr et al., 335–42. Madaba Plains Project Series 2. Berrien Springs, MI: Andrews University Press, 1990

———. 1996. "Preliminary Report of the 1994 Season of the Madaba Plains Project: Regional Survey, Tall El 'Umayri and Tall Jalul Excavations (June 15–July 30, 1994)." *Andrews University Seminary Studies* 34:65–92.

Zapassky, Elena et al. 2009. "Computing Abilities in Antiquity: The Royal Judahite Storage Jars as a Case-study." *Journal of Archaeological Method and Theory* 16:51–67.

Zevit, Ziony. 2001. *The Religions of Ancient Israel: A Synthesis of Parallactic Approaches.* New York: Continuum.

Index of Ancient Documents

PERIPHERAL AKKADIAN DOCUMENTS

El Amarna Texts

7:73–82	49
8:13–41	49
14	42
16:37–42	49
60	18
68:12–18	18, 43
69:12–28	41
71:10–32	41
71:10–31	18
71:20–26	45
73:14–33	18
73:23–33	39
73:26–29	43
73:32–33	43
74:17–19	45
74:19–45	38
74:19–41	18
74:19–21	43
74:25–29	43
74:34	42
74:35–36	43
74:36	47
74:42	47
75:10–17	45
75:10–11	18
75:25–34	39
75:25–29	40
76:7–20	18, 41
76:33–37	43
77:21–37	18, 43
77:26–29	43
77:36–37	39
79:7–29	18, 41
79:18–26	43
81:6–13	18, 41
81:9–13	39
81:11–13	43
81:33–41	42, 45
82:5–13	19
82:33–45	39
83:15–20	41
83:23–27	19
85:10–15	42
85:63–82	18
85:63–69	19
85:69–74	43
87:18–24	43
88:29–34	18, 43
89:10–32	39
90:5–25	18, 41
90:36–44	45
91:3–26	18
91:13–26	41
91:14–15	41
101	18
101:29–31	18, 45
104:17–54	18
104:37–45	41
104:49–54	42
104:51–52	43
104:52–54	47
106:13–16	18
111:17–21	43
112:10–12	39–40
112:43–47	18

El Amarna Texts (*continued*)

114:20–22	41
116:37–38	43
117:35–40	18
117:56–64	18
117:56–58	43
117:89–94	42, 43
117:92–94	18, 43
118:21–39	18, 41
118:21–37	43
121:19–23	43
125:25–30	41
130:30–43	41, 43
130:31–33	39
130:36–42	18
131:18–30	39
132:43–50	39
138:9–14	39
139:12–15	39
139:33–40	39
140:10–14	39
144:22–32	18
144:24–33	43
148:20–23	49
148:45	43
161:51–53	18
179:20–22	43
185	45
185:9–64	41
185:42–49	46
186	45
189:9–18	43
195:24–32	18
207:19–21	43
215:9–17	43
243:19–22	42, 47
244:8–33	48
245:11–18	43
246 rev.:5–10	18, 42, 48
248	42
248:9–22	42
250	48
252	48
253	48
254	48
254:31–46	48
255:8–25	49
264:5–25	49
271:9–21	18, 40
272:10–17	18, 41
272:14–17	43
273:8–24	18, 40
273:11–14	43
286:16–60	18
287:14–24	18
287:29–31	48
288:36–47	40
288:36–47	40
288:36–46	18, 41
288:44	43
289:5–29	48
289:5–24	41
290:12–13	43
292	47
298:20–27	44
299:17–26	18
305:21–24	18
318:8–15	18
335:7–20	40
362:31–42	41
366:11–26	18

PRU

III.116	73

UGARITIC DOCUMENTS

KTU

1.1:3.1	168
1.3:6.15–16	168
1.4:7.35–37	13
1.4:8.12–14	168
1.5:2.15–16	168

HEBREW BIBLE

Genesis

	70
4:20	169
10:2	188
10:3	188
14:12	168
18:1	168
19:1	168
23:10	168
24:3	168
24:37	168
24:62	168
25:27	169
28:10–22	240
33:19	196
34:25–31	31
37:28	196
39:5	74
45:8	171
47:19	196
49:5–7	31
49:24	240

Exodus

	20, 118
2:11–15	31
2:14	172
3:1–6	59
3:5	59
11:5	168
12:29	168
18:13–27	240
18:14	168
20:17	67–68, 74, 79–80
21:1—22:17	115
21:1–11	106, 115
21:7–11	198
21:16	69
21:17	72–73
22:24	196
22:25–27	106
32:25–29	31
34:12	169
34:15	169
34:24	69, 71

Leviticus

15:6	169
19:35–36	77
25	118–19
25:8–55	106, 118
25:26–27	112
25:8–55	118
25:37	196
25:50–52	112

Numbers

13:18	169
13:19	169
13:28	169
13:29	169
14:14	169
14:25	169
14:45	169
21:1	168
21:34	168
22:5	169
33:40	168

Deuteronomy

	52, 56–57, 59, 62, 69, 72, 79, 118
1:4	168
1:5	62
1:7	61
1:20	60
1:21	61
1:25	60
1:38	58, 62
1:44	169
2:5	61
2:9	61
2:19	61
2:29	60
3:2	168
3:12–22	61
3:20	60
3:21	58
3:28	61–62
4:1	60

Deuteronomy (continued)

4:5	60
4:8	62
4:14	60
4:21	60
4:22	60
4:26	60
4:40	60
4:44	62
4:46	168
5:16	60
5:17b	73
5:19	72
5:21	67–68, 72, 74, 79–80
5:31	60
5:32	63
6:1	60
7:1–5	63
7:1	60
9:1	60
9:5	60
11:8	60
11:10–11	60
11:17	60
11:24–25	60
11:24	61
11:25	60
11:29–30	53
11:29	60
11:30	169
11:31	60
12–26	52, 55
12	56
12:9	60
12:10	62
13:12	60
15	119
15:1–18	106, 118
15:4	60
15:7	60
15:9–10	112, 118
16:1–8	56, 64
16:5	60
16:18–19	62
16:18	60
16:20	60
17:2	60
17:11	63
17:14	60
17:18–20	62
17:18–19	62
17:20	63
18:9	60
19:2	60
19:3	62
19:10	60
19:14	60, 78–79
20:14	64
20:16–18	63–64
20:16	60, 64
20:17	63
21:1	60
21:14	196
21:22–23	63
21:23	60
23:15–16	36
23:19–20	106
23:20	60, 196
24:4	60
24:6	106
24:7	69
24:10–13	106
24:16	62
24:17–18	106
25:9	195
25:13–16	77
25:15	60
25:19	60
26:1–2	60
27	78
27:2–8	53
27:2–3	60
27:3	62
27:8	62
27:11–26	53
27:17	78
27:26	62
28:8	60
28:14	63
28:21	60
28:58	62
28:61	62
28:63	60
29:7–8	61

INDEX OF ANCIENT DOCUMENTS

29:21	62	2–22	58
29:29	62	2	32
30:16	60	2:1–24	63
30:18	60	2:2–7	33
31:3	58	2:9a	33
31:6–8	61	2:9b–11	33
31:7–8	58	2:10	63
31:7	62	2:12–14	33
31:9–13	53	2:14	33
31:9	62	2:14b	33
31:10	106	2:15	33
31:11–12	62	2:16	33
31:13	60	2:18–19	33
31:14–15	58	2:18	33
31:23	58, 61	2:20–21	33
31:24–29	53	2:20	33
31:24	62	2:22	33
31:26	62	2:23	33
32:36	165	2:24a	33
32:46	62	3–5	31
32:47	60	3–4	34, 60
33:15	198	3:1	60
		3:7	59–60

Joshua

	7, 32, 34, 35, 51–66	3:10	63
		3:13	60
		3:17	60
		4:1	60
1–12	4, 6, 51	4:5–7	65
1	9, 52, 58	4:11	60
1:1–18	51	4:12–13	61
1:1–9	58	4:14	59–60
1:2–9	59	4:18	60
1:2	60	4:20–24	65
1:3–5ab	60	4:23	59
1:4	61	4:24	60
1:5	58, 60	5:6	60
1:5c–7a	61	5:10–12	64
1:6	62	5:11	197
1:7	62–63	5:12	197
1:7bc–8	62	5:13–15	59
1:8	62	5:15	59
1:11	60	6	33
1:12–18	61	6:2	34
1:13	60	6:5	60
1:15	60	6:9a	33
1:17	58, 60	6:12–14	33
1:18	61	6:14	33
1:19	61	6:14b	33

Joshua (continued)

6:16	33
6:17–18	63
6:17	63
6:17b	33
6:18–19	33
6:18	33
6:19	63–64
6:20–21	33
6:20	33
6:21	63
6:22–23	63
6:22	33
6:23	33
6:24	63–64
6:24a	33
6:25	63
6:25b	33
7:1	63
7:3	60
7:6–9	64
7:9	60
7:11–13	63
7:15	63
7:23	60
7:24	60
7:25	60
8:1	61
8:2	63–64
8:8	63
8:15	60
8:21	60
8:24–25	63
8:26	63
8:27–29	63
8:27	64
8:29	63
8:31	62
8:32	62
8:34	62
8:35	62
9–10	34
9:1	63
9:3–27	63
9:6	172
9:7	169, 172
9:24	60, 63
10–11	4, 7, 9
10:1	63
10:8	61
10:15	60
10:20	63
10:21	60
10:24	60
10:25	61
10:27	63
10:28	63
10:29	60
10:30	63
10:31	60
10:32–33	63
10:34	60
10:35	63
10:36	60
10:37	63
10:38	60
10:39–40	63
10:40–43	51
10:42	60
11:3	63
11:6	61, 63
11:9	63
11:11–12	63
11:14	63–64
11:15	63
11:16–23	51
11:17	63
11:20–21	63
11:22	63
11:23	60–62
12	34
12:1–24	51
12:1	61
12:2	168
12:4	168
12:6–7	61
12:8	63
13–21	51
13:1–13	61
13:1–7	51
13:7–12	61
13:14—21:42	61
13:15–32	61
14:1–5	51
14:2–4	61

14:9	60	10:1	168
16:10	169	11	50
17:6	169	11:21	169
17:18	3	15:10	172
18:1–10	51	16:9	168
18:3	60	16:12	168
18:5–7	61	17:7–9	31
19:51	51	19:1	31
21:5–6	61	20:20	172
21:27	61	20:36	172
21:43–45	51		
21:43	60	**Ruth**	
22	51	4:1–12	106
22:1–34	61	4:7	195–96
22:5	62		
22:20	63	**1 Samuel**	
23	51, 52, 58		20, 52, 57, 61
23:4–13a	61	1:9	168
23:5	60	4:4	169
23:6	62, 63	4:13	168
24	31, 34, 52	8	195
24:8	169	8:5	74
24:18	169	8:14	74
24:26	62	11:8	172
24:32	196	12:3	195–96
		13:17–18	97
Judges		13:19–22	13, 98
	32, 35, 52, 57, 61	14:2	168
1	3, 9	15:4	172
1:1	58	16:14	231–32
1:9	169	19:9	168
1:10	169	20:16	172
1:17	169	22:1–2	50
1:21	169	22:2	106
1:27	169	22:6–8	98, 153
1:29	169	22:6	168
2:6–15	58	23–27	35, 50
3:1–6	61	23:1	97
3:3	169	26:3	168
3:5	63	29–30	35, 50
3:20	168	30:24	169
4:2	168		
5	14, 35	**2 Samuel**	
7:23	172		52, 221
8:22	172	1:1	57, 58
9	50	3:1	173
9:55	172		

2 Samuel (continued)

3:6	173
5:6	169
5:10	232
6:2	169
7:2	168
8:15–18	101
8:16	101
8:18	101
9:13	168
10:6	172
10:8	172
11:1	168
12:1–14	167
12:8	173
14:5–17	167
16:3	168
16:20–23	186
16:24	196
18:24	168
19:9	168
19:15	172
19:17	172
19:42	172
19:43	172
19:44	172
20:4	172
20:23–26	101
20:23	101
23:8	168
24:24	196

1 Kings

	52
1:1–4	186
1:5–8	101
1:8	101
1:38	101
1:44	101
1:48	168
2:1–4	58
2:2	172
2:3	62
2:26–27	101
2:28–35	101
2:39–40	36
3:6	168
4:6	101
4:7–19	62, 101
4:22–28	100
4:28	100
5:1–11	100
5:13–18	100
5:14	101
8:12–45	62
8:25	168, 172
9:16	168–69
10:26	102
11–13	55
11:26–28	102
11:29–38	239
11:29ff.	102
12–13	240
12:1–20	55
12:1	238
12:4	101, 238
12:9–11	101
12:10–11	238
12:14	101
12:16	238
12:18	102
12:19	173
12:20	173
12:26–33	56
12:26	173
13	52, 56
13:2	56, 173
13:11	168
13:14	168
13:25	168
13:34	173
14:8	173
14:10	173
14:13	173
14:14	173
15:18	168
15:29	173
16:3	173
16:7	173
16:11	173
16:12	173
17:19	168
18:1–6	104
20:31	173
20:34	103

20:35–43	167	23:4–24	55
21	73, 158, 189	23:4–20	56, 64
21:22	173	23:4	56
22:19	169	23:15–20	56
		23:21–23	56, 64
		23:22	56
		23:24–25a	62
		23:25a	53, 57, 63
		23:25b—25:30	53
		23:26–27	53
		23:29	53
		25:27–30	52

2 Kings

	52, 59, 70, 209
1:9	168
2:18	168
4:1–7	106
6:1–7	103
6:32	168
8:1–6	106
8:3	74
8:5	74
8:18	173
8:27	173
9–10	189
9:7	173
9:8	173
9:9	173
10:10	173
10:11	173
10:30	173
10:31	62
13:6	173
14:6	62
16:10–18	54
17:7–18	58
17:13	62
17:21	173
17:34	62
17:37	62
19:15	169
21:3–7	54
21:8	62
21:13	173
21:19–26	55
22:1—23:25a	52
22:2	63
22:3–14	55
22:8	62
22:11–13	64
22:11	62
22:15–20	53
23:1–3	55
23:2	172

1 Chronicles

1:5	188
1:6	188
5:8	168
9:16	168
12:30	173
13:6	169
17:1	168
18:14–17	101
20:1	168
21:24	196

2 Chronicles

6:16	169, 172
9:25	103
10:18	102
10:19	173
16:2	168
18:18	169
21:6	173
21:7	173
21:13	173
22:3	173
22:4	173
22:7	173
22:8	173
22:10	173
26:10	105, 125, 151–52, 155, 207

Ezra

9:4	168

Nehemiah

5:1–13	119
5:3	199
5:4	196
5:7	119, 199, 201
5:10	196
5:11	196
5:13	106, 199, 200
10:31	106, 119

Esther

2:19	168
2:21	168
5:1–13	199
5:1	168
5:13	168, 201
6:10	168

Job

2:8	168
5:6	198
9:19	212
9:29	213
14:8	198
24:3	106
24:9	106

Psalms

2:4	169
4:3	172
9:12	169
15:5	106, 196
17:12	168
22:4	169
44:13	196
49:3	172
50:4	165
55:20	169
60:8	195
68:17	69, 71
69:26	169
80:2	169
91:1	169
99:1	169
108:9	195
112:5	106
122:5	173
123:1	169
132:2	240
132:5	240
135:14	165

Proverbs

3:29	168
11:1	77
12:25	217, 218
14:28	214
16:11	77
19:14	74
19:17	106
20:8	168
20:10	77
20:23	77
28:8	106

Isaiah

	121–22, 147, 179, 183, 186
1:24	240
3:12–15	165–66
3:12	165
3:14	167
5:1–7	131, 160–74, 182
5:2	164
5:3	160–61, 167–69, 171–72
5:7	160–61, 167, 172–73
5:8–10	146, 166–67
5:8	74, 80, 166
5:9	169
5:10	214
5:29	218
6:1	169
6:5	168
6:11	169
7:2	173
7:13	172, 173
8:12–14	170–71
8:14	173
9:8	170
10:24	169

INDEX OF ANCIENT DOCUMENTS 287

20:6	169	34:16	201
22:15	171	34:19	118
22:20-22	171	34:22	169
22:20	171	36:22	168
22:21	171, 173	36:30	169
22:22	173	38:2	169
24:17	169	38:4	74
25:12	217	38:7	168
26:5	217	40:10	168
26:21	169	44:2	169
28:6	169	44:22	169
33:24	169	46:19	169
37:16	169	47:2	169
40:22	169	48:9	169
43:24	196	48:43	169
49:19	169	49:19	212
49:26	240	49:19b	212
60:16	240	49:31	168
61:1	106	50:3	169
		50:44	212

Jeremiah

	212	50:44b	212
1:1	101, 239	51:29	169
2:15	169	51:37	169
2:26	173	51:62	169
4:7	169		

Ezekiel

4:29	169		201
7:12	101	2:6	168
7:14	101	7:7	169
9:10	169	8:1	168
16:5	186	12:2	168
21:9	169	18:7	106
21:12	173	18:8	106, 196
22:2	168	18:12	106
22:30	169, 172	18:13	106
26:6	101	18:16	106
26:9	101, 169	18:17	106
29:16	168, 169	22:12	106
29:32	168	27-28	248
32:6-15	106	33:15	106
32:15	74		
32:25	196		

Hosea

32:44	196		121-22, 135, 147, 175-90
33:10	169		
33:17	169, 172, 173	1-2	184
34	119	1	187
34:8-22	106, 118		

Hosea (continued)

1:2	185
1:4	173, 189
1:6	173
1:9	183
2	187
2:4	185
2:6	185
2:7	185
2:14	187
2:18	189
2:24	189
3:1	185
3:3	185
4–14	184
4:2	185
4:3	169
4:10	185
4:11–14	177
4:11	185
4:12	185
4:13	185
4:14	185
4:15	185
4:18	185
5:1	173
5:3	185
5:4	185
6:10	185
7:4	185
9	187
9:1	185, 187
12:1	247
12:7–8	77
13:7	183
13:10	183
13:14	183–84
13:14b	184

Joel

4:3	196

Amos

	121–22, 147, 179, 183
1:4	173
1:5	169
1:8	169
2	193, 204
2:6–16	193
2:6–8	193, 194
2:6	195, 196, 198, 201, 204
2:6b–8	191–204
2:6c–7	204
2:6c	193, 195–98, 204
2:7	196, 198–201, 204
2:7a	198
2:7b	198
2:8	201
2:9–12	202
2:13–16	191–204
2:13	202, 204
2:14–16	203
5:11	131, 163, 180
5:24	147
6:1–7	248
6:1	173
6:4	130
6:6	126
6:7	186, 248
7:9	173
8:4–6	77, 193
8:6	193, 195–96, 204
8:8	169

Micah

	121–22, 147, 179, 183
1–3	205, 219
1:8–16	146
1:13	146
2	80
2:1–5	80–81, 146
2:2	73–74, 80, 166
2:3	211
2:4	80, 82
2:5	80, 82
3:1–4	79
3:1	173
3:2	74
3:9	173
6:1–2	211

6:5	34
6:9–15	205–19
6:9	211–13, 216, 217, 219
6:9a	212–13, 217
6:9c	212–13
6:10–11	77
6:10	213, 216, 219
6:11	213, 219
6:12	213, 216–19
6:12a	216
6:13	219
6:14	216
6:16	173, 209, 218

Nahum

3:4	196

Zephaniah

2:5	169
3:5	81
3:6	169

Zechariah

7:7	168
12	170
12:7	170
12:8	170
12:10	170

APOCRYPHA

Sirach

11:3	198
46:19	195–96

NEW TESTAMENT

Luke

10:25–37	82

Romans

7:7	68
13:9	68

DEAD SEA SCROLLS

Temple Scroll

1QT 57:19b–21	74

Index of Names

Adler, Elaine June, 177, 253
Aharoni, Miriam, 253
Aharoni, Yohanan, 7, 13, 150, 164, 253
Albright, W. F., 7, 14, 23, 24, 27, 28, 65, 176, 253
Allen, Leslie C., 176, 253
Alt, Albrecht. 4, 6, 29, 37, 50, 65, 69–72, 78, 94, 154, 168, 253–54
Andersen, Francis I., 176, 182, 184, 188, 196, 209, 254
Anderson, Bernhard W., 251, 257
Artzi, P., 19, 38, 254
Astour, M. C., 16, 19, 254
Auld, A. Graeme, 195, 254
Austin, M. M., 112, 254
Avigad, Nahman, 124, 152, 166, 214,
Aviram, Joseph, 274

Bagnall, Roger S., 27, 254
Ballard, Robert D., 247, 254
Baltzer, Klaus, 106, 254
Baly, Denis, 3, 224, 254
Balz-Cochois, Helgard, 176, 255
Batto, Bernard, 259
Beentjes, Pancratius C., 195, 255
Ben-Barak, Zafrira, 98, 154, 255
Bender, S., 179, 255
Ben Zvi, Ehud, 209, 212, 255
Bess, S. Herbert, 29, 255
Biger, Gideon, 124, 267
Biran, Avraham, 274
Bird, Phyllis A., xii, 135, 177–78, 182, 187, 255
Blenkinsopp, Joseph, 134, 255

Blum, Jerome, 29, 255
Boecker, Hans Jochen, 115, 255
Boer, Roland, xiv, 140, 243–49, 255
Boling, Robert G., 53, 255
Boren, Henry C., 113–14, 255
Borowski, Oded, 129, 154, 230
Boserup, Ester, 126, 181, 255
Bossen, Laurel, xi, 135, 182, 230, 255
Bottéro, Jean, 110, 111, 255, 259
Botterweck, G. Johannes, 263
Bowen, Nancy R., 235, 255
Brenner, Athalya, 264
Bright, John, 7, 10, 30, 102, 118, 119, 149, 255
Broshi, Magen, 126, 146, 162, 181, 228, 245, 256
Brown, Francis, xvii
Brown, William P., 251, 257
Brueggemann, Walter, xiv, 82, 256
Brunt, P. A., 114–15, 256
Bucher, Christina, 177, 256
Bury, J. B., 112–13, 256
Butler, Trent C., 256
Buttrick, George Arthur, xviii, 255

Callaway, J., 24, 256
Campbell, Edward F., Jr., 13, 17, 22–23, 30, 46–47, 50, 126, 143, 145, 164, 181, 256
Carney, T. F., 107, 256
Carroll, Robert P., 118, 256
Cary, M., 114, 256
Cassuto, Umberto, 71, 256
Cathcart, Kevin J., 203, 217, 256
Chaney, Marvin L., 35, 65, 76–77, 92–94, 107, 109, 116, 117,

INDEX OF NAMES   291

121, 122, 125, 127, 129–35,
138–39, 149, 151–54, 158,
162, 179, 182, 192–94,
206–7, 214, 217, 222, 224,
229–31, 233–34, 246–48,
252, 256–58
Chaney, Rilla McCubbins, xiv, 1
Childe, V. Gordon, 93, 95, 258
Childs, Brevard S., 6, 65, 72, 258
Cho, Eun Suk, 223, 225, 258
Ch'oe, Yŏng-ho, 225, 258
Claburn, W. Eugene, 117, 258
Coogan, Michael D., 256
Coomber, Matthew J. M., 136, 258
Cooper, Jerrold S., 177, 258
Coote, Mary P., 107, 115, 117, 120, 179, 231, 258
Coote, Robert B., xi, xii, xiv, 1, 66, 104, 107, 115–17, 119–20, 149, 156, 162, 179, 183, 186, 191–93, 197, 202, 206, 231, 240, 258, 264, 271
Critchfield, Richard, 109, 132, 157, 258
Cross, Frank Moore, ix–x, 1, 10, 34, 52, 101, 168, 206, 256, 258
Crown, A. D., 172, 258
Crüsemann, Frank, 71, 115, 258
Cumings, Bruce, 225, 229–30, 236–37, 258

Dalman, Gustav H., 203, 259
Dar, Shimon, 126, 143, 164, 181, 259
David, M., 106, 118, 259
Davies, Graham I., 259
Davies, Philip R., 263
Davis, Ellen F., 136, 259
Day, John, 236, 259
Day, Peggy L., 255
Dearman, J. Andrew, 109, 153, 157, 159, 162, 179, 198, 259
de Bary, Wm. Theodore, 225, 232, 234, 240, 258, 266
Deuchler, Martina, 225, 230, 259, 262
Dever, William G., ix, 4, 7, 14, 76, 259
Diakonoff, I. M., 29, 246, 259

Dick, Michael B., 232, 259
Dietrich, Manfred, xix, 39, 259
Driel, G. van, 157, 259

Eckert, Carter J., 231, 259
Edelstein, Gershon, 131, 156, 164, 181, 259
Edwards, I. E. S., 253, 260, 261
Edzard, Dietz Otto, 110–11, 259
Efird, J. M., 274
Ehrman, A., 217, 259
Eitam, David, 126–27, 130, 143, 152, 162, 164, 181, 259, 260
Elat, Moshe, 150, 179, 259
Emerton, John A., 255, 258, 260
Emmerson, Grace I., 183, 260
Esler, Philip F., xiii, 252, 257

Faust, Avraham, xi, 125, 131, 137, 140–46, 193, 260
Finkelstein, Israel, 76, 126, 162, 181, 228, 245, 247, 256, 260
Finkelstein, J. J., 110–12, 260
Fisher, Eugene J., 177, 260
Flanagan, James W., 97, 260
Forbes, R. J., 13, 260
Fowler, Jeaneane D., 177, 260
Freedman, David Noel, xvii, 10, 70, 168, 176, 182, 184, 188, 196, 209, 251, 254, 256, 257, 258, 260, 268
Frick, Frank S., 6, 260
Fried, Morton H., 224, 260
Fritz, Volkmar, 34, 260

Gadd, C. J., 110–11, 260
Gamoran, Hillel, 106, 109, 261
García Martínez, F., 260
Garelli, Paul, 267
Gerraty, Lawrence T., 276
Gerstenberger, Erhard S., 78, 261
Geus, C. H. J., de, 3–4, 8, 10–11, 13–14, 16–17, 25, 261
Geva, Shulamit, 124, 151, 162, 179, 261
Gevirtz, Stanley, 173, 261
Gilmore, David D., 187, 261
Gitay, Yehoshua, 161, 261

Gitin, Seymour, 270
Gnuse, Robert, 72, 106, 110–11, 261
Goedicke, Hans, 263, 268, 269
Good, Robert M., 264
Gordis, Robert, 195–96, 261
Gordon, Robert P., 203, 256
Gore, Rick, 124, 261
Göterbock, Hans G., 260, 265
Gottwald, Norman K., ix, xiv, 1, 4–6, 9, 11, 13–15, 38, 65, 74, 92–95, 107, 168, 170, 179, 251, 257, 258, 261, 264, 271
Graeber, David, 132, 261
Graf, David F., 251, 257, 261
Graffy, Adrian, 167
Greenberg, Moshe, 36, 44, 46–48, 50, 69, 261
Grigg, David B., 126, 181, 262
Gruber, Mayer I., 177, 262
Guillaume, Philippe, xi, 137–41, 193, 246, 262

Habel, Norman, 212, 262
Haboush, Jayyun Kim, 225, 262
Halpern, Baruch, 34, 98, 154, 231, 235, 262, 267
Han, Young Woo, 225, 228–29, 232–34, 236, 262
Handy, Lowell K., 234, 262
Hanson, K. C., xiv
Harper, William Rainey, 202, 262
Harrelson, Walter, 68–69, 80, 262
Harris, Marvin, 9, 83, 89, 156, 223, 262
Hauer, Chris, Jr., 100, 262
Hauser, Alan J., 38, 262
Hayes, John H., 123, 167, 225–26, 231, 233–34, 237, 259, 262, 269
Hearon, Holly E., 252, 257
Helck, Wolfgang, 27, 42, 262
Heilbroner, Robert L., 127, 262
Heltzer, Michael, 28–29, 130, 260, 262
Hendel, Ronald, 184, 263
Herr, Larry G., 126, 162, 179, 228, 245, 263
Herrmann, J., 69–70, 263

Hesse, Brian, 127, 274
Hillers, Delbert R., 215, 263
Hobsbawm, Eric J., ix, 43–49, 263
Hoenig, Sidney B., 106, 263
Hoffner, Harry A., Jr., 67, 232, 263
Hoftijzer, J., 197, 263
Hohlfelder, Robert L., 228, 263
Holladay, John S., Jr., 15, 76, 124, 142, 162, 263
Holladay, William L., 118, 169, 263
Hong, Seong-Hyuk, 223, 263
Hooks, Stephen, 177, 263
Hopkins, David C., xi, 76, 124–25, 127, 129–31, 143–44, 150–56, 159, 162, 179, 203, 229–30, 263–64
Horsley, Richard A., xiv, 251, 257
Hossfled, Frank-Lothar, 71, 264
Houston, Walter J., xi, 137, 141–46, 193, 264
Humbert, Paul, 197, 264

Inge, Charles, 124, 166, 214, 264
Irvine, Stuart A., 167, 262

Jackson, Bernard S., 70–71, 264
Jackson, J. J., 261
Jacobsen, Thorkild, 260, 265, 272
Janzen, J. Gerald, 80, 264
Jeppesen, Knud, 217, 256
Jin, Duk-kyu, 225, 264
Jirku, A., 172, 263, 264
Jobling, David, 251, 257
Jones, Richard, 226–28, 268
Jongeling, K., 197, 263

Kaiser, Otto, 165, 170, 264
Kaufman, Ivan T., 126, 264
Kaufman, Stephen A., 115, 264
Kautsky, John H., 107, 264
Keefe, Alice A., xii, 135, 177–78, 182, 184–85, 187, 264
Kelly, Thomas, 251, 257
Kessler, Martin, 106, 118, 261, 264
Kessler, Rainer, 126, 131, 140, 195, 265
Kim, Jung Bae, 225, 265

Kim, Seong Hwan, 224–25, 228, 234, 265
Kim, Yong Bok, xiii
Kim-Renaud, Young-Key, 236, 265
King, Philip J., 176, 265
Kislev, Mordechai, 131, 156, 164, 181, 259
Klein, Ralph W., 125, 265
Klem, H., 71, 265
Kletter, Raz, 124, 265
Knoppers, Gary, 206, 265
Knudtzon, J. A., xviii, 18, 41, 265
Köhler, L., xviii, 37, 134, 265
Kramer, Samuel Noah, 110, 265
Kraus, F. R., 110, 265
Kraus, Hans-Joachim, 172, 265
Kupper, J.-R., 4–5, 265

LaBianca, Øystein S., 76, 266
Landsberger, Betty H., 266
Landsberger, Henry A., ix, 1, 15, 19, 23, 25–31, 39, 49, 139, 263, 266
Landy, Francis, 184, 266
Lane, Edward W., 203, 266
Lang, Bernhard, 109, 131, 133, 150, 156–57, 162, 179, 196–97, 266
Lapp, Paul W., 6–10, 14, 21–25, 32, 65, 266
Latron, André, 29, 266
Lee, Bae-yong, 225, 230, 235, 266
Lee, Ki-baik, 225, 227, 232–34, 236–37, 266
Lee, Peter H., 234, 240, 266
Lee, Warren W., xiii, 222
Lemche, Niels Peter, 106, 110–11, 115, 118, 266
Lenski, Gerhard E., ix–x, xiii, 1–3, 9, 14–15, 23, 25–26, 30–31, 33, 42, 75, 86, 88–89, 95, 101, 123–24, 127, 135, 139, 150, 152–53, 182, 220, 223–24, 228–30, 244–245, 248, 266–67
Lenski, Jean, 2, 9, 14–15, 23, 33, 42, 86, 88–89, 95, 150, 152–53, 267

Levenson, Jon D., 235, 262, 267
Levy, Thomas E., 259, 260, 263, 266,
Lewy, Julius, 106, 110–11, 267
Liphshitz, Nili, 124, 267
Liverani, Mario, 19, 246, 267
Long, Burke O., 6, 267
Loretz, Oswald, 218, 259,
Lorton, David, 27, 267
Luke, J. T., 5, 267
Lys, Daniel, 267

MacDonald, Nathan, 135, 144–45
Macintosh, A. A., 188, 267
Maddin, Robert, 13, 93, 95, 103, 267
Maier, Johann, 74, 267
Maisler (Mazar), Benjamin, 152, 267
Malamat, Abraham, 254, 260, 272, 274, 275
Maloney, Robert P., 106, 267
Marfoe, Leon, 129, 153, 267
Marks, J. H., 264
Marx, Karl, xiv, 248
Matthews, Victor H., 187, 267
Mayes, A. D. H., 53, 267
Mays, James Luther, 176, 183, 206, 209, 211, 267–68
McCarter, P. Kyle, Jr., 19, 168, 195, 231–32, 268
McEvedy, Colin, 226–28, 268
McKane, William, 209, 211, 213, 217, 268
McKenzie, Steven L., 231, 268
McLaughlin, John L., 186, 268
McMillion, Phillip E., 238, 268
McNutt, Paula M., 74, 179, 268
Mendenhall, George E., 4, 6–7, 11–12, 14–18, 20–22, 24, 34–35, 37–38, 43, 45, 47, 49, 65, 92, 268
Meyers, Carol L., 135, 170, 182, 230, 268
Meyers, Eric M., 170, 263, 268
Milgrom, Jacob, 201, 268
Miller, Cynthia L., 211, 268
Miller, J. Maxwell, 9, 13, 22, 25, 32, 123, 225–26, 231, 233–34, 237, 259, 269
Miller, Patrick D., 254

INDEX OF NAMES

Mittmann, Siegfried, 166, 214, 269
Moore, Barrington, Jr., ix, 26–29, 269
Moore, George F., 35, 172, 269
Moran, William L., ix, 1, 19, 38, 40, 72–74, 79, 269
Muhly, James D., 13, 95, 275

Na'aman, Nadav, 116, 269
Naveh, Joseph, 124, 166, 214, 269
Nelson, Richard D., 53, 61, 72, 117, 206, 269
Netting, Robert McC., 126, 181, 269
Neufeld, E., 106, 109, 112–13, 118, 269
Nicholson, E. W., 30, 269
Nielsen, Eduard, 70, 269
Noh, Tae Don, 225, 269
Nolan, Patrick, 123–24, 127, 135, 223–24, 228–30, 248, 270
Noll, K. L., 124, 140, 245, 270
North, Robert, 106, 118, 270
Noth, Martin, 4, 6, 8, 10, 32, 36, 52, 65, 254, 270

Oden, Robert, 177, 270
Oppenheim, A. Leo, 111, 270
Ord, David Robert, 119, 258

Palais, James B., 108, 225, 230, 270
Pang, Kie-chung, 227, 258, 270
Park, Chung-shin, 231, 270
Park, Eugene E. C., xiii
Park, Young-Han, 224, 227, 270
Parpola, Simo, 123, 270
Parsons, Talcott, 27, 88, 270
Paul, Shalom M., 14, 36, 69, 115, 163, 180, 196–97, 201, 270
Payne Smith, J. (Mrs. Margoliouth), 187, 197, 270
Peckham, Brian, 53, 271
Perdue, Leo G., 74, 271
Petersen, David L., 176, 271
Phillips, A., 78, 271
Pintore, F., 46, 271
Plattner, Stuart, 255
Polzin, Robet, 59–60, 64, 271
Pope, Marvin H., 212, 218, 271

Postgate, J. N., 157, 271
Premnath, D. N., 77, 126, 152, 162, 164, 179, 181, 196, 201, 271

Rainey, Anson F., xviii, 18, 41, 125–26, 151, 162, 164, 271
Ramsey, George W., 134, 271
Renger, Johannes M., 177, 271
Richard, Suzanne, 274
Richards, Ivor A., 185, 271
Richards, Kent H., 259, 263, 274
Ricoeur, Paul, 185, 271
Riemann, Paul Alfonso, 6, 271
Ringgren, Helmer, 263
Roberts, J. J. M., 263, 268, 269
Roberts, Kathryn, 259
Rofé, Alexander, 79, 271
Roncace, Mark, 146, 271
Rosenbaum, Jonathan, 116, 272
Rowton, Michael B., 3–4, 13, 16–17, 20, 43–44, 47–48, 272
Runions, Erin, 209, 211, 272

Sakenfeld, Katherine Doob, 257, 264, 271, 273
Sanmartin, Jaoquin, 259
Sarna, Nahum, 85, 106, 118–19, 272
Sasson, Jack M., 1, 15, 272
Schloen, J. David, 74, 179, 272
Schottroff, Willy, 272
Schwienhorst-Schönberger, Ludger, 115, 272
Scott, James C., 138, 215–16, 272
Scullard, H. H., 256
Seeligmann, I. L., 6, 65, 272
Service, Elman R., 224, 272
Shaw, Charles S., 211, 272
Sheppard, Gerald T., 272
Sherwood, Yvonne, 178, 272
Shiloh, Yigal, 152, 272
Shin, Michael D., 227, 258, 270
Silver, Morris, 150–53, 155, 162, 272
Simkins, Ronald, xi, 251, 257
Sjoberg, Gideon, 3, 9, 23, 33, 42, 86, 272
Soden, W. von, xvii, 273
Soggin, J. Alberto, 33–34, 273
Song, Kiho, 225, 273

INDEX OF NAMES

Speiser, E. A., 195–96, 273
Stager, Lawrence E., 13, 94, 126–27, 129, 152–53, 162, 179, 273
Stamm, J. J., 70, 273
Stech-Wheeler, Tamara, 95, 273
Ste. Croix, G. E. M. de, 112–13, 273
Stein, Siegfried, 106, 109, 273
Stern, Ephraim, 253, 256,
Stivers, Robert L., 251, 257
Stone, Ken, 187, 273
Sweeney, Marvin A., 174, 183, 197–98, 206, 273

Talmon, Shemaryahu, 6, 273
Tcherikover, Victor, 27, 273
Thompson, Harry O., 181, 273
Thompson, Thomas L., 38, 273
Tigay, Jeffrey H., 177, 273
Toby, Jackson, 270
Toews, Wesley I., 239–40, 273
Torczyner (Tur-Sinai), Harry, 163, 180, 273
Tsevat, Mattitiahu, 97, 274
Tucker, Gene M., 32–34, 274
Turkowski, Lucian, 130, 155–56, 158, 203, 274
Turnham, T. J., 115, 274
Tushingham, A. D., 224, 254

Vaux, Roland de, 102, 274
Vidal-Naquet, P., 112, 254
Volz, Paul, 253

Wacholder, Ben Zion, 106, 118, 274
Waetjen, Herman C., xiv
Waldbaum, Jane C., 93, 95–96, 274
Walsh, Cary Ellen, 126, 130, 164, 181, 274
Wapnish, Paula, 127–28, 274
Watson, Wilfred G. E., 168, 274
Watts, John D. W., 170–71, 274

Weber, Max, 35, 274
Weill, H. M., 106, 274
Weinfeld, Moshe, 72, 110, 274
Weippert, Manfred, 4–5, 8, 13, 16–20, 38–39, 43, 65, 274
Wellhausen, Julius, 203, 211–12, 274
Wertime, Theodore A., 95, 275
Westbrook, R., 110, 275
Westenholz, Joan Godnick, 177, 275
White, Marsha C., 189, 209, 275
Whitelam, Keith W., 66, 107, 109, 134, 159, 258, 275
Wildberger, Hans, 165, 167, 170–71, 275
Williams, Gary Roye, 275
Willis, John T., 167, 275
Wilson, Robert R., 87, 275
Wire, Antoinette Clark, xii
Wise, Michael O., 74, 275
Wiseman, D. J., 39, 275
Wittfogel, Karl, 224, 275
Wolf, Eric R., ix, 6, 25–27, 29, 75, 91, 95, 139, 156, 236, 275
Wolff, Hans Walter, 176, 193, 197, 209, 211, 275
Wolff, Samuel R., 127, 152, 273
Woo, Taek Joo, 186, 223, 257, 275
Wright, Christopher J. H., 74, 106, 117–19, 275
Wright, G. Ernest, x, 7–8, 10, 34, 65, 101, 116, 275

Yadin, Yigael, 3, 74, 275
Yee, Gale A., 167, 183, 206, 275
Yeiven, S., 275
Younker, Randall W., 76, 181, 266, 275

Zapassky, Elena, 247, 276
Zevit, Ziony, 177, 276

www.ingramcontent.com/pod-product-compliance
Lightning Source LLC
Chambersburg PA
CBHW021651230426
43668CB00008B/583